Conversation Analysis

Language in Society

GENERAL EDITOR

Peter Trudgill, Chair of English Linguistics, University of Fribourg

ADVISORY EDITORS

J. K. Chambers, Professor of Linguistics, University of Toronto

Ralph Fasold, Professor of Linguistics, Georgetown University

William Labov, Professor of Linguistics, University of Pennsylvania

Lesley Milroy, Professor of Linguistics, University of Michigan, Ann Arbor

Launched in 1980, *Language in Society* is now established as probably the premiere series in the broad field of sociolinguistics, dialectology and variation studies. The series includes both textbooks and monographs by Ralph Fasold, Suzanne Romaine, Peter Trudgill, Lesley Milroy, Michael Stubbs, and other leading researchers.

1 Language and Social Psychology, *edited by Howard Giles and Robert N. St Clair*
2 Language and Social Networks (second edition), *Lesley Milroy*
3 The Ethnography of Communication (third edition), *Muriel Saville-Troike*
4 Discourse Analysis, *Michael Stubbs*
5 The Sociolinguistics of Society: Introduction to Sociolinguistics, Volume I, *Ralph Fasold*
6 The Sociolinguistics of Language: Introduction to Sociolinguistics, Volume II, *Ralph Fasold*
7 The Language of Children and Adolescents: The Acquisition of Communicative Competence, *Suzanne Romaine*
8 Language, the Sexes and Society, *Philip M. Smith*
9 The Language of Advertising, *Torben Vestergaard and Kim Schrøder*
10 Dialects in Contact, *Peter Trudgill*
11 Pidgin and Creole Linguistics, *Peter Mühlhäusler*
12 Observing and Analysing Natural Language: A Critical Account of Sociolinguistic Method, *Lesley Milroy*
13 Bilingualism (second edition), *Suzanne Romaine*
14 Sociolinguistics and Second Language Acquisition, *Dennis R. Preston*
15 Pronouns and People: The Linguistic Construction of Social and Personal Identity, *Peter Mühlhäusler and Rom Harré*
16 Politically Speaking, *John Wilson*
17 The Language of the News Media, *Allan Bell*
18 Language, Society and the Elderly: Discourse, Identity and Ageing, *Nikolas Coupland, Justine Coupland, and Howard Giles*
19 Linguistic Variation and Change, *James Milroy*
20 Principles of Linguistic Change, Volume I: Internal Factors, *William Labov*
21 Intercultural Communication: A Discourse Approach (second edition), *Ron Scollon and Suzanne Wong Scollon*
22 Sociolinguistic Theory: Language Variation and Its Social Significance (revised edition), *J. K. Chambers*
23 Text and Corpus Analysis: Computer-assisted Studies of Language and Culture, *Michael Stubbs*
24 Anthropological Linguistics, *William Foley*
25 American English: Dialects and Variation (second edition), *Walt Wolfram and Natalie Schilling-Estes*
26 African American Vernacular English: Features, Evolution, Educational Implications, *John R. Rickford*
27 Linguistic Variation as Social Practice: The Linguistic Construction of Identity in Belten High, *Penelope Eckert*
28 The English History of African American English, *edited by Shana Poplack*
29 Principles of Linguistic Change, Volume II: Social Factors, *William Labov*
30 African American English in the Diaspora, *Shana Poplack and Sali Tagliamonte*
31 The Development of African American English, *Walt Wolfram and Erik R. Thomas*
32 Forensic Linguistics: An Introduction to Language in the Justice System, *John Gibbons*
33 An Introduction to Contact Linguistics, *Donald Winford*
34 Sociolinguistics: Method and Interpretation, *Lesley Milroy and Matthew Gordon*
35 Text, Context, Pretext: Critical Issues in Discourse Analysis, *H. G. Widdowson*
36 Clinical Sociolinguistics, *Martin J. Ball*
37 Conversation Analysis: An Introduction, *Jack Sidnell*

Conversation Analysis

AN INTRODUCTION

Jack Sidnell

WILEY-BLACKWELL
A John Wiley & Sons, Ltd., Publication

This edition first published 2010

Blackwell Publishing was acquired by John Wiley & Sons in February 2007.
Blackwell's publishing program has been merged with Wiley's global Scientific,
Technical, and Medical business to form Wiley-Blackwell.

Registered Office
John Wiley & Sons Ltd, The Atrium, Southern Gate, Chichester,
West Sussex, PO19 8SQ, United Kingdom

Editorial Offices
350 Main Street, Malden, MA 02148-5020, USA
9600 Garsington Road, Oxford, OX4 2DQ, UK
The Atrium, Southern Gate, Chichester, West Sussex, PO19 8SQ, UK

For details of our global editorial offices, for customer services, and for information
about how to apply for permission to reuse the copyright material in this book
please see our website at www.wiley.com/wiley-blackwell.

Library of Congress Cataloging-in-Publication Data

Sidnell, Jack.
Conversation analysis : an introduction / Jack Sidnell.
p. cm. — (Language in society)
Includes bibliographical references and index.
ISBN 978-1-4051-5900-5 (hardcover : alk. paper) —
ISBN 978-1-4051-5901-2 (pbk. : alk. paper)
1. Conversation analysis. I. Title.
P95.45.S54 2010
302.3'46—dc22
2009026815

A catalogue record for this book is available from the British Library.

Set in 10/12pt Ehrhardt by Graphicraft Limited, Hong Kong
Printed in Singapore by Ho Printing Singapore Pte Ltd

1 2010

Contents

The truth is, the science of Nature has been already too long made only a work of the brain and the fancy: It is now high time that it should return to the plainness and soundness of observations on material and obvious things.

Robert Hooke (1635–1703)
Micrographia, 1665

Acknowledgements

Although I am listed as the sole author of this book it would not have been possible to write it without contributions of various kinds from many other people. I first encountered CA as a graduate student in the writings of Chuck and Candy Goodwin. Their work initiated me to the discipline of close observation and formed the basis for my continued study of social interaction. Later, while I was a visiting professor at UCLA, Candy encouraged me to take Manny Schegloff's classes. His influence has been massive and there is evidence of it on every page of this book. Chuck, Candy and Manny are not only towering scholars of social interaction: they are also wonderful people who have been incredibly generous with their time. Thanks here is small recompense for all that I have taken from them.

I had the good fortune of attending the Advanced Summer Institutes in the summers of 2002, 2003 and 2005. During this time I learned much not only from the instructors – John Heritage, Gene Lerner, and Manny Schegloff – but also from my student peers. Some of the analyses presented in this book developed out of discussions that took place at these institutes, others have their beginnings in notes I took during Manny's classes or in data sessions at UCLA. My own academic generation (broadly defined) is rich with brilliant conversation analysts – in classes and data sessions I have learned especially from Becky Barnes, Ignasi Clemente, Rod Gardner, Makoto Hayashi, Trine Heinemann, Mardi Kidwell, Celia Kitzinger, Chris Koenig, Irene Koshik, Anna Lindström, Harrie Mazeland, Lorenza Mondada, Geoff Raymond, Jeff Robinson, Federico Rossano, Marja-Leena Sorjonen, Tanya Stivers, Erik Vinkhuyzen, Sue Wilkinson, and many others. To all, many, many thanks.

Tanya Stivers, my collaborator on many projects, provided insight, encouragement and support. She read the entire manuscript and provided comments and suggestions that improved it immensely. She also arranged a meeting and data session with Gail Jefferson – an event that significantly shaped my own conception of what conversation analysis is all about.

Federico Rossano has been a source of inspiration since we first met in 2003. One shortcoming of the present work is that it does not adequately take into account his cutting-edge work on interaction and visible conduct. Federico's unstinting friendship and constant good humor (not to mention his love for and appreciation of good food) have seen me through many difficult times and made the good ones that much more enjoyable.

I am grateful to many other CAsts for comments on parts of this book: thanks especially to Ceci Ford and Anna Lindstrom who used an earlier version in their courses. Thanks also go to all the Toronto-area CAsts with whom I've enjoyed many lively discussions and energetic data sessions – Jeffrey Aguinaldo, Pam Hudak, Clare MacMartin, Tanya Romaniuk, Linda Wood.

A very special thanks to the many students who have read chapters from the book or participated in lectures upon which they were based. I must single out Norie Romano especially who transcribed many of the conversations I present.

At Wiley-Blackwell, I'd like to thank Glynis Baguley, Kelly Basner, Julia Kirk and especially Danielle Descoteaux.

Finally, I thank my beautiful and loving wife and our two daughters Sula and Ginger for providing the supportive and joyful environment within which it was possible to write this book. More importantly, I thank them for their conversation . . . the nuances of which never cease to amaze me.

The book is dedicated to the memory of a great conversationalist: Phyllis "Dee" Greene (1941–2007), my mother-in-law and dear friend.

Transcription Conventions

I. Temporal and sequential relationships

Overlapping or simultaneous talk is indicated in a variety of ways.

[
[— Separate left square brackets, one above the other on two successive lines with utterances by different speakers, indicate a point of overlap onset, whether at the start of an utterance or later.

]
] — Separate right square brackets, one above the other on two successive lines with utterances by different speakers, indicate a point at which two overlapping utterances both end or where one ends while the other continues, or simultaneous moments in overlaps which continue.

= — Equal signs ordinarily come in pairs, one at the end of a line, and another at the start of the next line or one shortly thereafter. They are used to indicate two things:

(1) If the two lines connected by the equal signs are by the same speaker, then there was a single, continuous utterance with no break or pause, which was broken up in order to accommodate the placement of overlapping talk.

(2) If the lines connected by two equal signs are by different speakers, then the second followed the first with no discernible silence between them, or was "latched" to it.

(0.5) — Numbers in parentheses indicate silence, represented in tenths of a second; what is given here in the left margin indicates 0.5 seconds of silence. Silences may be marked either within an utterance or between utterances.

(.) — A dot in parentheses indicates a "micropause", hearable, but not readily measurable without instrumentation; ordinarily less than 0.2 of a second.

II. Aspects of speech delivery, including aspects of intonation

. ? , ¿ — The punctuation marks are not used grammatically, but to indicate intonation. The period indicates a falling, or final, intonation contour, not necessarily the end of a sentence. Similarly, a question mark indicates rising intonation, not necessarily a question, and a comma indicates "continuing" intonation, not necessarily a clause boundary. The inverted question mark is used to indicate a rise stronger than a comma but weaker than a question mark.

:: — Colons are used to indicate the prolongation or stretching of the sound just preceding them. The more colons, the longer the stretching. On the other hand, graphically stretching a word on the page by inserting blank spaces between the letters does not necessarily indicate how it was pronounced; it is used to allow alignment with overlapping talk.

- \- A hyphen after a word or part of a word indicates a cut-off or self-interruption, often done with a glottal or dental stop.

word Underlining is used to indicate some form of stress or emphasis, by either increased loudness or higher pitch. The more underlining, the greater the emphasis.

word Therefore, underlining sometimes is placed under the first letter or two of a word, rather than under the letters which are actually raised in pitch or volume.

WOrd Especially loud talk may be indicated by upper case; again, the louder, the more letters in upper case. And in extreme cases, upper case may be underlined.

° The degree sign indicates that the talk following it is markedly quiet or soft.

°word° When there are two degree signs, the talk between them is markedly softer than the talk around it.

Combinations of underlining and colons are used to indicate intonation contours:

_: If the letter(s) preceding a colon is (are) underlined, then there is an "inflected" falling intonation contour on the vowel (you can hear the pitch turn downward).

: If a colon is itself underlined, then there is an inflected rising intonation contour.

↑ or ^ ↓ The up and down arrows mark sharper rises or falls in pitch than would be indicated by combinations of colons and underlining, or they may mark a whole shift, or resetting, of the pitch register at which the talk is being produced.

>< <> The combination of "more than" and "less than" symbols indicates that the talk between them is compressed or rushed. Used in the reverse order, they can indicate that a stretch of talk is markedly slowed or drawn out. The "less than" symbol by itself indicates that the immediately following talk is "jump-started", i.e. sounds like it starts with a rush.

hhh (hh) °hh °hh Hearable aspiration is shown where it occurs in the talk by the letter *h* – the more *h*'s, the more aspiration. The aspiration may represent breathing, laughter, etc. If it occurs inside the boundaries of a word, it may be enclosed in parentheses in order to set it apart from the sounds of the word. If the aspiration is an inhalation, it is shown with a dot before it (usually a raised dot) or a raised degree symbol.

III. Other markings

(( )) Double parentheses are used to mark the transcriber's descriptions of events, rather than representations of them: ((cough)), ((sniff)), ((telephone rings)), ((footsteps)), ((whispered)), ((pause)), and the like.

(word) When all or part of an utterance is in parentheses, or the speaker identification is, this indicates uncertainty on the transcriber's part, but represents a likely possibility.

( ) Empty parentheses indicate that something is being said, but no hearing (or, in some cases, speaker identification) can be achieved.

1
Talk

Talk is at the heart of human social life. It is through talk that we engage with one another in a distinctively human way and, in doing so, create what Erving Goffman (1957) once described as a "communion of reciprocally sustained involvement." We use talk to argue, to complain, to woo, to plead, to commemorate, to denigrate, to justify, to entertain and so on. Clearly, if we didn't talk we would not have the lives we do.

This book offers an introduction to "conversation analysis" (CA): an approach within the social sciences that aims to describe, analyze and understand talk as a basic and constitutive feature of human social life. CA is a well-developed tradition with a distinctive set of methods and analytic procedures as well as a large body of established findings. In this book I aim to introduce this tradition by guiding readers through a series of topics including turn-taking, action formation, sequence organization and so on. In this introductory chapter I attempt to give some of the flavor of the approach by examining a few fragments of conversation, sketching out in broad brush strokes some basic ways in which they are organized. My goal is essentially twofold. First, and most importantly, I hope to convey at least some of the immediacy of conversation analysis – the fact that what is most important for conversation analysis is not the theories it produces or even the methods it employs but rather the work of grappling with some small bit of the world in order to get an analytic handle on how it works. Secondly, I want to make a point about the way that conversational practices fit together in highly intricate ways. In the interests of clarity I have divided this book into chapters each of which focuses on some particular domain of conversational organization. In point of fact, of course, these different domains of organization are fundamentally interconnected. This interconnectedness creates something of a problem for a book like this one. It means that if we start off talking about the way turns at talk are distributed we soon find it necessary to make reference to the ways in which troubles can be fixed and this then requires some discussion of the way sequences of actions hang together. As Schegloff (2005: 472) suggests, it seems as though one can't do anything unless one knows everything! Where then to begin? We have to start somewhere and since the book in its entirety is an attempt to come to terms with the interconnectedness of practices in talk-in-interaction, here I just want to jump into the water. My aim for now, then, is simply to show that, in conversation as in talk-in-interaction more generally, one thing truly is connected to a bunch of other things.

Intersecting Machineries

And so, to that end, here is a bit of conversation. To understand it, you'll need to know that Ann and her husband Jeff had been entertaining two old friends and their young child. The friends had stayed overnight, for breakfast and into the early afternoon. After some rather extended goodbyes, the couple left and Ann and Jeff came back into the house. The following exchange then occurred:

(1) Visit – FN
01 Ann: That was fun,
02 (0.4)
03 Jeff: mm
04 Ann: ish.

This short fragment may seem at first glance unremarkable but, as I hope to show in the following pages, it illustrates many important features of conversation. It also exemplifies the principle of interconnectedness that I've already alluded to. Another way to put it is to say that, if we take any bit of talk, such as that presented in the example above, we find that it is the product of several "organizations" which operate concurrently and intersect in the utterance, thereby giving it a highly specific, indeed unique, character. At this point, a term like "organizations" may seem a bit obscure, but what I mean is actually pretty straightforward. Basically there is an organized set of practices involved in first getting and, secondly, constructing a turn, another such organized set of practices involved in producing a sequence of actions, another set of practices involved in the initiation and execution of repair and so on. Harvey Sacks who, along with Emanuel Schegloff and Gail Jefferson, invented the approach to social interaction now called "conversation analysis", sometimes used the metaphor of machines or machinery to describe this.

> In a way, our aim is . . . to get into a position to transform, in what I figure is almost a literal, physical sense, our view of what happened here as some interaction that could be treated as the thing we're studying, to interactions being spewed out by machinery, the machinery being what we're trying to find; where, in order to find it we've got to get a whole bunch of its products. (Sacks 1995, v. 2:169)

The machinery metaphor is quite revealing. What we get from it is a picture of speakers and hearers more or less totally caught up in and by the socially organized activities in which they are engaged. This is a highly decentralized or distributed view of human action that places the emphasis not on the internal cognitive representations of individuals or on their "external" attributes (doctor, woman, etc.) but on the structures of activity within which they are embedded.

It will be useful to keep this metaphor of machineries in mind as we move into the analyses of this chapter. Our inclination as ordinary members of society and as language users is to think of talk in a much more individualistic, indeed, atomistic way. Here's a fairly pervasive view of the way that talk works: The words that I produce express thoughts which exist inside my mind or brain. These thoughts-put-into-words are sent, via speech, to a hearer who uses the words to reconstruct the original thoughts. Those thoughts or ideas are thus transferred, by means of language, from a speaker to a hearer. Although this is not the place to discuss this commonplace view of language and communication I mention it here so as to draw a contrast with the view Sacks proposes when he speaks of "machineries".[1]

If we think about this little fragment in these terms, that is, as the product of multiple, simultaneously operative and relevant organizations of practice, or "machineries" for short, we can get a lot of analytic leverage on what may at first seem somewhat opaque.

Let's start by noting that there is an organization relating to occasions or encounters taken as wholes. For a given occasion, there are specific places within it at which point particular actions are relevantly done. An obvious example is that greetings are properly done at the beginning of an encounter rather than at its conclusion. Similarly, introductions between participants who do not know one another are relevant at the outset of an exchange. If I meet a friend on the street and do not fairly immediately introduce her to the person with whom I'm walking, I may well apologize for this – saying something like "Oh, I'm so sorry this is Jeff" – where the apology is specifically responsive to the fact that the introduction has not been done earlier. When an action is done outside of its proper place in conversation it is typically marked as such (with "misplacement markers" like "by the way . . ." and so on). Now I think most people will agree that one of the things people regularly do when their guests leave is to discuss "how it went". Notice then that Ann's utterance can be heard as initiating just such a discussion. It does this by making a first move in such a discussion, specifically by positively evaluating or assessing the event. Of course, an utterance like this not only assesses (or evaluates) what has just taken place; it also, in doing so, marks its completion. This utterance does that in part by explicitly characterizing the event as past with "was". So, to begin with, we can see this utterance as coming in a particular place within the overall structural organization of an occasion – at its completion.

Let's now consider this fragment in terms of turns-at-talk. This first thing to notice is that there is something about "That was fun" that makes it recognizable as a possibly complete turn, whereas the same is not true for "that was", or "that", or "that was fu" etc. In English, turns can be constructed out of a sharply restricted set of grammatically defined units – words, phrases, clauses and sentences. In the example we are looking at the turn is composed of just one such "sentential" unit (even with "ish" added) but in other examples we will see turns composed of multiple units. In characterizing the turn as "possibly" complete we are not hedging our bets but rather attempting to describe the talk from the point of view of the participants. Jeff may anticipate that the turn will end with "fun" but he can't be sure that it will; as it turns out this is both a possible completion and the actual completion of the turn, but as we'll see it's quite possible to have a *possible* completion which is not the *actual* completion (indeed, the addition of "-ish" here extends the turn, retrospectively casting the turn as *not* complete at the end of "fun").

Now, the possible completion of a turn makes transition to a next speaker relevant in a way it is not during the course of that unit's production. So we call such places "transition relevance places" and we'll see, in chapter 3, that speaker transition is organized by reference to such places. The point is, of course, that when Ann finishes her utterance – "That was fun" – she may relevantly expect Jeff to say something by virtue of the way turn-taking in conversation is organized. So we have two more organizations – the organized sets of practices involved in both the construction and the distribution of turns – implicated in the production of this fragment of conversation.

We noticed that the completion of "That was fun" is a place for Jeff to speak. If he had spoken there what might he have said? Although the range of things that Jeff *could* have said is surely infinite, some things are obviously more relevant and hence more likely than others. One obvious possibility is "yeah, it was" or just "yeah". Either such utterance would be a "response" to "That was fun" and would show itself to be a response by virtue of its composition. A response like this would then give us a paired set of actions – two utterances tied together in an essential way as first action and its response. In chapter 4 we will see that actions are typically organized into sequences of action and that the most basic such sequence is one composed of just two utterances – a first pair part and a second pair part – which form together an "adjacency pair". The utterances which compose an adjacency pair are organized by a relation of "conditional relevance" such that the occurrence of a first member of the pair makes the second relevant, so that if it is not produced it may be found, by the participants, to be missing (where any number of things did not happen but were nevertheless not "missing" in the same way).

"Yeah, it was" is more than just a response; it is a specific kind of response: an agreement. We will see that responses to assessments and other sequence-initiating actions (what we will call "first pair parts" like questions, requests, invitations and so on) can be divided into preferred and dispreferred types. We must postpone a detailed discussion of this issue until later (chapter 5). For now I will simply assert that, after an assessment such as "that was fun," agreement is the preferred response. Any other kind of response in this context may be understood, by the participants, not just for *what it is* but for *what it is not*, that is, as something specifically alternative to agreement with the initial assessment. Where agreement is relevant, a kind of "with me or against me" principle operates such that anything other than agreement is tantamount to *dis*agreement. We will see that even delay in responding to an assessment like "That was fun" can suggest that what is being withheld – what is *not* being said – is disagreement.

In fact, this example provides some evidence for that claim. So here, when Ann's assessment meets first with delay and subsequently with "mm", Ann is prompted to modify her original assessment to make it easier for Jeff to agree with if, indeed, he did not agree with its original formulation. So the organization of assessment sequences and the general patterns of preference can tip Ann off here. From Jeff's delay in responding and from the character of the response he eventually does produce, Ann can infer that he does not agree with her original assessment. She can then modify it in such a way that disagreement is avoided. So we have two more organizations implicated in this fragment of talk – the organization of actions (like assessments and agreements) into sequences and the general patterns of preference (here for agreement).

Ann has produced an utterance, and brought it to completion. Jeff's response is delayed and when it is eventually produced it is noncommittal: does Jeff agree or not with the assessment "That was fun"? At this point Ann does not produce an entirely new utterance; rather she modifies what she has already said. As noted already, this appears to be prompted by a lack of appropriate uptake by Jeff. We can see this addition of "-ish" to Ann's utterance as a form of self-repair. With this she not only modifies what she has said, she responds to problems with her original utterance which Jeff's delay in responding implies. As we will see in chapter 7, there is a preference in conversation for troubles, problems of speaking, errors and so on to be fixed or remedied by *the speaker of the trouble* rather some other participant. In this example we see that, though Jeff does not fully agree with the assessment "fun" and might perhaps be more willing to describe the visit as "fun-ish", he does not correct Ann. Rather, he delays his response, and in this way allows Ann a chance to repair, modify or correct her own talk. There is another way in which repair is involved here. One of the things a turn's recipient can always do at the possible completion of some bit of talk addressed to them is to initiate repair with something like "what?" or "it was what?" or "that was what?" or, again, "that *was* fun?" or "that was *fun*?" etc. Because this is an ever-present possibility, the fact that it is *not* done can be taken to imply that the talk was understood. So by the fact that Jeff does not initiate repair of Ann's turn, Ann may infer that Jeff (believes he) understood what she has said and that a lack of understanding therefore does not explain his delay in responding. So we have another organization of practices – the organization of repair – implicated in this short fragment of consideration.

Although there is much more we could say about this fragment the larger point should by now be clear: Any utterance can be seen as the unique product of a number of intersecting machineries or organizations of practice. This is an alternative then to the commonsense, "individualist" view, that sees the utterance as the product of a single, isolated individual speaker. It is also an alternative to the "externalist" view which sees the utterance as the product of intersecting, *external* forces such as the speaker's (or the recipient's) gender, ethnic background, age, class or whatever else.

So far we have seen that this exchange involves practices for taking and constructing turns, building sequences of actions, repairing troubles and for speaking in ways fitted to the occasion. There is one more organization of practices that should be mentioned here – those involved in selecting the particular words used to construct the turn. Now you might think that people don't select words at all; they just use the words that are appropriate for what they are talking about – they simply "call a spade a spade". The problem with this view is that for anything that one talks about, multiple ways are available to describe or refer to it. We can ask, for instance, why Ann says "that" in "that was fun" instead of "Having Evan, Jenny and Reg" or "The last twenty-four hours" or whatever else. This brings us to a central principle of conversation which Sacks and his colleagues termed "recipient design": "the multitude of respects in which the talk by a party in a conversation is constructed or designed in ways which display an orientation and sensitivity to the particular other(s) who are the co-participants" (Sacks, Schegloff & Jefferson 1974: 727). This is an obvious yet absolutely crucial point, that speakers design their talk in such a way as to make it appropriate and relevant for the persons they are addressing. Recipient design encompasses a vast range of phenomena – everything from the banal fact that a speaker will increase the volume of her talk to address a recipient at the back of the room to the subtle nuances of word selection which reflect what the speaker assumes the recipient knows. So with an expression like "that" in "that was fun" the speaker clearly presumes that the recipient will know what she means to refer to in using it. If Ann had said this to someone who phoned after her guests had left, that person might respond with "what was fun?" since they would have no idea what "that" was meant to refer to. This allows us to see the way "that" in "That was fun" was specifically selected for Jeff.

Think also about the way you would refer to the same person in talking to different recipients. With one recipient that person is "Dee", with another "your Mom", with another "Ms Greene" and with another "Nana" and so on. Why? Apparently, we select the name by which we presume our recipient knows the person to whom we want to refer. The name we use then is specifically designed for the particular recipient – it is recipient-designed.

I have concluded the discussion of the talk between Jeff and Ann with a consideration of recipient design for a reason. When we talk of "machineries" of turn-taking, of action sequencing or of repair it's easy to get the sense of these abstract "organizations" operating independently of the real persons engaged in talking to one another. And, of course, there's a sense in which that's absolutely correct. Indeed, that is, surely, just the point that Sacks wanted to drive home with the metaphor of "machines". However, a focus on these context-free organizations or systems, these intersecting machineries, obviously does not tell the whole story since, as Sacks, Schegloff and Jefferson (1974) note, whatever happens in conversation happens at some particular time, in some particular place, with some particular group of persons, after some particular thing has just taken place. In short, anything that happens in conversation happens within some particular, ultimately unique, context. As it turns out, although the structures that organize conversation are context-free in certain basic and crucial respects, they are at the same time capable of extraordinary context-sensitivity. We've had a glimpse at this in our consideration of recipient design here – enough, I hope, to suggest that CA involves tacking back and forth between the general and context-free on the one hand and the particular and context-sensitive on the other.

Historical Origins of Conversation Analysis

CA emerged in the 1960s through the collaboration of Harvey Sacks, Emanuel Schegloff and Gail Jefferson. Although CA can be seen as a fresh start within the social and human sciences, it drew inspiration from two important sociologists, Erving Goffman and Harold Garfinkel.[2] Goffman's highly original and innovative move was to direct sociological attention to "situations" – the ordinary and extraordinary ways in which people interact with one another in the course of everyday life. Through a series of analyses Goffman attempted to show that these situations, and especially what he would describe as focused encounters, could be studied as in some ways orderly systems of self-sustaining activity. In a card game, for example, each participant pays attention so that she knows whose turn it is, what has been played, what point the players have reached in the hand and in the game and so on. If one of the players becomes distracted and misses a turn or delays in taking it, others may complain that she is not paying attention, so there are built-in mechanisms for addressing problems that arise as the activity is taking place. Of course, what applies to a card-game applies equally well to conversation:

> We must see . . . that a conversation has a life of its own and makes demands on its own behalf. It is a little social system with its own boundary-maintaining tendencies; it is a little patch of commitment and loyalty with its own heroes and its own villains. (Goffman 1957: 47)

Goffman insisted that the organization of human interaction, what he would come to call the "interaction order" (1983), constituted its own social institution. Moreover, according to Goffman, face-to-face, co-present interaction is the basis for all other social institutions that sociologists and others study. Hospitals, asylums, courts of law, households and so on can be seen as environments for various forms of social interaction. What is particularly remarkable about Goffman is that at the time he was writing virtually no one in sociology or anthropology paid any attention to social interaction. A few psychologists, particularly those associated with Roger G. Barker (e.g. Barker & Wright 1951, Barker 1963), whom, by the way, Sacks had read, had begun to treat the "stream of behavior" as a topic of analysis. A number of linguists (e.g. Pittenger 1960, McQuown 1971) had also advocated a study of language as it was actually spoken. And there were murmurs within Anthropology too from people such as Gregory Bateson (e.g. Bateson & Mead 1942, Bateson 1956, 1972), who was interested in gesture and the body as well as the differences and similarities between animal and human communication. But many of these approaches were reductive in the sense that the authors were concerned to show how talk – or speech, or behavior – was organized by reference to something else, such as individual psychology. Others were concerned with talk only in so far as it was relevant to some larger theory. In contrast, in his most lucid moments, Goffman was very clear on the point that interaction had properties specific to it and had to be studied on its own terms. He noted, in "The Neglected Situation" (1972) and elsewhere, that this work had hardly begun. In one of his earliest published papers, Goffman (1957) described the various ways in which participants in interaction can become alienated from it. There he remarked (1957: 47):

> I want to consider the ways in which the individual can become alienated from a conversational encounter, the uneasiness that arises with this, and the consequence of this alienation and uneasiness upon the interaction. Since alienation can occur in regard to any imaginable talk, we may be able to learn from it something about the generic properties of spoken interaction.

In other words, Goffman was interested in "psychological" phenomena such as "alienation" and "uneasiness" precisely for the light that they might throw upon the organization of human interaction. What Goffman showed in addition to the various ways in which a person can become alienated in this special sense was that, to run smoothly, interaction demands a kind of unselfconsciousness. Interaction works best when the participants are engaged without being over-involved or otherwise distracted. "Conjoint spontaneous involvement is a *unio mystico*, a socialized trance" (Goffman 1957: 47). If you sit there trying to count the number of Mondays from August until Christmas you are more or less guaranteed to lose the gist of what a speaker is saying and, moreover, to fail to behave in ways appropriate to a recipient (see Bavelas, Coates & Johnson 2000). Moreover, the speaker will almost certainly notice it and orient to that failure as evidence that you are not *really* listening. Inversely, if a speaker becomes over-involved in what they are saying, the manner in which they are saying it can come to distract the recipient from what is actually being said.

To summarize, Goffman thought of face-to-face interaction as simultaneously its own institution and the foundation of everything else in society. This "interaction order", as he called it, is itself a moral ordering: a complex web of standards, expectations, rules and proscriptions to which people orient in their attempts to show deference, adopt a demeanor appropriate to a given situation, avoid embarrassing themselves and others and so on. According to Goffman, face-to-face interaction is an incredibly delicate thing. To maintain the fiction of ease (and to fend off the looming potential for interactional "uneasiness") each participant must dutifully do her part by attending to the right things at the right moments and conveying just the right degree of involvement. In his studies, Goffman attempted to describe different aspects of this balancing act by which we engage in a "reciprocally sustained communion of involvement".

In a more or less independent but parallel movement, in the late 1950s and early 1960s Harold Garfinkel was developing a critique of mainstream sociological thinking that was to develop into ethnomethodology (see Garfinkel 1974). Garfinkel had studied with Talcott

Parsons in the social relations program at Harvard but was deeply influenced by the phenomenology of Alfred Schutz and Edmund Husserl. Parsons was concerned with what he described, in a monumental study, as the "structure of social action", and developed a model in which, to put it very crudely, actors employed means to achieve ends within particular circumstances (Parsons 1937; see Heritage 1984b). For Parsons, social order is a result of socialization and the internalization of norms. If it weren't for the fact that people internalized norms, the argument goes, they would simply do whatever they needed to further their own ends and satisfy their own interests. Garfinkel challenged this conventional wisdom not by arguing with the model of human nature it implies but by suggesting that, to the extent that social life is regulated by such norms, this rests upon a foundation of practical reasoning. People, Garfinkel suggested, must determine what norms, precedents, traditions and so on apply to any given situation. This being so, an explanation of human conduct that involves citing the rules or norms being followed is obviously inadequate since the question remains as to how it was decided that *these* were the relevant rules or norms to follow! Moreover, how did the people involved decide how decisions were to be made in the first place? The underlying substratum of practical reasoning, argued Garfinkel, had all but escaped sociological notice despite the fact that it seemed to constitute the very precondition of society in the first place.

Followed through to its logical conclusion, practical reasoning always seems to result in infinite regress, since you end up having to say that behind each rule or norm is another that governs its application, and so on and so on (infinitely). Language presents a special case of just this kind of thing. For instance, if people frequently mean more than they say, which of course they do (e.g. "I'm not happy", "Well! That was interesting"), how are we able to determine what they mean in any given case? On this view, the meaning of any utterance can seem radically indeterminate. Garfinkel, however, noted that in fact, in the course of their everyday activities, ordinary members of society do not *typically* encounter problems of radical indeterminacy. The reason for this is twofold. First, the meaning of an utterance normally appears indeterminate only when that utterance is removed from the context of use within which it was produced (so if we know that "Well! That was interesting" was said by one friend to another after a chance meeting with a mutual acquaintance from work, what it means becomes obvious). And of course, ordinary persons encounter words within these rich contexts of use that provide for their intelligibility. Second, in the course of their ordinary activities, members of society adopt an attitude toward everyday life that seems to largely circumvent potential problems of indeterminacy. For instance, unless given reason not to, people generally assume that things are as they seem. They trust, that is, in ordinary appearances.

Drawing on Schutz and other phenomenologists, Garfinkel argued that everyday activities are made possible by a range of "background expectancies". Garfinkel tested what happens when these basic assumptions and expectancies of everyday life are challenged. For instance, in one experiment, students were asked to "spend from fifteen minutes to an hour in their homes imagining that they were boarders and acting out this assumption. They were instructed to conduct themselves in circumspect and polite fashion. They were to avoid getting personal, to use formal address, to speak only when spoken to" (Garfinkel 1967: 47). The results were dramatic. The student experimenters reported that family members were "stupefied" and "vigorously sought to make the strange actions intelligible and to restore the situation to normal appearances." Moreover, there was an obvious moral dimension to the family members' reactions:

> Reports were filled with accounts of astonishment, bewilderment, shock, anxiety, embarrassment and anger, and with charges by various family members that the student was mean, inconsiderate, nasty or impolite. Family members demanded explanations: What's the matter? What has got into you? Did you get fired? Are you sick? What are you being so superior about? Why are you mad? Are you out of your mind or just stupid? One student acutely embarrassed his mother in front of her friend by asking if she minded if he had a snack from the refrigerator. "Mind if you have a little snack? You've been eating little snacks around here for years without asking me. What's gotten into you?" One mother, infuriated when her daughter spoke to her only when she was spoken to, began to shriek in angry denunciation of the daughter for her disrespect and insubordination and refused to be calmed by the student's sister. A father berated his daughter for being insufficiently concerned for the welfare of others and for acting like a spoiled child. (Garfinkel 1967: 47–8)

Not surprisingly, students found it hard to sustain the pretence and reported feelings of relief at being able, at the conclusion of the experiment, to slip back into "normal" patterns of behavior.[3]

By the early to mid-1960s Harvey Sacks was deeply immersed in themes that Garfinkel and Goffman had developed. It is common, and not entirely inaccurate, to say that conversation analysis emerged as a synthesis of these two currents: It was the study of practical reasoning (à la Garfinkel) applied to the special and particular topic of social interaction (à la Goffman). There are at least two problems with this view. First, while certainly influenced by both Garfinkel and Goffman, Sacks, Schegloff and Jefferson also had their own distinctive approach and early CA cannot be reduced to either the influence or the confluence of these two seminal thinkers. Although some of his early work shows the clear influence of either Garfinkel (see Sacks 1963, 1967, Garfinkel and Sacks 1970) or Goffman (see Sacks 1972), by the late 1960s Sacks was clearly doing something quite distinctive. Schegloff's "Sequencing in conversational openings" (1968) remains to this day a model of CA method and analysis and bears little resemblance to the studies of Goffman and Garfinkel. Second, in addition to Goffman and Garfinkel there were a number of slightly less prominent but nevertheless important influences on the development of CA. Let me take up this last point before returning to the issue of the way in which Sacks, Schegloff and Jefferson's vision departed from that of Goffman and Garfinkel.

Reading Harvey Sacks's lectures one is immediately struck by the enormous range of work in the social sciences and humanities that he engaged with at a serious level. Obviously, I can't review that range of work in its entirety here and so instead I'll just mention a few streams running through the lectures. First, the anthropological stream: At one point, Sacks describes Evans-Pritchard's (1937) *Witchcraft, Oracles and Magic among the Azande* as "one of the greatest books in the social sciences" (1995a: 34). What was it that Sacks saw in this work seemingly so different from his own? In this book, Evans-Pritchard set about describing the Azande's use of various oracles in their everyday lives. Basically, when misfortune befalls an Azande he or she figures that its cause is witchcraft, and in fact Evans-Pritchard tells us these people have no concept of luck or chance. So, if a granary collapses one looks for the ultimate cause not in the termites that are known to inhabit the supporting posts of the structure but rather in the malevolence and general ill will of a neighbor or a kinsman.[4] Of course, any Azande is well aware that termites can weaken the strength of supporting beams, but then, how did the termites get there in the first place? And what caused the granary to collapse at the particular moment when someone was sleeping under it? The details of Evans-Pritchard's fascinating study need not concern us here. We should ask, instead, what Sacks saw in it relevant to the analysis of conversation. Sacks discusses the Azande example in relation to calls to a suicide prevention line. There he suggests that suicide is "a device for discovering if anybody cares", and he notes that among the Azande the oracle "is a device which is routinely employable for checking out how it is that others attend to your ill- or well-being" (1995a: 35). Beyond this rather surprising parallel, Evans-Pritchard's study resonates with conversation analysis in a more general sense. First, it is obviously based on close and detailed observation of what people do in their ordinary lives. Evans-Pritchard is a master of artful and subtle observation – just the kind of skill Sacks, Schegloff and Jefferson sought to cultivate in examining conversational materials. Second, Evans-Pritchard takes what looks like clearly irrational and bizarre behavior and, by putting it into an appropriate interpretive context, shows that it is perfectly rational and logically sound. There is a parallel again with CA, which has always been concerned to illustrate the underlying rationality and logic of ordinary human practice, refusing to ironicize them by comparing them to some standard imported from another setting (e.g. scientific procedures).

By the 1960s there were of course a number of other quite relevant things happening in anthropology. First, there were various attempts to tap into the "cognitive revolution" which, spurred on by Noam Chomsky's work in *Aspects of a Theory of Syntax* (1965) and *Syntactic Structures* (1957), was already in full swing within linguistics. In anthropology, this included such approaches as ethnoscience (from which Garfinkel had borrowed the name "ethnomethodology") and componential analysis (see Garfinkel 1974, D'Andrade 1995). The formal analytic character of this work appealed to Sacks and likely influenced his thinking about categories and what he would term "membership categorization devices". Also within anthropology at this time there was an emerging awareness of the importance of studying language use as part of the social and cultural world. People like Dell Hymes and John Gumperz – later to become important if short-lived advocates of CA – were developing an approach known as the ethnography of speaking which involved describing the particular ways in which people used language as part of a distinctive cultural repertoire in, for instance, marriage requests and rituals, in prayer and so on (see Gumperz and Hymes 1964, 1972, Bauman and Sherzer 1974). In short, from its earliest days, conversation analysis had always had a rather intimate, though at times fraught, connection with anthropology (see Sidnell 2008). This is seen not only in the emphasis on close observation of everyday activities but also in a common concern for the role language plays in the organization of those activities.

Another current in both Sacks's lectures and Schegloff's earliest writings was Sigmund Freud and the theory and practice of psychoanalysis more generally (see for example Schegloff 1963, Sacks 1995a). With his clear emphasis on the deep and hidden recesses of the human mind, Freud would seem on the surface an unlikely source of inspiration for an approach that takes seriously the public and fundamentally interactional character of human conduct and talk in particular. But this gross contrast obscures important points of convergence. For one thing, Freud was, like Evans-Pritchard, an extremely astute observer of human behavior. Indeed one could argue that Freud's greatest contribution was simply in getting people to see the importance of things that initially seemed utterly inconsequential, things that slip our notice most of the time. In fact, Freud starts the famous *Introductory Lectures* with an extended argument about the relevance of examining apparently small things (Freud 1975). For Freud, what needed defending was the study of apparently trivial slips of the tongue and apparently unintentional occurrences of arriving late or forgetting one's hat, all of which he grouped together under the term "parapraxes".[5] Freud of course argued that such things were far from random. Rather they were expressions of a hitherto little-understood domain of mental life: the unconscious. In a remarkably similar way, Sacks found himself defending his own studies of "small" phenomena. He writes (Sacks 1984a: 24, see also 1995a: 26–31): "It is possible that the detailed study of small phenomena may give an enormous understanding of the way humans do things and the kinds of objects they use to construct and order their affairs."[6]

Of course CA is neither anthropology nor Freudian psychoanalysis. The only point I want to make here is that it emerged in dialogue with a range of perspectives within the social and human sciences. While the influence of Goffman and Garfinkel was obviously pivotal, the intellectual milieu within which CA emerged was a complex and multifaceted one that included themes from sociology, anthropology, linguistics, philosophy and other disciplines (see Schegloff 1995: xiv–xv for a useful description of this environment).

Sacks's First Lectures on Conversation

In 1963 Garfinkel invited Sacks to UCLA to work on a project with a suicide-prevention program. This work was important because it brought to Sacks's attention the possibilities of working with recordings, and it also forced him to deal for the first time with some basic features of talk-in-interaction. The first lecture in Sacks's collected lectures is titled "Rules of Conversational Sequence". He begins with three examples of telephone openings to the suicide-prevention line:

(2) From Sacks, "Rules of Conversation Sequence"
A: Hello
B: Hello

(3) From Sacks, "Rules of Conversation Sequence"
A: This is Mr. Smith may I help you
B: Yes, this is Mr. Brown

(4) From Sacks, "Rules of Conversation Sequence"
A: This is Mr. Smith may I help you
B: I can't hear you
A: This is Mr. Smith.
B: Smith

Sacks notes that a fundamental problem the call-takers faced had to do with getting callers to give their name. He reports that one of his earliest findings, on reviewing the tapes, was that if the staff member opened with "This is Mr. Smith may I help you" any answer *other* than "Yes, this is Mr. Brown" meant that the staff member would have serious trouble getting the caller to give his or her name.

This led to an important discovery. It's obvious that the first and second turn in each of the first two exchanges constitutes some kind of unit (an "adjacency pair"). But beyond this Sacks noticed that there was a "fit" between the two parts, so that if the first person says "hello" then so does the second, if the first person says "this is Mr. Smith" then the second tends to say "this is Mr. Brown", etc. This is important enough but it also leads to another, equally significant, observation. Namely, if there is a tendency to fit the form of the return to the form of the initiating action in any of these greeting ("hello") or introduction ("This is Mr. Smith") pairs, then there exists a way of getting someone's name without asking for it. Rather than saying "what is your name?" one can say "This is Mr. Smith", and this will establish the relevance of the other giving his or her name. So Sacks was making an observation about the multiple ways of doing an action. That, Sacks goes on to note, is important also for the following reason. If the staff member asks "Would you give me your name?" the caller can reply "Why?" or "What for?" That is, the caller can ask the staff member to provide a reason for asking for the name. In this book, and in CA more generally, we tend to talk about "accounts" rather than "reasons", and in this first lecture Sacks (1995a: 4) notes "what one does with 'Why?' is to propose about some action that it is an 'accountable action'. That is to say, 'Why?' is a way of asking for an account." Sacks goes on to suggest that accounts "control activities".[7] What he means by that, I think, is that a person can be asked why they are doing an action and if they can't come up with a reason they may have to abandon it. The important point here is that "This is Mr. Smith, may I help you?" may be a way of getting the other person to provide her name, but it is not an accountable action in that respect; one cannot say in response "Why do you want my name?" because the name was never asked for.

What about the third example? Sacks would later describe turns like "I can't hear you" as initiating repair, but in this early lecture he notes only that turns such as "your name is what?" and question-intoned repeats like "My helplessness?" are "occasionally usable" (see chapter 7). He explains: "That is to say, there doesn't have to be a particular sort of thing preceding it; it can come at any place in a conversation." Moreover, with "I can't hear you", Sacks notes, the caller essentially skips a turn and, thus, the position in which giving the name is relevant never occurs. Of course, it's not as if this is a device for avoiding giving one's name: on the contrary, the primary use of repair is fixing problems of speaking, hearing and understanding. The point is that it can be used that way in part because there are very few, if any, restrictions on where it can go in a sequence.

Understanding in Conversation

Intersubjectivity – joint or shared understanding between persons – is typically explained in terms of convergent knowledge of the world. On this view, the world exhibits objective characteristics and, to the extent that different persons apply identical and valid procedures for generating knowledge of the world, they will converge in their knowledge and understanding of their circumstances (Heritage 1984: 26). In the social sciences, a related solution to the problem of intersubjectivity invokes the notion of a common culture as the resource through which "the individual's grasp of reality is mediated" (Schegloff 1992a).[8] In contrast, conversation analysts have developed a rather different account. In talk-in-interaction each utterance displays a hearing or analysis of a preceding one and, thus, the very organization of talk provides a means by which intersubjective understanding can not only be continually demonstrated but also checked and, where found wanting, repaired. Consider then the following case from the opening of a telephone call between two friends:

(5) Deb and Dick – Telephone opening.
01 Deb: Hello:(hh)?
02 Dick: Good morning=

Deb: =Hi:, how are ya.
Dick: Not too bad. How are you?
Deb: I'm fi::ne.

Here, then, Deb's response to Dick's "How are you?" in line 05 displays a number of basic understandings of that turn (Schegloff 1992a). By starting to talk at this moment (and not a few milliseconds earlier) Deb shows an understanding that Dick's turn was possibly finished. By producing an answer, Deb shows that she has heard the previous turn to be a question. By answering with a description of her personal state, Deb shows that she has heard the question to be a wh-question (involving a question word like "who," "where," "how" etc.) rather than a yes–no interrogative. By responding with "fine" rather than "terrible", or "absolutely fabulous", Deb shows an understanding of what this question is doing in this environment (a routine opening inquiry, not meant to be taken literally) and so on.

The turn-by-turn organization of talk provides then for a continuously updated context of intersubjective understanding, accomplished *en passant* in the course of other activities (see chapter 4). These publicly displayed understandings are provisional and contingent and thus susceptible to being found wanting, problematic, partial or simply incorrect. Where a first speaker finds the understanding displayed by a second speaker's turn inadequate they have recourse to a mechanism for correcting it – an organized set of practices of repair (see chapter 7).

This suggests that in conversation understandings emerge in the course of interaction and are revisable in light of what subsequently happens. With this in mind, consider the following case. Here three 4-year-olds are playing with blocks. Erika has created a tower-like structure and when Jude accidentally bumps the table she produces the turn in line 01:

(6) KIDS_02_02_06(1of2)JKT1.mov 10:55
Erika: Ju::de: yer makin' (me) knock it dow:n.
(0.4)
be more careful next time.
Jude: I: wi:ll:. I we:ll, I will, I will.
Tina: He sounds like a (actin) hhh
kinda like (ss) (0.2) ba:(h):by,
(0.8)
Jude: Ba::by?
(0.4)
Tina: he he ha ha oh .hhhh
Jude: sshhh.
(0.2)
You sound like a baby (to Adult)

This fragment begins, then, with Erika complaining that, by shaking the table, Jude is making her knock down the structure she is building. She enjoins him to "be more careful next time" to which he responds with "I: wi:ll:. I we:ll, I will, I will." Now although in saying this Jude acquiesces and accepts responsibility for "not being careful", the manner in which he says it – with multiple repetition and a whining intonation – conveys also that he is treating the complaint as less than completely serious.

Tina picks up on the somewhat peculiar way Jude says this in her talk at lines 05–06, remarking that Jude "sounds like – kinda like a baby". You can imagine, I think, how children of this age might respond to being called a "baby" or to having their behavior characterized as "like a baby". At four years, these children have really only just stopped being "babies". Moreover, though they are no longer infants, much of their behavior is in fact quite "baby-like". As such, Tina's turn at lines 05–06, which she produces with considerable hesitation, is hearable, I think, as a rather grave insult. Notice though that she allows a hint of laughter to infiltrate the word "baby". Gail Jefferson (1979) showed that such inserted laugh tokens are often treated as invitations to laugh by their recipients and so this might be seen as blunting the possible insult of "baby". However, that analysis is complicated here by the fact that Tina has addressed her remark not to Jude but to Erika. Thus the invitation to laugh may be treated as an invitation to laugh *at* Jude rather than *with* him (see Glenn 2003). Jude may hear in this then not only an insult but, in addition, a hint of ridicule.

Notice then, that when Jude questions the characterization "baby" by repeating this word with rising intonation, Tina withdraws the seriousness of the insult with laughter, treating her own talk and perhaps also Jude's at line 04 as a joke. Unlike the earlier laugh token, because of its position in a sequence initiated by Jude's questioning repeat this bout of laughter is clearly appreciative rather than ridiculing. Notice also that in line 13 Jude repeats this bit of talk but now directs it at the only adult in the room, in this way making its status as a joke unequivocal.

The point here is that the meaning, sense, and import of Tina's talk at lines 05–06 emerges over the course of this short interaction. Jude's "baby" marks this part of Tina's talk as potentially problematic and Tina's subsequent laughter retrospectively casts a possible insult as a joke.

We've seen then that talk-in-interaction provides an apparently unique methodological lever in the form of next utterances: in responding to a previous utterance a recipient necessarily displays a hearing or understanding of that utterance. Participants of course use those displayed understandings to see if and how they were understood, and we analysts can use them too. So in our last example, we can see that Jude, in answering with "I will . . .", hears Erika's "be more careful next time" as a request, Tina hears Jude's "I will . . ." as something other than a straightforward acceptance of that request, and so on. The analyst then can draw on the methods of the participants themselves and in so doing largely avoid the otherwise very real problems of indeterminacy and interpretation that afflict other approaches to language and discourse.

Conversation and Intrigue

In the examples discussed up to this point, I've stressed the importance of practical reasoning in the achievement and maintenance of understanding. This is an important underlying theme in conversation analysis and of course some degree of mutual understanding, or at least the presumption of such, is prerequisite to anything else that gets done in and through conversation. But there's more to social interaction than understanding.

In his analyses, Goffman tended to emphasize the way in which participants position themselves in relation to one another (see for instance Goffman 1956). Goffman often talked about this in terms of "face" (see Goffman 1955). Everybody presents a face to the world, a face that they want to have accepted and publicly ratified by others. According to Goffman social interaction is organized in such a way as to allow for the maintenance of face. This is a kind of group collusion in which each person must play his or her part. We treat one another, says Goffman, as ritual, sacred objects by carefully showing respect for the various "territories of the self".

Conversation analysts do not accept all these ideas about face nor do they embrace Goffman's methods. Some of the disagreement about these and other ideas came out in an exchange between Goffman and Schegloff. Late in his career, Goffman (1976) wrote a thinly veiled critique of conversation analysis called "Replies and Responses", and Schegloff (1988a) later responded in an effort to correct a number of misunderstandings. The exchange as a whole highlights many important differences between these two approaches. So while CA does not adopt a Goffmanian approach towards the individual that revolves around face-needs and the self as a "ritual object", it does attend to the very real ways in which people negotiate who-we-are-to-one-another in conversation and other forms of interaction (see for instance Heritage and Raymond 2005). Despite the fact that of the three co-founders of CA, Jefferson was the only one who didn't study with Goffman, she is known for highlighting this aspect of social interaction in her analyses. Indeed, Jefferson is reported as saying that she was always more drawn to the "intrigue" than to the "system" of conversation.

With this in mind then let's turn to consider one more fragment of conversation. Here two friends – 12-year-old girls – are talking on the phone. It's the day before Halloween and Betty has called Sue. The call begins with a report by Betty about what a group of girls at Betty's current, and Sue's former, school intend to dress up as for Halloween. The two girls converge on a strongly negative evaluation of these girls and their costume choices before a younger sibling, who is watching television in the same room she is talking on the phone, distracts Betty. The instruction to "watch smart guy" in line 108 is apparently addressed to this sibling. After a confusion on this score is cleared up, Betty returns to the topic of Halloween remarking "=>°no<, but I wan-I wanna go trick er treating with you=but like (.) yeah."

(7) YYZ: Halloween

Betty: watch smart guy.
(2.0)
Sue: are you talkin' to m:e?
(1.0)
Betty: yeah
Sue: oh::haha.HHH I'm like who the hell is she talking to? .hh
anyway ummm::=
Betty: → =>°no<, but I wan-I wanna go trick or treating with you=but
like (.) yeah.
Sue: .hhh(hhh) yeah bu-are=yu- wait are you going with like
Sarah Maxine an' st(hhh)uff hhh
Betty: no.
Sue: No::?
Betty: n::o=
Sue: =>okay well let's go together then<.
Betty: mmm Kay=
Sue: =kay (0.2) °just– [
Betty: [okay so let's go around like (0.2) OUR,
neighbourhood?
Sue: yeah. co[me down he::re
Betty: [°mmm k]
(1.0)
Sue: .hhh 'cause I don't wanna- [
Betty: [So h:ow's everybody
doing::? >at your house.

The turn at line 115 is transcribed with various symbols used to indicate some of the details of the way in which it was said and many of these will be unfamiliar to some readers at this point. Let's just note that Betty initially ends the turn with "but like" and subsequently recompletes it with "yeah". As I'll discuss in more detail in chapter 4, a very basic kind of question we can ask about a turn in conversation is simply, "What is the speaker doing in saying this and in saying it in this way?" So what is Betty doing here? There are various ways we could answer that question. For one thing she's resuming a topic that was interrupted by the talk at lines 108–13. Betty might also be reasonably described as saying "what she wants", which is to go trick or treating with Sue. If we consider *the way* she says this, we can go on to note that although she's saying what she wants to do, with "but like (.) yeah" she seems to be suggesting that what she wants may not be possible. So what, in the end, is she doing here? Recall Sacks's discussion of call-takers trying to get callers' names by saying "This is Mr. Smith" rather than by saying "What is your name?" The point there was that there are various ways in which speakers can achieve their goals in conversation. Similarly, here we can ask why Betty does what she does in this way rather than some other possible way. For instance, why doesn't Betty just ask Sue "Do you want to go trick or treating with me?" Let's look in more detail at this bit of talk.

(8) YYZ: Halloween (DETAIL)
115 Betty: =>°no<, but I wan-I wanna go trick or treating with you=but
116 like (.) yeah.
117 Sue: .hhh(hhh) yeah bu-are=yu- wait are you going with like
118 Sarah Maxine an' st(hhh)uff hhh
119 Betty: no.
120 Sue: No::?
121 Betty: n::o=
122 Sue: =>okay well let's go together then<.

So, starting with the obvious, one of the things Sue and Betty seem to be doing here is working out a plan to go "trick or treating" together. What's interesting is that they do this without either of them issuing an explicit invitation or anything of that sort. What Betty does rather is simply to reinvoke the topic after a bit of a break by saying that she wants to go with Sue. Notice though what she does at the *end* of her turn. Now it might seem like this "but like (.) yeah." is pretty inconsequential stuff, just rambling or mumbling inarticulateness. "What, after all, does this mean?", one might ask. But asking what this bit of the turn "means" gets the question wrong. We should ask instead what it *does*. In that respect, we will see at various points in this book that turn endings are important because, as Sacks (1987 [1973]) pointed out, turn endings establish what kind of a response is most immediately relevant for a recipient.

So what kind of thing does Betty leave for Sue to respond to? Betty actually completed the turn with "but like", she then added "yeah" after that. Sue then could have responded to the "but like" part, but by holding off on her response she ends up giving Betty another chance to speak, and Betty takes this opportunity to produce "yeah."

By ending the turn with "but like" Betty seems to anticipate a possible obstacle – a reason why these two can't go trick or treating together. We can imagine then various ways in which she might have finished this off, for instance "but like you're not going around here", "but like I have to go with Sarah, Maxine and stuff . . .", "but like it's too late to get it organized" and so on. The point is that by leaving the obstacle she has anticipated unarticulated,

Betty invites Sue to guess at what it might be that she has in mind. This puts Sue in an interesting position. If there's a reason why she can't go with Betty or if she doesn't want to go with Betty she can simply go along with the anticipated obstacle, filling in the blanks as it were. But if there's no problem or obstacle on *her* end, Sue can show that, and this is precisely what she does. That is, she talks in a way that shows she thought they were prevented from going together by the fact that Betty already had plans with others. Now there's a lot more we could say about this, but we are now at the point where we need to cover some basic points before we can go much further. The larger point, however, should be clear enough even from this preliminary analysis: Sue and Betty manage to make their plans without either having to "go out on a limb" interactionally by issuing an explicit invitation which might have been rejected. The anticipated, but apparently fictional, obstacle is a very delicate and rather ingenious way of coming together on this issue without risk to either party.

Conclusion

In this chapter I've tried to introduce some principles of CA through exemplification rather than argument or description. Rather than engage in a detailed discussion of findings or methods, I've focused on a few bits of conversation in the hope of conveying the conversation-analytic approach. This way of going about introducing the field itself embodies a central principle: at its core CA is about close observation of the world. In the actual practice of doing CA such close observation is coupled with a method for collecting, organizing and analyzing patterns across instances; it is to this set of methods that we turn in the next chapter. To conclude the current discussion we should take note of the ways the CA approach differs from other approaches to language and social interaction.

One alternative, associated with anthropology, is to examine talk and interaction in relation to culture. One can ask how, in the details of some interaction, participants embody, enact, challenge, or resist basic cultural themes, which is to say ideas and values around and through which some particular group of people can be seen to identify themselves. While an analysis of this kind can be revealing and make a significant contribution to a theory of culture it typically does little to illuminate the details of the way interaction itself is organized. For this reason perhaps, much work in anthropology, and especially linguistic anthropology, incorporates ideas from conversation analysis in order to develop an account of interaction, combining the structural analysis of talk with in-depth ethnography. Some recent work along these lines has considered the organization of repair (Sidnell 2008) and making reference to persons (see Levinson 2007, Enfield and Stivers 2007).

Another alternative is to examine interaction for what it can say about individual psychology. There are of course many variants of such an approach. Consider for the moment one possible psychological account of the hitches, pauses, restarts and so on that characterize Sue's talk at lines 117–18.

(9) YYZ: Halloween (DETAIL)
115 Betty: =>°no<, but I wan-I wanna go trick or treating with you=but
116 like (.) yeah.
117 Sue: .hhh(hhh) yeah bu-are=yu- wait are you going with like
118 Sarah Maxine an' st(hhh)uff hhh

One kind of psychological account might take these perturbations in the talk as evidence that Sue was nervous, unsure, or perhaps even insecure. This is a psychological account in so far as it seeks to explain aspects of the talk in relation to the state of mind of the speaker. A more sophisticated version, a cognitively based one, might attempt to explain the talk by reference to processing limitations or production issues (see e.g. Levelt 1989). From the perspective adopted in this book, however, such accounts are beside the point. Rather than asking what is going on in the speaker's head (or mind, or brain) we should be asking (as we have) what is being accomplished in interaction by speaking in just this way. We've already started to do this for Betty's "but like (.) yeah" and in later chapters we will sketch an interactional explanation for other features of talk that are often understood as reflecting the speaker's mental state. Of course we do not deny that there are important and interesting things happening in terms of individual psychology and within the minds/brains of individuals. We only refuse to let such potentially interesting things distract us from the task of analyzing interaction on its own terms *as interaction*.

A final contrasting approach is a – broadly speaking – "sociological" and "correlative" one in which the emphasis is on "external" characteristics of the participants and the world in which they live, for example their social class, gender, and race. Again, that the world is so structured is uncontroversial, though it's not at all certain how that structure should itself be understood. Indeed the social world is multiply structured according to many different axes of differentiation. Moreover, there is a situational dimension to this multiplicity such that in one context a speaker's gender is made relevant and in another her age, race or class or even her height is what's most important. This then raises an important issue, one that Sacks discussed in a number of his lectures: in any society persons are categorized in at least two ways. The anthropological literature suggests for instance that in all societies persons are categorized, minimally, in terms of gender (e.g. male vs. female) and age (e.g. infant, child, adult, elder). Of course, many more category sets are used in any society for which adequate documentation is available but, for the sake of argument, we only need to posit two category sets. For once we recognize that more than one categorization is possible (i.e. a person is always *both* an X and a Y – e.g. a child and a male) it becomes reasonable to question any explanation in terms of one or the other. That is, although a woman may be speaking, she may not be speaking *as* a woman. Rather, she may be speaking as an adult, a mother, a doctor, a vegetarian, a Belgian, a dog-lover and so on and so on. I take up some of these issues in chapter 12 but for now let's just note that while talk may be correlated in various ways with the external characteristics of the speaker, the recipient or any other participant, discovering such correlations tells us little about the way that talk is organized in the first place. This brings us back to Goffman, who wrote, in "The Neglected Situation":

> Your social situation is not your country cousin. It can be argued that social situations, at least in our society, constitute a reality *sui generis* as He [Durkheim] used to say, and therefore need and warrant analysis in their own right, much like that accorded other basic forms of social organization.

Notes

1 See Reddy (1979), Volosinov (1973).

2 It's a bit problematic to call Goffman a sociologist plain and simple since, though he clearly was one, he was other things as well. Goffman was trained in large part by anthropologists

(Birdwhistell and Hart at Toronto and Warner at Chicago), he conducted fieldwork in a society different from his own (the Shetland Islands), his intellectual heroes were Durkheim (equal parts sociologist and anthropologist) and Radcliffe-Brown and his influence was perhaps greatest among linguistic anthropologists and sociolinguists (with whom he affiliated in the last ten years of his life at Penn).

3 For further discussion of Garfinkel's work see Heritage 1984, Sharrock and Anderson 1986, Livingston 1987, Sharrock 1989, Francis and Hester 2004 and of course Garfinkel 1967.

4 Evans-Pritchard explains that such ill will generates witchcraft spontaneously and, in some cases, with the witch being quite unaware of it. The system thus appears to discourage directed feelings of ill will while encouraging feelings of suspicion. Sacks compares the system of oracles, which of course is a device for discovering persons who harbor hostility or enmity for another, with suicide, which Sacks describes as a "device for discovering if anybody cares" (Sacks 1995a: 32–9).

5 This points to another domain of resonance: many of the phenomena that Freud considered under the rubric "parapraxes" are handled by conversation analysts as instances of self-repair (i.e. word searches, word replacements, mis-speakings of various kinds). Here see, inter alia, Goodwin 1987, Schegloff, Jefferson and Sacks 1977, Schegloff 1979b. For other conversation-analytic studies that touch on areas of concern also to psychoanalysis see Sacks 1973, Schegloff 2003.

6 But there are problems involved in describing the relevant phenomena as "small" or "micro" in the first place; Schegloff 1987a explains why.

7 On this idea see Antaki 1994.

8 While this is obviously something of a simplification and the actual arguments for this or that view of intersubjectivity are considerably more nuanced than this suggests, it is nevertheless true that these two variants represent, in broad outline, the standard and most common approaches to the "problem of intersubjectivity" across a range of disciplines.

2

Methods

At its core, conversation analysis is a set of *methods* for working with audio and video recordings of talk and social interaction. These methods were worked out in some of the earliest conversation-analytic studies and have remained remarkably consistent over the last forty years. Their continued use has resulted in a large body of strongly interlocking and mutually supportive findings – findings that this book attempts to review. While the focus of the book, then, is on those findings, it is important to begin with a clear sense of the methods that produced them. And so in this chapter I briefly outline the basic methodological principles of CA. This is not, however, a "how-to guide", for several reasons. First, I do not believe that it is possible to provide a set of instructions for doing CA. Because it is fundamentally about discovering things we don't already know, CA requires some kind of apprenticeship or guided instruction from an already experienced practitioner. A book simply cannot teach this. Second, there are several other books that provide a more "hands-on" approach and I doubt very much whether they can be improved upon (ten Have 2007, Hutchby and Wooffitt 2008).

Different conversation analysts have different ways of working, so what is described here will not match exactly the methods of every practitioner. Moreover, different projects impose different methodological requirements. The point is not to set up a system of inviolable rules then but rather to suggest some possible strategies for working.

Acquiring Data

The first step is of course to acquire recordings of talk-in-interaction. In a lecture published, in edited form, as "Notes on Methodology", Sacks (1984a) explains the importance of working with actual, mechanically recorded, instances of talk-in-interaction.

> I want to argue that, however rich our imaginations are, if we use hypothetical, or hypothetical-typical versions of the world we are constrained by reference to what an audience, an audience of professionals, can accept as reasonable. That might not appear to be a terrible constraint until we come to look at the kinds of things that actually occur. Were I to say about many of the objects we work with "Let us suppose that this happened; now I am going to consider it," then

> an audience might feel hesitant about what I would make of it by reference to whether such things happen. That is to say, under such a constraint many things that actually occur are debarred from use as a basis for theorizing about conversation. I take it that this debarring affects the character of social sciences very strongly.

There are then several reasons why conversation analysts insist on working from actual recordings of conversation rather than imagined, remembered or experimentally produced examples. Heritage (1984b) summarizes these issues nicely. He notes that the following example is not unusual in its level of complexity:

(1) NB VII:2
01 Edna: =Oh honey that was a lovely luncheon I shoulda ca:lled you
02 s:soo[:ner but I:]l:[lo:ved it.Ih wz just deli:ghtfu[: l.]=
03 Margy: [((f)) Oh:::] [°( ) [Well]=
04 Margy: =I wz gla[d y o u] (came).]
05 Edna: ['nd yer f:] friends] 'r so da:rli:ng,=
06 Margy: = Oh ::: [: it wz:]
07 Edna: [e-that P]a :t isn'she a do:[:ll?]
08 Margy: [iY e]h isn't she pretty,
09 (.)
10 Edna: Oh: she's a beautiful girl.=
11 Margy: =Yeh I think she's a pretty gir[l.
12 Edna: [En that Reinam'n::
13 (.)
14 Edna: She SCA:RES me.=

This level of complexity can be readily recovered from recordings of actual conversation, but could it be invented or recollected? That seems unlikely. In fact, we don't have very good intuitions for this kind of thing, nor do we tend to remember the precise way in which someone pronounced a word (e.g. whether they said "thuh" or "thee"), though such details can turn out to be quite consequential for the way that an interaction unfolds.

In the quotation above, Sacks raises another important consideration. Specifically, Sacks notes that if one works with invented examples (or even recollected examples) one is constrained "by reference to what an audience, an audience of professionals, can accept as reasonable." The problem is that we know from studying recordings of conversations that many apparently counterintuitive and unexpected things actually do happen. If invented instances of such occurrences were presented to an audience people might well object, "but people don't say such things", "People don't talk like that" and so on. As Sacks notes, then, the use of recordings can open up a whole range of phenomena that no one would have ever suspected even existed.

> Our business will be to proceed somewhat differently. We will be using observation as a basis for theorizing. Thus we start with things that are not currently imaginable, by showing that they happened. We can then come to see that a base for using close looking at the world for theorizing about it is that from close looking at the world we can find things that we could not, by imagination, assert were there. (1984b: 25)

There is another important consideration involved in the insistence on using actual recordings. Thus as Sacks notes in the same set of remarks:

> I started to work with tape-recorded conversations. Such materials had a single virtue, that I could replay them. I could transcribe them somewhat and study them extendedly – however long it might take. The tape-recorded materials constituted a "good-enough" record of what happened. Other things, to be sure, happened, but at least what was on the tape had happened. It was not from any large interest in language or from some theoretical formulation of what should be studied that I started with tape-recorded conversations, but simply because I could get my hands on it and I could study it again and again, and also consequentially, because others could look at what I had studied and make of it what they could, if, for example, they wanted to be able to disagree with me.

As these remarks suggest, conversation analysis is a deeply empirical tradition. From its beginnings in Sacks's lectures, a strong emphasis has been placed on providing readers (or listeners) with the resources they need in order to check on the analyses being reported. In oral presentations of conversation-analytic work it is customary to play back for the audience recordings of the data being referred to. Not only does this again allow others to check the analyses against the data for themselves, it also allows for new, unanticipated noticings by others. Today, the internet has made it possible to provide readers of conversation-analytic research with access to the audio and video files which are being drawn upon. However, it is not always possible to make our data public in this way since participants in our recordings rarely give permission for such uses.

Sharing data in this way may seem like a perfectly obvious thing to do. In the natural sciences it is, of course, considered crucial that others are able to replicate the results being reported and this often requires making the data on which the analysis is based public if it is not already. But in the social sciences – in anthropology and sociology for instance – this is not so common. Anthropologists rarely share their fieldnotes with others. Anthropologists face another problem, since it is often the case that the anthropologist who conducted the research is the only person who has the experience and knowledge required to fully assess the arguments and analyses he or she is presenting. Members of the audience or readers are at a disadvantage because they do not speak the language and are not familiar with the cultural values operating or the social practices that the anthropologist claims are relevant to an understanding of the phenomenon of analytic interest.

For conversation analysis to work as Sacks intended, then, members of the analytic community must share access to the materials being studied. This explains the preference, among English-speaking analysts, for working on English materials (and likewise for Finnish materials among Finnish-speaking analysts, etc.). This situation provides a group of analysts with at least comparable access to the data being examined. This is not to say that English-speaking analysts are incapable of studying materials in other languages. It is simply to register what this entails. Essentially the conversation analyst must learn at least some of the language in order to work with such materials, since working via translations clearly won't do.[1]

Obviously, there are many ways to acquire data. For various reasons, perhaps the best way is to actually go out and video-record face-to-face interaction. Today, those of us who work at universities have to go through a rather complex set of legal and ethical reviews to do this. The results are, however, often worth the hassle. When it captures relatively naturalistic interaction, video-tape provides an extremely rich source of data that allows the conversation analyst to examine not just talk but also the use of the body and especially gaze and gesture in the organization of interaction. It is, for the moment, as close as we can get to recording just what the participants themselves had available to them as resources for producing and understanding the interaction. There are many complications involved in video-recording interaction that cannot be reviewed here. The reader is referred to the excellent article by Charles Goodwin (1993) and Duranti's (1997) chapter on methods in *Linguistic Anthropology*.

Another way to collect data is through the use of a telephone audio recorder. A great deal of conversation-analytic work has been based on recordings of telephone conversation. Obviously this sets up a number of quite consequential constraints, the most obvious being that the participants cannot see one another and thus cannot make use of gesture and gaze as communicative devices (though they may of course continue to gesture). Moreover, the number of parties, at least for traditional telephone talk, is limited to two, a matter of some consequence for the organization of turn-taking among other things (see chapter 3 and Sacks, Schegloff, and Jefferson 1974). These constraints obviously limit what can be done with telephone conversation but they also make it much easier to work with at least in some respects. In co-present interaction between three or more parties, sequences of action can become exceedingly convoluted and complex. While two-party telephone conversations have their own complexities, a number of complicating factors are bracketed out in such a way as to make some aspects of the organization of interaction more visible. At the same time, with the exception of certain practices that are clearly tied to the technology (such as recognizing and identifying one another through voice samples at the beginning of a telephone call – see chapter 10) just about all the findings based on telephone conversation appear to hold up for co-present, multi-party interaction as well. So there are some very good reasons to collect telephone calls. Moreover, it is often possible to collect an extended corpus of calls – from a single home for instance – and this can allow for a much more nuanced analysis based on a detailed knowledge of the persons involved and their relationships to one another. Some of these corpora are Newport Beach (NB), Santa Barbara Ladies (SBL), the Holt or Field corpus, etc.

The public domain can also be a rich source of data for the conversation analyst. It is often possible, for instance, to collect data from courtroom settings by tapping into public television broadcasts. Even so-called "reality" television shows may offer potential data for study, although caution must be exercised as interactional sequences have typically been edited in such a way as to make it difficult to tell exactly where cuts have been made. Certainly, talk shows can provide interesting and potentially rewarding sources. Another rich source is provided by radio. Today many radio shows are archived and publicly available on the internet so that many hours of data can be collected quite easily.

Transcribing and Making Observations

Doing conversation analysis involves making transcripts of recorded talk. People sometimes think of transcribing as laborious, mind-numbing grunt-work, something that only novices should have to do. For conversation analysts, nothing could be further from the truth. It's not just *having* the transcript that is crucial to conversation-analytic work, but the actual process of working from recordings, replaying them sometimes hundreds of times in an attempt to hear precisely what is being said. To do conversation analysis you have to train yourself to listen to talk in a different way. One has to learn to hear the sometimes very subtle nuances of intonation and breath and pacing because these can turn out to be consequential for the way in which talk is heard by its recipients, for the way they respond to it and thus for the way that it is organized. As ordinary members of the society, as conversationalists rather than conversation analysts, we apparently hear such details without being fully conscious or aware of them. This is a good thing since it's likely that we would not be able to engage in conversation were we fully aware of all the details of its production.[2] But as analysts we must train ourselves to hear and become aware of the details. The single best way of doing this is to do transcription and lots of it, indeed, as much as possible.

It is said that when Harvey Sacks hired Gail Jefferson to start producing transcriptions of the recordings he had been collecting (at one point she was listed as his "data recovery technician") he gave her a single instruction: "just write down what you hear." That is, he did not presume to know what level of detail was going to be relevant to his investigations, and thus Jefferson was left with the task of determining what might be relevant to and consequential for the participants and therefore what should be included in the transcript. Over a period of several years, Jefferson developed a system of conventions to represent various details of talk-in-interaction. At first glance a transcript produced with this system can seem tremendously complicated. Here is a snippet of a transcript from a radio interview in which Shealagh Rogers is talking to Frank Iacobucci, then interim President of the University of Toronto, to illustrate.

(2) Sounds like Canada – Iacobucci 20/4/05
FI: [mmhm
SR: [(an' tuh-) this is a retur:n to you fer
thee- t'the University uh Toronto.
FI: That's right I: ah: I was: uh u-in the university
fer nearly twenty yea:rs then went to Ottawa,
(.)
°h uhto do things there: an' [(turn)]
SR: [hhh hha: ha]
to do thi(h)ngs the:re.=
FI: =right.
SR: ri[ght.
FI: [(uh huh)=
SR: to do ↑big things the[re.
FI: [we:ll I- uhm I- I was:
Look.=I've been very fortunate. I: been very
very fortunate to have had the opportunities
to serve.
(0.2)
an' that's what I emphasize it's to serve

Here is another way in which this snippet might have been represented:

(3) Sounds like Canada – Iacobucci 20/4/05
SR: and this a return for you to the University of Toronto?
FI: That's right. I was in the University for nearly twenty years and then went to Ottawa to do things there.
SR: (laughs) To do things there.
FI: Right.
SR: Right. To do big things there.
FI: Well I was- Look I've been very fortunate. I've been very fortunate to have had the opportunities to serve and that's what I emphasize it's to serve.

So what's the point of the first transcript? Why include all those mysterious-looking symbols? It obviously makes the transcript a lot less readable. One obvious reason for putting in the detail is simply that it's there in the recordings, in other words, that that's just the way the talk was produced. It's a matter of being faithful to reality. But this is not, in the end, a very good answer. Jefferson (1985: 25) explains why:

> when we talk about transcription we are talking about one way to pay attention to recordings of actually occurring events. While those of us who spend a lot of time making transcripts may be doing our best to get it right, what that might mean is utterly obscure and unstable. It depends a great deal on what we are paying attention to. It seems to me, then, that the issue is not transcription per se, but what it is we might want to transcribe, that is, attend to.

In the same paper, Jefferson goes on to note that one of the things we might decide to attend to is laughter. She compares the treatment of laughter in earlier and later versions of a transcript she made. Here are the two versions:

```
(4)  [GTS:I:1:14, 1965]
01   Ken:     And he came home and decided he was gonna play with his
02            orchids from then on in.
03   Roger:   With his what?
04   Louise:  heh heh heh heh
05   Ken:     With his orchids. [He has an orchid-
06   Roger:                     [oh heh hehheh
07   Louise:  ((through bubbling laughter)) Playing with his organ yeah
08            I thought the same thing!
09   Ken:     No he's got a great big[glass house-
10   Roger:                          [I can see him playing with his
11            organ hehh hhhh

(5)  [GTS:I:2:33:R2, 1977]
01   Ken:     An'e came home'n decided'e wz gonna play with iz o:rchids.
02            from then on i:n.
03   Roger:   With iz what?
04   Louise:  mh hih hih[huh
05   Ken:                [with iz orchids.=
06   Ken:     =Ee[z got an orch[id-
07   Roger:      [Oh:.         [hehh[h a h   ·he:h] ·heh
08   Louise:                        [heh huh ·hh] PLAYN(h)W(h)IZ O(h)R'N
09            ya:h I[thought the [same
10   Roger:         [·uh::       [·hunhh ·hh ·hh
11   Ken:                        [Cz eez gotta great big[gla:ss house]=
12   Roger:                                             [I c'n s(h)ee ]
13   Ken:     =[(          )
14   Roger:   =[im pl(h)ay with iz o(h)r(h)g ·(h)n ·uh
```

Focusing just on the laughter, we can note with Jefferson that in the first version Louise's laughter is simply noted at the beginning of the turn ("through bubbling laughter") at lines 07–08. The later version shows something much more precise – the laughter is actually quite localized and infects just the segment of talk represented in standard orthography as "with his organ". Jefferson notes that in one influential account, advocated by Goffman (1961), laughter is explained in terms of "flooding out" – a speaker cannot contain his or her laughter and it infiltrates the talk in progress. But Jefferson asks whether "on this occasion, laughter in the course of talk is not flooding out but has been put in" (1985: 30). She notes that the presence of laughter can make an utterance, or, as here, some specific portion of an utterance, difficult to hear. It thereby sets the recipients the task of figuring out what it is the speaker is trying to say. In order to figure out what someone is saying we rely on our sense of what is a possible or probable thing to say in this context (Sacks 1995a: 722–9). Thus, as Jefferson puts it, "*playn wz orn* is an object that may specifically require, rely upon, and refer its recipients to their own guilty knowledge in order to analyze out of the distorted utterance what is being said" (1985: 31). So by allowing laughter to infiltrate the talk and forcing her recipients to recover what it is she is saying from her distorted utterance, the speaker co-implicates her recipients in her "perverse" hearing of Ken's talk in lines 01–02. Jefferson notes also that although Louise employs a standard turn format (repeat + yeah) "by which a recipient, repeating a prior utterance, acknowledges a prior speaker's authorship and marks accord with that utterance" (Jefferson 1985: 31), in this case, no one else, and specifically not Roger, has said the thing that Louise here casts as a repeat ("playing with his organ"). Rather, it seems, Louise imputes to Roger this thought on the basis of his "with iz what?" (a repair initiator that can convey "I think you said something that I did not expect", i.e. surprise; see chapter 7 and Wilkinson and Kitzinger 2006) and his subsequent laughter after Ken provides the repair "with his orchids".

So for laughter there is evidence that simply naming the phenomenon risks obscuring an orderly and consequential phenomenon. Moreover, by representing the talk as "Playing with his organ" in the first transcript the transcriber is actually performing the task that was set by the speaker for the recipients (the task of recovering from the distorted talk the words being produced).

So these details can matter a great deal. Let's take another example. This is the opening of a telephone call between two co-workers:

(6) YYZ_4_Allison & Clara
01 Allison: Hello:
02 (.)
03 Clara: Hi=Allison,
03 Allison: Hi:
04 Clara: It's Clara, howyadoin',=
05 Allison: =Good.How are you Clara.
06 Clara: U:m: I'm oka:y. I::: nee:d to tell you that I'm not
07 gonna have t(h)i(h)me t(h)o(h) d(h)o this budget next
08 week.=
09 Allison: Oh hh
10 Clara: U[h:m]
11 Allison: [.hh]
12 Clara: an' I: I- I actually have to go to David today and sa:y (.)
13 something needs to com:eoff: my plate here.
14 [cuz] stuff's gonna start to slip for Molson=
13 Allison: [huh]
15 Clara: =so: [°hh
16 Allison: [Okay

17 Clara: uhm:, so he said you should talk to him about that
18 (.)
19 budget which I don't know that yer- (.) gonnabe- really happy
20 uh- (.) bout=
21 Allison: =uh [h(hh)uh
22 Clara: [huh huh
23 Allison: °hhhh okay::
24 Clara: I'm really sorry,=
25 Allison: =That's oka:y,

In this example we again find laughter infiltrating specific words. Consider for instance lines 06–08. As we'll see in later chapters, this talk is an important position: it comes directly after greetings and an exchange of what we will call "personal state inquiries". This is a position typically reserved for announcing the reason for the call. It wouldn't make sense to go too far into an analysis of this utterance here but let's note that Clara seems to be delivering some rather bad news. And notice that Allison can see that it's bad news from the way it is introduced with "I need to tell you . . .". Now, interestingly, a crucial part of the news is infected with laughter – "time to do" at line 07. Clara is delivering a bit of bad news here to be sure, and this piece of the talk does a rather specific job: It provides a reason or account for Clara not doing the budget, the reason being that she doesn't have time to do it. Now what might Clara be doing here by inserting laugh tokens into this portion of the talk and thereby posing for Allison the task of "recovering" what it is she is saying? If Allison can come up with "insufficient time" as a possible reason for Clara not doing the budget, that is, if she can recover this in the distorted utterance, she shows that this is at least a possible and maybe a reasonable excuse for not getting the job done. So here again, laughter may be a way of co-implicating the recipient in what is being said.[3]

Now we noticed that at line 06 Clara marks her talk as something she "needs to tell Allison". With this Clara conveys a certain reluctance to tell the news. Later in this segment, Clara does something somewhat similar in a completely different way.

(7) YYZ_4_Allison & Clara ((Detail))
17 Clara: uhm:, so he said you should talk to him about that
18 (.)
19 → budget which I don't know that yer- (.) gonnabe- really happy
20 → uh- (.) bout=
21 Allison: =uh [h(hh)uh
22 Clara: [huh huh
23 Allison: °hhhh okay::
24 Clara: I'm really sorry,=
25 Allison: =That's oka:y,

Here then Clara does several things to delay the completion of her turn-at-talk. First of all, she doesn't just end it after "budget" which was, after all, quite possible. But more remarkable I think is the way, at line 20, she pauses *within* the final word of the turn. The word is "about" and it has been represented in the transcription as two units: "uh" (.) "bout". As we'll see in the next chapter, the possible completion of a turn-at-talk (such as after "about") is a place where it may be relevant for another (here Allison) to take a turn which specifically responds to that which came before. Now, clearly, at some point Allison is going to respond to this so there's really no reason for Clara to delay the completion of the turn. But by delaying it and delaying it in just this way, Clara conveys something to Allison over and above what she is explicitly saying. The analogy I find myself going to here is a verbal "wince"; that is, by delaying between the first and second syllables of "about" Clara seems to be displaying that she anticipates a negative reaction to what she is saying and is preparing herself for it. Delays like this that are built into a single word (rather than coming between two words) are not common and thus Clara is doing something remarkable, noticeable and, possibly, laughable here. That is, in producing the talk in just this way, Clara has done something to be appreciated by the recipient as funny, quirky or odd. Moreover, she has done this in the course of delivering another bit of bad news, as an attendant activity that is simultaneous with the official business of the utterance.[4]

This turn appears to make two quite different actions simultaneously relevant for Allison in next position. First there is the report of bad news which Clara formulates as "he said you should talk to him about that budget which I don't know that yer- (.) gonnabe- really happy uh- (.) bout=". Allison responds to this, apparently accepting the commitment to talk to David, with "okay." Clara *also* makes appreciation of the markedly odd and possibly humorous way in which she *delivers* the news relevant. To this Allison responds immediately with laughter at line 21 and Clara subsequently joins her at line 22. So Clara produces this in such a way as to make laughter the most immediately relevant next response from the recipient despite the fact that it is bad news that she is hearing.

We can see then that something like a slight delay between two sounds within a word can be an important detail of the talk *for the participants*, important, that is, for how they understand and respond to it. If a detail like this is consequential for the participants, we have good reason, indeed something of an obligation, to include it in our transcription. Another way to put this is to say that Allison orients by laughing to this detail in the way the talk is produced. If we do not include the delay in the transcript we will have trouble understanding and explaining Allison's subsequent laughter, which is apparently responsive to it.

Observation as a Basis for Theorizing

Returning to the quote from Sacks cited earlier, I want to consider what is involved in taking "observation as a basis for theorizing". Observation is central to CA precisely because CA does not set out to prove this or that theory but rather to get a handle on, and ultimately to describe in some kind of formal language, something in the world. Although Sacks initially talked simply about real events (see above), over the years CA has come to focus more or less exclusively on the organization of talk-in-interaction, that is, on one class of real events. The premium set on making observations through close looking is consistent with the goal of discovery which is central to CA. What we want to do is to locate and describe the practices of human conduct. A further goal is to examine the way these practices are part of larger organizations of turn-taking, turn organization, sequence organization, repair and so on. This makes CA closer in many ways to the natural sciences (like biology for instance) than the social sciences, in which it is common to start with some kind of hypothesis or theory of how the world works and then attempt to find the data that will support it. Goffman (1983: 6) made the analogy with natural history when he suggested that one goal of his studies was "to try to identify the basic substantive units, the recurrent structures and their attendant processes", and to answer the question of "what sorts of animals are to be found in the interactional zoo? What plants in this particular garden?"

Now obviously part of this involves, as Sacks puts it, "close looking". The great advantage of working with recordings and transcriptions is that the same fragment may be examined repeatedly – resulting in different noticings. Often the first few inspections of a recording will turn up a range of potentially interesting but somewhat amorphous observations. On later listenings the same phenomena may be seen with greater clarity and thus allow more subtle and more nuanced observations.

Making observations is a skill that needs to be cultivated through practice. More experienced practitioners who have looked at more data are at a distinct advantage since they have been better primed to make detailed and robust observations that can ultimately provide the basis for a search procedure, a collection and eventually a publishable analysis. It is thus hard to stress enough the importance of working with data, as much as possible as a disciplined kind of exercise – Schegloff sometimes describes it as calisthenics. Still, although much turns on exposure and practice, it may be possible to set out some potentially useful guidelines.

As a practice and discipline, CA is rooted in local communities of practitioners and many people find it quite difficult to do this kind of work in isolation. A community of practitioners provides an audience for trying out observations. A CA community is greater than the sum of its parts and typically generates collaboratively built observations, and even the beginnings of analyses, that belong to no single author. One way CA community is enacted is through "data sessions". There are different ways in which data sessions can be organized. One common way is for one person to bring in a piece of data – such as a telephone call or video recording – and associated transcript. The data is then viewed repeatedly, at least two or three times depending on length. A decision is then made about where in the data segment to focus observations. This can be a turn, a small sequence or any other noticeable feature of the talk. Once a decision is made the participants take time to make their own observations. Once everyone has had time to make notes, observations are shared among members of the group. The following are some suggestions for making and articulating observations in data sessions:

1 Stick as closely as possible to the data itself. That is, try to describe what the participants actually say (or gesture, or do). Typically this will involve quoting the talk and referencing the line number in which it is represented on the transcript.
2 Avoid motivational and other psychologically framed descriptions such as "she wants to get off the phone", "He's trying to make himself sound important", "He's not very confident", and so on. While it is inevitable that we will notice such things they tell us little about the talk itself, which should be the focus of our observations.
3 Describe what a thing *is* rather than what it is like. Avoid descriptions such as "he is doing something like a request". Although such hedges are sometimes necessary in order to articulate an only partially formed observation, they can lead to a kind of informal coding procedure which obscures what Garfinkel (Garfinkel and Wieder 1992, Garfinkel 2002), following the medieval philosopher Duns Scotus, called the "haecceity" or "thisness" of the thing being examined (its particularity).

These are some basic principles that people may find helpful in cultivating observational skills and in communicating those observations to others. But the question remains as to what one should be noticing in the first place. Ultimately, I believe, the only thing to do is to "go with your gut", because different analysts will notice different things, and this is a strength rather than a weakness of the method. However, advice such as "go with your gut" is likely to be of little practical assistance in this context, so here are some suggestions, again not inviolable rules but suggestions.

1 Patterns across data samples: Here the observation is of the form "I've seen one of these before" or "I've seen something like this before" (see Schegloff 1996b, 1997a, Jefferson 2004). Obviously, to be useful, an observation of this kind should include some details about the case to which comparison is being made. These, however, are rarely at hand in a data session (although laptop computers make this possible). After careful and repeated listenings one often comes to memorize sometimes extensive fragments of conversation and these can provide the basis for observations like this.[5]
2 Patterns within the data: There are obviously many different kinds of patterns. For instance, one can note instances of "repetition" either in next positioned utterances or across long stretches of talk (see Schegloff 1997a). Another, quite distinct, pattern involves reuse of a term where, for instance, a "pro-form" (such as "it") would have been possible (Schegloff 1996a).
3 Selecting formulations: Looking at repetition involves focusing on the forms used. Another way to get at patterns within a given spate of talk involves focusing not on the forms used but on the referents, the things being talked about. So we can track the various forms selected to refer to or formulate some referent (e.g. "my dog" vs. "Soul", "here" vs. "in Toronto" etc.). Now, clearly, each formulation is selected from an indefinitely large class of possible alternatives. While this is true and can form the basis for observation, we can make more robust observations by focusing on the selection of an alternative among a range of terms *actually* used in this spate of talk.
4 Selecting formats: Just as it is possible to talk about the selection of formulations, so we can observe speakers selecting different formats for doing an action. For instance, speakers may be seen to select among different formats in other-initiating repair (see chapter 7), choosing between, for instance, "what?" and "you went where?" and "you went to the *park*?" and so on. Similarly, speakers may select between different formats for accomplishing requests: "I was wondering if you could . . . ?" vs. "Could you . . . ?" and so on (see, inter alia, Goodwin 1990, Curl and Drew 2008). Now, again, the best and most robust observations will be those that are based on alternate format selections within a single data fragment or across instances within a constrained set of examples. We may note, for instance, how a request is formatted at the beginning of a call as opposed to how it is formatted at the end of a call. Alternatively, we may observe the ways in which requests are formatted at the beginnings of calls in general as opposed to how they are formatted at the ends of calls and so on.

Keys: Another Way to Access the Technical Features of Talk-in-Interaction

Our observations as conversation analysts are intended to take us beyond a vernacular sense of what is happening in a given spate of talk. Another way to achieve the same result is "to rough up the surface of the talk" using one of several "keys".[6] For instance, one way to unlock some features of a data segment is to go through it noticing all the "points of possible utterance completion". Such an approach forces us to make explicit what it is we mean to be referring to by this phrase. It forces us to look at each instance in all its particularity and decide whether it is in fact such a point, and, if it is, what makes it so. So this can help us to get a better handle on some particular phenomenon such as "possible utterance completion", but it also frequently makes visible quite other phenomena. Here are some other possible keys we can use in this way:

1 Possible utterance completion – see chapter 3.
2 Next-speaker selection – see chapter 3.
3 Turn construction – see chapters 3 and 8.
4 Self-repair – see chapter 7.
5 Other-initiated repair – see chapter 7.
6 Sequence organization – see chapter 6.
7 Overall organization – see chapter 10.
8 Action-formation/formatting – see chapters 4 and 8.

Making Collections

Once a potentially interesting phenomenon has been located through the use of the techniques described above, one can start gathering instances of it into a collection. Why make collections? Why not base the analysis on the first or the most interesting case one can find? One important reason is that different cases reveal different aspects or features of a phenomenon. Indeed, one's sense of what one is looking at typically changes as a collection of instances grows. A very quick sketch should suffice to illustrate the importance of looking across collections of instances.

Consider then that one of the ways some participant other than the speaker can initiate repair (see chapter 7) is through a question-intoned repeat of some or all of a previous turn as in (8), (9) or (10).[7] Here are three examples:

(8) Mary the tax Lady_ XTR1
01 ((click))
02 A: Hello: ¿
03 B: hHello, Ma:ry?
04 A: (0.2) ((kids speaking)) No:
05 (0.3)
06 B: No, not Ma:ry? hh
07 A: No, it's not Ma:ry=there's no Mary he:re (.) I don' think: hh
08 ((someone speaking)) (3.0)
09 B: Th' tax lady:
10 (0.2)
11 A: → The ^tax lad(h)y::?
12 B: Ya hhh=
13 A: =Nop-. Wha number were you callin'.
14 B: (3.0) (Is) she there.
15 A: Pardon:?
16 B. Is she the:re?

17 A: ^No no, no, no. I think you hav' the wrong number.
18 B: oh ma' god:
19 A: °.hh[hh]°
20 B: [o'] (hh) I'm so:rry=
21 A: =th(hh)at's okay:
22 B: °buh bye.°
23 A: b(h)ye:.
24 ((click))

(9) YYZ

((Telephone rings))
01 A: What do you want me to pick up?
02 B: Nothi:ng but I want to know how you boil an egg.
03 (1.0)
04 (h)hard boil.
05 A: Oh oka::y and I just read this you know
06 because I always let the water boil but
07 you're not supposed to (.hh) put it in and
08 you (.hh) bring it to a boil (.) but then
09 turn it down 'cause you're really not
10 supposed to boil the e::gg
11 (0.4)
12 you let it (.) uh simmer or you know on me:dium,
13 B: Ri:ght
14 A: fo:r [t w] elve minutes.
15 B: [((sniff))]
16 B: → Twelve minutes?
17 A: Well I always do it faster than th(h)at (hh)
18 B: okay=
19 A: =I just boil the shit out of it [but]
20 B: [How]
21 do you know when it's done?

(10) GTS:III:42(r)ST
01 Ken: Hey (.) the first ti:me they stopped me from selling
02 cigarettes was this morning.
03 (1.0)
04 Lou: From selling cigarettes?
05 Ken: Or buying cigarettes.

In each case we see one participant repeating some portion of the previous turn with questioning intonation. At the completion of the repeat, the repeating speaker stops and the first speaker responds. Here we are concerned with the importance of looking across a collection of instances rather than basing an analysis on just one, perhaps particularly interesting, case. In this respect consider the range of responses that such a questioning repeat may engender. So, in (8), "the tax lady" elicits a simple confirmation "ya." In (9), after A repeats "twelve minutes", B significantly modifies her advice. And in (10), Ken responds to Lou's "From selling cigarettes" with a correction, "Or buying cigarettes." So this range of responses is suggestive of the different actions a single practice, here a questioning repeat, may be understood to embody: from a request for confirmation in (8), to an expression of skepticism or a challenge to the accuracy of some prior statement as in (9), to an invitation to self-correct in (10). These examples illustrate the normal situation in which there is no one-to-one mapping between a given practice (i.e. question-intoned repeat) and a given action.

So by considering individual cases as part of larger collections we can see the range of actions a given practice can implement. Moreover, particular instances of a phenomenon within a collection can reveal participants' own orientation to specific aspects of the device. Staying with the example of questioning repeats, consider the following case from a recording of three 4-year-old children:

(11) KIDS_02_16_06(1of2)JKT6 (QT00:17)

01	Mikey:		There's no ponies inside fa:r:ms.=
02	Tina:		Ye:s. so:me.
03			(0.2)
04			I went to a real farm bef[ore
05	Grace:		[an' once (.)
06			I: rode on a pony.
07			(0.2)
08			I really did. ((looks to adult))
09	L:		(mhm)
10	Grace:		At centre island I rode on a pony.
11			(0.8)
12	Mikey:		(how [ )
13	Tina:		[( ) centre island?
14			(0.4)
15	Grace:		yes.
16			(0.6)
17	Mikey:	→	centre island?
18	Grace:		yes. I've been there. (.) On: a ferry.
19			(0.8)
20			a ferry boat.

This fragment – and the recording – begins with Mikey challenging Tina's prior claim that there are ponies on farms (this was not recorded). When Mikey asserts that there are "no ponies inside farms", Tina replies "Ye:s. so:me." After a short pause she continues by grounding her claim in prior experience, saying, "I went to a real farm before". At line 05, Grace begins a turn in which she proposes "an' once (.) I: rode on a pony.". When this receives no uptake from the other children, Grace turns to the adult in the room saying "I really did." The adult produces a minimal acknowledgement token and Grace continues by providing the name of the place where she rode on the pony – Centre Island. Tina picks up on this mention of Centre Island saying something partially inaudible which is confirmed by Grace with "yes" at line 06. Mikey then produces a questioning repeat of "Centre Island?" and Grace responds with a confirmation. Now, the important part of this for present purposes is the "I've been there" at line 18. This appears to be specifically oriented to the challenge which Mikey's questioning repeat is heard to embody. It is clear that part of Grace's claim involves her having been to Centre Island: if this is where she rode on a pony, then she surely must have been there. So in responding to Mikey's questioning repeat with the clearly defensive "Yes. I've been there" and then continuing with more of the same ("on a ferry. a ferry boat.") Grace displays an orientation to the challenge which that questioning repeat conveys.

Managing a Collection and Developing an Analysis

Once a collection is assembled one can really get to work on developing the analysis. To do this one has to organize the data in such a way as to make the relevant features of the talk visible. There are many ways to do this. Here are some suggestions.

1 Copy each case onto its own page and give it a number. Annotate this with any observations that seem possibly relevant.
2 Select your best two or three cases of the phenomenon and work on an analysis of them, concentrating on turn composition and design, sequential positioning and so on. Try to work up these analyses of the data on their own terms. That is, do not focus on the particular phenomenon you are collecting at this stage; just try to get a sense of what is going on for the participants. By "best cases" I mean those in which the phenomenon of interest is most visible, clear or "uncontaminated" by other things happening within that bit of talk.
3 Working your way through the entire collection, sort the cases into subsets according to whatever criteria seem possibly relevant. So, for instance, the cases may be sorted according to the types of responses they engender or the positions in which they occur. Obviously the ways in which you sort the data will depend very much on the type of thing you are collecting. When working with larger collections (more than 20 or so) I have found it helpful to use index cards to do this. For instance, in a study of other-initiated repair I had one card for cases in which repair was accomplished via repetition of the trouble source and another for cases in which the repair was an alternate formulation of the trouble source. Instances are sorted using their case numbers (see 1). This allows the analyst to see intersections: groups of cases that fall into more than one subset. For instance, you might find that many of the cases in which repair is accomplished via an alternate formulation also occur after significant delay. Such intersections can lead to new observations and a more profound analysis.

Working this way it sometimes feels as though everything suddenly falls into place and the analysis reveals itself with little effort from the analyst. Clearly this is partly an illusion, since a lot of work goes into making the initial observations, making the collections and subsequently working with them. But there is something very satisfying in things coming together with a kind of ineluctable force. That this happens suggests that what is being described is not the product of a clever analyst's fancy but something in the world that has real integrity (see Schegloff 2005). And, of course, the opposite situation is also possible. Sometimes an incipient analysis collapses under the weight of its own collection. By this I mean that as one begins to collect instances of a possible device or practice it becomes apparent that there's no practice there at all. But failures of this sort are not necessarily a bad thing, since they show that the method is rigorous and that proper use of it can detect analytic non-starters.

Concluding Remarks on Conversation-analytic Methods

In this chapter I've tried to introduce some core principles of CA through exemplification rather than argument. This way of going about introducing the method and the field itself embodies a central principle: CA is a way of working with recordings of talk-in-interaction and treats these as naturalistic records of real-world events. The method allows the analyst not only to describe the events and activities that make up the world of everyday life, but also to discover phenomena there that we did not previously know existed.

To summarize the main points of this chapter, CA is a rigorously empirical approach to social interaction that involves working with recordings of conversation and other forms of talk. In his lectures, Harvey Sacks laid out the rationale for working with such recordings; I summarized the argument at the beginning of the chapter. Sacks recognized that a rigorous study of conversation would have to deal with the recalcitrant details of what actually happened. Of course, many approaches in the social and human sciences involve a methodological step (by coding, by experimental design, by extracting what is considered "good" data from what is considered "noise") in which the stubborn details of real events are filtered out. The conversation-analytic stance towards the preservation of and attention to detail explains the importance placed on transcription. The transcript is not a substitute for the recording. Rather it is an aide-mémoire and a guide to others. In making or working closely with a transcript one comes to hear details of the talk that otherwise remain inaccessible. Including those details in a transcript allows others working with the recording to locate the details that were heard in transcribing it.

In the last part of this chapter I discussed some ways of cultivating and developing the observational skills that Sacks argued were crucial to the analysis of conversation. I then turned to offer some suggestions for taking an analysis further, moving from a bunch of observations to a more developed analysis based on a collection of instances.

Notes

1 Conversation analysts have had success working with native-speaker collaborators (see, for instance, Lerner and Takagi 1999, Fox, Hayashi, and Jasperson 1996).

2 Indeed, becoming overly engrossed in the way someone is speaking is one of the potential sources of alienation from interaction that Goffman described (Goffman 1957).

3 Moreover, by laughing, Clara also invites Allison's reciprocal laughter. Even if she does not actually elicit laughter from Allison, Clara has provided an alternative way for Allison to respond: Allison can respond to this as something laughable rather than simply as "bad news".

4 I take the notion of attendant activities from Jefferson 1987.

5 Of course, given the limitations of human memory, it is important to review the data to make sure that what is being remembered is remembered correctly.

6 The phrase "roughing up the surface of the talk" is one I have borrowed from John Heritage. I do not know who first used the term "keys" in the way I use it here but suspect it originates with Manny Schegloff, who used it in this way at the summer institutes of the early to mid-2000s.

7 Such repeats need not be produced with questioning intonation in order to initiate repair. In courtroom contexts, where lawyers are understood to be engaged exclusively in questioning, next-turn repeats that initiate repair are typically produced with final, falling intonation (see chapter 7 for some examples).

3

Turn-Taking

One of the most obvious things about conversation is that it involves people taking turns at speaking. Any form of coordinated, joint activity, from conversation to ballroom dancing, from road work to open heart surgery, requires some way of organizing and managing the contributions of the various persons who are engaged in it. In conversation, opportunities to participate are distributed through a turn-taking system. The purpose of this chapter is to describe the basic features of that system.

While the fact of turn-taking is obvious, how people actually bring it off is a matter of some considerable complexity. Moreover, as we shall see, the implications of turn-taking are far-reaching indeed. This is, perhaps, the most fundamental feature of conversation, and the facts that we talk in turns and that turns are distributed in a specific way among participants shape a vast range of phenomena in conversation. Although this chapter can only hope to scratch the surface of the topic, it will become clear, I think, that turns and turn-taking provide the underlying framework of conversation. Simply put, turns are the basic unit of conversation and, as Sacks, Schegloff and Jefferson (1974) pointed out, they are distributed within an "economy" of opportunities to speak.

Before we launch into a somewhat technical account of turn-taking in conversation, it is important to deal with some rather widely held assumptions about this topic. We are sometimes told, by Emily Post and others, that turn-taking in conversation is a matter of politeness and good manners. Those that *have* good manners dutifully await the completion of whatever their interlocutor is saying before offering their own contribution. Less mannered types are, in contrast, prone to jump in whenever it suits them. So, there is a widely held view that turn-taking is characteristic of "polite" conversation. The second widely held and sometimes explicitly articulated view is that certain groups of people (e.g. West Indians, Jews, Native Americans) simply do not take turns in conversation. *Their* conversations, we are told, are "contrapuntal", "anarchic", "disorderly" and so on. This, it is sometimes suggested, provides evidence that conversational turn-taking is a human "invention": the product of a particular group of people of a particular historical period (e.g. the salons of the European bourgeoisie in the eighteenth century, the English aristocracy, coffee-drinking customers of Starbucks). As it turns out, however, wherever rigorous and reliable research has been done, it has tended to undermine rather than support such ideas. In the first place, it is quite possible to be altogether rude, while at the same time coordinating one's turns-at-talk with those of the other participants (see for instance M. Goodwin 1983). Indeed, one way to be rude is to specifically exploit the properties of the turn-taking system so as either to completely exclude some person from a conversation (disallowing them any opportunity to speak) or to withhold a response to what someone else has said and in this way to ignore them. As will be seen, both forms of rudeness presuppose rather than disprove the existence of a turn-taking system of the type described in the following pages. In the second case, regarding certain "ethnic" groups who constantly interrupt one another, the stereotype is simply not borne out by the research. As I have addressed precisely this issue elsewhere (Sidnell 2001) I will not belabor the point here but only suggest that perhaps it might be not the facts of turn-taking and conversation which are "socially constructed", but rather our perceptions and representations of others, including our ideas about the ways in which they speak (on this distinction see Hacking 1999).

A turn-taking system of the kind described in what follows provides for the coherence and orderliness not just of "chit-chat" around the water cooler but also of surgeons' talk in the course of open heart surgery or physicists working to describe the movement of subatomic particles. Some system for turn-taking is a requirement of *any* coordinated action and thus of human society (see Levinson 2006). It is hard to imagine a society in which people don't organize their conversations this way and, in fact, none have been found.

The One-at-a-Time Rule and its Exceptions

When Sacks first started to work out the organization of turn-taking in conversation he wrote: "For conversation, preservation of 'one party talking at a time' is organizationally primary" (Sacks 2004: 37). By this, Sacks meant that the machinery of turn-taking is organized so as to minimize both gaps in which no one is talking and overlaps in which more than one person is talking at the same time. Of course, there are exceptions (see Schegloff 2000a). For instance, if I enter a room to find several people who should properly greet me, it is quite likely that they will do this in unison. There are other such "choral" occasions. Assessments, for example, are often produced in overlap with other talk (other assessments or the assessable item itself); indeed, there is some evidence to suggest that this is precisely where they are supposed to be done (see for instance C. Goodwin 1986b). Laughter too is something that people often do together (see Jefferson, Sacks and Schegloff 1987). Clearly, it would be bizarre if people, in responding to a joke for instance, laughed one after another rather than as a group![1] And, of course, there *are* cases in which people simply talk at the same time thus producing sometimes quite extensive stretches of overlapping talk. So there are certainly exceptions to the one-at-a-time rule. However, as we will see, when we look at some of these in detail, even in overlap (perhaps especially in overlap) participants' contributions are finely coordinated with one another (see Schegloff 2000a). More importantly for now, the exceptions are just that – "exceptions to the rule". Massively "one party talking at a time" *is* preserved. It is that massively more common situation which we must first account for before turning to consider the exceptions.

Awaiting Completion: A Possible Solution?

The answer to Sacks's question, "how is 'one-at-a-time' preserved?", may seem entirely obvious: While one person is speaking the other (*assuming* just two participants) simply waits for him or her to reach completion and, at that point, begins his or her own turn. But if you think about it for a moment you'll see that "one-party-talking-at-a-time" cannot, in fact, be achieved by each participant *waiting* for the other to finish. There are several reasons why this won't work. First, even in the simplest situation where just two people are talking, waiting would clearly result in the production of a gap between the end of one turn and the beginning of the next. Secondly, were conversation organized this way, some kind of unambiguous "turn-completion signal" would be required. After all, how, in the absence of such a signal, will the recipient distinguish between a pause *within* the course of a turn-at-talk from a pause at its completion? Such signals appear not to exist in English conversation.[2]

Notice that there *are* systems that work this way. When people talk on VHF radios for instance, a next speaker must wait until the current speaker finishes before starting their own turn since it is not possible to listen and broadcast simultaneously: once the "talk" button on the VHF radio is depressed it is no longer possible to hear anything on that channel. Not surprisingly, talk on VHF radios is characterized by the occurrence of significant gaps between turns. Moreover, although they are not always used, "turn-completion" signals such as "over" are available in this type of talk.

So if "waiting until the other is finished" won't work, how does it happen that one-at-a-time is generally preserved? The solution that Sacks developed not only solved the problem, it also accounted for the vast majority of exceptions to one-at-a-time, that is, the vast majority of instances of gap and overlap in conversation.

Grossly Apparent Facts of Conversation

So far we have considered one "grossly apparent fact" of conversation, namely, that one party talks at a time. As Sacks, Schegloff and Jefferson pointed out, there are several other such features for which any model of turn-taking should be able to account. For instance:

1 Speaker-change recurs, or at least occurs.
2 Overwhelmingly, one party talks at a time.
3 Occurrences of more than one speaker at a time are common, but brief.
4 Transitions (from one turn to a next) with no gap and no overlap are common. Together with transitions characterized by slight gap or slight overlap, they make up the vast majority of transitions.
5 Turn order is not fixed, but varies.
6 Turn size is not fixed, but varies.
7 Length of conversation is not specified in advance.
8 What parties say is not specified in advance.
9 Relative distribution of turns is not specified in advance.
10 Number of parties can vary.

11 Talk can be continuous or discontinuous.
12 Turn-allocation techniques are obviously used. A current speaker may select a next speaker (as when he addresses a question to another party); or parties may self-select in starting to talk.
13 Various "turn-constructional units" are employed; e.g., turns can be projectedly "one word long", or they can be sentential in length.
14 Repair mechanisms exist for dealing with turn-taking errors and violations; e.g. if two parties find themselves talking at the same time, one of them will stop prematurely, and thus repair the trouble.

Taken together these features suggest that the turn-taking system for conversation is, as Sacks, Schegloff and Jefferson (1974) described it, "locally managed" and "party-administered". It is *locally managed* since it organizes only current and next turn and not, for instance, what will happen in thirty seconds, in five minutes or tomorrow.[3] It is *party-administered* in the sense that there is no "referee" to determine who should speak next and for how long. Rather, the participants themselves work this out. Again, it is worth noting that there are forms of talk that are not organized in this way. In formal debate for instance, the order of the speakers and the length of the turn is decided, to some extent at least, in advance. In classroom discussion, the order of the speakers is decided, in part, by the teacher who selects students to speak next. Such systems provide a useful contrast since a moment's observation will reveal that conversation is simply not organized in this way (see Greatbatch 1988).

Constructing Turns-at-Talk

If we agree, then, that in conversation people are involved in taking turns, we can go on to ask a very simple but very important question: what is a turn or, more specifically, what is a turn-at-talk? One way to approach this question is to ask whether there are any restrictions on what will count as a turn in particular situations. To use a term that will become increasingly relevant in the following chapters, are there restrictions on what is *hearable*, by the participants, as a turn?

At this point it is helpful to consider some examples from recorded conversation. In the following instance "Tourist" is talking to "Parky" and "Old Man".

(1) Parky (cited in Sacks, Schegloff and Jefferson 1974)

01	Tourist:	Has the park cha:nged much,
02	Parky:	Oh:: ye:s,
03		(1.0)
04	Old Man:	Th'*Fun*fair changed it'n [ahful lot [didn'it.
05	Parky:	[Th- [That-
06	Parky:	That changed it,

The fragment begins with Tourist asking about their current surroundings, "the park". Notice that her question does not select a particular recipient to speak next. Rather, if we assume that both Parky and Old Man know about what the park was like in the past (an assumption that seems to find some support in what happens here), either could quite reasonably be expected to provide an answer to the question.[4] It is Parky who initially responds with "Oh:: ye:s," at line 02, thus confirming the supposition embedded in the question (notice that by including "much" in the question, the questioner presupposes that it *has* changed). After a pause, Old Man offers a contribution, suggesting that the "funfair" was the agent responsible for the change. At line 06 Parky agrees, saying "that changed it."

Let's begin our consideration of the turns out of which this talk is built by looking at Tourist's turn in line 01. I said earlier that the first thing we have to notice is that speakers can't construct turns out of just anything. So for instance, this turn could *not* have been:

(2) Parky – Detail
01 Tourist: Has the

or,

(3) Parky – Detail
01 Tourist: Has the park

It should be pretty obvious that neither of these would be *hearable* by the co-participants as constituting a turn, at least in this sequential environment. However, the following surely would have been hearable in this way:

(4) Parky – Detail
01 Tourist: Has the park cha:nged

What accounts for this? Why will some strings of words work as turns-at-talk while others will not? To oversimplify slightly there seems to be something like a "grammatical well-formedness" principle at work here. Every language of course has grammatical rules and these appear to shape what will and what will not count as a turn-at-talk. The problem with (2) then is that, in English, you can't get a definite article "the" (what linguists call a "determiner") without a noun following it (at least not in this context). In (3), the problem has to do with the lack of a verb the place for which is established by the fronted auxiliary and the grammatical subject "the park". We needn't get into the intricacies of English grammar here to see this since any fluent speaker can hear that there is something not quite right with these (non-)turns and, of course, it was not linguists or grammarians but rather ordinary people who participated in these conversations and located what actually was the turn, and they used only their native intuitions about grammar to do that.

But there are obvious and quite severe limits on how far grammar will take us in this area. Consider that, if we think only about grammar, the following also does not look like a very good turn:

(5) Parky – Detail
01 Tourist: Has

However, if we put it in a different context, a perfectly legitimate turn we will get:

(6) Parky – Constructed
00 Parky: Did you say "has" or "jazz"
01 Tourist: Has

Though invented, this example suggests that, while grammar constrains in a basic way what will count as a turn and what will not, the context (or better the *sequential* context) in which a given utterance occurs plays a decisive role. Of course, intonation is also relevant. Consider that although "Has the park changed" makes a perfectly good turn in terms of grammar, Parky did not in fact hear the completion of "changed" as the completion of the turn. What allowed him to hear "past" the grammar as it were and to find that the turn had one more word? Intonation, and prosody more generally (which includes the intonation, the volume and the pacing of the talk), offers crucial resources in this respect. You can see the importance of intonation in, for instance, lists which are a common feature of talk (see Jefferson 1990).

(7) NB:VII Power Tools
01 Margy: Hello:,
02 Edna: Hello Margy?
03 Margy: ↑Ye:[ah,
04 Edna: → [.hhhh We do pai:::nting, a:nti[qui::ng,=
05 Margy: [.hh
06 Margy: =I(h)s tha:t ri:ght.=
07 Edna: =Ehhhh[hhhhhhhh [#hh]#hh ((# indicates a squeak))
08 Margy: [hmh-hmh-[hmh]
09 (.)
10 Edna: → ihh -hn:h- hn.hh-hn [keep] people's pa:r too:::ls=
11 Margy: [.hhh]

Notice Edna's turn at line 04. Here she starts a list with "We do painting, antiquing . . .", which has its final item in line 10 ("Keep people's powertools"). And notice that it is in part the distinctive intonation contour of lists that allows Margy to hear that the turn will not end with "painting".

Returning to the issue of grammar, we find that turns are constructed out of a sharply delimited set of possible unit-types: single words, phrases, clauses and sentences. Consider the following example.

(8) Debbie and Shelley 5:35–40
35 Debbie: whatever:an [.hhh
36 Shelley: [you were at the halloween thing. Sentential
37 Debbie: huh? Lexical
38 Shelley: the halloween p[arty Phrasal
39 Debbie: [ri:ght. Lexical

Shelley's talk at line 36 exemplifies the use of a sentential turn constructional unit. Debbie's turns at lines 37 and 39 are both composed of single lexical items. Shelley's turn at 38 illustrates the use of a single phrase to construct a turn. Sacks, Schegloff and Jefferson (1974: 702) write that these unit-types "allow a projection of the unit-type under way, and what, roughly, it will take for an instance of that unit-type to be completed." So, the idea here is that turns are themselves constructed out of units which Sacks, Schegloff and Jefferson called, unsurprisingly, "turn-constructional units" (TCU). A single turn-at-talk may be built out of several TCUs. Here is an example:

(9) Virginia 4:1–8

01	Prudence:		I[t's s o frustrating havin' a mothuh]
02	Mom:		[If you saved yer- if you saved yer al]lowan[ce,
03	Prudence:		[hhh ·hhh
04	Mom:		[(if you) save yer allowance, an:' um: you could get=
05	Prudence:		[w(h)ith a °sho°°(p) ((°° = mid-word trailoff))
06	Mom:		=these little extr[a things.
07	Virginia:	→	[A(h)llo::wan(h)ce? I o(h)nly g(h)et fi(h)ve
08			d(h)ollars a week.That's rid(h)i(h)c(h)ul(h)ous.

In the talk leading up to this fragment Virginia has been asking her mother to let her have a dress which her mother has in her shop. The request has been turned down and Virginia has expressed her disappointment. At line 01 of the fragment, Prudence, Virginia's brother's girlfriend, says, somewhat ambiguously, that "it's so frustrating having a mother with a shop."[5] In overlap with Prudence, Mom suggests that if she saved her allowance Virginia could get "these little extra things" (e.g. the dress). This sets the stage for Virginia's turn at lines 07–08. Virginia rejects Mom's suggestion in three parts each one of which is its own TCU. The first TCU looks back to Mom's turn locating in it something problematic, "allowance" (see Schegloff 1997b: 533). The second component gives some grounds for rejecting what Mom has said (that the amount is too little). The third comments on the suggestion, assessing it by characterizing it as "ridiculous", and, in so doing, lodging what is, in effect, a complaint – here a complaint about what Mom has said. As a complaint, this TCU establishes what kind of a response is relevant next.

We said earlier that turn-taking in conversation cannot be based on one person waiting for the other to be finished. However, at the time, no plausible alternative to "waiting" was offered. We now have the beginnings of an alternative. Potential next speakers do not wait for the completion of a turn-at-talk. Rather, they "project" its possible completion and coordinate their own contributions with what that projection allows them to anticipate.

Points of Possible Completion Create Transition-Relevant Places

Various kinds of evidence converge (see Sacks, Schegloff and Jefferson 1974) to indicate that the system allocates rights to produce one turn-constructional unit at a time – be it lexical, phrasal, clausal or sentential. At the completion of each unit, transition to a next speaker *may*, but need not, occur. Thus, unless special provisions have been made, at the possible completion of a current turn unit, transition to a next speaker is relevant. Sacks, Schegloff and Jefferson (1974) called this, again unsurprisingly, a transition relevance place (TRP).

Both current speakers and potential next speakers can be seen to orient to the relevance of speaker transition at possible completion. For instance, *speakers* who produce multi-unit turns display an orientation to the relevance of speaker transition at possible unit completion by increasing the pace of the talk through such places and in this way foreclosing the possibility of another self-selecting (see Schegloff 1982, 1998, Walker 2003, Local and Walker 2004). *Recipients* orient to the relevance of speaker transition at possible completion by targeting just those points as places at which to start their own turn. Consider then the following example:

(10) Parky (cited in Sacks, Schegloff and Jefferson 1974)

```
01  Tourist:   Has the park cha:nged much,
02  Parky:     Oh:: ye:s,
03             (1.0)
04  Old man:   Th'Funfair changed it'n [ahful lot [didn'it.
05  Parky:                             [Th-       [That-
06  Parky:     That changed it,
```

In this example Parky begins an incipient next turn at the first point of possible completion in Old Man's turn. Parky starts up here and again at the next point of possible completion not by virtue of any silence (by the time he starts there is no hearable silence) but by virtue of the *projected* possible completion of the turn constructional unit which constitutes a potential transition relevance place. Evidence such as this leads to the conclusion that "transfer of speakership is coordinated by reference to such transition-relevance places" (Sacks et al. 1974: 703).

We can see then that hearers monitor the syntactic, prosodic and broadly speaking pragmatic features of the current turn to find that it is about to begin, now beginning, continuing, now coming to completion.[6] That is to say, they monitor talk not only to *find* possible points of completion but to *project* and *anticipate* them before they actually occur. A point of possible unit completion is a place for possible speaker transition – what Sacks, Schegloff and Jefferson (1974) define as a transition relevance place.

How Turns are Distributed in Conversation

Speaker transition at such transition-relevant places is organized by a set of rules to which the participants themselves orient. The rules can be summarized as follows: A next speaker may have been selected to speak next by the current turn (e.g. an addressed question). If this is the case, the one so selected should speak at the first point of possible completion. If, however, no speaker has been selected by the current turn, at its possible completion any other party may self-select. If no speaker has been selected and no other party self-selects at the possible completion of the current turn, the current speaker may continue. The rules, more formally stated, are given below (from Sacks et al. 1974: 704):

> Rule 1 – applies initially at the first TRP of any turn (C = current speaker, N = next speaker)
>
> a If C selects N in current turn, then C must stop speaking, and N must speak next, transition occurring at the first possible completion after N-selection.
> b If C does not select N, then any (other) party may self-select, first speaker gaining rights to the next turn.
> c If C does not select N, and no other party self-selects under option (b), then C may (but need not) continue (i.e. claim rights to a further TCU).
>
> Rule 2 – applies at all subsequent TRPs.
>
> When Rule 1(c) has been applied by C, then at the next TRP Rules 1 (a)–(c) apply, and recursively at the next TRP, until speaker change is effected.

The rules are thus *ordered* and this ordering is crucial to the way in which they organize the distribution of turns-at-talk. Specifically, a party wishing to invoke rule (b) must start early, before rule (c) is invoked. In contexts involving the participation of more than two parties, there are additional motivations for an early start since more than one potential next speaker may target a given transition relevance place as a place to start her own turn. This, in part, explains why next speakers often start before the actual completion of a turn. Recurrently, such early starts result in short segments of overlapping talk. Early starters may begin "at the final sound(s) of the last word of what constitutes a possibly complete utterance" (terminal overlap) or at a "recognition point" where although the utterance has not yet been quite completed, "that which is being said within and through it has been made available" (Jefferson 1984). Consider in this respect the following examples:

(11) Virginia:15
Mom: ·hhh ^Well that's something else. (0.3) ^I don't think that
you should be going to the parties that Beth goe:s to. She is
eighteen years old.An' you are fou:rtee:n, da[rlin'.
Virginia: [I KNOW::, BUT
A:LL THE REST OF MY: PEOPLE MY AGE ARE GWAFFS.I
promise.they are si:[ck.
Mom: [They're what?
(.)
Virginia: GWAFFS.

At lines 3 and 4, Virginia's turn starting with "I know" overlaps Mom's "darling". At lines 6 and 7 Virginia's "sick" is overlapped by Mom's "They're what?" These are just the kinds of exceptions to the "one-at-a-time" rule which provide further evidence of its operation. Thus consider that in both cases the overlap occurs very close to the actual completion of the turn. Moreover, in the first case, Virginia's "I know" overlaps an addition to the turn, specifically, an address term. It seems likely that, in this case, the overlap resulted from a misprojection of the turn's completion which Virginia may have expected to coincide with the completion of "fourteen". In the second example, by lengthening the word "sick", Virginia extends the turn a little bit further than might have otherwise been anticipated and it is this little bit that is overlapped by Mom's "They're what?" These are, then, two "overlap-vulnerable locations" in conversation: post-positioned address terms (and tags) and lengthened final words. Thus, this example displays some of the systematic bases for overlap, which is to say, bases for overlap within a system designed to achieve "one-speaker-at-a-time". Note also that when Mom reaches a point of possible completion (between "years old . . ." and "and you are . . ." in line 03) *within* her turn she does not allow any silence to develop between the end of one unit and the beginning of another. In this way she forecloses the possibility of self-selection here. This is represented in the transcript by the absence of a space in this position.

To summarize, conversation is composed of turns-at-talk. Participants monitor the unfolding course of a turn to locate points within it where it is possibly complete. Such points of possible completion constitute discrete places in the talk at which transition to a next speaker is a relevant possibility. These are transition relevance places. At each of these points a set of rules operates to allow for transfer to a next speaker either by current-selects-next technique (such as an addressed question) or by self-selection. Where transfer is not so effected, the current speaker may continue. It is important to see that the rules are still operating even if transfer is not effected. Clearly a crucial role is accorded to the "transition space" by this system. Since this is where much of the action of turn-taking actually happens we will devote some attention to it. First however we must discuss practices of next-speaker selection which have been alluded to but not yet described.

Practices of Next-Speaker Selection

In discussing the rules of turn allocation above, reference was made to the possibility of "selecting a next speaker": techniques whereby a "current speaker" selects a "next speaker". According to Sacks, Schegloff and Jefferson (1974: 716–17), the fact that there are such techniques is suggested by such obvious cases as "an addressed question", which clearly selects its addressee to speak next. Consider the following case in which Vivian and Shane are hosting Nancy and Michael for dinner. Shane has complained that his potato is not fully cooked and, at line 41, Nancy weighs in saying that hers "seems done". Nancy then poses the question of Michael addressing the question to him by use of his name.[8] The question thus selects Michael to speak next and he does so at line 44.

(12) Chicken Dinner p. 5
38 Vivian: It's not do:ne? th' potato
39 Shane: Ah don't think so,
40 (2.2)
41 Nancy: → Seems done t'me how 'bout you Mi[chael,]
42 Shane: [Alri'] who cooked
43 this mea:l
44 Michael: → .hh Little ↓bit'e e-it e-ih-ih of it isn'done
45 Shane: Th'ts ri:ght.

Sacks, Schegloff and Jefferson suggest that, like questions, other sequence-initiating actions may select a next speaker when combined with some form of address. They cite, for instance, the following case in which Ken selects Al as next speaker by addressing a complaint to him.

(13) Sacks, Schegloff and Jefferson (1974: 716) – [GTS:1]
01 Ken: Hey yuh took my chair by the way
02 an' I don't think that was very nice.
03 Al: I didn' take yer chair, it's my chair.

And in the following instance from the same occasion as example (12), Michael's request, which takes the form of a question, selects Nancy to speak next.[9]

(14) Chicken Dinner p.3
01 Michael: Nance kin you- kin you ↓cut my chicken.↓
02 (0.3)
03 Nancy: Do yer own cut(h)'n(h)n(h)n

Sacks, Schegloff and Jefferson explain that, whether they be questions as in (12), complaints as in (13) or requests as in (14), such sequence-initiating actions "set constraints on what should be done in a next turn". However, they go on to note that such first pair parts (i.e. sequence-initiating actions) do not *by themselves* allocate next turn to some specific next speaker. In order to do this a first pair part must be combined with some form of address. Notice then that first pair parts need not be addressed to anyone in particular and, as such, need not select a next speaker (e.g. "Who can tell me who wrote this poem?", "Can someone give me a ride downtown?", "Oh great! Someone ate the last piece of cake!").

So if the basic technique for selecting next speaker involves addressing a sequence-initiating action to some particular co-participant, we can ask, what are the techniques or practices for doing address?[10] How does a speaker show that they are addressing what they say to some specific co-participant? In (12) and (13) we see one technique: the use of an address term. While this may seem like the most effective way to ensure that others recognize to whom the utterance is addressed, it is actually not very common. Much more often, it would seem, address is signaled by gaze (see Lerner 2003). Such "explicit" means of addressing as use of an address term and directed gaze can be contrasted with more tacit and context-tied methods. For instance, in the following case it has already been established in prior talk that Mike was the only of the co-participants who attended the races the night before. Curt's question in line 01 asks for an eyewitness report and thus tacitly selects Mike as the next speaker (see Lerner 2003).

(15) [Auto discussion]
01 Curt: Wul how wz the races las'night.
02 (0.8) ((Mike nods head twice))
03 Curt: Who w'n [th'feature.]
04 Mike: [A l w o n,]
05 (0.3)
06 Curt: [(Who)]=
07 Mike: [A l.]=
08 Curt: =Al did?

Lerner points out that it is also possible for a turn to tacitly select a next speaker by eliminating all but one of the co-participants. He gives the following example from the dinner group consisting of Vivian, Shane, Nancy and Michael. This talk follows discussion of what time the two couples (Vivian and Shane on the one hand, Nancy and Michael on the other) will go to a swap meet the next day. At line 02, Nancy asks a question that includes reference to Vivian and Shane ("They") thus eliminating them as possible addressees. This leaves only Michael as a possible addressee and so this turn selects him as next speaker via a process of elimination.

(16) [Chicken dinner]
02 Nancy: Soo w'time sh'd they c'm over t'°morruh.°
03 Michael: (Sniff)
04 (1.5)
05 Michael: I don'know wuh ti-:me

There are a number of other ways in which next speaker may be tacitly selected. Indeed, because such techniques can involve an indefinite range of context-specific features and characteristics of the participants it's obviously not possible to give an exhaustive list of techniques. Rather, the analyst must be attentive to whatever features of context a speaker might invoke in order to achieve next-speaker selection in some particular situation.[11]

Where the Action is: The Transition Space

The turn-taking model has been criticized for being too formal and too mechanical.[12] Some critics have been led to ask, "Where are the human beings in this? The ones who are actually using the system to make sense with each other, ask questions, make requests, lodge complaints and such." In a way this is a funny kind of criticism that seems premised on a basic misunderstanding of what Sacks and his colleagues were doing in describing the organization of turn-taking for conversation. The model we have just sketched is not the *end* point of the analysis. Rather, it is a set of tools meant to be used to gain analytic leverage on any particular occasion of people talking together. Sacks, Schegloff and Jefferson gave the system a highly abstract and highly formal treatment precisely so as to allow for its application to virtually any situation. It is in that application of the formal system that we see the life and the intrigue, the human beings doing things. You can think of the system as a "metric": a system or standard of measurement. Through its operation, the system defines and delimits units of social life: turn-constructional units, gaps, increments and so on. Considered from this angle, we can see that each transition space is a locus of action.

Recall then that, unless special provisions are made by a current speaker (see chapter 9), a projected point of possible completion constitutes a "transition relevance place" or TRP. Such TRPs are, for the participants, "discrete places in the developing course of a speaker's talk [. . .] at which ending the turn or continuing it, transfer of the turn or its retention become relevant" (Schegloff 1992b: 116). Let us briefly return to the example of Parky, Tourist and Old Man, reproduced for convenience below:

(17) Parky (cited in Sacks, Schegloff and Jefferson 1974)

Tourist:	Has the park cha:nged much,
Parky:	Oh:: ye:s,
	(1.0)
Old man:	Th'*Fun*fair changed it'n [ahful lot [didn'it.
Parky:	[Th- [That-
Parky:	That changed it,

To review what we've already said about this example: here Parky begins an incipient next turn at the first point of possible completion in Old Man's turn. Parky starts up here and again at the next point of possible completion not by virtue of any silence but by virtue of a projected possible completion of the turn constructional unit which constitutes a potential transition relevance place. Now consider the following from a telephone call between two female college friends:

(18) TG

Ava:		I'm so:: ti:yid.I j's played ba:ske'ball t'day since the
	→	firs' time since I wz a freshm'n in hi:ghsch[ool.]
Bee:	→	[Ba::]sk(h)et=
		b(h)a(h)ll? (h)[(°Whe(h)re.)

Although there are points within this turn that are possibly complete on syntactic grounds (after "ti:yid" or "ba:ske'ball" or "t'day" etc.) the speaker produces them so as to show to the recipient that she is *not*, in fact, coming to completion. For instance, after "ti:yid" she launches immediately into the next TCU without allowing any silence, which the recipient might hear as a possible completion, to develop. In contrast, when she produces "hi:ghschool" the vowel in "high" is what Schegloff (1998) calls a pitch peak. It is produced with noticeably higher pitch and greater volume than the surrounding syllables. There is some evidence that such pitch peaks signal to a recipient that the turn is going to end at the next point of possible completion and here it does just that.

So what does an example like this tell us? Conversationalists are not at the mercy of points of possible completion. That is to say, there are ways in which the transition space can be obscured or even eliminated (between "tiyid" and "I") so as to prevent speaker transition via self-selection. Alternatively, the transition space can be extended and exaggerated so as to invite or re-invite speaker transfer. What we want to see then is that the transition space has boundaries that can be manipulated. It can be "opened early" or "closed late". The length of the transition space may also be either extended on compressed.[13] So while many transition spaces are produced as "nothing out of the ordinary" this is not automatic. The system is locally managed and participant-administered even at this, incredibly fine, level of detail.

The Transition Space: A Closer Look

Consider the following example from the beginning of a telephone call.

(19) Deb and Dick

			(ring)
			(r[
01	Deb:		[Hello:?hh
02	Dick:		Good morning.=
03	Deb:		=Hi:, howareya.
04	Dick:		Not too ba:d. Howareyou?
05	Deb:		I'm fi::ne
06	Dick:		Howdit g[o?
07	Deb:	→	[.h Oh: just grea:t,<everybody:st- still
08			here.
09	Dick:		Oh really(h)=
10	Deb:		=Yeah
11	Dick:		Oh they stayed. Okay.
12	Deb:		Yea:h

There are several unremarkable transition spaces here. In some of these transfer to a next speaker occurs (e.g. between lines 04 and 05), while in others it doesn't (e.g. line 04, between "not too bad" and "Howareyou?"). There are also several transitions which are compressed, that is, slightly shorter than normal. The one that we'll consider in detail occurs at line 07 between ".h oh: just grea:t" and "everybody:st- still here." Let's begin by noticing that this turn comes after a question (line 06 "Howdit go?"). One way in which people respond to a question is by answering it and we will want to consider whether that is one of the things this turn might be doing. Before we do that though, we need to consider briefly where this question occurs. In chapter 10 we will describe sequences of talk such as are represented by lines 01–05 as "opening sequences". In openings talk is directed to the accomplishment of several distinct tasks such as the identification and recognition of the parties, greetings, and initial inquiries such as "how are you?". So one way of describing the position of the question in line 06 is "directly after the opening sequence". Now as it turns out, callers routinely use this position to display why they are calling. For this reason it is sometimes called the "reason for the call" or "anchor" position (see chapter 10, Schegloff 1986).

For present purposes it is enough to note that this is a particularly important position in the structure of a call. By producing this question here and by designing it in the way he does, Dick shows that he is attending to what is happening in Deb's life. Consider then the design of the question, "Howdit go?". What is Dick doing by phrasing the question in this way and specifically by using "it"? "It" is a pronoun or what grammarians describe as an anaphor, which means that is meant to substitute for a noun where that noun has already been used (e.g. "John bit the apple. When he found that it was rotten, he spit it out."). But where is the noun for which this pronoun substitutes? There isn't one. By using a pronoun here, without a preceding noun, Dick suggests that Deb will know what he is talking about even though he hasn't referred to it explicitly. In effect, with this "it" he shows that he knows what is important to her. And notice that Dick gets it right in so far as Deb knows exactly what he is talking about. That is, she treats the meaning of "it" as utterly transparent. Talk further on in the call reveals that this "it" refers to a party which took place the night before.

There is one more thing we should notice about Dick's turn. Although not immediately obvious from the transcription, Dick's question employs the past tense: "How *did* it go?" he asks. Clearly, with this Dick locates the party in time, specifically, a time prior to the point at which this conversation is taking place.[14] Although we can't here deal with exactly how it does this, past tense in this context conveys that the thing being talked about (the "it", the party) is over and complete.

As it turns out there is a problem with the way in which Dick has formulated his question, since it is not quite right to say that the party is over. The guests have stayed and thereby continued the event, as Deb indicates in her response at lines 07–08. And yet, at the same time, the question *is* answerable as it stands. Dick has asked how it went and, for all practical purposes, it is over. Thus there are two different actions that are relevant next:

1 Answer the question.
2 Correct a problem in how the question has been formulated.

As we shall see in chapter 4, anything that occurs in the slot after a question ("they're still here" for instance) may be inspected by a recipient for how it answers or at least responds to that question. If it cannot be heard as answering the question it may be inspected by the recipient for how it accounts for not answering the question. In short, anything that occurs here can be inspected for its relevance to the question asked and can thus serve as the basis for further inference.

Imagine this pair of utterances without the "just great" such that "everybody's still here" comes as a response to "Howdit go?". Simplifying things somewhat, the problem with this is that "everybody's still here" could easily be heard by a recipient as "it didn't go well" or "it went on too long" or "I'm trying to get them out". In chapter 5 we will begin to see *why* anything other than a positive assessment (such as "just great") could be heard in this way. For now we will simply register that there is a built-in reason for answering this question in a straightforward way because any *other* way of responding might suggest a negative assessment and invite further inquiries.

At the same time, if she chooses simply to answer Dick's question and respond with "just great" alone, Deb has let the mistaken assumption that the event is over go unchallenged and uncorrected. This too is something to be avoided. Consider then that there are certain things that become relevant at the completion of an event: a report to interested parties, an assessment, the reporting of news and so on. By locating the event in the past, Dick's question proposes the relevance of these activities, indeed it invites them. But to the extent that the event is not, in fact, over, these activities are not the relevant ones to do.[15] There are then a number of intersecting reasons why Deb would like to do this assessment ("just great"), first as a response to Dick's question but, at the same time, so as not to allow the problematic assumption contained in Dick's question to pass without being corrected.

So what in fact happens? Deb produces the correction, "everybody:st- still here.", without releasing the turn after "just great". Sounds like the last consonant in "great" can be produced either with or without a release of air. Here, rather than produce this last sound (aspiration) of the last segment ("t") of the last word ("great") of this turn unit, Deb moves immediately into the first sound of "everybody". So one resource for talking through a possible completion is to withhold the production of the actual completion of the turn constructional unit and move directly into the next component of the turn. In this way a speaker can talk in such a way that a projectable point of completion never actually occurs.

Here is another example that I noted in passing. This happened in a faculty meeting and the person was talking about the administration of a large university:

(20) They always try to do tha- it's- it's just the way that they work.

Here the speaker is clearly coming to a point of possible completion with "that" but manages to avoid this by never actually producing the last sound of the word, substituting instead the first sound of the next turn unit. Returning to the example with Deb and Dick, we can see that Deb uses this practice to get two relevant tasks done in a single turn-at-talk without risking the possibility of Dick self-selecting at the first possible completion. We thus have some interactional motivation for this compressed transition space.[16]

Let's now consider an example in which the transition space is extended. This fragment is from the same conversation as the last example. It begins with Deb asking "so don't you have all your family coming today?" The question is answered but with some qualification in lines 24–8 and importantly, as Raymond (2003) has shown, without a "yes" or "no".[17] They *are* coming but perhaps not "all" of them.

(21) Deb and Dick
Deb: [s]o don't you have all your
family coming today?
Dick: We:ll they're coming around two and I °hhh left
messages with Brian an:d my dad to(uh) see if
→ they wanted to come but=ah:
(0.2)
°hh that's all I could do was leave messages.
Deb: owh
(0.4)
Dick: °Gotsome° °hhhh five pound lasagna thing to(hh)
throw in the oven=an
Deb: o(h)h(h)=huh (.) well: I'm sure you'll have a

good time.=
Dick: =[oh=
Deb: =[at least it's inside. And it didn't rain
yesterday so we were lucky [l- looking at it
Dick: [mmhm yeah
Deb: today god. woulda been awful.

Consider what happens after Dick says, "to see if they wanted to come". The turn is grammatically complete at this point and, with this, Dick has answered Deb's question. Notice, though, that he has answered it in a particular way. Specifically, he has concluded the turn by describing a failed attempt to get in touch with his own son and father so as to invite them to a family gathering at his house. There is something perhaps worthy of sympathy here then. (See discussion in chapter 4.)

When Deb does not talk at the initial completion of Dick's turn ("wanted to come"), he continues it with "but ah".[18] When Deb does not talk in the space provided after "but ah", Dick goes on to reiterate what he has said, this time characterizing it as "all he could do", once again recompleting the turn. Notice that he now ends the turn with the complainable item "leave messages" (rather than "wanted to come"). Moreover, with "all I could do" he hints at a certain desperation in this.

Although Deb now responds to what Dick is saying, they way she does this is entirely consistent with her withholding of "sympathy" earlier. Thus, rather than register the troubles contained within Dick's report, Deb merely registers the information with "oh". This receipts the information but does not take a stance towards it. More specifically it does not convey to Dick that Deb hears what he is saying as "bad news" or as "troubles talk" (see chapter 4 for further discussion of this fragment).

What we want to see then is that each point of possible completion is a place where certain things may relevantly happen. Moreover, people talk in such ways so as to prepare a possible completion – and the transition space associated with it – for certain things to happen there or *not* to happen there.[19] In the first example we considered, (19), completion at the end of "just great" was obscured and the transition space compressed. We noted an interactional motivation for this in that in this context there appear to be two jobs that need to get done in this one position. In the second example, (21), Dick talked in such a way as to extend the transition space, thereby providing Deb with additional opportunities to talk and thus for transition to take place.

So conversationalists are not at the mercy of points of possible completion determined by syntax. On the contrary, they talk in ways that obscure, eliminate or highlight the possible completion of a turn so as to compress or extend the transition space. A point of possible completion then is something that a speaker constructs and prepares for the recipients as a discrete place within the ongoing course of talk.

Overlap and Interruption

There is a pervasive view that conversation is filled with interruptions, that people frequently "talk over one another", not listening to what the other is saying. The evidence provided by recorded conversations suggests otherwise. Firstly, overlapping talk, though common, tends to occur in a highly restricted set of places in conversation. Secondly, most overlap appears to be a product, rather than a violation, of the system of turn-taking described above. Thirdly, conversationalists typically treat overlap as a potential source of impairment and seek to resolve and repair it. Thus, overlapping talk is typically not, in fact, the product of conversationalists "not listening to one another". On the contrary, extended episodes of overlapping talk provide some of the most remarkable displays of fine-grained orderliness in conversation. Specifically, we find in overlap evidence that participants attend to one another's talk syllable by syllable, beat by beat (Schegloff 2000a).

According to the turn-taking model, the norm is "one speaker at a time". So, do instances of overlap invalidate that model? Not at all. Rather, departures from one-at-a-time often provide further evidence for the operation of the turn-taking system. In order to see this we must inquire as to where overlap typically occurs. Overwhelmingly, this is at transition relevance spaces. For instance, many cases of overlapping talk occur when the beginning of a next turn starts just before the prior has come to completion:

(22) Virginia: 28
07 Virginia: ^Yer the one- (0.4) -who got bo:mbed at graduation so
08 bad couldn' even see:[:.
09 Beth: [Well graduation.'s some'in
10 else.don'tchyou think so¿Wesley¿

Here the completion of Virginia's turn is slightly extended by her lengthening the final sound of "see". This of course extends the turn slightly beyond the point at which Beth may have projected it to be complete. It is precisely this "extra length" which is overlapped by the beginning of Beth's turn. Another systematic basis of overlap is exhibited in the example from Tourist, Parky and Old Man which we have already considered:

(23) Parky (cited in Sacks, Schegloff and Jefferson 1974)
01 Tourist: Has the park cha:nged much,
02 Parky: Oh:: ye:s,
03 (1.0)
04 Old man: Th'*Fun*fair changed it'n [ahful lot [didn't it.
05 Parky: [Th- [That-
06 Parky: That changed it,

Here Parky's contributions overlap slightly with Old Man's continuing turn. This can be seen to result from the coincidence of rules 1b (next speaker self-selects) and 1c (current speaker continues). That is, as already noted in our earlier consideration of this fragment, Parky's incipient turn-starts occur at points of possible, though not actual, completion within Old Man's turn. As points of possible completion these are transition-relevant and thus activate the rule set described above. Note that in both cases the overlap is quickly resolved (after one beat/syllable) by one of the speakers dropping out. Here is another example exhibiting multiple instances of overlap.

(24) TG, 2:10–27
01 Ava: I'm so:: ti:yid.I j's played ba:ske'ball t'day since the
02 → firs' time since I wz a freshm'n in hi:ghsch[ool.]
03 Bee: → [Ba::]sk(h)et=

04 b(h)a(h)ll? (h)[(°Whe(h)re.)
05 Ava: [Yeah fuh like an hour enna ha:[lf.]
06 Bee: [·hh] Where
07 Bee: → didju play ba:sk[etbaw.]
08 Ava: → [(The) gy]:m.
09 Bee: In the gy:m? [(hh)

The overlap at lines 02–03 is a case of terminal overlap similar to that in example (15). The overlap at lines 4–5 appears to be the product of the coincidence of rules 1b and 1c at a transition relevance place, as in example (16). The overlap at 07–08, however, is somewhat different. Here Ava makes a more significant incursion into Bee's turn. With respect to this example let us make two initial observations. First, Ava has initiated the talk here by announcing that she "just played basketball" (line 01). Second, Bee's overlapped turn at lines 06–07 is a question and Ava's overlapping turn at 08 is an answer to that question. So notice then that, at the point at which Ava overlaps Bee's turn, it is perfectly clear what Bee is going to say. That Ava played basketball has already been established and the syntax of the turn clearly indicates that this is a question. So at the point where Ava interrupts Bee's turn she is already able to recognize what Bee is saying. For this reason, Jefferson (1983) used the phrase recognitional overlap to describe instances like this.

So far we have considered the three types of overlap which account for the vast majority of cases in conversation. These are "turn-terminal", "turn-initial" and "recognitional". None of these are really "interruptive" in the usual sense of that word, as they actually promote the progress of the action embodied in the talk. Moreover, these kinds of overlap clearly involve one participant closely monitoring another's talk. So what of interruption? We can all attest to being interrupted. Can we find some instances which seem to involve not just overlap but one speaker interrupting another? Here is a possible case:

(25) Sidnell: Call 04. 2003
((Ring))
01 Cld: °hh He:llo::¿
02 Clr: Hello:,=my name is Naomi=from <u>con</u>:quest research?
03 one of [Cana
04 Cld: [No::. I'm sorry.
05 Clr: °No problem°
((Hang up))

Notice that unlike the examples of overlap examined so far, in this one the overlap does not occur in the vicinity of a turn's possible completion. The called party can likely hear that "one of" is on its way to becoming "one of Canada's leading telemarketing research firms" or something along those lines. In this respect, this case is similar to the third instance in example (24), since in both cases overlap occurs at a point where the remainder of the turn is "recognizable" or "expectable". There is, however, a crucial difference between the two examples. In (24), Ava has enough of the turn available to anticipate *precisely* what Bee is going to say and build a response – an answer – to her question. In contrast, in (25), the called party can only project the *kind of* turn which is in progress. This surely allows her to see what kind of an action the caller is engaged in and thus what kind of activity is being initiated. Notice, however, that, rather than use this "projection" to further that activity, her turn at 04 arrests its progress and declines to participate in it.

So what is it about this case that makes it recognizable as interruption? Not just the occurrence of overlap but also the actions in which the participants are engaged seem to be important. Specifically, this example suggests that for an overlap to be heard as interruptive it must involve competing trajectories of action and perhaps also evidence of disaffiliation.[20]

Let's take a look at another potential case of interruption. This one is not from conversation but rather from an interview of George Bush Sr. by Dan Rather in the wake of the Iran–Contra affair (see Schegloff 1988d).

(26) Bush–Rather
074 Rather: .hhhh And- a member of your own sta:ff Mister Craig
075 Fuller.-((swallow/(0.5))) has verified. And so did
076 the o:nly other man the:re, Mister Ni:r. Mister
077 Amiron Nir, .hh who's the Israeli's .hh to:p anti-
078 terrorist man,
079 Bush: [Ye: [s
080 Rather: [.hh [Those two men >were in a meeting with you an'
081 Mister Nir not once, < but three: times. three times,
082 underscored with you that this was a straightout
083 arms[fer hostages swap.] = .h h h]=
084 Bush: [W h a t t h e y::] (.) were doing.]
085 Rather: → = Now [how do you- How] do you reconc-] I have (sir)]
086 Bush: → [Read the memo] Read the memo.] What they::]
087 were doing.
088 Rather: How: can you reconci:le that you were there<Mister
089 Nir a- underscored three:: separate occa:sions, .hh
090 that it was a- arms fer hostages swap an' to:ld you
091 we were dealing with the most ra:dical elements in

There are several relevant observations we can make about this fragment. First, like (25), it involves disalignment and disaffiliation (these are terms that will be discussed in greater detail in subsequent chapters). This is recognizable from the first significant overlap at 084. Clayman and Heritage (2002) have shown that, in news interviews, interviewees typically wait until a recognizable question has been articulated before beginning their own turn; this waiting for the question is, of course, one way in which the participants jointly construct and sustain the interaction as an interview (see chapter 12). Now, at line 084, Bush is breaking this basic ground rule of interview by talking before the question has been asked and, in the process, overlapping the interviewer's turn.

Looking at the arrowed turns at 085–086, we can notice a very common thing: overlapped talk gets repeated. Often, an overlapped fragment of talk will be repeated so that it is eventually produced "in the clear". Example (27) provides an example:

(27) Chicken Dinner: Michael's Father, Part 1.
17 Nancy: But (0.4) yihknow w[it t h e h e l l]
18 Shane: [Like yih said you][wuh feelin ↓goo]d,=
19 Michael: → [M y ↓fa:ther-]
20 Michael: → =·hhh ↑My ↓fa:ther we w'r in Manners Big Boy.ih( )
21 Big Bo[y back E]a:st?
22 Shane: [Yea:h?]
23 (0.3)

Here the beginning of Michael's turn at line 19 is overlapped by the continuation of Shane's. Michael then repeats the overlapped portion of talk in the clear at line 20.

In example (26), neither speaker is able to repeat the overlapped portion of their talk completely in the clear. Even so, the fact that speakers typically repeat talk which is overlapped suggests that they see this as a problem and a source of possible impairment. Repetition in this sense is a repair mechanism (Schegloff 1987).

Let us make one more observation about example (26) before moving onto the final example of this chapter. Notice that at line 085, Rather remarks "I have (sir)". This is clearly a response to Bush's instruction to "read the memo". Notice that Bush has said this completely in overlap with Rather's "how do you- How do you reconc". This, then, is *prima facie* evidence that speakers do monitor one another's talk even as they overlap it with their own.

We have seen that a particularly common place for overlap is at and around possible turn completion. Overlap is common here because these are places where speakers "collide" as it were – one continuing and one self-selecting. The following example is from a call-in radio show called Cross Country Check Up. Notice what happens at lines 07 and 08.

```
(28)  Cross Country Check Up
01  Cr:   frankly I was s:pee::chless beyond
02        (.)
03        belief when I read the interview=
04        =because I said uh oh::=
05  Cd:   =yea[h
06  Cr:       [°h here comes Chretien=
07  Cd:   =[°ts[h we[ll  [uh
08  Cr:       [°hh [an:[d uhm I-I-I-I think
09        that justice Gomery has done a wonderful
10        job so fa:r: °hh I-I jus' think that
11        he is (.) he::: (.) had a moment of
12        intemperance. which=
13  Cd:   okay.
```

The caller has a reached a point of possible completion at the end of line 6 and appears to have paused momentarily, perhaps for dramatic effect. However, the radio host targets this as a place for speaker transition and begins a turn-at-talk.[21] In response, the caller *continues* his turn with "and". Notice that the overlapping talk here exhibits a beat-by-beat organization. The overlap begins gently enough with both participants producing "pre-turn" components that display an intention to speak next without actually beginning a turn (see chapter 8). The radio host is the first to begin speaking in earnest with "well" and this is overlapped by the caller's "an:d". The sound stretch on "and" is the first competitive move in this battle for the floor. The radio show host starts to back off a bit and the caller produces a further competitive increment with a loud "uhm". The caller, now speaking in the clear, produces a string of repeated "I"s, almost stuttering, before continuing his turn. Such "post-overlap" hitches are very common. One thing they may be doing is defending the beginning of a turn against further incursion. We may use this observation to locate occasions in which participants orient to the *possibility* of overlap even where none occurs. Thus notice that *at the next point of possible completion* in the caller's turn (after "fa:r:"), he once gain produces a "stuttered" "I". With this, might he be defending against any further attempt by the radio host to self-select? One further thing to note about this example has to do with where precisely the caller leaves pauses in his talk at line 11. Whereas transition relevance places are particularly vulnerable to overlap and incursion by self-selecting next speakers, such points as these offer current speakers more control by virtue of being recognizably *incomplete*. That is, after "he is" and "he" the caller's turn is clearly not complete. Schegloff (1982) has described places like this within the unfolding course of a turn as "points of maximal grammatical control."

Conclusion

We are now in a position to appreciate the following passage from Sacks, Schegloff and Jefferson (1974: 700):

> In sum, turn-taking seems a basic form of organization for conversation – "basic", in that it would be invariant to parties, such that whatever variations the parties brought to bear in the conversation would be accommodated without change in the system, and such that it could be selectively and locally affected by social aspects of context. Depiction of an organization for turn-taking should fit the facts of variability by virtue of a design allowing it to be context-sensitive; but it should be cast in a manner that, requiring no reference to any particular context, still captures the most important general properties of conversation.

Underlying everything else that happens in conversation is an organization for turn-taking. This is not simply a "traffic management" system. The turn-taking system defines the basic units out of which all conversations are built – turn constructional units. As Sacks, Schegloff and Jefferson note, the system is basic and abstract, so that it can work for two, three, four or more participants without modification.[22] Moreover, the system works for conversations between co-workers, parents and children, bosses and employees and any other category of person. In this sense it is invariant. However, the system allows for extreme context sensitivity, becoming adapted to the minute details of particular situations, relationships and the particular persons involved from Deb and Dick on the one hand to Bush and Rather on the other.

We began this chapter with a sketch of some of the most basic features of conversational turn-taking – what Sacks, Schegloff and Jefferson characterize as "grossly apparent facts". Any model or "systematics" should of course be able to account for these features, and if you return to that list you'll see that the one described here does in fact account for them.

The Sacks et al. model of turn-taking rests on the basic yet crucial observation that the system is locally managed and party-administered. Moreover, in conversation, "one-at-a-time" is organizationally primary as Sacks put it, meaning the whole system is designed to preserve this. So the question then becomes, what kind of a locally managed, party-administered system for turn-taking will minimize gap and overlap while at the same time preserving "one-at-a-time" and accounting for the other "grossly apparent facts" of conversation?

Following Sacks, Schegloff and Jefferson we sketched out such a system that involves a turn-constructional component and a turn-allocation component. In this system participants monitor a turn-at-talk to find that it is now beginning, now continuing, now approaching completion. Participants listen for and target points of possible completion as places at which to begin their own talk. The result is a dynamic and highly sensitive system that confers upon conversation a distinctive temporal signature: it provides a metric within which a silence may be heard as resulting from some particular person not speaking.

With this established we can now turn to consider how participants use the opportunities to speak – distributed within the system just described – to get things done.

Notes

1 On the organization of laughter in conversation see Jefferson 1979 and Glenn 2003.

2 Tanaka (2000) has argued that certain particles in Japanese are essentially "turn-completion" signals. See Goodwin (1979a) for a discussion of this issue in relation to alternative models of turn-taking.

3 There are a few apparent exceptions to the "organizes only current and next" feature of the turn-taking system. For instance, if A introduces B to C, the sequence may run off like this (see chapter 4, example (10), for an instance):

A: Bob, this is Curt
C: Hi Bob
B: Hi Curt

And thus it looks as though A's introduction has organized not just the next turn but also the turn after that. However, as Sacks argued (1995 vol. 2: 524), this is not a real exception. A's introduction only selects a next speaker, Curt. Curt's greeting then selects Bob as next speaker.

4 Of course we are assuming, in the absence of a video record, that Tourist did not select a next speaker by the use of gaze (see Lerner 2003).

5 The ambiguous character of this utterance is discussed in Schegloff 2005.

6 By pragmatic features I mean that the recipient can listen to the talk to find whether the turn-so-far can be heard as a possibly complete, locally appropriate action in the immediate sequential context.

7 The obedience to these rules is normative rather than categorical – that is, violation of them is something recognizable and accountable. See chapter 4 (and Schegloff 1992b) for discussion of the differences between normative and categorical rules.

8 Nancy also redirects her gaze here first from her own plate to Michael's (her gaze reaches his plate at "you" in "how 'bout you") and subsequently to Michael's face after he does not immediately respond. She withdraws her gaze, returning it to her plate, just before Michael produces the talk at line 44.

9 While Michael says this he looks from his plate to find that Nancy is visibly engaged in eating and not available to look at him. It is at precisely this point that he cuts off the production of "you" and restarts the request. See Goodwin 1979b, 1980 and chapter 7 on the use of self-repair to elicit recipient gaze. See also Lerner 2003 on the use of pre-positioned address-terms in cases where the availability of the recipient is uncertain.

10 We should really say that selecting a next speaker involves addressing a sequence-initiating action at some specific *party* and in doing so leave open the possibility that the party in question may in fact consist of more than one participant as in questions such as "What did you guys think of the movie?" addressed to a couple, for instance.

11 Schegloff tells the following story as an illustration: A group of four are in the car. The driver and her daughter have been sharing some peanuts – the other two passengers have not had any. When the driver asks "you want some more nuts?" she has tacitly selected her daughter to speak next as the only other person who has already had some and thus as the only other person who could potentially have "more".

12 By Moerman (1988) for instance.

13 Such descriptions as "opened early", "closed late", "extended" and "compressed" rest upon a comparison with a "normal", unmarked transition space.

14 Such linguistic devices, which work by relating something to the current event of speaking, are called "deictics". See Levinson 1983, Sidnell 2005.

15 Moreover, there is the issue of announcing the presence of other hearers so that the recipient can know that whatever is said has been designed in part to be heard by someone else in the room, and so to establish a warrant for getting off the phone (see chapter 10).

16 There are other resources for getting past a possible completion. "Rush-throughs" were discussed earlier in this chapter. Another resource is the "pivot" construction described in, for instance, Walker 2006.

17 Raymond (2003) shows that what he calls type non-conforming responses to yes–no interrogatives – that is responses that contain neither a "yes" nor a "no" and therefore do not conform to the grammatical format of the question – are produced "for cause". Looking at this example we can see that Dick orients to a problem with the way in which the question has been formulated. Specifically, Deb has asked whether Dick has "all" his family coming. As Dick indicates in his response, it is unclear whether some members of his family are indeed coming.

18 Local and Kelly (1986) analyze pauses after conjunctionals such as "but" and "well" and find that in some the pause begins with glottal closure which is held until the beginning of the next word after the pause. Such pauses are associated with the speaker holding the turn. In others, there is no glottal closure at the beginning of the pause. Rather there is often some audible outbreath. These kinds of pauses are associated with turn transfer and are heard as "trail-offs". See also Jefferson (1983).

19 This is part of what Schegloff and Sacks meant in their (1973) discussion of "close ordering".

20 In fact, talk need not even involve overlap in order to be heard by the participants as interruption. Consider, for instance, the following case:

(30) David and Robin, 1:1–29

Ring rin-
Robin: Hello.-
David: Ro:bin?
(.)
Robin: Yeah.
David: Hi:.
(0.8)
Robin: You have one hell of a nerve.
(0.2)
David: (.hhhh)/(hhhh)
(0.8)
Robin: Now listen ta me.=I jus' wanna tell you one thing.
(.)
David: Yeah? ((Weakly; without lower registers of voice))
(0.8)
Robin: Y'to:ld me on Sunday, (.) that you were coming home on
Thursday.
David: → pt. .hhhhh=
Robin: → =Y'didn't te- wait don't:(.)[inte]rrupt me.
David: [ok-]
David: O:okay,=
Robin: =Y'didn' tell me how: you were coming,(1.0) y'could've come
by pla:ne, y'could've come by ca:r,=y'could've been
hitchhiking.

21 Talk not shown here suggests that he is ready to bring the call to a close.

22 Although the number of parties introduces certain "biases" (see Sacks, Schegloff and Jefferson 1974).

4

Action and Understanding

In the previous chapter we examined one kind of organization in conversation: the organization of turns-at-talk. That organization is largely *serial*, by which I mean, simply, that turns follow one another in a series. As we have already seen, this is not the only way in which talk is organized. Turning our attention from turns to actions, we find that the latter are not arranged serially, one after the other, like so many marching penguins. Instead, they come grouped together in various ways. An answer, for instance, responds to a question and the two form together a paired unit. In this chapter, then, we examine the ways in which actions are grouped together and related to one another so as to form sequences of actions. This leads to a consideration of the distinctive way in which understanding is achieved and sustained in conversation.

Let's begin by looking at a very brief recorded telephone conversation. Here, Anne is called by Janet whose daughter is at Anne's house.

(1) xtr. 1

<<ring>>=
Anne: =Hello::
Janet: Oh=hi:_=it's Janet_ [Cathy's mo]m
Anne: [hi: Janet]
How eryou(h) .h hh
Janet: I'm goo:d,how are y[ou
Anne: [I'm fi:ne.h[we're actually: uhm
Janet: [°good°
(0.2)
Anne: we're running a bit late=but we're
(.)
on our wa(h)y:.
Janet: a→ Do you want me to come an' get her?
Anne: Uhm:, it doesn't matte:r, like(hh)
(0.4)
.hhhhh
Janet: a→ I- I could.it's very easy.
so rather than you h:av(h)e(h)
(.)

19 you know (.) tuh get everybody ou[t
20 Anne: [.hhh
21 Janet: I'll justa
22 (0.2)
23 come dow:n.=
24 Anne: =we:ll,my mom's here, so I don't have to uhm::
25 (.)
26 I don't have to put my kids in the ca:r.
27 Janet: a→ I'll ju[s- I'll just come down.
28 Anne: [bu
29 b→ ↑Oka(h)y(h)=
30 Janet: =yeah
31 Anne: ok(h)ay
32 Janet: uh what's yo[ur number again?=
33 Anne: [.hhhhh
34 =It's seven-seven eight.
35 Janet: Okay great.
36 Anne: ↑Oka:y [thanks]
37 Janet: [thanks]
38 Anne: bye.

There are many ways this brief conversation could be analyzed. For instance, one could focus on the topics of the conversation – what these people were talking about (Anne's mom? Anne's kids? the car?). Alternatively one could consider the talk in terms of the identities which the participants enact (e.g. "mother") or the particular face arrangements which their talk implicates. What distinguishes the conversation-analytic approach from these alternatives is a focus on the participants' own understandings as these are revealed in the talk itself. So the first thing we need to ask is what these people understood themselves to be doing here, what actions they were bringing off in talking the way they did. Let's begin with the talk at line 12, reproduced here for convenience as (2):

(2) XTR 1 – Detail
12 Janet: a→ Do you want me to come an' get her?
13 Anne: Uhm:, it doesn't matte:r, like(hh)
14 (0.4)

The turn at line 12 could be characterized in several different ways. If we look at the linguistic form of the turn, we find that the auxiliary verb "do" occurs before the pronoun "you" and thus the sentence involves subject–auxiliary inversion (see Quirk, Greenbaum, Leech, & Svartvik 1985). Moreover, the turn at line 12 is produced with a markedly rising intonation contour, indicated by the question mark at its completion. These are two ways in which speakers of English convey that they are asking a question (see Schegloff 1984). If the talk in line 12 is a question, it seems likely that Anne's response at line 13 is an answer to it. The question and answer pair together form a small sequence, an adjacency pair. Or do they?

That Janet's talk at line 12 poses a question is clear enough, but she seems also to be doing something else. Specifically, Janet seems to be *offering* to come and pick up her daughter from Anne's house. In a moment we will review several types of evidence for the claim that, in saying "Do you want me to come an' get her?", Janet is making an offer. However, before doing so, it may be useful to briefly consider the relationship between the question and the offer in this example. Describing this turn as a question captures something important about its design, specifically about the use of recurrent and stable features of English grammar (and intonation) which distinguish "Do you want me to come over and get her?" from "I'm coming to get her" etc. Because these are relatively stable features which recur across a wide range of utterance types and actions, we will call them "practices of speaking" or, simply, "practices". Describing this turn as an offer, on the other hand, captures something important about what this speaker, on this occasion, is *doing*. An offer, after all, is an action. Analysis typically involves attention both to the actions which are being accomplished by a turn *and* to the practices of speaking which make those happen within some particular context.[1] We've already seen (in our consideration of question-intoned repeats in chapter 2 for instance) that there is typically not a one-to-one mapping between practice and action. That is, although some practices of speaking are strongly associated with some particular action (e.g. "Hello" with greeting) even these can perform other actions in specific contexts. So, although typically used as a greeting, "hello" can be used on the telephone to check whether the recipient is hearing the speaker.[2] In the vast majority of cases the relation between some practice of speaking and some particular action is wholly contingent. That is, what some practice of speaking is doing on some particular occasion is a function of the context in which it is produced. As Schegloff (1993: 121) puts it, "both position and composition are ordinarily constitutive of the sense and import of an element of conduct that embodies some phenomenon or practice."

So what evidence, beyond our own intuitions, do we have for the claim that Janet is making an offer when she says "Do you want me to come an' get her?"? First, we can quite readily find other examples of just this construction used in apparently similar ways. For instance:

```
(3)  Heritage 1:3:3
01   Ilene:         =Wellnow look.
02             →    d'you want me ti[h come over'n get her?=or wha:t.
03   Lisa:                          [°(              )°
04   Lisa:          ↑Just please yerself dear we were g'nna t-bring'er
05                  ↑back b't chor very wel[come
06   Ilene:                                [No well when you- when you
07                  going to bring her ↓ba:ck.=
```

Or

```
(4)  Holt 5/88:2:4:
01   Deena:    →    So: are you going to go ¯back that night or d'you want
02                  (.) a bunk bed or somethi[ng
03   Mark:                                   [nNo we'll go back thank you
04                  very much it's not very far
05                  (.)
06   Deena:         Are you su:re becuz we're not having anybody to stay
07                  here I mean we (.) we c- (.) we could accommoda[te you:=
08   Mark:                                                         [.hhhhhh
09   Deena:         =uh:[m
10   Mark:              [n:No:: (.) no it's alright it's not (.) not
11                  particu'rly fa:r a couple of hours 'n we're home again.
```

Here are two more cases in which speakers use the "do you want X" construction to make an offer. Notice that this kind of evidence involves a focus on the "practices of speaking" involved in our example and requires that we look across a collection of instances.[3] A second kind of evidence is provided by what comes next in the sequence. That is, we can look to see how the participants themselves treated the utterance in responding to it. Consider example (4) in this respect. Here Deena has invited Mark, her cousin, to stay overnight after her daughter's wedding. She does this by offering "a bunk bed or something". Mark's response answers the question which is the vehicle for the offer ("no") while, at the same time, accounting for not accepting it with "we'll go back."[4] Moreover, Mark's "thank you very much" responds to Deena's turn explicitly in terms of its status as an offer by appreciating it.

We can access a third type of evidence by looking at the relation between the focal turn and the previous one. We can look, that is, at the talk to which the focal turn was itself designed as a response. In this respect, it can be observed that offers are frequently produced in response to a description of speaker-trouble (e.g. "my car is stalled"). Notice then that Janet's offer to "come and get her" follows directly on the heels of Anne's "we're running a bit late". To summarize, we can draw on three kinds of evidence, beyond our own intuitions, in making claims about what a given utterance is doing. First, we can collect other instances of the same construction or, more generally, the same practices of speaking to see if they do the same or similar jobs in those other cases. Second, we can look at the response which the focal turn elicits from a recipient. Third we can examine the interactional circumstances which occasion the focal turn and, in particular, the immediately preceding turn to which it is built as a response.

In example (4) we saw an offer rejected. In example (1), Anne seems neither to accept nor reject Janet's offer in the immediately subsequent turn. Rather, Anne's "Uhm: it doesn't matter" withholds a response to the offer. Moreover, after coming to completion of her turn, Anne starts again, only to trail off the production of "like", in this way providing Janet with another opportunity to speak. By neither accepting nor declining the offer, with her talk at line 13 Anne puts the ball back in Janet's court, so to speak.

(5) XTR 1 – fragment 3

12	Janet:	a→	Do you want me to come an' get ↑her?
13	Anne:		Uhm:, it doesn't matte:r, like(hh)
14			(0.4)
15			.hhhhh
16	Janet:	a→	I- I could.it's very easy.
17			so rather than you h:av(h)e(h)
18			(.)
19			you know (.) tuh get everybody ou[t
20	Anne:		[.hhh
21	Janet:		I'll justa
22			(0.2)
23			come dow:n.=
24	Anne:		=we:ll,my mom's here, so I don't have to uhm::
25			(.)
26			I don't have to put my kids in the ca:r.
27	Janet:	a→	I'll ju[s- I'll just come down.
28	Anne:		[bu
29		b→	↑Oka[(h)y(h)=
30	Janet:		=yeah
31	Anne:		ok(h)ay

There are various ways in which an offer may be declined. Although declination may be accomplished by a simple "no thank you", often this kind of thing involves the recipient giving a reason or account for why the offer is not being accepted (see chapter 5). For instance, the recipient may claim not to want or not to need the thing being offered, as in example (4). Alternatively, the recipient of an offer may decline it on the basis of the burden acceptance would create for the one making it. The one making the offer may themselves orient to potential grounds for declining it. Here, in line 16, Janet's "I- I could.it's very easy" pushes the offer forward by characterizing the task as a minimal inconvenience to her. Janet then goes on to contrast the course of action which she is proposing with the alternative of Anne coming to Janet. She concludes with, "I'll just come down", which, in this context, transforms the offer so that it no longer hinges on Anne's wants. In this sense it is strongly built towards acceptance, which it subsequently elicits from Anne with "okay".

We can thus see how this talk forms a sequence of action initiated with an offer by Janet to Anne and eventually brought to completion with an acceptance of that offer by Anne. Now that we have seen something of this organization in action, we can turn to describe its technical features.

Adjacency Pairs and Conditional Relevance

A great deal of talk is organized into sequences of paired actions or "adjacency pairs". For instance, a question creates a "slot", "place" or "context" within which an answer is relevant and expected next. Schegloff (1968: 1083) noted that such paired actions pose two basic problems for analysis. First,

> How can we rigorously talk about two items as a sequenced pair of items, rather than as two separate units, one of which happens to follow the other?

And secondly,

> How can we, in a sociologically meaningful and rigorous way, talk about the "absence" of an item; numerous things are not present at any point in a conversation, yet only some have a relevance that would allow them to be seen as "absent."

Recognition of these problems led Schegloff (1968: 1083) to introduce the concept of conditional relevance:

> By the conditional relevance of one item on another we mean: given the first, the second is expectable; upon its occurrence it can be seen to be a second item to the first; upon its non-occurrence it can be seen to be officially absent – all this provided by the occurrence of the first item.

So, for instance, questions are not always followed by answers. However, the conditional relevance that a question establishes ensures that participants will inspect any talk that follows a question to see if and how it answers that question. In other words, the relationship between paired utterance types such as question and answer is a norm to which participants themselves orient in finding and constructing orderly sequences of talk (see Goodwin and Heritage 1990, Heritage 1984b). Paired utterance types, such as question and answer, request and granting, offer and acceptance, greeting and greeting, complaint and remedy, form what Sacks called "adjacency pairs" (Sacks 1995b: 521–41). Schegloff and Sacks (1973) identified four defining characteristics of the adjacency pair. It is composed of two utterances that are:

1 Adjacent.[5]
2 Produced by different speakers.
3 Ordered as a first pair part (FPP) and a second pair part (SPP).
4 Typed, so that a particular first pair part provides for the relevance of a particular second pair part (or some delimited range of seconds; e.g., a complaint can receive a remedy, an expression of agreement, a denial as its second).

Discussing the last feature in this list, Schegloff (2007) writes:

> the components of an adjacency pair are pair-type related. That is, not every second pair part can properly follow any first pair part. Adjacency pairs compose pair *types*; types are exchanges such as greeting–greeting, question–answer, offer–accept/decline, and the like. To compose an adjacency pair, the FPP and SPP come from the same pair type. Consider such FPPs as "Hello," or "Do you know what time it is?" or "Would you like a cup of coffee?" and such SPPs as "Hi," or "Four o'clock" or "No thanks." Parties to talk-in-interaction do not just pick some SPP to respond to a FPP: that would yield such absurdities as "Hello," "No thanks," or "Would you like a cup of coffee?" "Hi." The components of adjacency pairs are "typologized" not only into first and second pair parts, but into the *pair types* which they can partially compose: greeting–greeting ("Hello," "Hi"), question–answer ("Do you know what time it is?" "Four o'clock"), offer–accept/decline ("Would you like a cup of coffee?" "No thanks," if it is declined).

What kind of organization is the adjacency pair? It is not a statistical probability and clearly not a categorical imperative. Rather, the organization described is a norm to which participants hold one another accountable. The normative character of the adjacency pair is displayed in participants' own conduct in interaction. For example, as the principle of conditional relevance implies, when a question does not receive an answer, questioners treat the answer as "noticeably" absent. Questioners' orientation to a missing answer can be seen in three commonly produced types of subsequent conduct: pursuit, inference and report.

The following example provides an illustration of both pursuit and inference (from Drew 1981). Here Mother asks the child, Roger, what time it is.

(6) Drew 1981: 249
01 Mother: What's the time- by the clock?
02 Roger: Uh
03 Mother: What's the time?
04 (3.0)
05 Mother: (Now) what number's that?
06 Roger: Number two
07 Mother: No it's not
08 What is it?
09 Roger: It's a one and a nought

After Roger produces something other than an answer at line 02, Mother repeats the question at line 03. Here then we see that a failure to answer prompts the *pursuit* of a response (see Pomerantz 1984b). When this second question is met with three seconds of silence, Mother transforms the question, now asking, "what number's that?". Note that the first question, "What's the time?" poses a complex task for the child. The child must first identify the numbers to which the hands are pointed and subsequently use those numbers to calculate the time. Here, in response to a failure to answer, Mother takes this complex task and breaks it down into components. Mother has inferred that the child did not answer because the question as initially put was too difficult. Mother's subsequent simplification of the task is informed then by an inference that the child did not answer because he was not able to do so.

Although it does not happen here, questioners may also report an absent answer by saying such things as "you are not answering my question", or "he didn't answer the question", or "she didn't reply", etc. In public inquiries and other courtroom contexts, lawyers commonly suggest that the witness is not answering the question that has been asked of them (see Ehrlich and Sidnell 2006, Sidnell 2004, Sidnell 2010a).

It is important to see the difference between an absence on the one hand and an "official", "noticeable" or "accountable" absence on the other. Obviously, an indefinite number of things can be accurately described as absent after the occurrence of a first pair part. The next speaker did not blow his nose, scratch his head, jump up and down, sing "O Canada", etc. The point here is that the first pair part of an adjacency pair has the capacity to make some particular types of conduct noticeably or relevantly absent, so that their non-occurrence is just as much an event as their occurrence.

Would-be answerers also orient to a missing answer. Thus, the non-occurrence of an answer typically occasions an account for not answering. One particularly common account for not answering is not knowing. The following examples from Heritage (1984b) illustrate this:

(7) From Heritage 1984 (W:PC:1:MJ(1):18)
01 J: But the trai:n goes. Does th'train go o:n th'boa:t?
02 M: °h °h Ooh I've no idea:. She ha:sn't sai:d.

(8) From Heritage 1984 (Rah:A:1:Ex:JM(7):2) – simplified
01 M: Is he alri:ght?,
02 J: W̲ell he hasn' c'm ba-a̲ck yet.

In the first example the speaker accounts for not answering by saying she has "no idea" and subsequently accounts for not knowing by saying "she hasn't said.". In the second example, the speaker produces only an account for not knowing and by this implies a corresponding account for not answering. To summarize, at the heart of many sequences are adjacency pairs which organize two turns via a relation of conditional relevance. An orientation to the normative character of adjacency pairs is revealed in various aspects of the participants' own conduct (questioners' pursuit, inference and report as well as answerers' accounts).

Let's take a moment to register the broader implications of what we have so far said about the organization of action. Many explanations of human conduct involve people learning or otherwise internalizing patterns, scripts, procedures, ideologies, cultural values and so on. On this view, it is by virtue of individuals internalizing norms and values that social cohesion and social order are possible. However, scholars in a number of traditions have recently pointed to the difficult questions about "structure" and "agency" to which such explanations inevitably lead.[6] The question arises as to how much of what we do is a matter of conscious decision-making and how much is a matter of shaping by a hidden hand. As long as the questions are posed in this way it seems as though we must either be puppets or gods. Our brief consideration of adjacency pairs hints at the distinctive way in which the issue is conceptualized within conversation analysis. CA is not deterministic, since people may or may not do the normatively called-for action. On the other hand, neither is it just a matter of people doing whatever they want. Rather, in making sense of what others are up to, conversationalists are also holding them accountable to the dictates of normative structures. Looking at the sequential organization of talk we see that "conversationalists are . . . not so much constrained by rules or sanctions, as caught in a web of inferences" (Levinson 1983: 321).[7] Whereas in the classical social theory of Emile Durkheim (e.g. 1964, and following him Parsons 1937, Radcliffe-Brown 1954, Goffman 1971 and others) compliance with norms is encouraged by the fact that those who deviate from them may face various forms of negative social sanction, the analysis of conversation suggests that in talk-in-interaction the issue is more one of generating inferences. So, if a question is not answered, the questioner is likely to draw the inference that the recipient does not know the answer (or has some other reason for not answering, e.g. the answer may incriminate the recipient, insult the questioner and so on). Again the point is that, in this context at least, deviance from norms does not so much attract negative sanction (though it may of course do that *too*) as generate, perhaps unwanted, inferences.

"A context of publicly displayed and continuously updated intersubjective understandings"

The relatedness of the two turns in an adjacency pair has both a prospective and a retrospective dimension. Thus, as discussed above, the occurrence of a first pair part creates a slot for a specific second pair part. At the same time, a second pair part displays its speaker's understanding of the first to which it responds. Adjacency pairs allow then for a framework of understanding that is constructed and sustained on a turn-by-turn basis. If a speaker responds to a first part with an inappropriate second part, the speaker of the first part can see that she has not been properly understood. In such a situation the speaker of the first part can initiate repair in "third position" (see chapter 7). This is precisely what happens in example (9).

(9) Third-position repair – from Schegloff 1992a.
01 Annie: Which one:s are closed, an' which ones are open.
02 Zebrach: Most of 'em. This, this, [this, this ((pointing))
03 Annie: → [I 'on't mean on the
04 → shelters, I mean on the roads.
05 Zebrach: Oh!
06 (0.8)
07 Zebrach: Closed, those're the ones you wanna know about,
08 Annie: Mm[hm
09 Zebrach: [Broadway . . .

Here, Annie and Zebrach are looking at a map together and, at line 01, Annie asks Zebrach "which ones" are closed and which are open (this is first position). In his response at line 02, Zebrach indicates which of the "shelters" are open (this is second position). This turn reveals a misunderstanding of the question and specifically the reference with "which ones" in line 01. Zebrach's response reveals to Annie that he has understood her to be asking about the shelters when in fact she meant to be asking about the roads. The problem is addressed via third-position repair at lines 03–04 (see Schegloff 1992a, 1997a).

Examples such as this indicate that participants in conversation look to a next turn to see if and how they have been understood. As analysts we can exploit the same resource. This is sometimes called the next-turn proof procedure. Consider the following fragment from one of Sacks's recordings of the Group Therapy Sessions.

(10) (Sacks 1995b vI: 281).

01	Roger:		On Hollywood Boulevard the other night they were giving
02			tickets for dirty windshields ((door opens))
03	Jim:		hh
04	Therapist:		Hi, Jim [c'mon in.
05	Jim:		[H'warya
06	Therapist:		Jim, this is uh Al,
07	Jim:		Hi
08	Therapist:		Ken,
09	Jim:		Hi
10	Ken:		Hi
11	Therapist:		Roger.
12	Roger:	→	Hi
13	Jim:		Hi
14	Therapist:		Jim Reed.

Sacks draws attention to "the *prima facie* evidence afforded by a subsequent speaker's talk" in his analysis of the therapist's turns at 08 and 11 as recognizable introductions. Thus, when, at line 12, Roger responds to the

> utterance with his name [. . .] not with "What" (as in an answer to a summons), indeed not with an utterance to the therapist at all, but with a greeting to the newly arrived Jim, he shows himself (to the others there assembled as well as to us, the analytic overhearers) to have attended and analyzed the earlier talk, to have understood that an introduction sequence was being launched, and to be prepared to participate by initiating a greeting exchange in the slot in which it is he who is being introduced. (Schegloff 1995: xliii)

Thus a response displays a hearing or analysis of the utterance to which it responds. As noted, such a hearing or analysis is "publicly available as the means by which previous speakers can determine how they were understood" (Heritage 1984b). The third position in a sequence is then a place to accept the recipient's displayed understanding or, alternatively, to repair it. Heritage (1984b: 259) writes:

> By means of this framework, speakers are released from what would otherwise be an endless task of confirming and reconfirming their understandings of each other's actions . . . a context of publicly displayed and continuously updated intersubjective understandings is systematically sustained. . . . Mutual understanding is thus displayed . . . "incarnately" in the sequentially organized details of conversational interaction.

There is, of course, significant room to maneuver within this framework. Thus, Goodwin and Goodwin write that "rather than presenting a naked analysis of the prior talk, next utterances characteristically transform that talk in some fashion – deal with it not in its own terms but rather in the way in which it is relevant to the projects of the subsequent speaker" (Goodwin and Goodwin 1987: 4). Consider for instance the following instance in which Dick is reporting trouble in getting his family over for the holidays.

(11) Deb and Dick
Deb: [s]o don't you have all your
family coming today?
Dick: Well: they're coming around two and I °hhh left
messages with Brian an:d mydad to(uh) see if
they wanted to come but=ah
(0.2)
°hh that's all I could do was leave messages.
Deb: owh
(0.4)
Dick: °Gotsome° °hhhh five pound lasagna thing to(hh)
throw in the oven=an
Deb: o(h)h(h)=huh (.) well: I'm sure you'll have a
good time.
Dick: [oh
Deb: [<at least it's inside. And it didn't rain
yesterday so we were lucky [l- looking at it
Dick: [mmhm yeah
Deb: today god. woulda been awful.

At lines 22–3 Deb asks whether Dick's family is coming to visit. In response, Dick indicates that although some members of the family are expected, he has been unable to get a hold of "Brian" and his "Dad". The answer concludes with Dick saying, "that's all I could do was leave messages.". The selected extreme case formulation (see Pomerantz 1986) might well have elicited an expression of sympathy. Instead, however, Deb registers the report with a prosodically non-committal "owh". After a pause, Dick continues saying, "°Gotsome° °hhhh five pound lasagna thing to(hh) throw in the oven=an". The selection of "some", rather than "a", and "throw", rather than "put", endow Dick's description with a sense of pathos. By adding "thing" to the description of the food, Dick does not even allow it to be categorized unequivocally as "lasagna". Moreover, Dick's description of the lasagna in terms of its weight characterizes it as something to be eaten but not necessarily enjoyed. Taken together these choices in description convey Dick's negative stance and strongly suggest that he may have "troubles" to tell Deb. Deb, however, blocks the projected troubles-telling by saying, "I'm sure you'll have a good time" and "at least it's inside.". The "at least" here is a device for retrieving the good in otherwise bad news. Used here, it also allows Deb to move stepwise into her own topic. In this example, then, Deb resists being aligned as a "troubles recipient" (see Jefferson 1988) by dealing with Dick's talk, as Goodwin and Goodwin say, "not in its own terms but rather in the way in which it is relevant to the projects of the subsequent speaker". Since this is a point of crucial importance, one further illustration will be considered.

In the following, Deb has invited her cousin Mark to her daughter's wedding. She has decided not to invite Mark's mother (her aunt), after whom Dee is asking in line 01.

(12) Holt 5/88:2:4:3

Dee: You doh-uh how is she[Mark.
Mark: [.hhh We:ll she's-:-: r-
physically n-: she is: gettin' a bit o:ld you
kno:w, uh::m .hhhhhh she can't get around quite
so much although she still does 'er shopping
still looks a:fter 'erse:lf I mean it's amazing
really, u-uh::: .hhhhhh She drives us nu:ts but
stihhhll[h-h .hu .hu
Dee: [Oh I know love I do know the feeling
you've got my every sy[mpa
Mark: [phhh! ↑heh heh e-[he
Dee: [( ).
Mark: .hhhhhh[hh
[We: had it,
(.)
believe you me we had[it.
Mark: [hI: kno:w.[hYe:s

Dee has phoned to tell Mark that she has decided not to invite his mother to her daughter's wedding ostensibly so as not to inconvenience Mark and his wife.[8] As such, Dee has something invested in hearing, in response to her query at line 01, that Mark's mother is not well, this having been presented as grounds for not inviting her to the wedding. In his response, Mark seems initially to align with Dee's evaluation of his mother's health (with, for example, "a bit old" and "can't get around") but at line 04 he moves in the opposite direction, detailing the extent to which she is, in fact, able to "do her shopping" and "look after herself". Note that there are several points within the turn at which Dee might have treated Mark's report about his mother's heath as possibly complete. Dee, however, holds off responding until the point at which Mark remarks that his mother "drives us nuts". "Drives us nuts" confirms in no uncertain terms Dee's already expressed conviction that the mother would hamper Mark and his wife's enjoyment of the wedding. It is *here* that Dee responds with an empathetic "Oh I know love . . .". A report of this kind then can be seen as the product of an interaction between a speaker and a recipient (see chapter 8). The recipient plays an active role in the production of the report in at least two ways. In the first place, Dee selects a particular place in the course of Mark's talk at which to begin a response and thereby helps to construct its completion. Secondly, of the many ways in which she might have responded – with optimism, with surprise, with skepticism, etc. – Dee's expression of sympathy ("Oh I know love I do know the feeling you've got my every sympathy") treats Mark's report about his mother's health as a complaint. Dee hears in what Mark says here a description of the ways in which the mother has become a burden and it is *this* hearing that she displays in her response to it.

Heritage (1984b), from whom I have borrowed a great deal for the discussion in this section, notes that "observations concerning the way a turn's talk displays an analysis, appreciation or understanding of a prior turn do not simply apply to . . . responses or 'reactive' second utterances. They also apply to 'first' or initiatory actions . . . which, in their own various ways, also display analyses of the 'state of talk'." As Heritage notes and as we shall see in chapter 10, a speaker who initiates the pre-closing of a call with "well::", or some other "possible pre-closing", displays an analysis of that " 'there and then' as an appropriate place for that to occur." Indeed, any utterance can be heard as, in some sense, exhibiting its speaker's sense of the current state of talk and the context in which that talk is produced.

Irony in Conversation

In conversation speakers frequently talk in such a way as to convey something other than what their words "literally" mean. Irony is a case in point. Irony involves the expression of one's meaning by using language that normally signifies the opposite. For instance, responding to the news that your plane's departure has been delayed, you might say "oh great", thereby producing a negative assessment through the use of positive terms. Given that irony involves the use of words to convey other than "literal" meanings, it presents something of a test for the maintenance of intersubjectivity. If intersubjectivity is to be maintained, a recipient of a possibly ironic utterance is required to show that they understood not only what the words mean but, moreover, what the speaker meant in using those words (see Clift 1999, Hutchby and Drew 1995). Recipients have available to them two basic practices for accomplishing this task. One practice involves treating the ironic utterance as something humorous and appreciating it with laughter. Alternatively, the recipient of an ironic utterance may build on to it in their response, thereby both acknowledging and sustaining the irony it embodies.

The following case illustrates the first of these practices. Here Rich is telling long-distance girlfriend Hyla that he is at work from three to eleven thirty. Hyla, registering this as a less than optimal arrangement, responds with "oh: yer ki::dding.", following up with "That's terrible hours." Hyla receipts Rich's qualification, "jest today en yesterday.", with "oh" and then produces another assessment. Rich responds to this with the apparently ironic "Oh but the pay is grea:::t." Hyla's laughter in line 33 shows an appreciation.

(13) Hyla_&_Rich_p2_qt2:00

Rich: Well I go in en outa work from about three to eleven thirt[y.
Hyla: [tch
oh: yer ki::dding.
(0.3)
Hyla: That's terr[ible hours.]
Rich: [Jes- jes fe]r (.) jest today en yesterday.
Hyla: O:h.
(.)
Hyla: Those're aw:ful hour:s.
Rich: → Oh but the pay is grea[:::t.]
Hyla: → [hehuhuh]=

The case given as (14) is similar. Here Hyla is talking to her friend Nancy. The two have plans to see a show in the evening, and at line 05 Hyla proposes that they go for a drink afterwards. Nancy accepts the proposal, and continues saying that she "owes" Hyla a drink. This offer is accepted and confirmed. Hyla then remarks, at line 16, that she "can't drink too much" because she is driving. Nancy responds to this with the ironic "I said one drink" and, after this is appreciated with laughter by Hyla, "You think I'm made of money or something." This elicits further laughter from Hyla which Nancy joins at lines 23 and 26.

(14) HN_25
05 Hyla: =·hh Maybe we c'n go out fer a drink t'night.
06 (·)
07 Nancy: Ye::ah. That soun- Yeh I owe y'a dri:nk.
08 (·)
09 Nancy: Ah wanna buy y'a dri:n[k.
10 Hyla: [Aow. A'ri[:ght,
11 Nancy: [Oka : y¿ So we will fer sure.=
12 Hyla: =A'ri[ght.]
13 Nancy: [A f]ter, (·) the pl[ay,]
14 Hyla: [·hh]
15 (·)
16 Hyla: I can't drink too much cz I'm dri-i-vhh[i(h)i(h)ng,]=
17 Nancy: [O k a : y,]=
18 Nancy: → =(Look,) (0.2) I said one dri[nk.
19 Hyla: [hhheeh ·heh ·eh [·hh
20 Nancy: [You think I'm
21 made a' money er shhomehhn-hhn=
22 Hyla: =·e·e=
23 Nancy: =·hhi::[::hh]
24 Hyla: [·t·k]°h-h°
25 (0.3)
26 Nancy: ·hhheh[hh
27 Hyla: [·hhhOh en yihknow w't I wan'my book ba:::ck.=

As noted, an alternative practice involves a recipient displaying an understanding of a previous utterance as ironic by actively contributing to the sequence of talk in which it participates, building a next utterance which not only appreciates the first but also builds on to it, thus sustaining the irony across a series of turns. A rather simple case is shown in (15) below. Here Hyla is reporting to Nancy that she has to go to "Robins" to return a birthday gift from her brother. When Nancy asks "Whud'e buy you" Nancy responds saying a "li'l shorty, nightgown" and continues saying "yihknow en this forty degree weather I nhheed a shorty ni'gown.". The point is clearly that Hyla neither needs nor wants a "nightgown" given the weather conditions and thus this utterance is ironic. Equally ironic is Nancy's response – "Yeah r i :ght,=".

(15) HN_p.11
16 Hyla: =Nen I('ve) gotta go tuh Robins'n return *u-h-h* birthday
17 gift *my* brother (·) bot me,=
18 Nancy: =Mmmi. Whud'e buy you,
19 (·)
20 Hyla: ·tch·hhh u-him'n Nancy got me this, nightgown, li'l shorty,
21 (·)
22 Nancy: [Uh hu:h,]
23 Hyla: → [nightgown] yihknow en this forty degree weather I nhheed a
24 shor[ty ni'gown.]
25 Nancy: [Yeah r i :]ght,=

A final example nicely illustrates the way participants can collaborate to sustain a sense of irony across a series of turns-at-talk. Earlier in this call Edna has invited Margy to dinner, saying "Why don't I take you'n Mo:m up there tuh: Coco's. someday fer lu :nch." This comes up again later in the call when Margy says "why don't we all do that.W'l go up en eat et Coco's? er will go someplace e:lse.=", to which Edna responds with an endorsement of Coco's, suggesting that it's "fun" and "yuh look down it's so pretty" and finally "An it's cheap." This is appreciated with laughter from Margy, and Edna starts to talk again saying "I'm on retirement." However, this is overlapped by Margy saying "yer not taking us Edna." This leads to an extended sequence of talk in which Edna denies that she meant to withdraw the invitation by saying that she's "on retirement." This denial is winding down at the point where the fragment given as (16) begins. Here Edna is repeating that she's on retirement and elaborating by saying that, because of this, she can't take Edna to the "Country Club", in this way implying that she *can* take Edna to Coco's (which, it has already been observed, is "cheap"). Margy responds to this with the ironic utterance "I wanna go t'the Stu:ff' Shi:rt". A "stuffed shirt" is an idiomatic expression for a pompous or arrogant person and is apparently used here to refer to an expensive restaurant.[9] Notice that Edna first appreciates this with laughter which Margy joins in at line 33. Edna, going along with and thus sustaining the irony of Margy's proposal, says "Ah'll pack a lunch.". After this is appreciated with more laughter, Edna continues with "I'll pack a lunch 'n buy yih a ma:rti:ni.". Margy, sustaining the irony for one further turn, accepts this proposal with "o::kay,".

```
(16) NB:VII_Power_Tools_p10–11_qt7:56
26 Edna:        =You know I'm on re[t(h)I:[:REM'NT I: C](h)AN'T=
27 Margy:                          [( )  [ih-heh-yhehh  ]
28 Margy:       =((f)) hhn- [hnh   ] .ikhh-] .ekhh.ku]
29 Edna:                    [TAKE] y i h  ] to  the- ] .hhh COUNTR(h)Y C(h)LU[:b?]=
30 Margy:                                                                   [.hh]=
31 Margy:  →    =I wann[a go t'the S  ]tu:ff' Shi:rt [E : d n a  ]=
32 Edna:               [°huh-hih- hn]               [°hh-uh- eh]=
33 Margy:       =.hhhhN(h)[uhhhh]
34 Edna:                  [O_H: ]hhhhhuh-huh-° hu
35              (0.4)
36 Edna:   →    Ah'll pack a lu[:nch. ]
37 Margy:                      [nh-hn]u- HAH-hnf hn:h=
38 Margy:       =h-.h [Hee whi(h)z-z]
39 Edna:              [nh  nh  nh  nh]unh=
01 Edna:   →    =.t.hhhhh I'll pa:ck a lunch['n buy yih a ma:r[ti [:ni.   ]
02 Margy:                                   [.hhhhh             [#-[E(h)y]o::kay,=
```

As Hutchby and Drew note (1995) in a subtle single-case analysis of irony, a focus on the "ironical form and ironical uptake" of utterances reveals that "indirect actions such as ironical reference are not simply properties of individual speech acts but are situated features of interaction, achieved in local space and real time." Irony provides a particularly vivid illustration of the way in which intersubjective understanding is a contingent *achievement*, accomplished on a turn-by-turn basis, as a by-product of other activities in which the participants are engaged.

The Power of Sequential Analysis

The discovery of sequential organization in the mid-to-late 1960s more or less coincided with the emergence of conversation analysis as a field. Others, including rhetoricians, playwrights, novelists, philosophers and linguists, had pointed to the existence of paired actions such as question and answer, greeting and greeting. What Sacks and Schegloff discovered was the normative order or logic that undergirds such paired actions. This made it possible to examine not just paired actions *per se* but conversational sequencing and conditional relevance.

Early in this chapter we made a distinction between "practices of speaking" and the actions which those practices are used to accomplish within some particular bit of talk. The distinction plays an important role in conversation analysis and distinguishes it from many other approaches to language use in the human sciences which, for the most part, emphasize *either* practices of speaking (such as repetition, or clause structure) or actions (promises and such). Conversation analysis, on the other hand, examines the relation *between* practices of speaking and actions-in-talk within sequences. Nowhere is the power of such an analysis displayed more clearly than in Schegloff's study of "confirming allusions". The phenomenon Schegloff examines in that paper appears, at first glance, perfectly simple: repetition. Here are two examples:

(26) Berkeley II: 103–14 – simplified (from Schegloff 1996b: 174)

Evelyn:		=Hi: Rita
Rita:		Hi: Evelyn:. How [are y'
Evelyn:		[I hadda come in another room.
Rita:		Oh:. Uh huh.=
Evelyn:		=I fee:l a bi:ssel verschickert.
		(0.2)
Rita:		W- why's 'a:t,
		(0.4)
Rita:	→	uh you've had sump'n t'drink.=
Evelyn:	→	=I had sump'n t'dri:nk.
Rita:		Uh huh.

(27) MDE, Stolen (from Schegloff 1996b: 185)

Marsha:		=He's flying.
		(0.2)
		En Ilene is going to meet im:.Becuz the to:p wz ripped
		off'v iz car which is tih ssay someb'ddy helped th'mselfs.
Tony:	→	Stolen.
		(0.4)
Marsha:	→	Stolen. Right out in front of my house.

Schegloff shows these repetitions to be instances of a previously undescribed action – "the practice of agreeing with another by repeating what they have just said is shown to constitute the action of confirming an allusion – that is, confirming both its 'content' and its prior inexplicit conveyance" (Schegloff 1996: 161). In (26), Evelyn reports that she "hadda come in another room" and goes on to remark "I fee:l a bi:ssel verschickert.". Schegloff notes that there is an ambiguity here in the Yiddish word "verschickert", which may refer either to a state brought on by the consumption of alcohol, "tipsy", or one arrived at without – "groggy" might serve as a translation for the latter. After Rita offers the understanding check "you've had sump'n t'drink.", Evelyn produces the repetition. "In confirming with a repeat, Evelyn not only verifies the supposition as to how she came to be in the state she is in, but invokes the presence of that meaning in her own immediately prior talk" (Schegloff 1996: 186). In (27), Marsha is telling her ex-husband, Tony, that their son is flying, rather than driving, back to northern California where Tony is. She accounts for what is a change of plan by saying that the "to:p wz ripped off'v iz car" and, apparently catching the possible ambiguity of "ripped off" between an idiom for robbery and the act of tearing, extends her turn with "which is tih ssay someb'ddy helped th'mselfs." However, although this is meant to disambiguate, it is again not to be taken literally. As Schegloff says, "the sense of what has happened has, then, been conveyed without being given its 'common name.' When Tony offers 'stolen' as literally what happened, Marsha not only confirms that that is what has happened, but does so with a form that confirms as well that that is what she was conveying in her prior talk" (Schegloff 1996: 185).

The action of confirming allusions could not have been noticed without careful examination of the sequences in which it occurs since, without attention to the sequence of which these repetitions are a part, it would not have been possible to see the "allusive" character of the talk that gets confirmed. Moreover, by bringing together instances of the practice into a collection, Schegloff is able to specify "environments of relevant occurrence" – that is, interactional environments in which the action *could* be done, even if it is not in that instance. This in turn allows Schegloff to identify a case in which the speaker appears to specifically avoid repetition in order *not* to confirm an allusion: the speaker comes to "the very verge of a possible allusion-confirmation before veering away" (Schegloff 1996: 194). Schegloff (1996: 199) remarks about such instances that "it is virtually certain that nothing of interest would have been seen at all were we not already familiar with the practice of confirming allusions and its environments of possible occurrence. Here then we may have some of the most distinctive fruits of inquiry in rendering what would otherwise be invisible visible in its very absence." This remarkable analysis is the product of many years of research, patiently tracking the phenomenon and allowing it to come fully into view as instances were collected and put side by side. It well illustrates the power of sequential analysis.

One way to begin an analysis of a fragment of talk is by blocking out the sequences that together compose it. This provides a point of entry – a way of accessing some of the technical details of talk – even if a more complete analysis, such as Schegloff's study of confirming allusions, requires attention not just to sequence organization but also to turn-design, turn-taking, repair and many other phenomena.

Conclusion

In this chapter we've reviewed a series of central and interconnected issues in conversation analysis. We started with a consideration of action. Here we developed a distinction between practices of speaking and the actions that they implement. Our focus in this discussion was the practice of speaking "Do you want X . . .", which, we saw, can be used to perform an offer. I discussed several types of evidence that can be marshaled to show that a given deployment of a practice (such as Janet's "Do you want me to come over and get her") is in fact performing some particular action. We need evidence such as this because the relation between practices and actions is contingent: there's typically no one-to-one mapping between some particular practice of speaking and some particular action. We then turned to consider a basic form of action sequencing: the adjacency pair. We saw that the two parts of such a pair (such as question and answer, offer and acceptance) are bound together by a relation of conditional relevance. As Schegloff demonstrated, given the occurrence of a first part, the non-occurrence of a second part is noticeable by the participants. That missing second pair part is "officially absent" and thus its non-occurrence is just as much an event as its occurrence. Next we considered the distinctive form of intersubjectivity that the sequential organization of conversation provides for – a context of publicly displayed and continuously updated intersubjective understandings, as Heritage (1984b) describes it. After showing how this works in a number of cases and discussing briefly the methodological lever it provides the analyst, we went on to press the case in a consideration of irony. Irony presents something of a challenge to this structure of understanding, in so far as it involves people using words to convey something other than what their literal meaning would seem to imply. Here we described the basic practices that recipients have available to them in responding to an ironic utterance and, in doing so, showing that they have understood it.

Of course there are other ways in which the turns-at-talk that constitute an adjacency pair are related. It is to one of these, the relation of "preference", that we turn next.

Notes

1 This is not to say that "questioning" cannot itself be the action with which a turn is occupied. For that reason it is useful to distinguish between interrogative "practices of speaking", which are recurrent features of grammar, and questioning, which is an action. Notice that a turn can do questioning even if it has no interrogative features.

2 And as Schegloff notes, when the detective stumbles over the body in the English crime drama, he says "Hello!" Finally, "hello" is used as an answer to a summons in telephone openings. See Schegloff 1986 for discussion.

3 Of course, although the construction "Do you want X . . ." is regularly used to make an offer, this does not contradict what we've said about the contingent relation between actions and practices, for two reasons. First, other practices of speaking are used in making offers, e.g., "Would you like X . . .", "Can I offer you X . . ." etc. (see Curl 2006). Secondly, the "Do you want X . . ." construction is used to accomplish various actions other than offers; for instance, it is used in invitations, threats, warnings and so on.

4 We'll see in chapter 5 that rejections are dispreferred actions and are often accompanied by accounts or explanations. Here the standard account for non-acceptance of an offer is used, specifically that the thing being offered is not needed.

5 See the discussion of insert sequences in chapter 6.

6 In this they echo philosophers who have long wondered about the problem in terms of "determinism" and "freewill".

7 Schegloff suggests that conditional relevance has the status of a social fact.

8 The following fragment directly precedes the talk under discussion:

(28) Holt 5: 82: 2: 4.
Mark: =three:,hh .h[h .h h h h h h hhhhhhhhh
Deena: [Yea:h (.) right. Anyway it's lovely to
hear from you How- By the way .hhhh Mark now I wuh-
will: say. I didn't put your mother (.) o:n becuz I

wasn't sure I mean okay. she should come, but I thought
→ .hhh you 'n Leslie are gonna 'av a 'ell'v a day if
→ you've gotta cart her abou[t.
Mark: [.t.hhh iYeah I don't know
whether she'd really be A Capable no:w,
(.)
Deena: You doh-uh how is she[Mark.

9 At the time this recording was made there was an expensive restaurant in Newport Beach called "The Stuffed Shirt".

5

Preference

Schegloff (2007: 58–9) writes, "In the vast majority of sequence types, there are not only alternative responses which a first pair part makes relevant and a recipient of a first pair part may employ; there are alternate *types* of response. These embody different alignments toward the project undertaken in the first pair part." Thus, a request can be either granted or rejected. Of course, there are many ways in which a request may be granted (e.g. "sure", "I guess", "of course, you needn't ask", etc.) or rejected ("I don't think that would be a good idea", "It's just not possible", "no way!"), but as Schegloff, again, points out, "accepting and declining, granting and rejecting, are fundamentally different *types* of responses and alignments." We will see in this chapter that these are not "symmetrical alternatives" as Schegloff and Sacks (1973: 14) put it. Rather, the response to the first pair part that promotes the accomplishment of the activity underway is, typically, "preferred".

Heritage and Atkinson (1984: 53) explain that the term "preference" here refers to the fact that, in conversation, choices between courses of action are "routinely implemented in ways that reflect an institutionalized ranking of alternatives". "Preference" in this context refers, then, not to psychological states of the participants but, rather, to observable regularities in their talk. Consider a situation in which you are invited to a dinner party at the house of someone you dislike and whose company you assiduously avoid. In such a situation you would obviously prefer, in the individual or psychological sense, to decline the invitation, but this does not alter the fact that acceptance is the preferred alternative in terms of the organization of the talk. A declination will likely require an accompanying explanation, for example that you are busy that evening, or that you have a rare and highly contagious fungal infection, whereas an acceptance will not. The point of an example like this is to show that the structural preferences that organize much of talk-in-interaction are quite independent of the individual, psychological preferences of the participants.

Schegloff (1988b, 2007) distinguishes two basic manifestations of preference in the structural regularities of talk-in-interaction. On the one hand, there are preferences related to the "character of the course of action" being implemented. Preference in this sense has to do with the success of an action. For instance, a request is an action by which one party attempts to get another to do or to give something. Success here involves getting the recipient to actually do or give the thing requested and the preferred response is the one that promotes this outcome. On the other hand, there is a sense of preference as it relates to the design or construction of turns-at-talk. We can isolate a set of features that regularly characterize preferred and dispreferred turns and we can thus see that speakers routinely design their turns *as* preferred or dispreferred alternatives. In order to see some of this we will begin by looking at responsive turns. Once we have some basic ideas about preference established we will proceed to consider how it operates over a broader range of action sequences in conversation.

Preferred and Dispreferred Responses

Consider the following example:

(1) SBL, T1/S1/C10, simplified
A: Uh if you'd care to come and visit a little while
this morning I'll give you a cup of coffee.
B: hehh Well that's awfully sweet of you. I don't
think I can make it this morning. .hh uhm I'm
running an ad in the paper and-and uh I have to
stay near the phone.

In this extract from a telephone conversation, A's turn at 1–2 is an invitation to B to come and visit "a little while" and have a cup of coffee. In this context, B's talk at lines 3–5 clearly constitutes a declination of the invitation. Notice, however, that B never says "no thanks". How then does this talk nevertheless *do* declining? What features of the talk make it clear to A that B does not accept the invitation? In fact, this turn collects together many of the features characteristic of dispreferred responses (see also Kitzinger 2000).

(i) Delays: B delays the production of the declination by prefacing the turn with audible breathing ("hehh") and "well" and "that's awfully sweet of you.". In terms of positioning, dispreferred responses are often delayed both by inter-turn gap and turn-initial delay. In our example above, the declination of the offer is significantly delayed by the talk that precedes it.

(2) SBL, T1/S1/C10, simplified
A: Uh if you'd care to come and visit a little while
this morning I'll give you a cup of coffee.
B: **hehh Well that's awfully sweet of you.** I don't
think I can make it this morning. .hh uhm I'm
running an ad in the paper and-and uh I have to
stay near the phone.

We can distinguish such "turn-initial delay" from "inter-turn gap", as in the following case:

(3) NB IV: 10, 41: 17–21
Lottie: F→ ↑Don't chu want me tih come dow:n getchu
dihmorr'en take yih dow:n dih the beauty parlor?
→ (0.3)
Emma: S→ What fo:r I ↑jis did my hair it looks like pruh-
a perfess↓ional.

(ii) Palliatives: It is common for dispreferred responses to contain some kind of appreciation, apology and/or token agreement by which the overwhelmingly "negative" valence of the turn is mitigated. Here the dispreferred response is accompanied by the appreciation "that's awfully sweet of you.". The declination is further mitigated by being framed with "I don't think . . .".

(4) SBL, T1/S1/C10, simplified
A: Uh if you'd care to come and visit a little while
this morning I'll give you a cup of coffee.
B: hehh Well that's awfully sweet of you. **I don't**
think I can make it this morning. .hh uhm I'm
running an ad in the paper and-and uh I have to
stay near the phone.

(iii) Accounts: Dispreferred responses typically contain explanations or justifications indicating why a dispreferred response is being produced (for example why an invitation is being declined). In our example, for instance, B explains that she is prevented from accepting the invitation by the fact that she is "running an ad in the paper" and thus must "stay near the phone.". With accounts of this sort, people typically suggest that they are unable to accept the invitation (or grant the request), not simply unwilling (see Drew 1984).

(5) SBL, T1/S1/C10, simplified
A: Uh if you'd care to come and visit a little while
this morning I'll give you a cup of coffee.
B: hehh Well that's awfully sweet of you. I don't
think I can make it this morning. .hh uhm **I'm**
running an ad in the paper and-and uh I have to
stay near the phone.

(iv) Pro-forma agreement: Where agreement is relevant, dispreferred, disagreeing responses may be preceded by what Schegloff (2007) describes as "pro-forma" agreement. One familiar form this takes is a turn beginning with "yes but . . .". Another manifestation is shown below:

(6) NB II 2 (Sacks 1987 [1973]: 63)
A: 'N they haven't heard a word huh?
B: Not a word, uh-uh. Not- not a word. Not at all.
Except- Neville's mother got a call . . .

Returning to the distinction between structural preferences of talk-in-interaction and "personal preferences" we can see from the invitation example, in (1), that they are quite different. There is no way for us to know whether B would "prefer" to accept or decline the invitation. On the other hand, it is clear that she builds her declination of the invitation as a dispreferred rather than preferred response.

Structural Consequences of Preference Organization

The features of dispreferred turns mentioned above, particularly delay, are resources which the speaker of a first pair part can use to project or anticipate the imminent production of a dispreferred response. Moreover, having anticipated a dispreferred response, the speaker of the first pair part may take measures to prevent it from being produced. Thus, the features of dispreferred second pair parts play a role in minimizing the chance that such a response will, in fact, ever be articulated. Consider,

(7) Levinson 1983: 320
01 C: So I was wondering would you be in your office
02 on Monday (.) by any chance?
03 → (2.0)
04 → Probably not

C's talk at lines 01–02 is apparently building towards some kind of request (although the exact nature of that request is not available to us). Moreover, the design of the question is constructed so as to prefer an affirmative answer: compare "I don't suppose you'll be in your office on Monday?" (see Sacks 1987 [1973]). Note that, after coming to possible completion after "Monday", the request is extended a little bit with "by any chance?".[1] When the recipient does not respond immediately, allowing a sizeable two seconds of silence to develop, C treats this as foreshadowing a negative answer and partially withdraws the (pre-)request by reversing the valence of the question with "probably not". Consider also the following instance:

(8) NB II: 2: 17–18
01 Emma: [Wanna c'm] do:wn 'av [a bah:ta] lu:nch w]ith me?=
02 Nancy: [°It's js] ( )°]
03 Emma: =Ah gut s'm beer'n stu:ff,
04 (0.3)
05 Nancy: → ↑Wul yer ril sweet hon: uh:m
06 (.)
07 Emma: [Or d'y]ou'av] sup'n [else °( )°
08 Nancy: [L e t-] I :] hu. [n:No: I haf to: uh call
09 Roul's mother, I told'er I:'d call'er this morning
10 I [gotta letter]'from'er en .hhhhhh A:nd uhm
11 Emma: [° (Uh huh.)°]

Here Emma issues an invitation in line 01, adding an extra incentive "Ah gut s'm beer'n stu:ff," (see below). Nancy's response is delayed and begins with an appreciation. This is enough to tip Emma off. Thus notice that before a rejection of the invitation can be done Emma has already anticipated a problem, saying, at line 07, "Or d'you'av sup'n else".

Alternatively, rather than withdraw the action in the face of a projected dispreferred response, the speaker can add further talk in an effort to make it more appealing or easier to accept. Consider:

(9) NB – cited in Davidson 1984: 105
01 A: C'mon down h*e:*re,=it's oka:y,
02 (0.2)
03 I got lotta stuff,=I got b*e:*er en stuff.

Here, a slight pause after the invitation reaches possible completion provides an opportunity for its speaker to "upgrade" the action being implemented – here by adding "beer".

In most cases the preferred response is the one which advances or aligns with the action launched by the first pair part. However, there are at least two kinds of exception to this general rule. First, there are certain actions that, by their very nature, inherently prefer disaligning responses. For instance, both self-deprecating assessments and compliments appear to prefer disagreeing rather than agreeing responses (see below and Pomerantz 1978).

Second, in addition to particular kinds of actions that prefer non-aligning responses, we must be alert to the potential for general preferences to be suspended or even reversed in certain contexts. For instance, although offers seem to generally prefer acceptances, they can also be built to prefer declines. An offer such as, "why don't I come over and pick her up" is built towards acceptance whereas one such as "do you want me to come an' get her" may not be. The emphasis placed on the recipient's needs or wants in the latter appears to invite special treatment. Consider the example which we discussed in chapter 4:

(10) XTR 1 -
Janet: Do you want me to come an' get ↑her?
Anne: Uhm:, it doesn't matte:r, like(hh)
(0.4)
.hhhhh
Janet: I- I could.it's very easy.
so rather than you h:av(h)e(h)
(.)
you know (.) tuh get everybody ou[t
Anne: [.hhh
Janet: I'll justa
(0.2)
come dow:n.=

Here Anne's turn at lines 13–15 is built as a dispreferred response. The turn begins with delay and does not contain either an acceptance or declination of the offer. Janet's talk at lines 16–23 suggests that she hears Anne's *dispreferred* turn as adumbrating an acceptance rather than a declination in so far as she actively pursues the matter in precisely this direction. This then suggests that the offer is built to prefer a declination.

Concurrent Preferences

So far we've seen that the maximally cooperative response is typically the preferred one. This can be observed also for sequences in which the first action is an assessment. In her initial work on this topic, Pomerantz (1975, 1978, 1984) found that agreement was often conveyed via second assessments that were upgraded relative to a first. In the following example, for instance, the second speaker's "gorgeous" is a clear upgrade of "beautiful".

(11) Pomerantz 1984: 59
J: T's-tsuh beautiful day out, isn't it?
L: Yeh it's just gorgeous

In the next example the speaker uses both word selection and prosody to upgrade a first assessment.

(12) Pomerantz 1984:60
01 A: Isn't he cute
02 B: O::h he::s a::DORable

In contrast, second assessments of the same or lower value, though they may accompany agreements, are often associated with disagreement. Consider the following:

(13) Pomerantz 1984:67
01 E: 'n she said she f- depressed her terribly
02 J: Oh it's [terribly depressing.
03 L: → [oh it's depressing
04 E: Ve [ry
05 L: → [but it's a fantastic [film.
06 J: [It's a
07 beautiful movie

Notice here then that a first assessment in line 01 initially meets with same-value assessment responses from both J and L in lines 02 and 03. Both, however, offer a competing and not altogether compatible assessment in subsequent talk ("fantastic", "beautiful").

In cases where an initial assessment is met by a downgraded or same-level second assessment the speaker of the first may produce a reassertion, the vehicle for which is a stronger assessment. The following example is typical:

(14) Pomerantz 1984: 69
01 G: That's fantastic.
02 B: Isn't that good.
03 G: That's marvelous

And in (15) Guy's less than enthusiastic second assessment "it's not too bad" is targeted for repair (see chapter 6 and 7 for further discussion of this example).

(15) NB: 1.1: 6, 18–27
01 Jon: Well I'm s:↑ure we c'get on et San Juan ↑Hi:lls ↑that's
02 ni:ce course ah only played it ↑o:nce.
03 Guy: °Uh huh?°
04 (0.6)
05 Guy: → .hhh °↑It's not↑ too bad,°
06 (0.4)
07 Jon: → Hu:h?
08 Guy: → 'S not too ba:d,
09 (.)
10 Jon: No:.

Thus we see that assessments typically prefer agreements. However, assessments are the vehicles for action and there are cases in which the action implemented by an assessment sets in motion another, distinct set of preferences. Consider the following for instance:

(16) SBL-2-2-2-3R, 51 (from Pomerantz, 1984: 85, retranscribed)
Chl: En I n:ever was a gr(h)ea(h)t br(h)idge [play(h)er]=
Cla: [Y e :: h]
Chl: =Cl(h)a [heh?]
Cla: =hhh [Well I] think you've always been real good . . .

Here the assessment is negative and directed at the speaker; this is what Pomerantz (1984) describes as a "self-deprecation". An agreement would, of course, constitute an endorsement of the self-deprecation. In cases like this a basic rule against insulting others appears to override any preference for agreement. You can see that following a self-deprecation the preference for agreement is reversed if you imagine a case in which someone says "God I look awful today". Any kind of delay in responding to this will be heard as suggesting agreement rather than disagreement.

Compliments: Concurrent Preferences

Compliments similarly involve concurrent and conflicting preferences. Whether they are accomplished through an assessment or some other turn-type, one set of preferences makes agreement with and acceptance of the compliment the preferred next action. However, Pomerantz argues that compliments set in motion another set of preferences having to do with the avoidance of self-praise. She writes (1978: 88) that "there is a system of constraints governing how parties may credit or praise themselves. Self-praise avoidance names a system of constraints which is enforceable by self and/or other, in that order." Pomerantz cites a number of illustrative cases. If a speaker does not enforce the constraint against self-praise on him- or herself, a next speaker may point out the violation in next turn:

(17) GTS:2:17 – Pomerantz 1978: 89
K: Y'see I'm so terrific,
A: Y'see folks, he is very vain, an' he realizes his
mature talents compared to our meager content of our minds.

(18) HS:S – Pomerantz 1978: 89
A: Just think of how many people would miss
you. You would know who cared.
B: Sure. I have a lot of friends who would come
to the funeral and say what an intelligent,
bright, witty, interesting person I was.
A: They wouldn't say that you were humble
B: No. Humble, I'm not.

And a speaker may themselves orient to the rule against self-praise by disclaiming or qualifying what they say:

(19) BC:III:28
B: So he- so then, at this- y'see, —I don't like to
brag but see he sorta like backed outta the
argument then.

(20) S.2 Pomerantz 1978
01 G: Ken gave that internship to Peter?! I'm much
02 better than he is! Well maybe I shouldn't say
03 that.

Extract (21) provides a rather more complex but nevertheless striking illustration of the norm against self-praise. This is taken from the television talk show Ellen (hosted by Ellen DeGeneres). The fragment of talk here comes from mid-way into an interview with TV actor Rashida Jones. The two (Jones and DeGeneres) have come to the end of one topic and at line 01 DeGeneres is raising the next thing to be discussed in this interview: Jones's new TV show with comedian Amy Poehler, *Parks and Recreation*. DeGeneres initiates the topic by inviting Jones to tell the audience about the show. She then gives the title before concluding the turn with "an' you an' Amy Poehler how- how great is that.". Notice then that this final part of the turn can be heard as a real information question – a request for Jones to specify how great "that" is. At the same time, this construction "How X is that?" is a familiar, idiomatic expression which, by virtue of the presupposition it carries, conveys "it's X" or, in this case, "it's great". Notice what happens.

(21) Rashida Jones on Ellen 04, 2009
01 Ellen: Al:right tell people about this hilarious
02 show. It's Parks and Recreation an' you
03 an' Amy Poehler how- How great is that.=
04 Rashida: =It's pretty great=
05 Ellen: =mm mh[m.
06 Rashida: [It's- uhm- it- I just mean it- ek-
07 experientially for me it's pr(h)etty
08 [gr(h)ea(h)t(h) [heh heh ha ( )
09 Ellen: [yeah. [no. an' but I mean it's
10 a- I ah- know what you mea[nt. But I: say
11 Rashida: [hih huh ha hah ha
12 [huh huh .hh hah
13 Ellen: [it's really great. The two of you.=
14 Rashida: nyeah.
15 Ellen: yeah. [an' it's about,
16 Rashida: [(it is)

So here at line 04, Jones treats DeGeneres's talk at lines 01–03 as a question and answers it with "it's pretty great". Again there are several ways in which this may be heard. If "that" in "how great is that" and "it" in "it's pretty great" are heard as referring to the TV show, Jones is clearly praising the show and thus, by extension, herself. If, however, "that/it" is heard as meaning "working with Amy Poehler" or "the two of you/us working together" then Jones's answer is not obviously self-praise but, rather, a compliment to Poehler. Jones, apparently orienting to the potential for the first hearing, begins an elaborate self-correction at line 06 landing on "experientially" at line 07. This unpacks, as it were, the second possible hearing, implying that it's a great experience to work with Amy Poehler. Notice Jones's laughter which marks her own mis-step and potential impropriety. DeGeneres also clearly orients to the unwanted and problematic possible hearing of what Jones has said and self-corrects (or at least clarifies the meaning of) her own "how great is that" by saying at lines 10–13 "but I: say it's really great. The two of you.". Two things worthy of note here are: First, DeGeneres emphasizes the first person pronoun "I", thereby indicating a contrast (i.e. not *you* – Rashida Jones – but me – Ellen DeGeneres – is saying "it's great") and thus marking what has transpired as a compliment rather than self-praise. And second, Ellen's "the two of you" draws out the second possible sense of "it's great" – that it is a great "partnership", a great experience and so on. This short fragment shows then the remarkable interactional gymnastics that participants engage in to avoid even the possible appearance of self-praise.

So compliments involve the concurrent operation of two conflicting preferences. On the one hand, there is the preference for agreement that operates across assessments and assertions more generally. This preference should of course result in recipients agreeing with and also accepting the compliment. On the other hand, there is the preference against self-praise. Pomerantz (1978: 92) writes that "instances of actual compliment responses display a sensitivity to these potentially incompatible sets of constraints." In responses to compliments then we can see various "solutions" to the problems posed by the two conflicting preferences.

First, there are cases in which the response takes the form of scaled-down agreement: this satisfies the preference for agreement while minimizing self-praise. If the compliment is done with an assessment, scaled-down agreement may be accomplished with a downgraded assessment as in the following:

(22) SBL:2:2:4 – Pomerantz 1978: 94
01 A: Oh it was just beautiful
02 B: Well *thank* you uh I thought it was quite nice.

Alternatively, the recipient of a compliment may prioritize the preference against self-praise over the preference for agreement/acceptance and disagree with the compliment. However, even in such cases, "recipients generally do not altogether negate or deny prior assertions but rather downgrade the prior terms" (Pomerantz 1978: 99). Recipients suggest, that is, that the compliments are overdone or exaggerated.

(23) NB:5 Pomerantz 1978: 98
01 A: you've lost so much weight
02 P: Uhhh hmhh uhh hmhh [well, not *that* much
03 A: [Aaghh Haghh Haghh

In other cases the recipient offers a qualification by way of response.

(24) Pomerantz 1978: 99
01 A: Good shot
02 B: Not very solid though.

Pomerantz notes that although these may be heard as disagreements they also display features of agreements: typically both agreeing and disagreeing responses involve "scale-downs". Thus they can be seen as a compromise between the two conflicting preferences, that for agreement, on the one hand, and that against self-praise, on the other.

Pomerantz discusses two other solutions to the interactional issues that conflicting preferences pose for compliment recipients. Both of these involve "referent shift". In the first, the object of praise is shifted to some object or person other than the recipient in such a way that there is a reassignment of praise. For instance:

(25) Wc:ycc:4 Pomerantz 1978: 102
01 R: You're a good rower, Honey.
02 J: These are very easy to row. Very light.

A second kind of referent shift is seen in "return compliments", a species of what Schegloff (2007: 16–19) describes as counters:

(26) NB:1:1
01 E: Yer lookin' good,
02 G: Great, so are you.

Pomerantz (1978: 106) writes "as a solution type, returns offer a procedure through which a kind of agreement is performed which simultaneously satisfies the constraint of self-praise avoidance."

Pomerantz's studies of compliments and self-deprecations thus illustrate the way in which concurrent and conflicting preferences help to shape a response. In both cases we see a range of recurrent "strategies" for dealing with that inherent conflict and minimizing violation.

Action-Based Preference vs. Design-Based Preference

So far we've considered preferences that organize the relationship between the actions embodied by the first and second parts of an adjacency pair. Continuing for a moment with this line of analysis, consider the following case taken from a recording of 5-year-old children who are playing with blocks.

(27) KIDS_11_29_05(1of2)T10.mov
01 Jeremy: Hey Benjamin wanna connect ours?
02 Benjamin: no

Here Jeremy's invitation prefers a granting response – like "sure" – though Benjamin rejects it. We can call this the *action-type preference* of an FPP: an invitation prefers an acceptance. It can also be observed that the vehicle for the invitation is a yes–no interrogative (YNI). This is a question which specifically calls for a "yes" or "no" answer. There is then another preference having to do with the *design* of the question. Specifically, Jeremy's invitation not only prefers an acceptance in terms of its action-type, but also a "yes" (rather than "no") response in terms of it's design. We can say that this question "anticipates" a "yes". This kind of *design-based preference* is quite independent of the action-type preference. To see this, consider the following case from a little bit further on in the same interaction.

(28) KIDS_11_29_05(1of2)T10.mov 3.21
01 Jeremy: You don't want to connect it?
02 Benjamin: No.

Here Jeremy's invitation still prefers an acceptance in terms of its action-type preference but now it has been designed to anticipate or prefer a "no" answer in terms of its design-based preference. The difference can be seen in questions such as "You didn't like that much, did you?" which is clearly built towards a "no" and "You liked that, didn't you?" which is built towards a "yes". We can see then that speakers can design or compose their YNIs to provide for a second type of preference – independent of the FPP's action-type preference.

Now notice that these two preferences can point in different directions, which is to say that a given turn may exhibit "cross-cutting" preferences (Schegloff 2007: 76–7). The following case illustrates:

(29) NB Sacks 1987 [1973]: 64

01	A:		Can you walk?
02			(0.4)
03	A:	→	W'd be too hard for yuh?
04	B:		Oh darling, I don't know. Uh it's bleeding a little,
05			'e j's took the bandage off yes'day.

Schegloff explains there is an invitation or offer of an outing in the works here and the question at line 01 (Can you walk?) is the pre-invitation. For the talk at line 1, the action-based preference and the design-based preference are congruent. The action-based preference is for an affirmative "go-ahead" response, and the design-based preference is for a "yes" answer to the question. However, when this turn meets with delay (at line 02), A revises the question and reverses the design-based preference. Schegloff (2007: 77) writes:

> "W'd be too hard for you?" allows that response to be done as an agreement. However, that agreement with "be too hard" would also constitute a dispreferred response to the pre-invitation – a blocking response to actually issuing it, adumbrating a rejection of it were it actually tendered.

Schegloff further calls our attention to the response that is produced to this in which B never actually says in so many words that it would be "too hard" but rather gives an account for not wanting to go based on the condition of her toe.

Type-Conformity Preference

Raymond (2003: 944) has suggested that, in addition to the action-based and design-based preferences we've considered so far, "the grammatical form of a FPP sets a third preference, one that can exert a more general constraint on the forms responding actions should take." The issue has to do with what Raymond calls "type-conformity". Thus a YNI establishes preferences for particular kinds of response based not only on the action it embodies and the manner in which it is designed, but also on the more basic fact that it is a YNI. A response to a YNI that includes a "yes" or a "no" is "type-conforming", one that does not is "non-conforming". Consider the following examples from the first visit to the new mother by a "health visitor" (see Heritage and Sefi 1992).

(30) [Hv 5A1] (HV = Health Visitor, Mom = Mom)
01 HV: How about your breast(s) have they settled do:wn
02 [no:w.
03 Mom: [Yeah they 'ave no:w yeah.=
04 HV: =( ) they're not uncomfortable anymo:re.

(31) [Hv 1C1] (HV = Health Visitor, Mom = Mom)
01 HV: Mm. =Are your breasts alright.
02 (0.7)
03 Mom: They're fi:ne no:w I've stopped leaking (.) so:
04 HV: You didn't want to breast feed.

Here in both cases the health visitor poses a question, the vehicle for which is a YNI, about the mother's breasts, and in both cases the mother reports that her breasts are fine by producing a preferred response – one that goes along with the expectation built into the question of a "no problem" answer. These responses differ, however, in that in the first case the response is type-conforming whereas in the second it is not. Raymond explains that this difference can be understood by considering the question to which the mother is responding in each case. Raymond (2003: 948) writes that in the first case the

> question incorporates (1) an explicit reference to the progress of the mother's breasts (that is, their change over time) and by extension (2) an implicit recognition that her breasts had been, in some way, painful, or problematic. As a consequence of this question's design, then, the response ("yes") "preferred" by its action-type, polarity, and grammatical form, allows the mother to confirm that her breasts have "settled down" while also indicating that she had suffered some discomfort prior to the visit.

In the second case, the health visitor merely asks whether mom's breasts are "alright". She thus does not include in the question anything about how the mother might have been feeling in the past. Notice then that the mother produces a non-conforming response – one in which "yes" and "no" are withheld – in answer to this question, and in doing so introduces the issues of change over time herself, remarking "they're fine *no:w* I've *stopped* leaking" (emphasis added). Raymond explains further that the mother

> treats the response options made relevant by (the question) as inadequate for conveying the status of her breasts since the choice between "yes" and "no" would only make reference to their current state. To respond with a "yes," would be to risk implying that her breasts had never been a problem; to respond with a "no" would be to claim that they currently are one.

YNIs then can grammatically encode presuppositions about how and when something happened. We can see in their responses that answerers orient to those presuppositions and may withhold a "yes" or "no" token in an effort to avoid confirming them (see also Ehrlich and Sidnell 2006). Consider a final example drawn from a call we have already considered in chapter 4.

(32) Deb and Dick
22 Deb: → [s]o don't you have all your
23 → family coming today?
24 Dick: → Well: they're coming around two and I °hhh left
25 messages with Brian an:d mydad to(uh) see if

they wanted to come but=ah
(0.2)
°hh that's all I could do was leave messages.
Deb: owh
(0.4)
Dick: °Gotsome° °hhhh five pound lasagna thing to(hh)
throw in the oven=an
Deb: o(h)h(h)=huh (.) well: I'm sure you'll have a
good time.
Dick: [oh
Deb: [<at least it's inside. And it didn't rain
yesterday so we were lucky [l- looking at it
Dick: [mmhm yeah
Deb: today god. woulda been awful.

In chapter 4 we discussed the way in which Deb constructed and placed her response to Dick's troubles telling in lines 24–32. We noted, specifically, that Deb disattends some aspects of the situation that Dick is describing (that he has not heard from his son Brian and his father as to whether they will be attending the get-together) and highlights others (the fact that it's being held inside). Bringing the analytic resources provided by Raymond's work on YNIs to bear on this extract, we can see that Deb's initial question – "so don't you have all your family coming today" – establishes a number of preferences. In terms of design preference, this is strongly built towards a "yes" response. Moreover, by virtue of its construction as a YNI it prefers a type-conforming "yes" or "no" response. As Raymond puts it, non-conforming responses such as Dick's in lines 24–32 are produced "for cause". And we can see that, in addition to everything else it does, Dick's non-conforming response conveys why he has not answered with a "yes" or "no". Deb's question made reference to "all your family", and notice that although "they're coming around two" suggests that more than one person is expected, Dick immediately follows up with a qualification of "all" by indicating that he is unsure whether "Brian" and "my Dad" are going to come.

Minimization and Recognition in References to Persons: Twin Preference Structure

In a lecture from 1971, Sacks (1995 vol. 2: 444) noted that in making initial reference to a person, a speaker selects between two basic options, each of which sets a different task for the recipient. On the one hand, a speaker may design the identification so that it proposes the recipient should be able to use it to find someone they know. Such *recognitional reference* forms "convey to the recipient that the one being referred to is someone that they know (about). The use of a recognitional reference form provides for the recipient to figure out who that they know the speaker is referring to by use of this reference form" (Schegloff 1996a: 459). Two common recognitional forms in English conversation are (personal) names and recognitional descriptors such as "the guy that always comes in here". Alternatively, the speaker may design the identification in a way that does not suggest the recipient should or could recognize the person being talked about with it. Such non-recognitional forms comprise a varied and heterogeneous set and include expressions such as "a guy", "someone", "this woman", as well as non-recognitional descriptors such as "a guy at work" and category terms such as "my professor", "this student", "the postman" etc. There is no one single or basic way of doing non-recognitional reference; rather, different interactional circumstances make alternate non-recognitional forms relevant.[2]

Sacks suggests that the procedure used for selecting identifications in ordinary conversation involves selecting between these two alternatives. He further suggests that there is preference for recognitional over non-recognitional references. Thus a speaker is expected to use a recognitional form if she believes that the recipient knows and can identify the person being talked about (Sacks 1995 vol. 2: 444).

In their later, co-authored paper, Sacks and Schegloff (1979) added another consideration. Specifically, they proposed that references to persons are organized in relation to two sometimes conflicting and sometimes convergent preferences. The first preference is for recognitionals over non-recognitionals, as Sacks had outlined in his lecture. The second is for single, minimal forms over complex ones. The concurrent operation of both preferences results in the massive use of personal names since a name satisfies both preferences. Where the preferences are in conflict, the second is minimized "step by step" so as to allow for recognition via more elaborate and less minimal forms. Sacks and Schegloff provide the following example as evidence of their claims.

(33) NB 1.1
01 Mrs: 'Ello:?
02 Guy: 'Ello is Curly there?
03 (.)
04 Mrs: Oo jis (.) e-Who:?
05 Guy: Johnny?h An[sin?]
06 Mrs: [Oo j]ista minnih,
07 (0.6)
08 Kid: ([ )
09 Mrs: [It's fer you dea:r,

A recognitional form may engender a sequence devoted to the pursuit and display of recognition. So for instance in the example above, Mrs. initiates repair of the recognitional form "Curly", and Guy then goes on to try several alternate names. The sequence is closed by Mrs.'s use of "oh" to mark her success in finding the person Guy is talking about.[3]

General Preferences in the Organization of Interaction

So far we've considered just those preferences that organize the relation between first and second pair parts of adjacency pairs and specifically those that bear on the production of the second pair part response. But preference organization is much broader and more profound than this. There are preferences that appear to operate quite generally across conversation, indeed social interaction in general. For instance in chapter 7 we'll see that repair is organized with respect to a preference of "self-" over "other-"correction. At an even more abstract level all interaction appears to be organized in relation to a very basic preference for "progressivity":[4]

> Among the most pervasively relevant features in the organization of talk-and-other-conduct-in-interaction is the relationship of adjacency or "nextness." . . . Moving from some element to a hearably-next-one with nothing intervening is the embodiment of, and the measure of, progressivity. Should something intervene between some element and what is hearable as a/the next one due – should something violate or interfere with their contiguity, whether next sound, next word or next turn – it will be heard as qualifying the progressivity of the talk, and will be examined for its import, for what understanding should be accorded it. Each next element of such a progression can be inspected to find how it reaffirms the understanding-so-far of what has preceded, or favors one or more of the several such understandings that are being entertained, or how it requires reconfiguration of that understanding. (Schegloff 2007: 17)

Schegloff (1979b) showed speakers' orientation to such a general preference in instances of multiple self-repair where we see them "displaying that each repair has made progress toward a solution of the trouble being addressed" (1979b: 278). In instances of multiple self-repair, then, the pervasive orientation of interactants to the principle of progress comes to the surface. Another place where we see it is in word searches. For instance, M. Goodwin and C. Goodwin (1986) show that if a participant is having difficulty finding a word, other participants routinely provide candidate words, in this attempting to help the turn progress.

Stivers and Robinson (2006) provide further evidence of this pervasive orientation to progress on the part of conversationalists. These authors begin by describing a basic preference for recipients of a question to respond with answers rather than non-answers. The evidence for this preference is seen in a number of related phenomena. First, in terms of turn-shape, non-answers typically include features typical of dispreferred turns:

(34) Trio 2
01 Mag: What happened at (.) wo:rk.
02 At Bullock's this evening.
03 Christina: .hh Wul I don' kno:^::w.

Here then the question first comes to completion at the end of "wo:rk.". Thus, it can be observed that Christina's response at line 03 exhibits both inter-turn gap and turn-initial delay. Furthermore the turn as a whole constitutes an account for not answering. Another piece of evidence for the preference for answers over non-answers is seen in the fact that non-answers (failures to respond) are treated as disaligning and may prompt reversals (see above). From the recipient's side we can see a preference for answers in the fact that, even where they lack information on the matter asked about, question recipients often work to provide an answer. Stivers and Robinson (2006: 374) illustrate with the following example in which the recipient of a question does not know the answer and turns to another party, apparently in an effort to gather the information required to answer the question posed:

(34) SBL:2.2 (analyzed by Pomerantz 1984: 58)
01 A: How is Aunt Kallie.
02 B: Well, I (suspect) she's better.
03 A: Oh that's good.
04 B: Las' time we talked tuh Mother she was uh better,
05 B: → Uh Allen, (she wants to know about),
06 (2.0) ((talking to someone off the phone))
07 B: → No, Allen doesn't know anything new (out there) either.

So it can be seen that there is a preference for answers over non-answers. The authors go on to discuss another preference: that for selected next speakers to respond to questions. As we saw in chapter 03, speakers have a number of techniques available for selecting a next speaker. Stivers and Robinson show that, in multi-party interaction, there is a clear preference for responses to be provided by such selected next speakers rather than some other participant. Again there are various kinds of evidence to support this. First, there is the quantitative evidence. In their study, Stivers and Robinson found that 97 percent of responses to questions that selected a specific next speaker came from that speaker. Second, there is the fact that when non-selected speakers did respond they responded with answers to the question, whereas selected next speakers sometimes responded with something other than an answer. The fact that non-selected respondents to questions restrict their responses to answers whereas selected respondents do not suggests that there is preference for selected next speakers to respond that is distinct from the preference to provide an answer (Stivers and Robinson 2006: 377). A final piece of evidence that Stivers and Robinson cite is that, even when a non-selected recipient is knowledgeable about the matter questioned, they rarely respond immediately following the question at the TRP. Rather, non-selected respondents of questions can be seen to "wait" to see if the selected next speaker will themselves respond. This was first documented in a study of pediatric medical visits. Stivers (2001) found that when doctors posed questions to children, parents, who were clearly in the know about the matter asked about, would nevertheless not immediately respond to those questions if they were not the selected next speaker. This was true even with children as young as 2 or 3 years.

Stivers and Robinson argue that when a question that has selected a next speaker reaches completion, these two preferences – for answers over non-answers and for selected next speakers over non-selected next speakers – are simultaneously relevant. In the default situation a selected next speaker provides a response and thus both preferences are satisfied. But what happens when a selected next speaker does not or cannot answer? The preference for answers over non-answers outranks the preference for selected next speakers over non-selected next speakers and non-selected speakers routinely provide an answer, as in the following:

(36) SNS 51:36
01 Stuart: a→ Bates ha- have you heard the PhD story.
02 b→ (0.4)
03 Luke: c→ Bates's heard it.
04 Stuart?: (°yeah.°)/(0.8)
05 Bates: Yieahp,

Here Stuart and Luke are sitting together around the breakfast bar when Stuart asks Bates, who is off camera, whether he's "heard the PhD story.". This question projects the telling of the story and makes a "yes" or "no" response relevant both as an answer to the question and as a go-ahead or blocking move to the projected story-telling. Bates does not respond immediately to the question and a silence ensues (arrow b). Luke, a non-selected next speaker, provides an answer which is subsequently confirmed by Bates in line 5.

In example (37), below, taken from a pediatric visit, the selected next speaker responds to the doctor's question not with an answer but with an account for not answering ("I don't know"). In this context the non-selected next speaker (Mom at arrow d) produces an answer.

```
(37) P110; six-year-old girl
01  Girl:             [I::'m si:ck,=[h
02  Doctor:           [.hh          [#u# Hu:h?
03                    (.)
04  Doctor:  a→       You're sick, Well what's u:p,
05           b→       (1.1)
06  Girl:    c→       I don't know[:,
07  Mom:     d→                   [B[etween yesterday and to[da:y: she-
08  Doctor:                          [How- hh               [-hh
09                    (.)
10  Mom:              You know it's (just)/(this)- nasal crap an'
11                    it's gotten it was gree:n_ it was [(uh) really
12  Doctor:                                             [Okay.
13  Mom:              =uh beautiful color this morning.
```

These examples show that, in situations where they are not concurrently satisfiable, the preference for answers over non-answers outranks the preference for selected next speakers over non-selected next speakers. It is worth asking just what these preferences bear upon. The preference for selected next speakers relates to the rights and obligations accorded to participants in interaction via the operation of the turn-taking system. The preference for answers over non-answers relates to the onward progress of action. That is, answers forward the action launched by the question whereas non-answers such as "I don't know" or the absence of any response do not. Thus the prioritizing of the preference for answers over the preference for selected next speakers in examples (36) and (37) reveals a "second order" preference for progressivity: the onward progress of action in conversation and other forms of interaction is privileged even to the extent that it results in a violation of the otherwise secure right of selected next speakers to respond to the question addressed to them.

Although we looked at second pair parts in this chapter – at preferred and dispreferred *responses* – it is also possible to describe at least some first actions within this framework. Although a detailed consideration of this matter is beyond the scope of this chapter (see Schegloff 2007: 81–96), we will encounter one such case of alternative first actions organized by a relation of preference in chapter 10 when we consider identification and recognition in telephone openings.

To conclude, we've taken a quick look in this chapter at biases or "preferences" that organize a broad range of phenomena in conversation. Taken together these preferences can be seen to constitute a kind of conversation inertia or momentum that anonymously pushes participants in one direction or another quite irrespective of their own wishes, desires, predilections, best intentions and so on. Preference is a structural rather than psychological force that operates independently of the particular participants in any given encounter.

Notes

1 This "by any chance" looks very much like what Davidson (1984) called a "monitor space".

2 The preference for recognitionals over non-recognitionals is evidenced most obviously in the overwhelmingly more common use of recognitional forms. Moreover, where there is uncertainty about the possibility of achieving recognition through a given form the speaker may use it with try-marking. Thus the anticipated possibility of failure does not prevent the pursuit of recognition;

rather, a special device comes into play. Further evidence of the preference for recognitionals is found in the fact that recognition may be pursued through several successive tries. Finally, the preference for recognitionals over non-recognitionals is treated as an accountable matter by the participants. So, for instance, if a non-recognitional form is used and later it is found that recognition might have been achieved, this can then become grounds for complaint or indeed, for the inference that the speaker is being purposively vague or even deceptive.

3 Later work by Schegloff (1996a) has extended and elaborated the earlier analysis by taking into account both initial and subsequent references. The original analysis of the concurrent operation of preference for recognitionals and minimization remains unaltered for locally initial references.

4 The term was first used in this sense in Schegloff 1979. As Heritage (2007) points out, the "principle of progressivity" can come into conflict with another basic principle – that of intersubjectivity.

6

Sequence

So far we have considered sequences composed of only two turns: a first and second pair part. Clearly, sequences can be much more complex than this. Much of this added complexity is the product of expansion. An adjacency pair can be expanded before the occurrence of its first part, after the occurrence of its first part but before the occurrence of its second, or after its second part. These possibilities are represented schematically in figure 6.1. Expansions are themselves typically built out of paired actions and can thus serve as the bases upon which further expansion takes place. It does not take much to see how this could result in sequences of considerable complexity and length (see Schegloff 2007). In this chapter I sketch out the basics of sequence organization beyond the adjacency pair. We begin with expansion before the first pair part of a base pair and proceed from there to consider insert and finally post-expansions.

Pre-expansion

As the name implies, pre-expansions involve an expansion of a sequence before the occurrence of a base first pair part. Pre-expansions are, in a basic sense, preparatory to some other, projected work to be done in the sequence and implemented by the first pair part of the base adjacency pair (the action of the first pair part).

Some pre-expansions are "type-specific" in that they project a specific base first pair part; for example, they are pre-invitations ("hey, are you busy tonight?"), pre-announcements ("Guess what happened to me?"), or pre-requests ("You wouldn't happen to be going my way would you?") (see Levinson 1983, Schegloff 1988b, 2007, Terasaki 2004 [1976]). Such type-specific pre-expansions typically check on a condition for the successful accomplishment

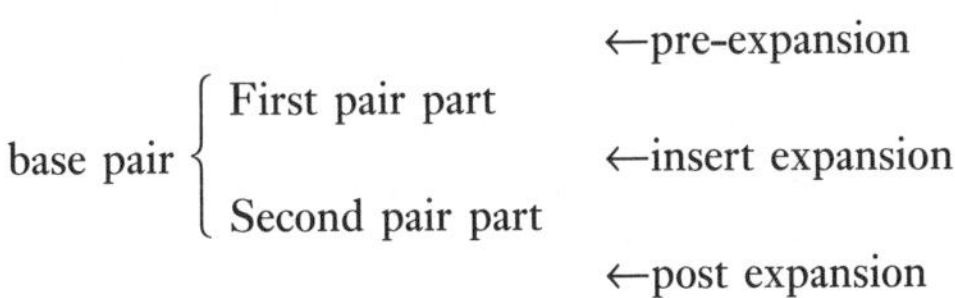

Figure 6.1

of the base first pair part. So, for instance, pre-invitations often check on the *availability* of the intended invitee. Consider the following:

(1) HS:STI,1

01	John:		Judy?
02	Judy:		Yeah,
03	John:		John Smith
04	Judy:		Hi John
05	John:		How ya doin'=
06			=say wh*a*t'r you doing.
07	Judy:	→	Well, we're going out. Why.
08	John:		Oh, I was just gonna say come out
09			and come over here an' talk about
10			this evening, but if you're going
11			out you can't very well do that.

We can make two observations about Judy's response in line 07. First, notice that she answers the question not in terms of what she is doing at this very moment but rather in terms of her plans for the immediate future. Second, observe that Judy's "why" displays an orientation to the preceding turn as something more than an information-seeking question. John's answer at lines 08–11 confirms this inference.

Pre-requests typically check on the availability of the item to be asked for. Consider the following example in which the participants have been talking about some fish tanks belonging to Vic. At lines 01–02, Mike inquires about one particularly large tank.

(2) US. 24

01	Mike:	→	Wuhddiyuh doing wh dat big bow-puh-tank.
02			Nothing?
03			(0.5)
04	Vic:		((cough))
05			Uh-h-h
06			(1.0)
07	Vic:	→	I'm not intuh selling it or giving it. That's it.
08	Mike:		Okay
09			(1.0)
10	Mike:		Dat wz simple. Khhhh huh-huh-heh=
11	Vic:		=Yeh.

We can see here that Vic hears Mike's inquiry at line 01 as building towards a request (or possibly an offer to buy the tank) and responds by indicating that it will not be granted. These participants, then, treat questions such as "Say what'r you doing." and "Wuhddiyuh doing wh dat big bow-puh-tank." as preliminary moves to other, projected, actions. Recipients of such questions are thus given an opportunity to show the way in which the action projected (invitation, request) will fare. Recipients of such pre-requests or pre-invitations can give a response which either encourages the other to go ahead with or to abort the projected action. Alternatively they can respond to the action as if it had already been articulated, as the recipients in both (1) and (2) do.

Notice also that in both cases, the second part of the pre-expansion blocks the doing of a projected first pair part (an invitation in (1) and a request in (2)). In this way, pre-expansions work to prevent the occurrence of dispreferred second actions (e.g. declinations, rejections). Pre-sequences may also be seen to contribute to the non-occurrence of dispreferred first actions. For instance, requests are dispreferred relative to offers.[1] Consider the following:

(3) Levinson 1983: 343
01 Charles: Hullo I was just ringing up to ask
02 if you were going to Bertrand's party
03 Roger: yes I thought you might be
04 Charles: Heh heh
05 Roger: Yes would you like a lift?
06 Charles: Oh I'd love one

Here, Charles asks whether Roger will be going to Bertrand's party. This is hearable as leading to a request such as "can I get a lift with you?". Indeed, it could be said to check on the availability of the service to be requested. Roger clearly anticipates this and, before the request is produced, produces an offer.

Announcements and story-tellings are also frequently initiated with pre-expansions: pre-announcements or story prefaces. It was suggested earlier that pre-expansions typically check on a condition for the successful accomplishment of the base first pair part. In the case of announcements and other tellings, perhaps the most important and basic of such conditions is that the recipient does not already know the thing to be told or announced (this is the principle of recipient design; see Sacks, Schegloff and Jefferson 1974, Sacks 1995 [1971]). It should thus come as no surprise to find that pre-announcements often take the form of questions about what the recipient knows.

(4) HG
01 Hyla: → D'you know w't I did t'day
02 I wz so proud a'my[s e l]f,=
03 Nancy: → [What.]
04 Hyla: =·hh I we:nt- (0.2) A'right like I get off
05 et work et one,=
06 Nancy: Uh hu:h,=

In (4), Nancy responds to Hyla's pre-announcement, "D'you know w't I did t'day", with a go-ahead response ("What.") which suggests that she does not know the thing to be told. In the following fragment, Vivian's preannouncement does not elicit an audible response from the co-participants but Vivian nevertheless produces the announcement in the following turns.

(5) Chicken Dinner
16 Shane: [Uh wz goi:n
17 crazy tihday uh on th'on the roa:d
18 (0.2)
19 Vivian: → We' yih know w't he di[↑:d?
20 Shane: [Wen'outta my
21 fuckin'mi[:nd.
22 Vivian: → [He maHHde
23 (.)
24 Vivian: a right- it wz- in Sanna Monig'yihknow

The following example is taken from a recording of a dinner-time conversation. The participants are three siblings, Virginia, Wes and Beth, their mother, and Wes's girlfriend Prudence.

(6)	Virginia		
37	Prudence:	→	You know what she said one ti:me?
38			(.)
39			((dog bark))
40			(0.4)
41	Prudence:	→	One [night we were talki- we had porkchops fer dinner an'=
42	Virginia:		[( )
43	Prudence:		=thuh next mornin' I went tuh wake her u(huh)p ·hm! an' she
44			was in thuh bed goin' (1.1) they're porkchops. They're all:
45			porkchops. £People are porkc(h)ho(h)ps sih hih high heh
46	Wes:		heh heh heh
47			(.)
48	Prudence:		·hhhh uhh! A(h)ll thuh p(h)eop(h)le a(h)re p(h)orkcha(h)
49			·hh ·uh ·h[hh

Story prefaces, such as Prudence's "You know what she said one time?", solve a problem generated by the turn-taking system. In telling a story, a speaker often reaches completion of a turn-unit (e.g. "we had porkchops for dinner" at 41, "I went to wake her up" at 43, "and she was in thuh bed" at 44) without thereby completing the story. This being so, in order to allow for the telling of a story in its entirety, the usual association of turn completion and transition relevance must be suspended. A story preface allows recipients to see that points of possible turn completion which fall within the scope of the preface are not transitionrelevant and do not constitute opportunities for another speaker to take a turn.

Notice that in all these cases the pre-announcement or story-preface takes the form of a yes–no question: "Do you know what I did today?", "You know what he did?", "You know what she said one time?". In responding to turns such as these, recipients must necessarily attempt to discern whether the turn is intended as a pre-announcement or is in fact a real request for information, and in some cases they get this wrong. Schegloff (1988c) discusses the following case:

(7)	From Schegloff 1988		
01	Mom:	'z everybody (0.2) [washed for dinner?	
02	Gary:	[yah	
03	Mom:	Daddy 'n I have t- both go in different	
04		directions, en I wanna talk ta you about where	
05		I'm going (t'night).	
06	Russ:	mm hmm	
07	Gary:	Is it about us?	
08	Mom:	Uh huh	
09	Russ:	I know where you're goin',	
10	Mom:	Where.	
11	Russ	To the uh (eighth grade)=	
12	Mom:	=Yeah. Right.	
13		Do you know who's going to that meeting?	←A
14	Russ:	Who.	←B
15	Mom:	I don't kno:w.	←C
16	Russ:	Oh::. Prob'ly Missiz McOwen ('n detsa) en	←D

17		prob'ly Missiz Cadry and some of the teachers.	
18		(0.4) and the coun[sellors	
19	Mom:	[Missiz Cadry went to the-	
20		I'll tell you . . .	

At line 13 Mother asks Russ, "Do you know who's going to that meeting?". In responding with "Who." in line 14 Russ treats his mother's question as a pre-announcement. This hearing is available because Russ assumes that Mother in fact knows who is going to the meeting and is proposing to tell what she knows to Russ. As it turns out, however, this is a misanalysis which Mother corrects with "I don't know". Russ registers the correction with "Oh" and proceeds to answer in a way fitting to a "real" question. Example (8) provides another, somewhat more complicated, instance:

(8) Pyatt and Bush

		((ring))	
01	Bush:	Hello¿	
02	Pyatt:	.h m- Mister Bush,	
03	Bush:	Yes.	
04	Pyatt:	Mister Pyatt.	
05	Bush:	Yes,	
06	Pyatt:	D'Yknow where Mister Bowdwin is.	←A
07		(0.2)	
08	Bush:	Wha:t?	
09		(·)	
10	Pyatt:	hhuh-hhuh-°hu-° [·hhh	
11	Bush:	[Do I know where who?	
12	Pyatt:	Leo is.	
13	Bush:	No.	
14	Pyatt:	Oh. Okay.	
15		(0.2)	
16	Bush:	He's down in Mexico or some'in¿	←B
17	Pyatt:	I don't know,	←C
18	Bush:	Oh:. Yer lookin' for him.	←D

Here, after a problem of person reference is repaired (see chapter 7), Bush responds at line 16 to Pyatt's question in line 06 with a turn that is marked as a guess by rising intonation and the tag "or some'in¿". He thus responds in such a way as to invite confirmation from the questioner and so shows that he has heard this question as a pre-announcement. So Bush apparently assumes that Pyatt knows where "Leo/Mr Bowdwin" is, and in line 17 Pyatt corrects this. Notice here, that in announcing his own ignorance on this matter, Pyatt heavily emphasizes the pronoun "I" in this way suggesting a contrast with "you"/Bush. At line 18 Bush articulates a new understanding of the turn "D'Yknow where Mister Bowdwin is." as a real request for information.

In both these examples, then, we see a recipient apparently mistaking what has been designed as a real request for information as a pre-announcement. In both cases it is possible to identify particular aspects of the context that may have encouraged the misanalysis. In (7) the conversation is between a mother and her child and the talk concerns a meeting at the child's school. While it turns out the child has a good idea of who, in fact, is attending the meeting, these are "adult" matters being talked about and the child may thus have expected that his mother was preparing to "tell" rather than "ask" about them. In the second instance, the utterance "Do you know where Mr Bowdwin is?" is in the position typically reserved to announce or convey the "reason for the call" (see chapter 10) and this may have led Bush to hear this as a pre-announcement rather than the real question it was intended to be.[2]

There is also evidence that it is not always obvious to a recipient what specific action is being projected by a given pre-sequence. Consider in this respect the following case in which Joyce asks brother Stan, "whatta ya doing like: s: late Saturday afternoo:n." While Stan appears to recognize this for the pre-sequence it is and accordingly responds by detailing his availability for the time-period asked about, his "why what's happening¿" at line 22 suggests that he has understood Joyce to be preparing the way for an invitation when in fact there is a request in the works. Notice in this respect that although Stan has indicated that an invitation would meet with an acceptance (in saying, for instance, "but S:aturday a:fter noon if it's not too: la:te"), once Joyce articulates the request in line 27 Stan essentially rejects it by saying "don't count on me,".

(9) Joyce and Stan (p. 8)

Joyce: [°Mm,
Stan: [·hhhh We:ll okay: at's about all I wannid tuh
(0.7)
bug you with. (tod[ay).
Joyce: [uhhahhahh hh Okay Stan:,
Stan: So are ^you okay?
Joyce: → Yeah, (0.4) um: (0.2) whatta ya doing like: s: late
→ Saturday afternoo:n.=
Stan: =·hhhhh Well late Sa- I pra- a friend a'mine just
called me a little while ago: an' he: uh:
(0.7)
he wannid'a do something.<so I said well:, it's a
( ) Saturday night why don't we go: uh: you know
(le's:)/(us:) catch a movie: er: ge[t something
Joyce: [Mm
Stan: to ea:t er: ballgame >er somethin' like tha[t<
Joyce: [°Mm
·hhhh but S:aturday a:fternoon if it's not too:
la:te I don't think [I ( )
Joyce: [No it'll it'll be like six.
o'clock.
Stan: → Oh: why what's happening¿
Joyce: Because I'm going down to San Diego.
(0.3)
Joyce: An' I'm gonneh- fly:.
(.)
Joyce: → And so I need somebody'ta drive me to the airport.
(0.4)
Joyce: And uh: Ma said she might but ˅yihknow,
(0.9)
Joyce: She'll tell me [la:ter;
Stan: [Oh I might be ableta manage it
I'll see:, but don't count on me, yih[know?
Joyce: [Arright well
I'll try an[d get someone else.

Stan: [Av: I wouldn' I wouldn' have a really
good idea until: uh timorrow or Saturday.
Joyce: Yeah, o[kay.

So far we've been talking about "type-specific" pre-sequences. Another kind of pre-expansion, the summons–answer sequence, is generic and checks on the precondition of any interactional project – the availability of a projected recipient to attend the talk for which he or she is selected as recipient. Example (10) provides an obvious case.

(10) Atkinson and Drew 1979: 46
Child: → Mummy
Mom: Yes dear
(2.1)
Child: I want a cloth to clean the windows

Here the child summons and thereby secures his mother's attention by addressing her in line 01. Mother responds with "Yes dear" in this way showing a willingness to attend further. As Schegloff (1968) noted, a summons projects further talk by the same speaker. Participants' orientation to this is seen in deferring (e.g. "wait a minute"), go-ahead (e.g. "what?") and blocking (e.g. "I'm not interested in what you have to say", "I know, take out the trash") responses. Go-ahead responses, in so far as they orient to imminent further talk, are minimal contributions (similar in this respect to continuers) that claim as little turn-space as possible. Taken to the extreme, this may result in the collapse of a sequence into a single turn with an adjustment in gaze direction being treated as equivalent to a summons's answer (see Schegloff 2007).

Another kind of pre-sequence, termed a "pre-pre", is shown in examples (11) and (12). The "pre-pre" turn is marked in each case by the "A" arrow(s).

(11) [#12, BC, Beige, 18–19]
Host: Good evening, W.N.B.C::,
Caller: Hi:: Brad, 'ow're you.
Host: I'::m fine thanks=
Caller: =Tell thet lady she sh'd drive 'n
not to be afraid.
((pause))
Host: Well, that's easy tuh say. But
not aways easy tuh do.
Caller: Y're, yer right deh.
Host: Meh!
Caller: I like tuh ask you something. ←A
Host: Shoot.
Caller: Y'know I 'ad my license suspended ←B
fuh six months,
Host: Uh huh
Caller: Y'know for a reason which, I
rathuh not, mention tuh you, in
othuh words, -a serious reason,
en I like tuh know if I w'd ←C
talk tuh my senator, or— ←C
somebuddy, could they help me ←C
get it back, ←C

(12) [FD, SP I

01	A:	I wuh- I would just like tuh ask	←A
02		y'a question, ·hh-	
03	B:	Yes ma[am.	
04	A:	[Uhm,	
05		I understand that there are no	←B
06		private ambulance services in this	←B
07		town. And that the fire department	←B
08		has a rescue wagon,	←B
09		[Is that right?	←B
10	B:	[Uh.	
11		We have the amb'lance service.	
12		Right.	
13		The rescue wagon.	
14		((pause))	
15	A:	<u>Oh</u>.	
16	B:	D'yuh ave[a t-	
17	A:	[Are you the only people	←C
18		that have this?	←C
19	B:	Right.	
20		you, call us [in case-	
21	A:	[-other than military?	
22	B:	Right.	

In these sequences we see an initial turn (at the A arrow) that takes the form "I'd like to ask you something" or "I'd just like to ask you a question". After this elicits a "go-ahead" response from the recipient ("shoot", "Yes maam") the speaker continues, but *not* with the question that was projected by the initial turn at the A arrow. Rather, in (11), the speaker follows not with a question but by telling the call-in radio host that he has had his license suspended. In (12), the speaker does follow with a question but not the one projected by the initial turn. Thus, before the speaker performs the action that has been projected, she first does something else. This something else appears, on closer inspection, to be some business that is recognizably *preliminary* to what will end up being asked about. Schegloff explains that in each case the projected action crucially involves reference to or talk about some person, place or thing and that this kind of pre-sequence allows the speaker to check whether the recipient will be able to recognize the person, place or thing being referred to before he or she actually asks the question. Schegloff (1980: 114–15) writes:

> Each of the projected actions will include, and ends up including, a reference or references to persons, places, or things. The preliminaries are occupied with securing the recognizability or understandability of those references. They do so by introducing the references in a turn or turns in which the reference is not used for the doing of the action that was projected. The recipient then has an opportunity for raising any problems of understanding or recognition or correction that these references pose. Typically they pose none, and the recipient exhibits this (as well as exhibiting a recognition that a larger unit is in progress, of which this is not the end) by use of a "continuer" – a token such as "uh huh" or "mm hm" or "yeah" – or a confirming answer if the preliminary was a question. After one or more such initial mentions or preparation of referents, the speaker does the projected action, employing in it terms that require reference to what was introduced in the preliminaries without rementioning them, for example by a pronoun or other pro-term reference, or by terms that require reference to an antecedent that

> is found in the preliminary. . . . In the preliminaries, then, terms are introduced without being used; in the projected actions, they are used without being mentioned. The work of "referring" and "what is being talked about" is extracted for separate, prior treatment from the doing of something – asking, telling, requesting – with respect to those referents.

We see then that all pre-expansion sequences are recognizably preliminary to some other action whose production they project. Different pre-sequences are distinguished in terms of the type of precondition which they are directed to checking. For instance, pre-invitations typically check on a person's availability. Pre-requests often check on the availability of a thing to be requested or the availability of the recipient where a service is being asked for. Pre-pres typically check whether a recipient will be able to recognize some person, place or thing to be talked about.

Insert Expansion

An adjacency pair consists of two adjacent utterances, with the second selected from some range of possibilities defined by the first. As discussed in chapter 4, this account of adjacency pairs is meant to describe members' own normative expectations. However, on some occasions, the two utterances of an adjacency pair are not, in fact, adjacent. In some cases this is because a sequence has been *inserted* between the first and second pair parts of an adjacency pair (see Schegloff 1972). Such insert expansions can be divided into post-firsts and pre-seconds (Schegloff 2007) according to the kind of interactional relevancy they address. The most common form of post-first insert expansion consists of a next-turn repair-initiator (NTRI) and its response (see chapter 7). For example, in (13), Rebecca is struggling to close the door and at line 01 Ann suggests that she should move a piece of clothing hanging on the door handle. Ann refers to this piece of clothing with "it", and rather than respond to the suggestion, in the next turn Rebecca initiates repair with "Move what.". Ann then repairs the reference with "that thing . . ." and Rebecca subsequently responds to the suggestion in line 04 with "okay.".

(13) KIDS_11_24_05(2of2)T7.mov @11:33
01 Ann: Maybe Rebecca, maybe you can move it,
02 Rebecca: → °Move what.°
03 Ann: Move that thing that('s in the lock)/(yo- in the door).
04 Rebecca: Okay.

So a sequence like this involves a sub-sequence embedded or inserted within another – between the first pair part and second pair part of the base sequence. Notice then that the sequence inserted within the base sequence is prosecuting not some independent trajectory of action but rather a task that is recognizably preliminary or prerequisite to what Ann is suggesting, in so far as Rebecca needs to know what "it" refers to in order to follow that suggestion.

Pre-second insert expansions are oriented not to trouble with the FPP but rather to trouble with an expected SPP. Such insert expansions routinely address issues that stand as preconditions to the doing of a preferred SPP (for instance, locating an object requested in the FPP). Consider examples (14) and (15).

(14) Merritt 1976: 325, cited by Levinson 1984: 361
01 Customer: Do you have Marlboros?
02 Seller: Yeah. Hard or soft?
03 Customer: Soft please
04 Seller: Okay

(15) Merritt 1976: 333, cited by Levinson 1984: 304
01 A: May I have a bottle of Mich?
02 B: Are you twenty-one?
03 A: No
04 B: No

In a rather more complicated case given as example (16) below, Bev and Ann are making arrangements for Ann to come to Bev's house. At lines 23–4, Bev asks at what time she can expect Ann to be at her house. Rather than respond to this question with an answer, Ann turns the question back onto Bev asking "what time am I to be there at" (treating the matter as ultimately up to Bev). After this is dealt with in the following turns, Ann responds to the initial question with "yeah I'll come around six thirty" at line 31.

(16) XTR
22 Bev: Okay wul listen ((smile voice))
23 .hh (.) >Are=you gonna be at my house at what time on ←FPP_1
24 ah Fri:- on Sund[ay? ←FPP_1
25 Ann: [What time am I (.) to be there at. ←FPP_2
26 Bev: I think a little before se:ven.= ←SPP_2
27 Ann: =Ya cause it's the (.) w[a l k]
28 Bev: [I waana] watch th-the
29 [runway:]
30 Ann: [°hhhhhh]
31 hhugh. yeah I'll come aroun six thirty. ←SPP_1
32 Bev: Okay. SCT

In insertion sequences, then, the participants maintain an orientation to the relevance of the base sequence though suspending that activity to engage in some ancillary or subsidiary matter.

Post-expansion

Post-expansions are highly variable with respect to their complexity. Schegloff (2007) suggests that they can be divided into minimal and non-minimal types. Minimal post-expansions consist of one turn. "Oh", for instance, can occur after a second pair part and thus minimally expand the sequence, as in the following example:

(17) HG:II:25:ST Hyla and Nancy – Heritage 1984: 286–7
25 Nancy: =·hhh Dz he av iz own apa:rt[mint?]
26 Hyla: [·hhhh] Yea:h,=

27 Nancy: → =Oh:,
28 (1.0)
29 Nancy: How didju git iz number,
30 (·)
31 Hyla: I(h) (·) c(h)alled infermation'n San Fr'ncissc(h)[uh!
32 Nancy: → [Oh::::.

"Okay" may also serve as a minimal post-expansion:

(18) YYZ 2 – Deb and Dick
55 Dick: Are they leaving today?
56 Deb I don't know
57 Dick: O(hh)ka(h)y

Heritage (1984) described "oh" as a change-of-state marker because, with it, a speaker can claim to have been informed and thus to have undergone a change of state from not-knowing to knowing. Consistent with this description, Schegloff (2007) suggests that as a minimal post-expansion – "a sequence closing third" – "oh" registers information receipt. In example (17), for instance, Nancy uses "oh" to show that she has been informed by the answers to her questions. Schegloff suggests a contrast with "okay" which is oriented more to the action being implemented in a sequence than the information being conveyed. In (19), Jane has called to invite Edgerton and his wife to have drinks. Edgerton's response is significantly delayed and he eventually responds by saying that he must confer with his wife, suggesting that whether they can accept the invitation depends on "what she's doing". When Edgerton returns to the phone he delivers a dispreferred non-acceptance of the invitation. Jane responds to this with "Okay.".

(19) Heritage I.
01 Jane: .h Uh:m I wz -wond'RING IF: you'n Ilene w'd like t'come ovuh
02 fer a (.) drink this evenin:g.h u-¯uh:: (.) Mahrgo hez come
03 fr'm Coventry.
04 (.)
05 Jane: .h End uh::
06 (0.2)
07 Jane: Yihknow I thought thet ih-'d (.) be nice if we cood get
08 t'gethuh,
09 (0.2)
10 ( ): .hh
11 (0.2)
12 Edgerton: Yah. Okay well let me ahsk huhr just a moment it depe:nds upon
13 [what she's doing ha[ng on.
. . .
14 Edgerton: Ja:ne,
15 Jane: Ye:s?
16 (0.4)
17 Edgerton: Ah must apologi::ze (.) the ahnswer is negative:.
18 Jane: SCT Okay,
19 Edgerton: S+ Bihcau:se uh: she's (0.2) she's feeling a little unduh the
20 weathah:

Notice that although, as a "sequence-closing third", "okay" proposes to end the sequence, Edgerton continues with an account. The point here is that although a sequence-closing third may propose closure, it need not effect this in any given case. In the following instance Nancy is finalizing arrangements with Hyla for a night out they have planned. When Hyla confirms that she'll come about eight, Nancy accepts it with "Okay.".

(20) Hyla–Nancy
22 Nancy: =You'll come abou:t (·) eight.Right?=
23 Hyla: =Yea::h,=
24 Nancy: =Okay.

And in the following case, when an offer of assistance is not accepted, the recipient goes to some lengths to give a rationale for this. When Pat concludes with "=Suh that'll sh'd take a mo:nth,=" the reponse is accepted with "=Okay,".

(21) Houseburning p. 9
21 Penny: → =.hhh[h well I wz g'nnuh-]
22 Pat: [(tuh)]
23 Penny: → if: we c'n help you with the Rover. .hh u::m with the space we
24 have in it.
25 (0.2)
26 Pat: → .t .hh Aww Thank you y-u::m, I (.) don't think we're gonna
27 do anything though unti:l, .hh[hh like fer a mo:nth, entil=
28 Penny: [.tlk!
29 Pat: =we find ou:t- It just doesn't pay t'do anything cz we can't do
30 anything 'ntil we get any (.) money frm the insurance company.
31 Penny: Ri:ght.=
32 Pat: =Suh that'll sh'd take a mo:nth,=
33 Penny: → =Okay,

So according to Schegloff, whereas "oh" is used to receipt some information (as per Heritage's 1984 analysis), "okay" seems to be more concerned with registering and acknowledging some bit of action. With this we can make sense of instances in which the two tokens are combined. In the following case, Ann and Bev are concluding a telephone call by finalizing arrangements for a get-together at Bev's house later in the week. When Ann proposes to call before she comes over to check what she can bring, the proposal is rejected by Bev on the grounds that she "won't be there" to receive the call. Notice that the "informing" character of Bev's turn is first acknowledged with "oh" and then the "rejection" character is acknowledged with "okay".

(22) XTR
36 Ann: I'll call you before then jus to see what I can
37 br[ing an' stuff]
38 Bev: [I won't be:] there [though
39 Ann: [Oh: okay
40 wul what should I bring?

We can use the analysis of the different jobs performed by "oh" and "okay" to make sense of some otherwise rather puzzling cases. For instance, in the following example Dick asks whether Deb's guests are leaving that day. On the surface this appears to be a simple request for information, but when Deb responds with "I don't know" Dick follows not with "oh" but with "okay". In this way Dick can show that what was at stake here was not simply a request for information but a proposal to get together which has been rejected.

(23) YYZ 2 – Deb and Dick

55	Dick:	Are they leaving today?
56	Deb:	I don't know
57	Dick:	O(hh)ka(h)y

Non-minimal post-expansions come in a variety of forms. One kind involves commentary upon the just prior sequence which it thereby expands. Consider again:

(24) US. 24

01	Mike:		Wuhddiyuh doing wh dat big bow-puh-tank.
02			Nothing?
03			(0.5)
04	Vic:		((cough))
05			Uh-h-h
06			(1.0)
07	Vic:		I'm not intuh selling it or giving it. That's it.
08	Mike:		Okay
09			(1.0)
10	Mike:	→	Dat wz simple. Khhhh huh-huh-heh=
11	Vic:	→	=Yeh.

After the request is blocked, the sequence is expanded by a short assessment sequence that involves Mike characterizing the interaction as "simple" and Vic agreeing. Post-expansions can, of course, be considerably more complicated. Schegloff (2007) notes that post-expansions include cases in which a recipient other-initiates repair of the base second pair part, topicalizes it, or challenges it. Example (25) illustrates the first of these possibilities.

(25) NB:1.1:6, 18–27

01	Jon:	Well I'm s:↑ure we c'get on et San Juan ↑Hi:lls	
02		↑that's ni:ce course ah only played it ↑o:nce.	←F_1
03	Guy:	°Uh huh?°	
04		(0.6)	
05	Guy:	.hhh °↑It's not↑ too bad,°	←S_1
06		(0.4)	
07	Jon:	Hu:h?	←OIR, post-expansion
08	Guy:	'S not too ba:d,	←repair
09		(.)	
10	Jon:	No:.	

Here Jon has recommended San Juan Hills by assessing it as a "nice course". Guy's responsive second assessment is delayed and downgraded and thereby suggests he does not fully agree. This is the second pair part of an adjacency pair and it is targeted for repair initiation by Jon in line 07 – a post-expansion.

The following fragment from the call between siblings Joyce and Stan shows a more elaborate post-expansion sequence.

(26) Joyce and Stan

25	Joyce:		B-he wanted one like an a:ll one color like
26			an engli:sh style.<So I got'im an all navy
27			[blue one.
28	Stan:		[Oh.
29	Stan:	A→	·hhhh Well where can I find something like
30		A→	that. Jess. I mean a good hat. yihknow I don't
31			care paying ten dolla:rs er so °er even more.
32			[Yihknow a good ha:t, [something that would look-
33	Joyce?:		[(pt) [((sigh))
34	Stan:		something tha'I'd- u:[I'd have a variety 'a
35	Joyce:		[Why don't
36	Stan:		things ta loo:k at[:,
37	Joyce:	B→	[Why don'tchoo: go into Westwoo:d,
38			(0.4)
38		B→	and go to Bullocks.
39			(1.2)
40	Stan:	C→	Bullocks? ya mean that one right u:m
41			(1.1)
42		C→	tch! (.) right by thee: u:m (.) whazit the plaza?
43		C→	theatre:: =
44	Joyce:	D→	=Uh huh,
45			(0.4)
46	Stan:		°(memf::)
47	Joyce:		°Yeah,
48	Stan:	E→	Why that Bullocks. Is there something about it?
49	Joyce:	F→	They have some pretty nice things. an' you could
50		F→	probly f[ind one you like(d) there,
51	Stan:		[(·hh ·hh)
52			(1.5)
53	Stan:	G→	Well I mean uh: do they have a good selection of hats?
54	Joyce:	H→	I on't know I n(h)ever l(h)ooked f(h)er hhats.
55	Stan:	I→	O[:h (I)
56	Joyce:		[you're ask(h)[ing me and I (jus-)

In this example, Stan's "well where can I get something like that" at lines 29–30 is a question soliciting a recommendation. This is significantly elaborated in subsequent talk by the same speaker. At lines 37–8 Janice responds with a recommendation to "go into Westwood and go to Bullocks" (see Heritage and Sefi 1992 on the formatting of "advising"-turns). There follows a series of post-expansions. Stan first initiates repair with "ya mean that one right u:m tch! (.) right by thee: u:m (.) whazit the plaza? theatre:: =". He then questions the rationale for recommending this particular store with "Why that Bullocks" at line 48. He pursues this further at line 53, saying "Well I mean uh: do they have a good selection of hats?" It is worth noting that each of these expansions consists of a question and an answer, and the last includes also a sequence-closing third, "oh", at line 55.

Conclusion

In this chapter we've seen how sequences are expanded beyond the adjacency pair. The recursive possibility of one sequence occurring before, within and after another results in a vast variety of actual sequences. Of course the *possibilities* are logically infinite even if *in practice* people tend to speak in relatively recurrent ways, the result being recurrent patterns of sequence organization. And of course there are limits imposed on the proliferation of sequences by virtue of other aspects of conversational organization. For instance, the proliferation of insert sequences can come into conflict with the preference for contiguity and the general principle of progressivity (discussed in the last chapter). Insertions of this kind not only generate inferences but also threaten to derail a course of action underway.

Notes

1 Showing that this is, in fact, the case would take us too far afield (see Schegloff 2007).
2 There is also something about the intonation of this turn, which "jokingly" echoes Pyatt's preceding turns, that suggests that it is a pre-announcement rather than a genuine request for information.

7
Repair

The examples we've considered in previous chapters provide ample evidence of the fact that when people talk together they frequently encounter problems of hearing, speaking and understanding. Troubles of speaking arise, for instance, when a speaker uses the wrong word or cannot find the exact word they want. Troubles of hearing arise when a hearer cannot make out what the speaker has said. Troubles of understanding arise within a wide variety of circumstances, such as when the hearer does not recognize a particular word used, does not know who or what is being talked about, or cannot parse the grammatical structure of an utterance. When conversationalists encounter such troubles they have recourse to a "repair mechanism". For example, if a speaker says that they are going to have a siesta, someone might respond by saying "a what?". The first speaker could then repair the reference either by repeating some portion of the original utterance (e.g. "a siesta") or by substituting another word (e.g. "a nap").

"Repair", then, refers to an organized set of practices through which participants in conversation are able to address and potentially resolve such problems of speaking, hearing or understanding. Episodes of repair are composed of parts (Schegloff 1997a, 2000b, Schegloff, Jefferson and Sacks 1977). A repair initiation marks a "possible disjunction with the immediately preceding talk", while a repair outcome results in either a "solution or abandonment of the problem" (Schegloff 2000: 207). That problem, the particular segment of talk to which the repair is addressed, is called the trouble source or sometimes the repairable. The trouble source must be distinguished from the source or basis of trouble, which can be anything from ambient noise or failing hearing to an esoteric word choice.

Repair can be *initiated* either by the speaker of the repairable item or by the recipient/hearer. Likewise the repair itself can be done by either the speaker of the trouble source or someone else. In describing the organization of repair it is usual to use the term "self" for the speaker of the trouble source and "other" for any other participant. Thus, we can talk about cases of self-initiated self-repair (see 1 below), other-initiated self-repair (see 2 below), self-initiated other-repair and other-initiated self-repair etc. In the following examples of recorded conversation, the arrow labeled (a) indicates the position of the repairable item or "trouble source", the arrow labeled (b) indicates the position of the repair initiator, and the arrow labeled (c) indicates the position of the repair or correction.

(1) Self-initiated self-repair (YYZ.5.1:22–6, 24)

Bev: Okay wul listen ((smile voice))
.hh (.) >Are=you gonna be at my house at what time on
a,b,c→ uh Fri:- on Sund[ay?
Ann: [What time am I (.) to be there at.
Bev: I think a little before se:ven.=

(2) Other-initiated self-repair (NB:1.1:6,18–27)

Jon: Well I'm s:↑ure we c'get on et San Juan ↑Hi:lls ↑that's
ni:ce course ah only played it ↑o:nce.
Guy: °Uh huh?°
(0.6)
Guy: a→ .hhh °↑It's not↑ too bad,°
(0.4)
Jon: b→ Hu:h?
Guy: c→ 'S not too ba:d,
(.)
Jon: No:.

These examples illustrate a number of important features of the repair mechanism. First, they illustrate the different ways in which repair is initiated. When repair is initiated by the speaker of the repairable item, initiation is typically indicated by perturbations, hitches and cut-offs in the talk (in (1), notice the lengthening of the vowel in "Fri:-" and the cut-off sound indicated by a dash).[1] Such repairs are routinely done in the same turn as the trouble source or in the transition space which directly follows the possible completion of that turn (the exception of third-turn repair is in fact not so exceptional as it may at first seem; see Schegloff 1997b). In other-initiated repair (such as in (2)), repair typically generates a small sequence. In example (2), repair is initiated in the turn directly following the trouble source ("It's not too bad"), and the repair itself follows in the turn after that. The repair as a whole constitutes a sequence inserted between the assessment at line 05 ("It's not too bad") and the response to it at line 10. When repair is other-initiated, this is typically done in the turn following that which contains the trouble source, by one of several available next-turn repair-initiators (NTRI).

The repair mechanism plays a vital role in the maintenance of intersubjectivity. As we've seen, in conversation, speakers address themselves to the talk contained in immediately preceding turns, and more specifically in the most immediately preceding turn (Heritage 1984b). In formulating their talk in this way, speakers can reveal to the co-participants understandings of the previous turn which the latter find problematic. Such misunderstandings can then prompt the initiation of repair in "third position", as in the examples below (see Schegloff 1992).

(3) Third-position repair – from Schegloff 1992.

Annie: Which one:s are closed, an' which ones are open.
Zebrach: Most of 'em. This, this, [this, this ((pointing))
Annie: → [I 'on't mean on the
→ shelters, I mean on the roads.
Zebrach: Oh!
(0.8)
Zebrach: Closed, those're the ones you wanna know about,
Annie: Mm[hm
Zebrach: [Broadway . . .

Here, in the turn at line 02, Zebrach displays an understanding of Annie's inquiry in responding to it. Annie surmises that there has been a misunderstanding of her talk in line 01 (what is at issue specifically, it seems, is the interpretation of "which ones"). In line 03, Annie repairs the problem and the course of action underway is then re-engaged on the basis of the new understanding which Annie's correction provides for.

The following case comes from interaction among 5-year-old children. Sasha and Robin are playing with plastic animal figurines, trapping them periodically under a plastic basket which they have decided is a jail. At line 01 Robin has trapped a gorilla figurine that Sasha had been playing with under the basket. When Robin declares at line 04, "He'll never see his mother and father again" he apparently means to refer to the now trapped figurine with "He" and several others arranged in front of him with "father" and "mother". After Sasha responds with "That's not- (0.2) his father.", Robin pursues the matter of how the figurine in the pretend jail is related to the others, first asking "is it 'is mother", and subsequently "wha' is it,". Sasha's responses to Robin's questions at lines 12 and 16 indicate that he has not properly understood what Robin is asking, and this leads to third-position repair, first at line 20 and then again at line 23.

(4) KIDS 11_05(1of1)T1.mov @17.10
01 Sasha: hahehe
02 Robin: hi- hee:[:.
03 Sasha: [heh.
04 Robin: He'll never see his mother and father again_=
05 Sasha: That's not- (0.2) his father.
06 (0.4)
07 Robin: padon,
08 (0.2)
09 Sasha: thas not his father.
10 Robin: is it 'is mother,
11 Sasha: no.
12 Robin: wha' is it,
13 (0.6)
14 Sasha: a chi:ld
15 (1.0)
16 Robin: → no de- no: wha i' di:s:,
17 (0.6)
18 Sasha: a gorilla:
19 (0.2)
20 Robin: → no. no what is it to him.
21 Sasha: monkey.
22 (0.8)
23 Robin: → no is it- is it (.) somethin- part of his family,
24 Sasha: yup.
25 Robin: what is it.
26 Sasha: a kid. Part of the family.
27 Robin: khis mother?
28 Sasha: no. his kid.

In this way, the repair mechanism operates to sustain an intersubjectivity that is the basis of any collaboratively built course of action (see Schegloff 1992a). So, given that speakers display in a current turn their understanding of a previous one, repair operates as a kind of "self-righting" mechanism where those displayed understandings turn out to be *mis*understandings (Schegloff, Jefferson and Sacks 1977). As Schegloff (1991a: 158) notes: "The ordinary sequential organization of conversation thus provides for displays of mutual understanding and problems therein, one running basis for the cultivation and grounding of intersubjectivity."

The Preference for Self-Repair

One of the central findings of early work on repair concerned the preference for self-correction. Schegloff, Jefferson and Sacks (1977) noted a "strong empirical skewing" which resulted in the vastly more common occurrence of self- over other-repair, more specifically, self-correction over other-correction. One purpose of the 1977 paper was to describe "an organization, operative in local environments and on a case-by-case basis, which cumulatively produced the aggregate orderliness of repair phenomena" (Schegloff, Jefferson and Sacks 1977: 374), including the bias toward self-correction. So what local organizations result in the vastly more common occurrence of self-repair and self-correction? First, the authors show that positions for self-correction precede positions for other-correction across a repair-opportunity space, and that not only are these positions ordered relative to one another but, further, the ordering is "organizationally designed". So the organization which produces the skewing of the aggregate in the direction of self-correction is seen in the positioning of other-initiation relative to the trouble-source turn.

Recall that the turn-taking system confers to the current speaker the right and obligation to produce a single TCU, that is, to talk to a first point of possible completion at which point transition to a next speaker may but need not occur. Because a trouble source or repairable typically occurs *within* a TCU, a current speaker has the first opportunity to both initiate and execute repair.[2] And of course, other initiations of repair routinely occur in one position: next turn. Indeed, according to Schegloff, Jefferson and Sacks (1977), other-initiations are routinely withheld a bit past the possible completion of the turn containing the repairable item. So withholding not only causes other initiations to be positioned in next turn, it can further cause "next turn" to be itself delayed slightly. The authors conclude from this that "in such cases, other initiations occur after a slight gap, the gap evidencing a withhold beyond the completion of the trouble-source turn – providing an 'extra' opportunity, in an expanded transition space, for speaker of trouble source to self-initiate repair" (Schegloff, Jefferson and Sacks 1977: 374). The second "local" organizational feature that results in a bias towards self-correction is found in the fact that others typically only *initiate* repair, leaving it up to the speaker of the trouble source to produce a repair or correction. Moreover, where other-corrections *do* occur, they are routinely modulated by, for instance, "I think" – further testament to their dispreferred status. A final piece of evidence relating to the dispreferred status of other-correction is found in the fact that unmodulated other-corrections are often treated by the participants as constituting, or at least as preliminary to, disagreement. Indeed, as we will see, even other-initiation can function as the harbinger of disagreement.

Thus, several strands of evidence converge to suggest the operation of a preference for self-correction in adult conversation. Indeed, the basic rule in conversation appears to be: correct only when required for understanding. Since other-correction entails a certain level of understanding, opportunities for its occurrence are rare. Schegloff, Jefferson and Sacks (1977: 380) write:

> When the hearing/understanding of a turn is adequate to the production of a correction by "other", it is adequate to allow production of a sequentially appropriate next turn. Under that circumstance, the turn's recipient ("other") should produce the next turn, not the correction (and, overwhelmingly, that is what is done). Therein lies another basis for the empirical paucity of other-corrections: those who could do them do a sequentially appropriate next turn instead.

The necessary and sufficient conditions for doing a correction are thus essentially the same as those for doing a sequentially appropriate next utterance which will advance the action already underway. Other-correction thus involves an, in some sense, *unnecessary* digression from the current course of action and, for this reason, invites inspection by the co-participants for what else, in addition to setting things right, it might be doing, e.g. instructing, admonishing (see Jefferson 1987 and below).

Self-repair

All repair involves a break, however small, in the continuity and progress of the talk underway and a digression from the action that that talk otherwise implements. A central question concerns how recipients are able to parse talk which is self-repaired. How, that is, do recipients know that what follows is not the next bit of what was, up to this point, in progress, but rather a correction or repair of what has already been said (or attempted). Relatedly, how do recipients know when the speaker has completed the repair and returned to what was in progress before repair was initiated? Given that all this happens in real time, in the course of people speaking to one another and without recourse to a time-out to "fix things", examined from either a cognitive (Levelt 1989) or an interactional perspective, self-repair is no mean feat.

Self-repair is made possible by the existence of what may be usefully termed a "technology" of repair. This technology consists of practices for marking the onset and completion of repair, for locating the repairable item(s) and for performing some operation upon them.

In English, self-repair is most commonly initiated by a cut-off that interrupts the talk-in-progress and resembles, phonetically, a glottal stop. In other cases, self-repair is initiated by an elongated sound or some other peculiarity of articulation. In some cases no initiation is observable. Self-repair is typically initiated in the same turn as the trouble source; however, exactly where in that turn self-repair is initiated is a matter of considerable variability. As many of the examples in this chapter illustrate, a particularly common place for the initiation of self-repair is directly after the first syllable of the repairable item (e.g. "on Fri:-" in example (1)). Self-repair may also be initiated after the possible completion of a turn, in the transition space, as in example (5) where "thought about this" is replaced by "done about this".

(5) As it happens. Feb 11.05.mov QT:7.56
01 A: is asking the president ↑questions.
02 Q: °hh but- uh wha- [so what has the
03 A: [crazy
04 Q: rest of the press gallery:
05 (.)
06 → thought about this.uh done about this.

Initiation marks the onset of repair. What Schegloff (2004) describes as "framing" is a technology for locating the repairable item via a repetition of some part of the prior talk. The frame can be a piece of the talk which precedes or follows the trouble source. The former results in "pre-framing", the latter in "post-framing". In (6), for instance, A replaces "has" with "works for . . .". The repair is pre-framed by repetition of "that".

(6) As it happens. Feb 11.05.mov QT:15.45

01	A:		Well I can't say that everybody gets a
02			question.°hh look. nobody's-nobody's
03			pa:ssed over: in favor of me. you know
04		→	that has- that works for a larger news
05			service that's got you know (.) better
06			credentials:, that's nonsense.

In line 06 of (7), "thought" is, as we saw, replaced by "done". Here the repair is post-framed by the repetition of "about this.".

(7) As it happens. Feb 11.05.mov QT:7.56

01	A:		is asking the president ↑questions.
02	Q:		°hh but- uh wha- [so what has the
03	A:		[crazy
04	Q:		rest of the press gallery:
05			(.)
06		→	thought about this.uh done about this.

Self-repair can operate on the prior talk in various ways. For instance, the repair can involve a replacement of one item by another. In (8), for instance, "on Friday" is replaced by "on Sunday".

(8) YYZ.5.1:22–6, 24

22	B:	Okay wul listen ((smile voice))
23		.hh (.) >Are=you gonna be at my house at what time on
24		ah Fri:- on Sund[ay?
25	A:	[What time am I (.) to be there at.
26	B:	I think a little before se:ven.=

In (9), "stu-" is on the way to becoming "students" but this is abandoned and replaced with "lawyers" (notice the pre-framing by "to the").

(9) Sounds like Canada – Iacobucci 20/4/05

01	FI:	→	As I used to say to the stu- to the lawyers in
02			the justice department. when I was there,
03			(.)
04			you can't get a better client than the people
05			of Canada.

Alternatively, self-repair can involve the insertion of an item (or items) into the prior talk. In (10), for example, the interviewer is apparently on the way to asking "Can you tell us who she is?". However, the final sound of "she" is cut off and the turn is repaired by an insertion of "you think".[3]

(10) Metro-Morning_Gillespie_April05
01 I: Can you tell us who she- who you think
02 she i:s, do you think she is a witness to:
03 sexual abuse,

An item can also be deleted from prior talk via the operation of self-repair. In the following example, Bee's self-repair serves to delete the almost completed production of "also" from her emergent turn-at-talk.

(11) TG 9: 32–9
32 Ava: =M[mm.
33 Bee: → [tuh go en try the:re. Because I als- I tried Barnes
34 'n Nobles 'n, (0.6) they didn' have any'ing they don' have
35 any art books she tol' me,

Another kind of operation performed by self-repair involves a reordering of words or phrases in the prior talk. In (12), for example, the interviewer employs self-repair to reorder the words "always" and "get".

(12) As it happens. Feb 11.05.mov QT:15.45
01 A: if you: watch any of the briefings you'll
02 see that am usually one of the last
03 people to get called on,
04 Q: → But do you get alwa-do you always get
05 called on?
06 A: not always, no.

So far we have seen self-repair operating on words and phrases to effect deletions, insertions, replacements and reorderings. A question arises as to what kinds of things besides words get repaired. Can intonation and stress, for instance, also be self-repaired? The following example (13) involves a phenomenon Stivers (2005) characterizes as a modified repeat. Thus, in line 04, the interviewer is objecting to the suggestion embedded in "we need to deal with this an' get on with it" that the issue she wants to discuss is less important than others. By stressing the "is" in "this is an important issue to a lot of people" the interviewer marks her position as in opposition to that of the interviewee. After the interviewee agrees, she begins to repeat the interviewer's words (replacing "this" with "it"). She twice starts her turn with a contracted form of the copula but these starts are abandoned and she eventually produces her turn with a fully formed and heavily stressed "is". Stivers's analysis (2005) suggests that a claim to epistemic rights is at issue here. Specifically, modified repeats which involve stressing and "un-contracting" an auxiliary or copular verb appear to be a practice for confirming something that a previous speaker has just said and thus for claiming primary epistemic rights to the thing being talked about.[4]

(13) As it happens
01 F: [the thing ( )
02 S: =we need to deal with this an' get on with [it.
03 F: [(yih)
04 F: this is an important issue to a lot of people.
05 S: → ah-ah I agree. it's a-it's-it is an important issue.
06 S: but there are many other important issues that we
07 S: must address as well.

This last example points to some of the interactional import of self-repair. In many cases it is extremely difficult if not impossible to say with any certainty *why* a speaker repairs her own talk. Many instances of self-repair involve alterations that add very little to what was said and do not appear to be necessary in terms of correcting something that was problematic or mistaken. However, in other cases it is possible to describe some of the interactional import of self-repair. One way to go about this is to begin by looking at local interactional environments in which self-repair is particularly common (Schegloff 1979b: 270–2). For instance, Schegloff (1987) and C. Goodwin (1980, 1981) have examined self-repair at turn beginnings.

Self-repair involves a break in the current course of action in order to return to and repair some prior bit of talk. The range of things upon which self-repair can operate is extremely broad and includes single words, phrases, whole turns, intonational contours and the placement of stress. Each self-repair necessarily involves the use of some technology for locating the repairable item (e.g. framing) and some operation which it accomplishes. Although the practices may *appear* humble and the phenomenon haphazard and unworthy of serious study, it is clear that self-repair plays an absolutely crucial role in the production of coherent stretches of talk and coordinated courses of action. Moreover, careful examination of actual instances of self-repair shows it to be, in fact, far from simple. On the contrary, self-repair is made possible by an extremely sophisticated ability to parse the emerging structure of utterances and to attend to multiple, simultaneous courses of conduct in interaction.

Other-Initiated Repair

So far we have considered self-initiated, same-turn self-repair (SISTSR). I now turn to consider other-initiated self-repair. As noted at the start of this chapter, whereas same-turn self-repair is contained within turns-at-talk, other-initiated repair engenders a sequence. As Schegloff, Jefferson and Sacks (1977: 377) note, this means that in "other-initiation, the operations of locating the repairable and supplying a candidate repair are separated. The techniques for other-initiation are techniques for locating the trouble-source."

Formats for the other-initiation of repair

Every language for which there is adequate documentation appears to have a set of devices used to initiate repair by some participant other than the one who produced the trouble source. For the sake of convenience, I refer to these as next-turn repair-initiators, despite the fact that work by Wong (2000) and Schegloff (2000b) suggests that positioning in next turn is a contingent outcome rather than a defining attribute.

The major forms of other-initiation have a "natural ordering" based on their relative power to locate a repairable (Schegloff et al. 1977: 369). At one end of the scale, open-class initiators such as "what?" and "huh?" indicate only that a recipient has detected some trouble in the previous turn and do not locate any particular repairable component *within* that turn. Question words such as "who?", "where?" and "when?" are more specific in that they indicate what part of speech is repairable. The power of such question words to locate some specific item in a previous turn is increased when framed by a repeat of some portion of that turn (e.g. "the what?"). Repair may also be initiated by a repeat without any question word.

Open class → Wh-word → Repeat + Wh-word → Repeat → Understanding check

WEAKER ——————————————————————→ STRONGER

Figure 7.1 The typology of other-initiation forms

Finally, repair may be initiated by "y'mean" plus a possible understanding of the prior turn. The typology of forms is represented in figure 7.1.

Schegloff et al. (1977: 369) note that "there are, of course, additional construction types for other-initiation". Specialized formats for the other-initiation of repair may be tied to features of a particular speech-exchange system.[5] For instance, in inquiry testimony, a witness sometimes initiates repair on the prior turn by saying that they "do not understand the question" as in example 14.

(14) Sponsorship – 20126 qt 25:55
01 Lawyer: So m-my-my (.) submission to you Monsieur Guité,
02 is the following.
03 (1.4)
04 that amount of $17 million had to have an
05 "encrage" of some sort in- in April of 1996 so
06 there must have been (.) dra:fts of a list
07 already ah: in existence in April of 1996.
08 (0.4)
09 totaling $17 million.
10 Witness: → No I-I don't understand your question.
11 (3.0)
12 Lawyer: On April 22nd, (0.2) 1996 there is a submission
13 signed by ((continues))

Here, at line 10, the witness responds to the lawyer by saying that he does not understand the question.[6] The lawyer then repairs the problem by re-asking the question in modified form (at lines 12–13 and continuing). Another kind of evidence for this analysis of witnesses' claims to not understand the question is provided in example (15). Here, after the lawyer completes the question, the witness first remarks that he does not understand the question and subsequently initiates repair by proffering a candidate understanding. The witness thus appears to be moving from a less to a more specific repair initiator.

(15) Sponsorship – 20458 qt. 23:40
01 Lawyer: uh but how did you actually look at these
02 amounts, how did your department analyze these
03 amounts (.) with a view to determine whether they
04 would give the amounts solicited, less, or even
05 perhaps more?
06 (0.8)
07 How was that process working?
08 Witness: → I-I don't- I don't understand your question. if-
09 How we evaluated the- the proposal?
10 Lawyer: Yes. [in terms] of dollars. (.) [to be granted.
11 Witness: [.hh ehm] my- [my staff- my
12 staff would talk to the agency

There are doubtless other "construction types" (i.e. formats). However, in what follows, I focus on the basic formats included in the typology depicted in figure 7.1.

A basic question that arises in the analysis of other-initiated repair, one of sufficient generality to be appropriately termed *the other-initiated repair problem*, can be put as follows: how is the speaker of the trouble source able to determine what *kind* of problem (hearing, problematic formulation, recognition) a given open-class repair initiator is meant to target and, relatedly, what kind of repair (repeat, reformulation or word substitution, alternate word) will fix the problem (see Jefferson 1972)?

Open-Class Repair Initiators

The most common formats for the other-initiation of repair are those we call "open class" following Drew (1997). These are repair initiators that indicate that there is a problem with the prior turn but do not locate some particular item as the trouble source. In English "what?", "huh?", "sorry?" and "pardon (me)?" are examples. It is sometimes supposed that use of such an initiator necessarily indicates a problem of hearing. Examples such as (16) lend support to such a view:

(16) Ex. 12 TG page 16
19 Bee: He asn' been there sih-since Christmas [so:. hHe's going.
20 Ava: [Mm.
21 (0.5)
22 Ava: Yeh w'l I'll give you a call then tomorrow.when I get in
23 'r sumn.
24 (0.5)
25 Bee: Wha:t,
26 Ava: <I'll give yih call tomo[rrow.]
27 Bee: [Yeh:] 'n[I'll be ho:me t'mor]row.
28 Ava: [When I-I get home.] I

Here, at line 22 Ava promises to give Bee a call "tomorrow" when she gets in. After a delay, Bee initiates repair with "Wha:t," and Ava then repeats the first portion of her talk (the second part is repeated after Bee's response). Repeats like this suggest that the participants themselves understand the trouble to have resulted from a problem of hearing (Schegloff 1997b: 507). Example (17) provides further evidence: here the occurrence of an overlap in the initial saying of the trouble source may provide the speaker with an additional warrant for supposing that the problem results from a failure to hear.

(17) Ex. 7 NB:I:1
36 Jon: Awright,h en ↑Biffer[d's the:re too:.
37 (Guy): [(a-)
38 Guy: → e:h?
39 Jon: ↑Bifferd is the:re too.
40 (0.4)
41 Guy: Oh izth'e?
42 Jon: Yihknow Al Bifferd?
43 Guy: Ye:ah?
44 Jon: He lives there too eez gotta place down'ere too:.=

Notice that the first solution offered here is a repeat which is clearly responsive to problems of hearing. It is only after this receives the lukewarm uptake of "Oh izth'e?" at line 41 that Jon addresses another possible source of trouble, i.e. that Guy does not know "Bifferd". In other cases only a portion of the trouble-source turn is repeated in response to the initiation of repair.[7]

(18) Debbie and Shelley 5:35–40
35 Debbie: [.hhh
36 Shelley: [you were at the halloween thing.
37 Debbie: → huh?
38 Shelley: the halloween p[arty
39 Debbie: [ri:ght.

(19) NB:I:1
22 Guy: Is Cliff dow:n by any chance?=diyuh -°know°?
23 (0.3)
24 Jon: Ha:h?
25 Guy: I:ss uh: Bro:wn down-e?
26 (.)
27 Jon: Yeah he's do:wn,

In (19), after a delay, Jon initiates repair of the turn at line 22, Guy does not produce a verbatim repeat. Rather, he substitutes for "Cliff" an alternate name – "Brown". This suggests that Guy understands the problem to have resulted not from inadequate hearing but rather from the use of a name which is unfamiliar to the recipient.[8] The following examples, (20) and (21), again from inquiry testimony, feature use of the open class repair initiator "pardon?" or "pardon me?". Here again the repair involves reformulation rather than repetition of the trouble source.

(20) Sponsorship – 20401 qt 9:09
01 Witness: I think when that happened it was out of the uhm:
02 the sponsorship budget if I [recall correctly.
03 Lawyer: [You- you stuck it
04 in the sponsorship.
05 (0.2)
06 b[udget?
07 Witness: → [Pardon?
08 Lawyer: You- you- you: deci:ded in '96 (.) to place these
09 (.) purchases in thee sponsorship account correct?
10 Witness: It's the only place I could place it

Here, after the witness initiates repair with "pardon?" in line 07, the lawyer produces a repair which is not an exact repeat of what he initially said. One important difference is that while in the first version the lawyer describes the witness as having "stuck" something in the "sponsorship budget", in the second he is said to have "placed" it there. The first version, with "stuck", implies that this did not actually belong in the sponsorship budget and was only put there as a matter of convenience. In contrast, "placing" something in the sponsorship budget implies forethought, care and deliberation.[9] Here, then, the repair initiator prompts a significant reformulation of the action being described. In his response to the initiation of repair, the lawyer displays an orientation to a possible problem with his talk which is not the product of a failure to hear. This example and others like it suggest that open class repair initiators invite the speaker of the trouble-source to monitor their prior talk not necessarily for something that was not heard but, more generally, for something potentially problematic from the recipient's point of view.

This would go some way to explaining why open class (and other) repair initiators frequently precede disaffiliative and/or disagreeing responses. Consider the following example, also from inquiry testimony.

(21) Walkerton – qt. W1:24.31

Lawyer: An'-an'- just I'm not gonna ta:ke you through it but-
uh- although thee-thee budget of the Ministry increased
substantially you would also agree with me that the
pro::grams performed by the Ministry an' the statutory
mandate of the Ministry, also increased substantially
.hh during the period nineteen eighty five [.h °( ) and
Witness: [It could have.
Lawyer: → following°. Pardon me?
Witness: It could have.
Lawyer: You don't know that
Witness: ah no, I wasn't in government from eighty-five to ninety
-five
Lawyer: But you were in opposition,
Witness: Yes.

Here at lines 21–6 the lawyer is working through a document which shows that the budget for the Ministry of the Environment increased substantially over time. The lawyer is concerned to have the witness confirm that the mandate of the Ministry also increased during this time and in various ways suggests that this fact is well established. First, he begins by saying that he does not intend to take the witness "through it", thereby conveying that although documentation is available its contents are a matter of common knowledge. Second, the lawyer does not employ an interrogative frame here but rather asserts that "you would agree with me . . .". Although this can be heard as a B-event requesting confirmation, it is much more tilted towards assertion than the comparable question "would you agree with me . . .". (On the design of questions in this context see Sidnell 2010a.)

At line 27, the witness responds with a less than confirming, "it could have.". The response here conveys, by implicature, that the witness is unsure about the facts in this case. The lawyer completes the question turn (with "and following") in overlap with the witness and subsequently initiates repair of the answer. "Pardon me?" elicits a repeat from the witness, and the implicature it generates (that the witness does not *know* the facts being reviewed) is subsequently challenged at line 30. So here the provision of a repeat treats the repair-initiator as conveying a problem of hearing. However, in the talk that follows, the lawyer indicates that this was in fact not the problem.

Consider now the following example (22) from a telephone conversation between two older men. Guy has called John to ask if he'd like to play golf. After John agrees, the issue of where they will play is dealt with in a series of three proposal sequences, this being the last. The prior two possibilities have been rejected more or less jointly and here Jon suggests that San Juan Hills might be a possibility. At lines 18–19, he recommends it by suggesting that, first, it should be possible to "get on" there, second, it's a "nice course", and third, he has only "played it once.". Guy registers the recommendation with "uh huh" at line 20 and, after a significant delay, produces an assessment which is a significant downgrade of Jon's "it's a nice course". As Pomerantz (1984) showed, second assessments which are equivalent or downgraded in relation to a first are regularly heard as embodying disagreement. "It's not too bad" not only disagrees with Jon's assessment of the course, but also projects a rejection of the proposal to play there.[10] It is in this context of emerging disalignment that we find Jon initiating repair with "hu:h?" in line 24.

(22) NB:I:1 – Example 3
18 Jon: Well I'm s:↑ure we c'get on et San Juan ↑Hi:lls ↑that's
19 ni:ce course ah only played it ↑o:nce.
20 Guy: °Uh huh?°
21 (0.6)
22 Guy: .hhh °↑It's not↑ too bad,°
23 (0.4)
24 Jon: Hu:h?
25 Guy: 'S not too ba:d,
26 (.)
27 Jon: No:.

Here the "hu:h?" is produced after a slightly longer than normal delay and perhaps invites Guy to monitor his talk for something problematic. Guy, however, does not withdraw the downgraded assessment. Instead, he repeats it, treating the issue as a problem of hearing and maintaining his stance on the course. Jon, however, treats Guy's "'s not too ba:d," as if it *were* a positive assessment and agrees with it with "no:.".

Rather than dealing with problems of hearing, then, many open-class repair-initiators seem to deal with problems related to the "action relevance" or "action implication" of some bit of talk. Consider in this respect the following examples from a telephone conversation between friends Pyatt and Bush. The first example comes from the opening of the call. Here, at line 06, Pyatt asks Bush "D'you know where Mister Bowdwin is.". As we saw in chapter 6, questions such as this are ambiguous: they can be heard either as "real" requests for information or as pre-tellings. Notice then that this gets dealt with, initially, through the use of an open-class repair-initiator. The response to this (laughter at line 10) reveals *another* action implication of the talk. Pyatt is apparently "joking around" by using a series of person-referring/address forms ("Mister Bush", "Mister Fiatt", "Mister Bowdwin") that are not only parallel but more "formal" than is warranted by the relationship.

(23) Pyatt and Bush TC II(b):#28 – example 1
01 Bush: Hello¿
02 Pyatt: .h m- Mister Bush,
03 Bush: Yes.
04 Pyatt: Mister Pyatt.
05 Bush: Yes,
06 Pyatt: D'Yknow where Mister Bowdwin is.
07 (0.2)
08 Bush: Wha:t?
09 (·)

Pyatt: hhuh-hhuh-°hu-° [·hhh
Bush: [Do I know where who?
Pyatt: Leo is.
Bush: No.
Pyatt: Oh. Okay.
(0.2)
Bush: He's down in Mexico or some'in¿
Pyatt: I don't know,
Bush: Oh:. Yer lookin' for him.

In the second example taken from the same call (24), Pyatt, with his "well I guess . . . Well I guess I'll jus sit back an wait for somebody to call me and tell me", is resigning himself to the fact that he will not be able to locate Leo. This triggers for him a complaint: why should he be able to locate Leo? His first attempt to convey this in line 33 is marked as a complaint by the inclusion of "Hell", but causes difficulty for Bush, who initiates repair at line 35. The problem, it seems, is that this "Hell I don't know what desert he's in" challenges the presumption of the question to which it was originally produced as a response (whether Pyatt actually said this or simply thought it we cannot tell). As a report to Bush it is a complaint about being asked a question which holds Pyatt accountable for knowing Leo's whereabouts. The repair at lines 36–7 makes this context available to Bush.

(24) Pyatt and Bush TC II(b):#28
Bush: I sure haven't seen Leo but- (1.0) I was gonna call him
yesterday an tell him to come over here.=
Pyatt: =Yeh.
(0.2)
Pyatt: Well I guess I'll jus sit back an wait for
somebody to call me and tell me [that-
Bush: [Yeah he'll probably
call you [(in the)
Pyatt: [Hell I don't know what desert he's in,
(0.5)
Bush: Huh?
Pyatt: u- u- I don't know. He says "diyou know where he might
be." Well- (0.2) I don't know what desert he's in.
Bush: Yeah,
Pyatt: I don't whether he went to S::- to the Sahara desert,
the Mohave, the-
Bush: eh heh

In both cases the open-class repair-initiation is used where there is some problem in understanding what action a speaker means to accomplish in talking in the way he does. In the first example that ambiguity cuts three ways between real question, pre-telling and joke (which perhaps accounts for the double repair initiation). In the second example, Pyatt has not provided Bush with the context necessary to see that what Bush is saying is a complaint about a question he was asked.

It has been noted that "pardon (me)?" and "excuse me?" are apology-based open-class repair initiators and thus appear to be "polite" versions of "what?" and "huh?". Robinson

(2006: 137) suggests that the distinction here is implicated in the negotiation of responsibility for the trouble to which the repair initiator responds. Specifically, Robinson argues that, while "context-free structures of interaction bias practices of repair such that other-initiated repair is vulnerable to communicating a stance that responsibility for trouble belongs to the speaker of the talk that inspired repair initiation", the apology-based format conveys that "responsibility belongs to repair-initiators, rather than to their addressees."

Class-Specific Question Words Used to Initiate Repair

Class-specific question words such as "who?", "where?" and "when?" may be used to initiate repair. Unlike "what?" (which is not class-specific and thus belongs with other open-class repair-initiators), these initiation formats identify a particular kind of item in the prior talk as in need of repair. Due to recurrent problems encountered in making recognitional reference to persons, "who?" is likely the most common of these. Consider the following example from the opening of a telephone call.

(25) NB:I:1
01 Mrs: 'Ello:?
02 Guy: 'Ello is Curly there?
03 (.)
04 Mrs: Oo jis (.) e-Who:?
05 Guy: Johnny?h An[sin?]
06 Mrs: [Oo j]ist↑a minnih,

When Guy asks for "Curly", Mrs. seems initially prepared to respond but subsequently initiates repair with "Who?". This is effected by the provision of an alternate name in line 05. In the following case, Bee announces that "Sibbie's sistuh" had her baby.

(26) TG page 19
01 Bee: Oh Sibbie's sistuh hadda ba:by bo:way.
02 Ava: Who¿
03 Bee: Sibbie's sister.
04 Ava: Oh really?
05 Bee: Myeah,
06 Ava: [°(That's nice.)/[°(Sibbie's sistuh.)
07 Bee: [She had it yestihday. Ten:: pou:nds.
08 Ava: °Je:sus Christ.

Bee's "Sibbie's sistuh" is produced with a noticeable derhoticization of the final syllable (indicated in the transcription by *sistuh* rather that *sister*). Ava's "Who¿" indicates trouble in finding a referent for this form while at the same time conveying that she has heard that a person-reference has been produced. Bee treats the problem as one resulting from insufficiently precise pronunciation and repeats the form – now with a fully rhotic final syllable – in the next turn. Ava's response in 04 to the news of the baby's arrival embodies a claim to have recognized the person being talked about. Consider, by way of contrast, the following case:[11]

(27) Holt 1:8
01 Leslie: And um .t (0.4) an' Janet's enga:ged?
02 (0.7)
03 Mum: Who:?
04 (0.3)
05 Leslie: Sa:rah's sister Janet.
06 Mum: ^Good gra:cious!

Here, Leslie's news announcement is produced in such a way as to suggest she thinks Mum should be able to recognize "Janet", indeed that "Janet" is someone about whom Mum should be updated with respect to important events such as marriages. Mum's delay in responding, in combination with the "who:?" she eventually produces, suggests that she has been engaged in a search for the person being referred to by "Janet". The evidence of a search provided by Mum's delay in initiating repair leads Leslie to figure that Mum's problem results not from mishearing but rather from a failure to locate a referent on the basis of the form used, and it is to *this* problem that the repair, "Sarah's sister Janet.", is addressed. With her self-admonishing "Good gra:cious!", Mum suggests that she should have been able to get the reference in the first place and thereby confirms the appropriateness of Leslie's initial selection of "Janet".

We can see then that the selection of a repair-type conveys the repairer's own sense of what trouble afflicts the talk (Schegloff 1997b: 507). Moreover, in attempting to determine what kind of repair (replacement by an alternative expression, repeat, etc.) will resolve the trouble in any particular case, speakers take into account not only the form used to initiate repair ("Who?", "Who's that?", etc.) but also the circumstances in which problems have arisen, as well as the evidence provided by the manner in which repair is initiated (e.g. after a significant delay).

Repetition With and Without a Question Word

As noted above, "what?" does not function as a class-specific question word in other-initiated repair in the same way as "who", "when" and "where" do. One of the things these class-specific question words do in other-initiated repair is identify a particular term or word as the repairable. But the unavailability of "what" leaves a hole here. In the case of problematic person, place and time references, repair may be initiated by the appropriate question word, but this accounts for only a small proportion of the things people talk about. A question arises as to how repair is initiated when these other kinds of references are found, by their recipients, to be problematic. One possibility is illustrated by (28):

(28) Virginia page 15
01 Mom: ·hhh ^Well that's something else. (0.3) ^I don't think that
02 you should be going to the parties that Beth goe:s to. She is
03 eighteen years old.An' you are fou:rtee:n, da[rlin'.
04 Virginia: [I KNOW::, BUT
05 A:LL THE REST OF MY: PEOPLE MY AGE ARE GWAFFS.I promise.they
06 are si:[ck.
07 Mom: → [They're what?

(.)
Virginia: → GWAFFS.
???: ( )
Prudence?: What's a gwaff.
(3.1)
Virginia: Gwaff is jus' someb'dy who's really (1.1) I just- ehh! ·hh
s- immature.>You don't wanna hang around people like tha:t.<

Here Virginia describes "all the rest of" the people her age as "gwaffs", and at line 7 Mom initiates repair of this term using a combination of repetition and "what?". Here the partial repeat of Virginia's turn frames the wh-word and thus locates, within the prior talk, the particular place where the repairable item occurred, i.e. directly after "are" in "people my age are gwaffs.". By framing "What?" with a repeat, Mom prevents this from being heard as an open-class repair initiator and instead targets a particular word as in need of repair. Note that the trouble here appears to result from the use of a word unfamiliar to the recipient. Although Virginia offers only a repeat of "gwaff" and in that sense does not solve Mom's problem, notice that she does not take "They're what?" to be targeting "they're sick", which is, after all, the most proximate possible trouble source. Thus Virginia can apparently see that it is her use of an unfamiliar word which has caused a problem (and see the talk at lines 11–14).

Sacks notes that what we get in cases like this is "the repetition of phrase plus the use of 'what' at the point where some not-heard or not-understood word occurs, as a way of locating for the person who has just spoken what part of what they said you didn't hear or didn't understand" (Sacks 1995a: 723). Sacks goes on to ask if it's the case that "any word" can be "asked for" in this manner or if perhaps it's the case that "only some sorts of words are ever asked for in that way?" So, for instance, it would seem that nouns and verbs are targeted in this way but prepositions and conjunctions are not. Sacks asks "Does that mean conjunctions are really easy to hear or easy to understand? Or does it mean perhaps, if you didn't hear them but you hear the rest, you can figure out what they were?" (Sacks 1995a: 724). Sacks is suggesting then that some words more than others are inferred as much as actually heard. Indeed, this, he suggests, is true for whole phrases such as "excuse me" which is regularly produced as little more than "sk'm", or something to that effect, without thereby presenting any problem of hearing. Sacks concludes on this point that "a great deal of what is said is not pronounced in radio English, but in such a way as to signal 'the thing that goes here has just been said' " (Sacks 1995a: 724). So the larger point here is that whether a word is heard properly depends not simply, and perhaps not even primarily, on how it was articulated or pronounced, but on what context is provided for it by the surrounding talk. Sacks gives a rather striking example to illustrate this in which the Group Therapy participants are questioning newcomer Jim (see chapter 4 in which we considered the introduction sequence that precedes the fragment to be considered here; the entire transcript can be found in Sacks 1995a: 268–80). There's been a series of questions relating to how Jim has come to be placed in Group Therapy. These are listed as, for instance, "first of all you must be crazy or you wouldn't be here.", "Secondly, you must be an under-achiever.", "Fourth you like to drive fast cars." There've been ten questions in all and to each of them, with one exception, Jim has responded with confirmation. Then comes the following:

(29) Group Therapy Session 2:2:70 (transcript revised from Sacks, Schegloff and Jefferson 1974: 708 and original audio)[12]

01 Roger: Are you just agreeing because you feel you wanna uh
02 Jim: Hm?
03 Roger: You just agreeing?
04 (0.4)
05 Jim: What the hell's that.
06 Al: It's- Agree[ing?
07 Roger: [Agreeing.
08 Jim: Agree::n.
09 Roger: Yeah
10 ( ): A[gree:n
11 Al: [With us. Just going' along with us.
12 Jim: No.
13 (0.4)
14 Roger: Saying 'yes, yes' [hehheh hh hehhh hh hehheh hh
15 Jim [Well, i-i-it's=it's true.
16 Everything he sai(h)d is true, so

Sacks asks why Jim is unable to hear this word "agreeing" for what it is despite the fact that it presents no difficulty to the other participants. He suggests that part of the problem may come from the prior context, which has, as it were, primed him to hear this as "a green". Notice then that Jim's response at line 05 suggests that he initially hears this as an unfamiliar word. We can imagine him supposing it is an "in group" term in use among these guys or, perhaps, that it is a technical term associated with group therapy. This would fit with what has gone before in a number of ways. First, in terms of the design of the turn itself, "Are you just a green?" exhibits a structure parallel to the earlier question "you must be an underachiever" and the later question "you a hood?" (see Sacks 1995a: 276). In these cases the turn is composed of a question beginning plus a noun which is a "category term" ("underachiever", "hood" are categories of persons). Second, in a more general way, these guys have been asking questions about who Jim is and not, until now, about what he is doing. Indeed, the question that Roger asks at line 01 represents a significant shift in the activity from "just questioning" to now "interpreting" Jim's behavior and specifically his answers to those questions. And finally, as Sacks notes (1995a: 268), "the core of this . . . segment . . . constitutes an 'initiation ceremony' " and "there are . . . features in it which the literature on initiation ceremonies proposes to be present in such events." Now if Jim can recognize this as an initiation ceremony of sorts he may well expect it to involve, among other things, an introduction to the mysteries of the group, including its esoteric terms, of which "green" is possibly one.[13] Let us also just register that, in the context in which he currently finds himself, Jim *is* "green" in the sense of being, as the *Oxford English Dictionary* has it, "Immature, raw, untrained, inexperienced".[14] It is not until Al provides a paraphrase in line 11 that Jim is able to figure out what is being said.

So, if it's true that much of what we hear is actually inferred from the context, an example like this suggests that that context includes not just the immediately preceding and following words but also the larger sequential context in which some bit of talk occurs. Sacks (1995a: 728) concludes: "what we see is that the very determination of what it is that somebody said in a given utterance, i.e. hearing what they said, may turn on an analysis of other things that have been said, perhaps by others, before that."

Returning to our discussion of different formats used in the other-initiation of repair, we should note that cases like (26), which are produced with rising intonation, are quite distinct from those that are produced with falling or final intonation. Example (30) is taken from a recording of 5-year-old children. Cathy has just closed the door and has returned to the table where the other two children are playing. When Anne says "maybe you can move it," she is apparently talking about a jacket that is hanging on the door handle and preventing the door from staying fully closed.

(30) KIDS_11_24_05(2of2)T7.mov @11:33
01 Anne: ((looks at door)) Maybe Cathy, maybe you can move **it**,
02 Cathy: → °Move what.°
03 Anne: Move that thing that('s in the lock)/(yo- in the door).
04 Cathy: Okay.

Example (31) is from the beginning of a telephone call. Notice that there is no identification by name (see chapter 10) here and the identification assumed at line 07 turns out to be wrong.

(31) From Schegloff 1979- p.45
01 Al: Hello?
02 Bob: Hello?
03 Al: Hi.
04 Bob: Hi, Howaryou.
05 Al: Okay, Howaryou.
06 Bob: I'm just fine thank you.
07 Al: Did you get the note? (CALLED)
08 (.)
09 Bob: → What note. (CALLER)
10 (0.6)
11 Al: Oh (this is) Gary,
12 (0.2)
13 Bob: Yeah,
14 Al: Oh I'm sorry.
15 Bob: ( ) that's okay.

Notice then that whereas Mom's question-intoned "They're what?" in example (28) queried the meaning of a specific word, Cathy's "move what." and Bob's "what note." indicate trouble not with the *meaning* of a word but rather with *finding a referent* for a word whose meaning is perfectly transparent. Expressions such as "the note" at line 07 of example (31) and "it" at line 01 of example (30) presuppose already established referents that speakers assume their recipients should be able to identify and this is exactly what these downwardly intoned repair initiators mark as problematic. Notice then that in (31), Al's assumption that his recipient will know what it is he is talking about is based on a misidentification which is revealed precisely by the fact that Bob cannot retrieve the referent for "the note".

Repeats without question words similarly target specific items in the prior talk as in need of repair (see the discussion in chapter 2). The following example is taken from the Group Therapy Sessions (see Jefferson 1987: 86).

(32) GTS:III:42(r)ST
01 Ken: Hey (.) the first ti:me they stopped me from selling
02 cigarettes was this morning.
03 (1.0)
04 Lou: From selling cigarettes?
05 Ken: Or buying cigarettes.

Lou's partial repeat targets a misspeaking by Ken and prompts the correction at line 05. Consider also the following case from a telephone conversation between mother and daughter:

(33) YYZ((Telephone rings))
01 A: What do you want me to pick up?
02 B: Nothi:ng but I want to know how you boil an egg.
03 (1.0)
04 (h)hard boil.
05 A: Oh oka::y and I just read this you know
06 because I always let the water boil but
07 you're not supposed to (.hh) put it in and
08 you (.hh) bring it to a boil (.) but then
09 turn it down 'cause you're really not
10 supposed to boil the e::gg
11 (0.4)
12 you let it (.) uh simmer or you know on me:dium,
13 B: Ri:ght
14 A: fo:r [t w] elve minutes.
15 B: [((sniff))]
16 B: → Twelve minutes?
17 A: Well I always do it faster than th(h)at (hh)
18 B: okay=
19 A: =I just boil the shit out of it [but]
20 B: [How]
21 do you know when it's done?

Here Betty's repeat of "twelve minutes" prompts Amy to significantly modify what she is saying. Thus whereas she begins at lines 05–10 by reporting what she has *read* about what one is *supposed* to do, in response to the repeat, she tells Betty what *she* actually does. The next example (34) again comes from inquiry testimony. Here the witness has been asked why he did not include particular information in an answer he gave earlier. He first responds by saying that he gave an answer "based on that time.". At line 51, the lawyer initiates repair by repeating the words "based on that time" and thereby marking them as problematic.[15] The witness hears this as a challenge to the adequacy of the answer and goes on, at lines 52–4, to recharacterize his answer as "fairly good". At lines 61–3, responding to another question, the witness explains that "it didn't come to mind". Once again the lawyer initiates repair by repeating the expression.

(34) Sponsorship –
44 Witness: Monsieur Fournier, what I did at the time is I gave an
45 answer: (.) based on-on
46 (0.2)
47 that time.

48 (0.2)
49 I can't say any more.
50 (0.8)
51 Lawyer: → Based on that time.
52 Witness: Well (.) I gave a fairly good answer, I think, and I did
53 include (.) th–th-thee quote unquote political influence
54 in the policy decisions. [ah::
55 Lawyer: [Not at the time, you did not.
56 Witness: No. (.) I know. An' I di:d last week apparently, and ( ) –
57 it's fine an' I would not change my mind.
58 (4.0)
59 Lawyer: An' I take it you cannot explain why you didn't gi:ve
60 the politi[cal influence at the time
61 Witness: [No. It probably, at the ti:me (.) uh: didn't come
62 to mi:nd t-t-to mention that area, that's is the only
63 explanation I can [give.
43 Lawyer: → [It didn't come to mind.
44 Witness: No.
45 Lawyer: Would you not consider that to be:: (.) somewhat
46 important in-in answering the question why was there
47 no price competition?

Claiming that something "didn't come to mind" of course carries the implication that it is not very important and it is exactly this implication that the lawyer challenges in his follow-up question. We can see then that the use of repetition to initiate repair often involves one speaker challenging the adequacy, accuracy or plausibility of what another has said in the prior (repeated) talk. Example (35), from a sexual assault case, provides even more compelling evidence. Here the lawyer, cross-examining the plaintiff, first establishes that, during the assault, neither party made any noise. The lawyer's follow-up question contains the characterization "you were doing it so quietly". Not only does this co-implicate the witness in an act which she claims was done *to* her, it also formulates her as intentionally, "quiet". Rather than confirm the lawyer's conclusion, the witness initiates repair with a repeat of the problematic expression followed by a claim to not understand.

(35) Chmura trial
01 Lawyer: and (.) when he was on the grou::nd. with you.
02 and he got up, he made no noise and you made no
03 noise.
04 Witness: no noise.
05 Lawyer: correct?
06 Witness: yes.
07 Lawyer: So thet if somebody was standin' right outside
08 the door listenin to you two move, (0.2) you
09 were doing it so quietly they wouldna heard
10 it right?
11 (2.5)
12 Witness: → we were doin' it so quietly we wouldn'av heard
13 I- I'm not sure -I'm following you [here
14 Lawyer: [didju get up
15 fast?

A final example well illustrates the special way in which a repeat may cast prior talk as problematic and in need of modification. This is taken from the reality television show *The Apprentice* in which contestants vie for a job with Donald Trump. At the end of each episode members of the losing side are required to come back to the boardroom to explain why they lost the task and to otherwise account for their actions. The fragment is taken from an episode in which teams were asked to sell candy bars on the street. At one point, one of the contestants, Ivana, pulled down her pants in order to attract customers and potentially sell more candy bars. In the fragment, taken from the boardroom portion of the show, Ivana is being questioned by Trump and his two aides (George and Caroline) about this action.

(36) The Apprentice: Boardroom
01 Trump: Ivana. (.) you flash:edt (0.4) a group of
02 people.=
03 Ivana: =look (.) [this]
04 Trump: [>no no no<] did that happen?
05 Ivana: it happened? but it happened for a reason.
06 Trump: wh:y.
07 Ivana: because I knew,- okay we had gone through
08 a lot of product (>we [only had<)]
09 Trump: [what does] flash mean.
10 you ripped down your pants? [what does that mean]
11 Ivana: [I was wearing-]
12 I was wearing a bikini
13 (0.4)
14 a:n- an let's not blow this out of proportion, (.)
15 <I was wearing bikini shorts .hh I wear
16 Caroline: we [haven=t] said anything yet [so: relax]
17 Ivana: [more>] [>I know (.) I know<]
18 I'm just really defensive a[bout this because]
19 Trump: [go ahead I'd like to hear at]
20 Ivana: um=
21 Trump: =but you did flash
22 Ivana: I did, (.) but it was a gimmick. (.) it was a gimmick,
23 just like [(girls)]
24 Trump: [did it work?]
25 (0.3)
26 Ivana: → it did work (.) [I sold a candybar for twenty bucks]
27 Trump: [(oh=rilly), but you're on the losing team]
28 (0.8)
29 George: → you sold a <u>ca:</u>ndybar for twenty dollars?
30 Ivana: hhhh look=
31 Caroline: =I would stop addressing him by look (.) it's not
32 [really professional]
33 (George): [(professional) I don't mind]
34 Ivana: [I'm sorry I'm sorry] I'm sorry
35 (0.5)
36 Trump: whose idea was it that you flashed
37 (1.0)
38 Ivana: it was- it was my idea it was my- it was my decision,=
39 Trump: =are you happy about it?

40 Ivana: u:m
41 (0.7)
42 you know thinking back I probably shouldn't't'ave done it
43 but at the time, (0.3) .hh I thought it was a good idea
44 because I knew we haddar- (.) raise our average selling
45 price=
46 Caroline: →→=but you weren't selling a candy bar.
47 (0.6)
48 →→wouldn't you agree <you were not selling a candy bar.>

The fragment begins with Donald Trump complaining that Ivana flashed a group of people. Ivana subsequently confirms this at line 05 and attempts to excuse the action, concluding at line 22 that it was a "gimmick". This prompts Trump to ask, "Did it work?" at line 24 and Ivana then answers that it did, accounting for her answer by saying "I sold a candy bar for twenty bucks." This utterance is targeted for repair by George's repeat at line 29. By initiating repair using a repeat, George suggests that there is something amiss in what Ivana has said and by marking the word "candybar" with special emphasis, he indicates that it is this word in particular that is problematic. Moreover, by maintaining the lexical and syntactic frame of Ivana's utterance ("You sold an X for twenty bucks") George not only highlights specific words within the turn, he also shows that he accepts part of what she has said. Indeed, George seems to be suggesting that Ivana sold something *else* for twenty bucks (see example (30) for a parallel case). Further evidence for this analysis is furnished by the talk at lines 46–8. Here, Caroline asks Ivana, "wouldn't you agree that you were not selling a candybar."[16]

Offering a Candidate

In other-initiated repair it is not uncommon for the one initiating repair to offer a candidate repair either in combination with another repair initiator or on its own as an understanding check. Example (37) illustrates the first possibility.

(37) Deb and Dick
13 Deb: [the pool] is kind of yucky but what can I say.
14 Dick: What. (0.2) The pool?
15 Deb: Yeah.
16 Dick: O[h]
17 Deb: [b] ut so's the Wymer's too so I think it was just the
18 -uhm -the rain an everything.
19 Dick: ( ) rain yeah mhm
20 Deb: yeah
21 Dick: Oh that's too ba[d]
22 Deb: [s]o don't you have all your family coming
23 today.

Here Dick has apparently encountered some trouble figuring out what it is Deb wants to describe as "yucky" and first initiates repair with a downwardly intoned "what." (see Schegloff 1997b). When this does not elicit an immediate response from Deb, resulting in a 0.2-second pause, Dick offers a candidate with "the pool?". This is then confirmed by Deb in line 15 and the sequence continues. In the next example, there is some confusion about the referent of "out there" at line 18. Repair is eventually initiated with the candidate understanding check, "oh, out here?" at line 25 and confirmed at line 26.

(38) Ex. 2. Pyatt and Bush TC II(b):#28 – example 2

Pyatt:		So I thought maybe he mighta come by and got a key
		from you for the desert er somethin, I don't know. what
		[the (hey)
Bush:		[No¿
		(0.4)
Pyatt:		He didn't come by en get one fr'm m:e.=I don't know w-
Bush:		D'ju you go out there last weekend?
Pyatt:		No_
		(0.2)
Bush:		Oh. I thought you were.=
Pyatt:		=I was going to. <I w's gonna go out there this weekend
		too but uh
Bush:		-heh hihih
		(1.0)
Pyatt:		I'jus c- c-can't get going aheheh
		(0.2)
Bush:		Oh you didn- you didn hear thuh the news didju.=
		=We were out there before Thanksgiving.
		(.)
Pyatt:		Oh, you were?
Bush:		Yeah
		(0.6)
Bush:		Were we?
		(1.0)
Pyatt:	→	Oh, out here?
Bush:		Yeah.=
Pyatt:		=Yeah. Yeah. Right. Right.=
Bush:		=Yeah. Annie's gonna have a baby.
Pyatt:		Oh really?
Bush:		Yeah.
Pyatt:		↓We:ll: congratulations.
Bush:		's'nat some'in. I [didn't think you- she's]=
Pyatt:		[Annie's gonna have a baby.]
Bush:		=she was keeping it all a secret until Thanksgiving.

Offering a candidate thus provides a way for recipients to check their understanding of a previous turn. That understanding may then be accepted or rejected in next turn.

Repair as a Vehicle for Action

Jefferson (1987: 88) suggests that: "In the course of the business of correcting we can find such attendant activities as e.g. 'instructing', 'complaining', 'admitting', 'forgiving', . . . 'accusing', 'apologizing', 'ridiculing', etc. That is, the business of correcting can be a matter of, not merely putting things to rights, . . . but of specifically addressing lapses in competence and/or conduct." The following provides a particularly clear illustration:

(39) [GJ: FN]
01 Pat: . . . the Black Muslims are certainly more provocative
02 than the Black Muslims ever were.
03 Jo: The Black Panthers.
04 Pat: The Black Panthers. What'd I
05 Jo: You said the Black Muslims twice.
06 Pat: Did I really?
07 Jo: Yes you di:d, but that's alright I forgive you,

Here we find that following the correction of a lapse, Jo "forgives" Pat. Consider also the following examples from inquiry testimony:

(40) Sponsorship – trans19899
01 L: uhm:
02 (0.4)
03 you will note at the top, thee: uhm fif:t (.)
04 uhm: inscription from the top (.) ah pertains to:
05 → a meeting on February, (.) uh twenty fifth nineteen
06 ninety six, (.) which would have been he:ld at uh le
07 Club Saint-Denis,
08 W: → twenty fift o' April.
09 L: twenty fift o' April, I'm sorry nineteen ninety six. .hh
10 (.) which you would have attended.

(41) Sponsorship – trans19975 qt:14:00 [Guite.day2.viii.(19966).mp3]
01 W: No, no,I knew when I was uh i-in public service that
02 he was doing some work with Mister Corriveau on exhibit
03 design.
04 (1.4)
05 L: → with Mister: (.) Lemay, you mean.=
06 W: =yes uh sorry Mister Lemay yeah.

Here in both examples a current speaker corrects a prior speaker. The correction is subsequently accepted by the original speaker and an apology – "I'm sorry" – for the error is offered.

In the paper already cited, Jefferson goes on to distinguish instances of what she calls *exposed* correction (such as in (39), (40), (41)) from those which she describes as *embedded*. Consider the following:

(42) GTS:II:60:ST
01 Ken: Well- if you're gonna race, the police have
02 said this to us.
03 Rog: That makes it even better. The challenge of
04 running from the cops!
05 Ken: The cops say if you wanna race, uh go out at
four or five in the morning on the freeway . . .

Here we have an initial reference term "police" (X) and an alternate reference term "cops" (Y) which is subsequently adopted by the first speaker. The pattern is thus: X, Y, Y. Precisely the same pattern is observable in examples (39), (40) and (41) – an initial term X (Black Muslims, February 25th, Mr. Corriveau) is corrected by another Y (Black Panthers, 25th of April, Mr. Lemay), and this is subsequently adopted by the first speaker. In (42), however, the correction and replacement is embedded and does not come to occupy a separate, digressive sequence of its own. Jefferson (1987: 95) remarks that when the correction is exposed "whatever has been going on prior to the offering of a correction is discontinued", whereas when it is embedded "the talk in progress continues." She notes further that, in the latter case, "the utterances are not occupied by the doing of correcting, but by whatever talk is in progress . . . correction occurs, but is not what is being done, interactionally. What we have, then is *embedded correction* as a by-the-way occurrence in some ongoing course of talk." Moreover, Jefferson (1987: 95) points out, while with exposed correction "we find attendant activities . . . , which specifically address lapses in competence and/or conduct, embedded correction has no place for such attendant activities . . . It might be said then, that 'embedded correction' is a means by which correction, and only correction, occurs in contrast to activities recognizable as 'correctings' which permit not only of correction," but other attendant activities as well.

A clear example of such attendant activities is seen in cases where repair is a vehicle for the expression of disagreement or disalignment more generally (see e.g. Drew 1997, M. H. Goodwin 1983). Egbert (1997) shows that other-initiated repair may serve as an entry or exit device to or from a conversation, and further that repair is often implicated in transformations of the participation framework in conversation in such a way that a single conversation becomes two simultaneous conversations. In an early paper, Jefferson (1974) showed that an error-correction format could be used to display self-monitoring (as when a speaker replaces a word such as "cop" with one such as "police officer" within the course of a single turn).

The extreme flexibility of the repair device and its potential to serve as a vehicle for a wide array of actions is, in part, a result of its omnirelevance and scope of application. In the first case, repair is always potentially relevant in conversation (Sacks 1995). It has been pointed out that, because repair is always a potentially relevant next action, continuers (mhm, uh huh) serve to pass the opportunity to initiate repair, thus acquiring the character of "acknowledgement tokens" (Gardner 2001, Schegloff 1982). Secondly, it appears that nothing in the talk is, in principle, excludable from the class of potential repairables. Thus, repair-initiators may "make" trouble just as they may locate it.

Conclusion

This chapter has only scratched the surface of an extremely generative topic within conversation analysis. As Schegloff (1992a) argued, an examination of the domain of repair in conversation leads immediately into central problems of social theory – most obviously, how it is that individuals come to know (or assume they know) a world in common. This "problem of intersubjectivity" is, arguably, the most basic problem of the social and human sciences:

> the problematics of intersubjectivity are anterior to most of the problems that sociological and social theory have treated as primary and fundamental, such as the so-called Hobbesian problem of order or the underlying engines of large-scale social change. Most simply put, without systematic provision for a world known and held in common by some collectivity of persons, one has not a misunderstood world, but no conjoint reality at all. That is, the problem of intersubjectivity (or cognitive order) is theoretically anterior to whatever formulations of problems of order or conflict are part of the tradition of social theory. Absent intersubjectivity, the terms of any social theory – whether they refer to interests or values, persons or roles, authority or power – by definition cannot name anything oriented to or effective with any regularity or commonality, for there could not be any common recognition of them. (Schegloff 1992a: 1296)

Whereas mainstream social scientists have typically attempted to solve the "problem of intersubjectivity" by positing some "common culture" through which the individual's grasp of reality is mediated, conversation analysts have discovered in the organization of conversation a "procedural" means by which intersubjectivity is established and maintained. Intersubjectivity is maintained, incarnately, in the sequential organization of turns-at-talk, each subsequent turn, necessarily, displaying its speaker's understanding of a previous one (see Heritage 1984b). This is done *en passant*, in the course of whatever action is being implemented by the talk, as a by-product "of bits of talk designed in the first instance to do some action such as agreeing, answering, assessing, responding, requesting, and so on" (Schegloff 1992a: 1300). Where a current speaker anticipates a problem of understanding, she can attempt to avoid it by means of same-turn self-repair, modifying the talk in its course so as to make its intended sense available to the recipient. Where a recipient is unable to arrive at an adequate understanding of a previous turn, she may initiate repair in next turn, employing the set of practices described as other-initiated repair. And, finally, where a recipient's next turn reveals a misunderstanding of the previous one, the speaker of a first turn may initiate repair in third position.[17] Thus, the sequential organization of talk provides not only for the ongoing display of understanding but also, through the operation of repair, for its defense where it is threatened.

Intersubjectivity, then, is not secured through the internalization of norms as is suggested by conventional social theory. Instead, it is built into the very fabric of social conduct (see also Wootton 1997).

> The achievement and maintenance of this sort of intersubjectivity is not treated in a theoretically satisfactory manner by invoking socialization as a mechanism, for intersubjectivity is achieved for a virtually inexhaustible range of types of events always contextually specified, for which no "distal" or "remote" socialization could provide. The solution surely is provided for by a resource that is itself built into the fabric of social conduct, into the procedural infrastructure of interaction. . . . [T]his involves a self-righting mechanism built as an integral part of the organization of talk-in-interaction – what has been termed the organization of repair. (Schegloff 1992a: 1299)

Repair then is a procedural, party-administered, locally managed, recipient-designed means by which understanding in talk is accomplished, maintained, and defended within the sequential contexts of talk-in-interaction (Schegloff 1992a: 1338).

Notes

1 It is also common to find hitches that premonitor upcoming trouble in the progress of the talk. In example (1), for instance, note the "uh" in "on uh Fri:-".

2 There are two obvious exceptions to this. First, a trouble-source may occur at possible completion as the last item in the TCU. Second, a trouble source may occupy more than one TCU in which case it does not occur *within* the TCU but across multiples thereof. Jeff Robinson (personal communication) offers the following cases to illustrate the second of these exceptions:

(43) MTRAc.90.2.33 [rev]
01 MAR: Hello:?
02 SUE: Hi.
03 MAR: Hi.
04 (.)
05 SUE: (Guess/Giss) wha:t.
06 MAR: What.
07 (.)
08 1→ SUE: °I have a low fever again. an' my eyeballs
09 1→ 're yellow.°
10 (1.0)
11 2→ MAR: Wha:t?
12 3→ SUE: I have a low fever again. an' my eyeba:lls
13 are yellow. hh ((laugh))
14 MAR: °.hhhhhhhhhhh° ((1.1)) We:ll hhhh
15 SUE: We:ll
16 MAR: I guess you should duh (0.4) cha::rge is (h)'at
17 th(h)uh w(h)ord on over to thee ess aych e:ss.

(44) HOLT:SO.88.II.1.1
01 MAR: He':ll drive to Wes'lands an' then 'e'll (.) tell me what
02 time tuh pick him up in thuh evening.
03 (.)
04 LES: .hhh Oh:.=
05 MAR: =After thuh meeting so that's fi:[ne.]
06 LES: [.hh]h Are you su::re,
07 MAR: Yes. so [I jus'] thought it might be easier
08 LES: [>.hhh<]
09 MAR: I th[ink [( )]
10 1→ LES: [Well [I'll come] with you in thuh evening, shall I:?
11 (.)
12 1→ LES: To pick him up?
13 2→ MAR: >Sorry?<=
14 3→ LES: =.hh Sh'll I come with you in thuh evening to pick him up?
15 MAR: Ooh:: yeah-=I mean I- (0.2) Yes. I think (.) I mean we'll
16 see how busy it is. will you >do you-< (.) is it easy
17 to find from you. I think ( ) quite
18 e:as[y.]
19 LES: [n]=I've never fo:und it. But I expect it is.
20 hh=[heh .hh I]'ll have=a look. .hh uhm: .tch ah is he
21 MAR: [h=hm::]
22 LES: staying for a meal in thuh e:vening?

3 For discussion of such epistemically framed questions and their interactional significance in news interviews see Roth 2002.
4 See Schegloff 2009 for further discussion of prosodic self-repair.
5 The notion of a "speech exchange system" is discussed in Sacks, Schegloff and Jefferson (1974).
6 The sense in which this is a "question" is not immediately obvious in so far as it does not contain any of the formal features associated with questions such as interrogative syntax or so-called question intonation. For discussion of this issue see Sidnell (2010a).
7 Notice also the substitution of "party" for "thing".
8 Of course, it need not be the case that the recipient does not know that name but only that that's not the name they use to refer to that person.
9 And notice that in the second version the lawyer characterizes this as a "decision".
10 On the formulation "too X" and "not too X" see Schegloff 2005.
11 I thank Jeff Robinson for providing me with this example.
12 This fragment is discussed in various places in the literature; see for instance Sacks 1995a: 726, as well as Sacks, Schegloff and Jefferson 1974: 708.
13 On "initiation ceremonies" see especially Van Gennep (1960). "Mysteries" associated with initiation are discussed on pages 89ff.
14 A sense which was certainly in use at the time the recording was made: the OED includes a use of "green" in this sense dating back to 1548! See "green", A.II.8.c, in the *Oxford English Dictionary*, 2nd ed., 1989. OED Online. Oxford University Press. At http://dictionary.oed.com/cgi/entry/50098386, accessed 19 Feb. 2009.
15 In this context repeats with falling or final intonation are regularly heard as initiating repair; see chapter 12 for discussion of some related features of talk in inquiry cross-examination.
16 For further discussion of repetition used in the initiation of repair see Sidnell 2010b, Schegloff 1997b, Robinson 2009, and Robinson and Kevoe-Feldman.
17 Fourth-position repair is also possible; see Schegloff 1992a.

8

Turn Construction

We've seen, in chapter 3, that turns are composed of turn-constructional units. In this chapter we will look inside those TCUs at their composition and design. This is a complex and crucial part of conversation analysis which concerns not only the way turns are constructed but also the ways actions are formed. Unfortunately, unlike the domains of turn-taking, action-sequencing and repair, which are relatively well described, our current understanding of turn construction is quite partial. As a result, our discussion in this chapter will be somewhat schematic and more suggestive than definitive.

Our task in this chapter, then, is to look more specifically at the internal organization and design of turns and the turn-constructional units of which they are composed. We begin by considering different positions within turns, looking in particular at turns composed of multiple-unit TCUs. We will then proceed to consider the ways in which turns-at-talk are products of an interaction between speaker and recipient.

The Anatomy of the Turn

We've seen in chapter 3 that turns are composed of TCUs and that a given turn may contain one or more of these. In their 1974 paper on turn-taking, Sacks, Schegloff and Jefferson noted a recurrent pattern exhibited in many multi-unit turns at talk. They write (1974: 722):

> Turns display gross organizational features that reflect their occurrence in a series. They regularly have a three-part structure: one which addresses the relation of a turn to a prior, one involved with what is occupying the turn, and one which addresses the relation of the turn to a succeeding one. These parts regularly occur in that order, an obviously rational ordering for an organization that latched a turn to the turns on either side of it.

The following is one of their examples:

(1) Sacks, Schegloff and Jefferson 1974: 722
01 D: Jude loves olives.
02 J: That's not bad.
03 D: → She eats them all the time.
04 I understand they're fattening, huh?

Here the first component of the turn "She eats them all the time" relates to the prior talk via the pro-terms "she" and "them". The second component advances the action, formulating an upshot of eating olives, and the third component, the tag "huh?", links to a next turn (selecting a next speaker to confirm "they're fattening"). So this is one common way in which multi-unit turns are constructed. And now consider Guy's turn at lines 10–11.

(2) NB 1.1.
08 Jon: .t.hhh Where d'yuh wanna go:.
09 [- - (0.9) - -]
10 Guy: Oh I d'know,h[hh. hhhhh] Wut about dat SAN JUAN ↑HILLS down
11 'ere. Yuh think we c'get on 'ere?
12 (.)
13 Jon: Ye:s I think so:,

Here the first component responds to the question asked, the second embodies a proposal to play at a particular place and the third makes the immediate relevance of the proposal for Jon explicit: he is being asked to confirm it as a possible place to play.

Notice that through this ordering, components of previous, current and next turns that "belong together" are "kept together" – that is, they are contiguous. Sacks went on to argue that there was a "preference" for contiguity in conversation (Sacks 1987 [1973]). This is seen for instance in the way dispreferred actions are often delivered with a break in contiguity (see chapter 5). It is also seen in cases where a single turn provides for the relevance of more than one subsequent action. Sacks illustrated this with the following example:

(3) Sacks 1987 [1973]: 59–60
01 A: Well that's good uh how is yer arthritis,
02 Yuh still taking shots?
03 B: Yeah. Well it's, it's awright I mean it's uh,
04 it hurts once 'n a while but it's okay.

The first turn here includes two questions: "how is your arthritis?" and "are you still taking shots?" Notice how B responds by first answering the second of A's questions (with "yeah") and only then giving an account of her arthritis. In this way, B's answer preserves the contiguity of the question ("Yuh still taking shots?") and answer ("Yeah") for at least one pair.

Sacks used such examples to show that turns at talk are constructed in a way that reflects their position in a sequence. At the same time, he illustrated that a turn could be broken down into components and the positions these occupy. The constituents of a turn are then organized into "positions". With this in mind we can now consider turn beginnings more specifically.

Turn Beginnings

We can begin with an observation from Schegloff (1996c) that a speaker's talk may start with something *other* than a beginning. Here is one situation in which this is the case:

(4) Sacks's Fall 1971 Lecture 4. *Lectures* vol. II: 437–43.
08 Ben: They must'v had some type of a showing.
09 A camper sho:w or uhm- [flea market
10 Ethel: → [At the great big
11 drive in theater.=

(5) Sacks's Fall 1971 Lecture 4. *Lectures* vol. II: 437–43.
16 Ethel: I mean it slowed up [a:ll, the traffic y' know
17 Ben: [An' there-there wz at least
18 ten mi:les of traffic bumper tuh bumper.
19 Ethel: → because a' that,

In these examples Ben and Ethel have just arrived at the home of Lori and Bill and are telling them about the traffic that they encountered on their way. In (4), Ben proposes a possible reason for the traffic. Ethel's talk here specifies the location where this proposed possible event was taking place. In (5), Ethel adds "because a' that" to Ben's "there was at least ten miles of traffic bumper to bumper.". So in both these examples Ethel produces something that is recognizably a continuation of what Ben has already said. As such, when Ethel starts to speak here she does not produce a turn beginning.

So once we have noticed that a speaker can design her talk as a continuation of what someone else has just said – that is, not as its own TCU but rather as an addition to one already produced – we can go on to register that what makes this recognizable as a continuation is that it does not start with a beginning (see Schegloff 1996 for further discussion). We can then ask, of any bit of talk, does it start with a turn beginning? And we can then, perhaps, go on to describe those beginnings. In another context, Schegloff (1987) has noted that turn beginnings are "sequence-structurally important places in conversation" for at least two reasons. First,

> Turn beginnings are an important initial place, and an important initial resource, for the projection of the turn-shape or the turn-type of the turn that is being begun at that turn beginning. Such projection is a critical resource for the organization of the turn-taking system for conversation. (1987: 71)

Secondly,

> "turn-initial position" . . . is a central place for a variety of sequential markers in conversation – little objects that do a piece of sequential work. . . . A misplacement marker, such as "By the way", is attached to a turn, typically at its beginning, to indicate that the talk that is going to occupy the turn thereby begun is something which has a proper place in conversation, but is about to be done outside its proper place; or, alternatively, that some turn type ought properly to go next, but the turn that is being started is not of that type. (1987: 72)

Heritage (2002: 197) notes in a similar way that:

> Turn beginnings are . . . a prime location for the placement of sequential markers that convey some relation between what the current speaker is about to say and what the previous speaker has just said. Turn components like *well*, *uh*, *but*, *so*, *oh*, and others are all used in this way. For example, turn beginning is the standard position for *well*, *uh*, and other markers used to index

a relationship of dispreference or disaffiliation between the position taken by a previous speaker and the position the current speaker is about to adopt. Similarly prefacing a question with "and" is a resource for conveying that the question to follow is part of a continuing activity initiated previously (Heritage & Sorjonen 1994).

Consider in this light the following fragment of conversation between Jon and Guy and specifically the beginnings of the turns. Guy has called Jon to see if he might want to play golf.

(6) NB 1.1
21 Guy: **Wt's** the name i-San Juan Hi:lls.huh?=
22 Jon: =hUh huh? .hhhh (0.6) I have the Hunningtin Seacli:ff?'n I
23 ha:ve uh.h (.) Shorecli:ffs'n I ha:ve (0.5) Sa[n Clemen[te.
24 Guy: [.hhh [**Hey**
25 ↑**how'bout** sh: 'ow bout She:rcliffs.c'n yih git on nere?
26 (0.7)
27 Jon: .khh I think so they ↑cha:rge too much Gu:[y
28 Guy: [**Oh** doh they?
29 Jon: Yeh ↑I ↓think so:,
30 Guy: **W't** a'they cherge.
31 (0.3)
32 Jon: f:Uh:: I think they cha:rge six ↑dollars ↓on Satur'ees'n Sundees.
33 Guy: °Mm:?°
34 (0.2)
35 Guy: °mWell thet's a° dollar too ↑much.
36 Jon: Ye:ah.hhh [U h :]
37 Guy: [(Fergi]t th[et)
38 Jon: [**How about** Hunningtin ↑Sea↓cli:ffs.

Consider first the turns at lines 21, 30 and 38:

21 Guy: **Wt's** the name i-San Juan Hi:lls.huh?=
30 Guy: **W't** a'they cherge.
38 Jon: **How about** Hunningtin ↑Sea↓cli:ffs.

Each of these begins with a component that strongly projects the kind of turn underway. "Wt's" and "W't" of course project that a so-called wh-question is being initiated whereas "How about . . ." projects a proposal.[1] One piece of evidence that recipients are able to use turn beginnings to project the type of turn underway comes from cases of "recognition point entry" (Jefferson 1983: 18–20) such as the following (see also discussion of "look" prefacing below).

(7) NB:II:3:R:2
01 Emma: How'r [you*:.
02 Lottie: [Oh:-
03 ·hh Oh fi:ne.
04 Emma: Good. Yih got comp'ny,
05 Lottie: Ye:h. Jist a minute. Waya min'.
06 (.)

07 Oh ah'll ((muffled-)) see. ez soon ez I[get dre:ssed.
08 ( ): [Yeah.
09 ( ): ([ )?
10 Lottie: [Nh hn,
11 (.)
12 Okay Ruth, ·hh A'right. (.) Bah bye hon,
13 (0.4)
14 Emma: Well ah: don'wanu ←a
15 (0.3)
16 [If- [y-
17 Lottie: [NO: [it's okay, ←b
18 (.)
19 Lottie No:. (.)
20 Emma: Getcher fam'ly the:re?

This comes near the beginning of a call in which Emma has called her sister Lottie. There are some voices in the background, and by line 04 here Emma has surmised that Lottie "has company". However, it appears that the guests are at this very moment leaving and at line 05 Lottie suspends the conversation with Emma in order to deal with the co-present participants' departure. At line 12, we and Emma can hear that the interaction at Lottie's end of the line has come to a close. Though this would seem to make Lottie available to talk on the phone, Emma begins a turn by which she apparently means to release Lottie from any obligation to talk. And notice that in this environment, the beginning of the turn – "Well Ah: don' wanu" – is sufficient for Lottie to determine where this is going. It is to this that she responds with "no it's okay" in line 17 though Emma subsequently completes the turn with "if- y' getcher fam'ly there?".

So the initial components of a turn can strongly project the type of turn underway. Returning to example (6), compare in this respect the turns at lines 21, 30 and 38 with those at 24, 28, 32 and 33:

24 Guy: **Hey** ↓how'bout sh: 'ow bout She:rcliffs.
28 Guy: **Oh** doh they?
32 Jon: **f:Uh::** I think they cha:rge six ↓dollars
33 Guy: °**Mm:?**° **(.2)** °**mWell** thet's a° dollar too ↓much.

In each of these examples the turn is prefaced by one of those "sequential markers that convey some relation between what the current speaker is about to say and what the previous speaker has just said" (Heritage 2002: 197). This is especially clear in the case of line 24 where, apart from beginning with "hey", the turn is structurally very similar to the turn in line 38 which we considered before. Putting these two turns side by side we can perhaps discern what distinctive work the "hey" is doing:

(8) NB 1.1
21 Guy: Wt's the name i-San Juan Hi:lls.huh?=
22 Jon: =hUh huh? .hhhh (0.6) I have the Hunningtin Seacli:ff?'n I
23 ha:ve uh.h (.) Shorecli:ffs'n I ha:ve (0.5) Sa[n Clemen[te.
24 Guy: → [.hhh [Hey
25 ↑how'bout sh: 'ow bout She:rcliffs.c'n yih git on nere?

(9) NB 1.1

Jon: .khh I think so they ↑cha:rge too much Gu:[y
Guy: [Oh doh they?
Jon: Yeh ↑I ↓think so:,
Guy: W't a'they cherge.
(0.3)
Jon: f:Uh:: I think they cha:rge six ↑dollars ↓on Satur'ees'n Sundees.
Guy: °Mm:?°
(.2)
Guy: °mWell thet's a° dollar too ↑much.
Jon: Ye:ah.hhh [U h :]
Guy: [(Fergi]t th[et)
Jon: → [How about Hunningtin ↑Sea↓cli:ffs.

In (8) Jon has returned from collecting his address book and is reporting on the numbers that he has found there. Notice the way he does this. Specifically, when Jon reports that he has first "Hunningtin Seacli:ff?" and then "Shorecli:ffs:" he does not pause after the name. On the contrary, he moves directly into the *next* item in his list, in both cases jamming "and" (transcribed as 'n) up against the name and, in so doing, blocking a possible transition space that might otherwise have been created (see pp. 48–51). So the way he designs his turn here is relevant to the kind of action he is producing: specifically he is *not* proposing these as places that they might play golf. And further notice where he *does* pause: at places that Schegloff (1998: 241) has described as points of "maximum grammatical control", that is, places where the turn is clearly not complete and thus where transition is not relevant. So it is in this context that Guy produces his "hey". This prefaces a turn that reaches back into what Jon has been saying, recovering from it "Shorecliffs" as something that Jon has "passed over". The "hey" here then is an *alert*, a response cry (Goffman 1978), triggered by something Jon has said.[2]

We can compare this example with the one in (9), where we find another turn beginning with "how about . . ." but now without the "Hey". And notice the very different sequential environment in which this turn occurs. Specifically, in this case, Guy has just agreed with Jon that what they charge at Shorecliffs is "a dollar too much". With this, he not only agrees with Jon's "they charge too much", he also aligns with Jon who has resisted the proposal to play golf at Shorecliffs. Guy withdraws the proposal explicitly with "forget that". So, in this case the proposal – "How about Hunningtin Seacli:ffs" – comes exactly where it should: as the initiation of the next sequence in a "sequence of sequences" (see Schegloff 2007). To summarize then, the comparison of these two turns suggests that the specific work of the "hey" preface is to reach back into a turn so as to recover something "passed over" in what the prior speaker has said. Of course, examination of other cases may support this initial analysis or perhaps provide grounds for an alternate and more general account.

Let's now consider the turn at line 28 – "oh do they?". Here it is again in a bit of context.

(10) NB 1.1

Jon: .khh I think so they ↑cha:rge too much Gu:[y
Guy: [Oh doh they?
Jon: Yeh ↑I ↓think so:,
Guy: W't a'they cherge.
(0.3)
Jon: f:Uh:: I think they cha:rge six ↑dollars ↓on Satur'ees'n Sundees.

In the course of several papers, John Heritage has provided us with a beautifully nuanced picture of this particle "oh". According to Heritage (1984a) its basic and canonical use is to indicate not surprise as is sometimes suggested but rather a "change-of-state" from not-knowing to knowing. An example such as 11 provides a particularly clear case:

(11) YYZ – Washer-Dryer
A: .hh Do you guys have a washer en dry:er er somethi:ng?
(0.6)
S: ah::=yeah, we got a little washer down here (.) °goin'°.
A: o::h. ok. [I didn']- I didn't know thet you guys ha:d tha:t
S: [water]

Here we have a question in line 01 followed by an answer in 03, and following this the questioner produces an "oh". As Heritage elsewhere (1984b) notes, with a question of this sort the speaker "proposes to be ignorant about the substance of the question and . . . projects the intended answerer to be knowledgeable about the matter. Thus the provision of an answer should, in such a context, commit the questioner to have undergone a 'change of state' from ignorance to knowledge." And notice that A conveys that change of state with "o::h." in line 04 before going on to explicitly announce that she has been informed by the answer. With this account of its basic function (as a change-of-state marker) it is possible to make sense of a great many occurrences of "oh" (see also pp. 104–7). Returning to Guy's "oh do they?" we can see that with this he is responding to the news that Shorecliffs charges "too much". Of course by responding with a question he is pushing Jon to specify exactly what he means by "too much", but notice what a difference the "oh" makes in a case like this. Without the "oh", "do they?" would be hearable as not merely requesting elaboration but also possibly challenging Jon, as suggesting that Guy and Jon have a different idea of what is an appropriate amount to pay for an afternoon of golf.[3]

So in this case the "oh"-prefaced turn comes in response to the delivery of news. That positioning turns out to matter a great deal for "oh" and other turn-initial particles (Heritage 1998). Heritage shows, for instance, that "oh"-prefaced turns may also come in response to questions. Such "oh-prefaced responses to inquiry" would seem to go against the "change-of-state" analysis since questions are not, on the surface at least, "informative". However, Heritage shows that in these cases the "change of state" consists not of a shift from not-knowing to knowing but rather of a shift of orientation or awareness. Specifically, the "oh" marks that the question asked about something that the questioner should have already known. Thus the question's recipient is "shifting attention" to something that was presupposed and in the background and thus was not the focus of attention prior to the question being asked. Heritage illustrates with the following case. Here Sir Harold Acton has been talking about teaching poetry at Beijing University.

(12) [Chat Show: Russell Harty–Sir Harold Acton]
Acton: . . . . hhhh and some of thuh– (0.3) some of my students
translated Eliot into Chine::se. I think thuh very
first.
(0.2)
Harty: Did you learn to speak (.) Chine[:se.
Acton: → [.hh Oh yes.
(0.7)
Acton: .hhhh You ca::n't live in thuh country without speaking
thuh lang[uage it's impossible .hhhhh=
Harty: [Not no: cour:se

Heritage writes:

> Given the environment of this question – that Acton taught modern poetry at Beijing University, and that his students were the first to translate T. S. Eliot's work into "Chinese" – it is evident that the interviewer's question is potentially problematic. Acton's "Oh yes." response, uttered with real finality, treats it as obvious that he would have learned the language, and thereby implies that the inquiry questions something that might have been presupposed in virtue of the prior talk.

So we've seen then that the general "change-of-state" meaning of "oh" is particularized according to the sequential context in which it occurs. As the third item in a sequence of question – answer – comment, "oh" clearly conveys that the questioner has been informed by the answer.[4] In response to questions, an oh-prefaced response conveys a shift of attention or focus occasioned by an inapposite or in some sense problematically formulated question (see also Heritage 2002, Heritage and Raymond 2005 for another particularization of "oh", in response to assessments).

Other items that preface turns are similarly particularized. For instance, first position turns prefaced by "look" – alone or in combination with other items – are used to launch new courses of action (Sidnell 2007). In (13), Ilene has called her friend and dog-groomer Lisa and opened the call with an inquiry "How's my madam?". This has led Lisa to give an extended report about the trouble she experienced removing knots from the dog's fur. In the fragment shown below, Ilene's turn at lines 06–07, by virtue of its timing and other aspects of its design, disattends Lisa's laughter and treats the foregoing report sequence as effectively complete. Moreover, Ilene's "look"-prefaced turn not only comes at the possible completion of talk on a topic, it initiates a new action sequence with an offer to come and collect the dog. The resultant arrangement making (involving a decision as to whether Lisa will deliver or Ilene collect the dog) is the apparent official reason for the call which has been diverted within the opening sequence by Lisa's response to Ilene's inquiry "How's my madam?".

(13) Heritage 1–3
01 Ilene: [.hhh
02 Lisa: [Yeh ah I'll tell you I'll give you
03 chapter'n verse,
04 Ilene: Right.
05 Lisa: ↑ehh heh heh[heh he-]hh=
06 Ilene: [Uh : m]
07 Ilene: → =Well now look d'you want me
08 ti[h come over'n get her? or wha:t.
09 Lisa: [°( )°

In the next example Edgerton has phoned Michael. At the completion of the opening sequence Edgerton announces the reason for the call with a "look"-prefaced turn.

(14) Heritage:OII:2:Call 4, 3:9 3:1–12 ((QT 1:01–12))
01 Michael: Woking three five one six?
02 Edgerton: Michael?
03 (.)
04 Michael: Hullo:?
05 Edgerton: This is Edgerton:.

06 Michael: Yes Edger[t ['n.
07 Edgerton: → [.h[Michael look ah::
08 I'm I'm phonin:g uh on
09 beha:lf of Ilene and myse:lf.
10 =We just heard abou:t
11 poor um (0.4) Margaret.
12 Michael: Yes ma:ddening isn't it.=
13 Edgerton: =Oh:hh Lord.< And we were wondering
14 if there's anything we can do to help<
15 Michael: [Well that's]
16 Edgerton: [I mean] can we do any shopping
17 for her or something like tha:t?

So in these examples we see a "look"-prefaced turn in first position launching a new course of action. We can compare this with the use of "look"-prefaced turns in second position, for instance in turns that respond to questions. Here is an example from a radio interview with a politician (Belinda Stranach).

(15) AIH – Belinda Stranach
01 F: is it going to divide your party badly?
02 S: → °hhh look there's division across the country on this issue
03 an' there's division in every par[ty
04 F: [mm-hm

Here the interviewer's yes–no interrogative "is it going to divide your party badly?" establishes the relevance of a type-conforming ("yes" or "no") answer (see Raymond 2003, chapter 5). Stranach, however, does not produce a straightforward, type-conforming answer to the question. Rather, she employs an extreme case formulation, suggesting that division is not a special characteristic of her party but rather of the country as a whole (on "extreme case formulations" see Sacks 1995a: 21–5, Pomerantz 1986, Edwards 2000, Sidnell 2004). In this way she avoids confirming the presupposition embedded in the interviewer's question. Consider also the following example in which Canadian Prime Minister Paul Martin is asked by the interviewer whether he is prepared to defer "corporate tax measures".

(16) As it Happens (25/4/05) Paul Martin
01 Interviewer: °hh wul you seem to be suggesting the door
02 is open and in fact one of your advisors
03 has been quoted today already as saying we
04 are prepared to discuss the possible deferral
05 of the corporate tax measures °hhh is that true
06 (.)
07 are you prepared to defer them
08 PM: → well (.) look. I'm not gonna speculate uhm:
09 beyond the principles that I have set out
10 uhm as I have said to you thet uhm part of that
11 corporate tax cut is small and medium size business
12 which I think is really essential. °hh to
13 ongoing uh job creation an' the strength of the
14 economy.

Here again the type non-conforming response to a YNI is prefaced first by "well" and then by "look". In his response, the Prime Minister refuses to "speculate" beyond the principles he has set out, in this way resisting the trajectory established by the YNI. And in the following case Det.-Sgt. Paul Gillespie is asked whether, by releasing the photo of a young girl, he might be putting her life in danger.

(17) Interview with Gillespie – Metro Morning.April05.aiff

01	Interviewer:		ho-ar-are you not putting her life in danger
02			though? by releasing this picture
03	Gillespie:	a→	°hh well: (y-) lookit let's be honest
04			(.)
05			we certainly have to be cognizant of-of things
06			could ohccur:
07			(.)
08			there certainly could be potential
09			safety issues in almost <u>an</u>ything we do, °hh

Once again the YNI receives a type non-conforming response prefaced by "well" and by "lookit".[5] Although the detective concedes that "we certainly have to be cognizant of-of things that could ohccur:", by going on to say that there "could be potential safety issues in almost anything we do" he suggests that his action in this instance is not remarkable. The extreme case formulation ("almost anything we do") suggests that potential safety issues are not unique to this particular case. Here then we have three examples in which "look" is used to preface a type non-conforming, and essentially evasive, response to a YNI. In so far as a YNI establishes the conditional relevance of a type-conforming "yes" or "no" answer, these responses can be seen to involve a redirection of the talk.

We can see participants' own orientation to the redirecting use of "look"-prefaced turns in second position in the following example from a conversation between a couple in a "long-distance" relationship, Hyla and Rich.

(18) Hyla and Rich p.9_qt7:40

30	Hyla:		Y- yeah well that's the whole thing that doesn't matter tch
31			.hh [we-] well so then (.) .h ah: so then you'll come down <u>he:</u>re.
32	Rich:		[hhh]
33			(.)
34	Rich:		Maybe yea:h.
35			(0.5)
36	Hyla:		t- But m<u>ay</u>be <u>no</u>: ch[heh
37	Rich:	→	[<u>Look</u>
38	Hyla:		Hehe I know I won['t] pin you dow[n (like that.)]
39	Rich:		[I] [I know we]ll <u>I</u> <u>don</u>'t
40			<u>kno</u>w I- it's <u>ok</u>ay.
41			(.)
42	Rich:		I h<u>ope</u> I come down.
43	Hyla:		t. Well yeah but I'm just sa[ying that
44	Rich:		[No question that's the cheapest
45			thing in the world.=
46	Hyla:		<u>Wh</u>at? hehe
47	Rich:		Have the company send me down there.
48	Hyla:		Yea:h.

Earlier in the call Rich has announced that, "Boss told me, h (0.2) that they wanna send me back to Rochester again" and reveals that this may conflict with an already planned rendezvous with Hyla. Rich, however, goes on to say, "I'm sure I could work something in though", and suggests that he may be able to visit Hyla in Los Angeles. After an intervening discussion, Hyla reinvokes Rich's suggestion to the effect that he could come to Los Angeles at line 31 with "ah so you'll come down he:re.". While the "ah"-prefacing marks Hyla's change of state, the "so" suggests that she is here formulating an upshot of what Rich has said (Raymond 2004). Formulating the upshot of another's talk invites their confirmation in next turn and Rich indeed responds in an appropriate though, by qualifying his "yeah" with "maybe", less than confirming way. Hyla's recompletion of Rich's utterance, "But maybe no:", makes the equivocal nature of it explicit and once again makes confirmation or disconfirmation a relevant next action. Rich begins to respond with a turn prefaced by "look" but, hearing only this component, Hyla effectively withdraws the relevance of confirmation which "But maybe no:" had activated, saying "I know I won't pin you down like that.". Here then we see a participant anticipating a course of action different from, indeed at odds with, that established by the conditional relevance of the first pair part *on the sole basis of a "look" preface*, this being the only component of the turn articulated by the time the response is produced.

Let us now consider a quite different way in which turns can begin – with "uhm". "Uhm" and similar non-lexical verbalizations (e.g. "uh" and "ah", what are sometimes described as "fillers") are often thought to reveal the uncertainty or nervousness of the speaker. As conversation analysts we will be concerned with these items not for what they might reveal about the psychology of the individual but rather for what they are being used to accomplish in interaction. In this respect, when they begin turns, items such as "uhm" seem to be doing the rather important job of claiming a turn-at-talk even though the speaker may not yet be able or inclined to produce it. Schegloff (1982: 81) writes:

> as Sacks pointed out years ago, participants sometimes begin a turn by producing an "uhm" just after the possible completion of a prior turn, then pausing, and then producing a turn, rather than just delaying the start of their turn until they are "ready." They may be understood to proceed in this fashion precisely in order first to show their understanding of the current state of the talk and their stance toward it (i.e. "a prior turn is over, it is an appropriate occasion for a next turn. I will produce one"), in some independence of the actual production of the turn they eventually produce.

In a related discussion in the turn-taking paper, Sacks, Schegloff and Jefferson (1974: 719) mention a class of items they describe as "appositionals". They begin by noting that there is a pressure for self-selecting next speakers to get an early start and that this, along with the possibility that the current turn will be extended by "optional elements" such as address terms and tag questions, means that a next turn's beginning is subject to multiple sources of potential overlap. Of course, if turn beginnings play the important role we have claimed for them in terms of projecting the type of turn underway and what it will take to be complete this can result in interactional difficulty – the beginning of the turn will be impaired by overlap and thus its recipients will not be able to recognize the type of turn being produced as early as they otherwise might.

> Therefore, the need to begin with a sentence's beginning (where a sentence is the planned unit) constrains the relative timing of its turn's start, for its analyzability may be affected if it

> overlaps. With regard to the 'begin with a beginning' constraint and its consequences, a familiar class of constructions is of particular interest. Appositional beginnings, e.g. "well," "but," "and," "so" etc., are extraordinarily common, and do satisfy the constraints of beginning. But they do that without revealing much about the constructional features of the sentence thus begun, i.e. without requiring that the speaker have a plan in hand as a condition for starting. Furthermore, their overlap will not impair the constructional development or the analyzability of the sentence they begin. Appositionals, then, are turn-entry devices or PRE-STARTS. (Sacks, Schegloff and Jefferson 1974: 719)

To this list of appositionals we can perhaps add "uhm" which can certainly be used, in overlap with the current turn, to claim next speaking position. Here is an example of that (one that we saw earlier in our discussion of "look"):

(19) Heritage 1–3

Ilene:		[.hhh
Lisa:		[Yeh ah I'll tell you I'll give you
		chapter'n verse,
Ilene:		Right.
Lisa:		↑ehh heh heh[heh he-]hh=
Ilene:	→	[Uh : m]
Ilene:		=Well now look d'you want me
		ti[h come over'n get her? or wha:t.
Lisa:		[°( )°

Straightforward enough it seems. Here Ilene disattends Lisa's laughter which she overlaps with "uhm" and then as, we've seen, launches into a new course of action. This kind of analysis, valid as it is, considers only one aspect of the organization of talk-in-interaction – specifically, the organization of turn-taking – but if you think back to the introduction of this book you'll remember that a basic idea of conversation analysis is that a turn-at-talk is always the product of multiple, intersecting organizations or "machineries". In order to understand this and "uhm"-prefaced turns like it we need to consider not only turn-taking but also the organization of talk into "occasions", or what we call "overall structural organization". We will consider the openings of telephone calls in more detail in chapter 10. For now, let's just notice that, in many calls, there is a position just after the opening sequence (in which greetings are exchanged, reciprocal personal inquiries made and answered, and the parties identified) where it is relevant for the one who made the call to announce or to otherwise convey *why* they are calling. Looking back at example (19), you'll remember that this is exactly what Ilene is doing in lines 6–8. And consider also the following cases:

(20) Geri–Shirley

Geri:		Howyih doin.h
Shirley:		Okay how'r you.
Geri:		↑Oh alri:[:ght,
(Shirley):		[(.hhhhhh)
Shirley:	→	Uh:m yer mother met Michael las'night.
Geri:		Oh rilly?=
Shirley:		=Ye:ah.
( ):		.hh-.hh
Geri:		↑Oh:::.=
Shirley:		=Yeah.She wz taking Shiloh out.just ez we w'r coming back
		fr'm dinner.

(21) Shawn and Ali pt. 2

01	Ali:		Hello::
02	Shawn:		Hi Ali?=
03	Ali:		=Yeah
04	Shawn:		It's Shawn downstairs
05	Ali:		Hi Shawn
06	Shawn:	→	Uhm:
07			(0.8)
08			When you asked us to not to run thu:h washing machine
09			again didju mea:n (.) just today er [(.) again.
10	Ali:		[°hhh
11			We:ll I don't rilly have the water fer you guy- see
12			when you guys moved in I toldja thet I had a water
13			issue with just even havin' you guys both showering
14			an' stuff °h[hh like when you run the washing
15	Shawn:		[mhmm
16	Ali:		machine I don't have any water at all in the house.
17			°h an' so it will- (0.2) pu- make my: (.) electricity
18			bill go up an' my water bill go up.

Of course there are other uses of "uhm". Here is an example which illustrates two of those other uses.

(22) YYZ.4.Alison and Clara1

01	Alison:		Hello:
02			(.)
03	Clara:		Hi=Alison,
04	Alison:		Hi:
05	Clara:		It's Clara, howyadoin',=
06	Alison:		=Good.How are you Clara.
07	Clara:	a→	U:m: I'm oka:y. I::: nee:d to tell you that I'm not
08			gonna have t(h)i(h)me t(h)o(h) d(h)o this budget next
09			week.=
10	Alison:		Oh hh
11	Clara:	b→	U[h:m]
12	Alison:		[. hh]
13	Clara:		an' I: I- I actually have to go to David today and sa:y (.)
14			something needs to com:eoff: my plate here.
15			[cuz] stuff's gonna start to slip from Molson=
16	Alison:		[huh]
17	Clara:		=so: [°hh
18	Alison:		[Okay
19	Clara:	c→	uhm:, so he said you should talk to him about that
20			(.)
21			budget which I don't know that yer- (.) gonnabe- really happy
22			uh- (.) bout=
23	Alison:		=uh [h(hh)uh
24	Clara:		[huh huh
25	Alison:		°hhhh okay::
26	Clara:		I'm really sorry,=
27	Alison:		=That's oka:y,

Clara's "uhm" at the 'a' arrow comes in the vicinity of the stated "reason for the call" but what it actually does here is to the break the contiguity between the question "How are you Clara." and the response "I'm okay.". Notice that this can convey to Alison that Clara has had to momentarily consider her response before she delivers it, and this can have significant consequences for how the interaction unfolds (see the discussion of Jefferson's "trouble premonitory responses to inquiry" in chapter 10). More generally, we can see that "uhm" can, like items such as "well" and silence, serve to delay a response and thus to convey its dispreferred status.

The "uhm"s at lines 10 and 17 occur in a rather different environment. Notice that in the first case, Clara has come to a clear possible completion with "next week", and indeed Alison has responded to this, the first part of a subsequently elaborated report of bad news, with a breathy "oh". Notice that this "oh" registers what Clara has said as news but only minimally responds to the laughter that has infected its production. So with her "uhm" at line 10, Clara may be providing Alison with some more room to respond before she continues the report. At line 17 we find another "uhm", now apparently marking the continuation of the report – or simply marking that Clara will continue speaking.

Turn Endings

Just as a turn-constructional unit need not start with a beginning so it need not end with a completion. Consider, for instance, the following example in which Lottie has asked Emma whether her husband Bud might want to join a chartered fishing trip that Lottie and her friend Adeline are organizing.

(23) NB:I:6:R:4
01 Lottie: [( )
02 Emma: [Well we'll talk about it yih haftih git booked up
03 rahght awa:y? er
04 ( ): °t °h
05 (0.2)
06 Lottie Oh:: no: but if I- I mean I'd like tuh: see how
07 many A:deline's got quite a few en I've got got quite
08 a fe:[w b't I] wanna getta depo:sit'n yih know=
09 Emma: [°Mm: hm°]
10 [°Mm: hm?°]
11 Lottie: [be sure] thet[: yih[know I c'n] ←
12 Emma: [°t °hh[W't boatch] 'u goin on.
13 Lottie: °hh It's call' the Cha:mp. It's a:: great big (.)
14 w- uh boa:t.

The key point to be made about this fragment for current purposes is that at line 11, Lottie never actually finishes the TCU that she began with "be sure". What's going on here? In asking whether Lottie needs to get it booked up right away, Emma can be heard as deferring on a decision as to whether Bud will join the party. This puts Lottie in a rather sticky situation. While to insist that Emma tell her here and now whether Bud will come or not would be clearly unreasonable, she may also not want to keep spots open for too long.

Indeed, it turns out that Lottie is asking for a deposit from those signing up for the fishing trip. Notice then that as she is saying this, Emma manages to shift the topic away from the pragmatic details of the deposit and on to the question of what boat is to be taken. By overlapping Lottie's ongoing talk, Emma treats what she has so far said as sufficient and Lottie stops speaking at a point where the TCU is not yet complete. Here then, a recipient's overlapping talk treats the current speaker's turn as sufficient and thus releases them from the obligation to produce a complete TCU.

There are other environments in which a current speaker may abandon the TCU before it reaches completion. In (24) Emma and Lottie have been discussing what America needs in terms of a political leader. While there is some evidence of common ground, the two sisters have found themselves in moderate disagreement: Emma is clearly more left (Democrat)-leaning than her outspokenly Republican sister Lottie.

(24) NB:II:1:R:11
Lottie: =becuz ah: (.) we need a(b) (.) a(b) p-p'litical
[↓leader we rilly do:.
Emma: [°°Yah°°
→ °We:ll ah duh- (.) MuhCarthy's kind of: I don'know
whether I like him er no[:t.°
Lottie: [I: ↓don::'. I: don'kno[:w.
Emma: [°°No,°°

Here then we want to notice that Emma begins a turn which projects an assessment of McCarthy ("MuhCarthy's kind of:") but rather than complete this with an assessment term, she abandons the TCU and ends up producing a quite different kind of completion: "I don't know whether I like him er no:t.". Notice that, unlike an assessment, this does not make agreement or disagreement relevant in next position. It does, however, allow Lottie to *align*, and she does this by saying the same thing. Now consider example (25). Here Emma and Nancy are talking just days after the assassination of Robert F. Kennedy (June 5th, 1968) and are complaining that the press has made a circus out of the event. In line 01, Emma is continuing with this already established theme and is apparently on her way to describing how the press followed the family to church to take pictures. However, she only produces the first sounds of the word "church", cutting this off in the course of its production in order to start a quite different TCU. It's only after Nancy revives the issue of the family's need for privacy that Emma returns to the description of the press at the church in line 09.

(25) NB:II:2:R:3–4
Emma: → Like yesterday showin um goin in the chu- ·hh ↑Ah mean so
much I: know it's sa:d but my God let's don't throw it et
the public °constantl[y°
Nancy: [·t·hhh We:ll I think it's sad thet they
don't ah:,h allo:w u-you know the fam'lies et least th'
decen[cy. of hav]ing s'm ↑privacy.
Emma: [e e Y a h]
(0.4)
→ Yeah'n the church yesterday thih .hhhh fla:shin the ca:m'ras
on um when theh w'r there yihknow went in tuh pr:a:y and an'
(.) ↑Go:d g-

And in the final example of this to be considered, Emma is asking Nancy whether she has any boyfriends. Nancy initially responds emphatically with "oh hell no" but then qualifies somewhat by saying that "I've gotta lot'v (0.2) frie:nds,". She goes on to offer an explanation which begins at line 09. Notice then that this explanation initially starts with "I don't wanna get" but this TCU-in-the-making is abandoned in favor of "I just am not emotionally" which is in turn abandoned when Nancy returns to the original format of "I don't wanna get involved . . .".

(26) NB:II:2:R:23
01 Emma: Y'got any(b) frie:nd boyfrie:nds? er any°thing
02 [goin:g [steady'r:°]
03 Nancy: [Oh::: [° ↓h*ell n]*o.↓°
04 Emma: °Nothin°
05 (0.3)
06 Nancy: ·t Oh I've gotta lot'v (0.2) frie:nds,=
07 Emma: =But n[othin'yer]dating.
08 Nancy: [But n o :]
09 → ·hhhh Oh hu-E:mma ↓I: don't wanna get↓ I=
10 Emma: =↓Y[eh
11 Nancy: → [just am: not emotion'lly:
12 Emma: °Mm-mm[:.°
13 Nancy: → [I: don't wanna get invo:lved I: don't wanna go ou:t
14 and ·hhhhhhhhh put myself in the p'sition whur: some ma:n's
15 gunnuh think oh boy she's rilly hard up yihknow,hh

So we've seen then that a TCU need not end with a completion. This can make visible to us the "unmarked" or default situation in which a turn *does* end in completion. We will not dwell on such unmarked completion here as that situation was already discussed in chapter 3. Rather, what I want to briefly consider are cases in which completion is "marked" in some special way. Such "marked completions" can perhaps be seen as parallel to the prefaces used to begin a turn.

Consider for instance tag questions which typically occur in turn-final position and in doing so mark its completion. For instance:

(27) Heritage 1:3
31 Ilene: → °¯Oh really they are casual aren't they.°
32 Lisa: → (Well he i[s.)
33 Ilene: [°Ye:h,°

Recipients' orientation to the completion-marking character of tag questions is seen in examples such as (28) and (29).

(28) Holt May 88: Side 2 Call 4 21:19–35, 30
28 Mark: [.h h h : h h : h h h h [hOtherwise
29 → it's a sheer waste'v money i'n'it rea[lly,
30 Dee: [Of course it is.
31 Dee: It's no good 'avin' swank- as I- I as I said you know
32 there['s no point in having a big .hhh (fancy) wedding=
33 Mark: [.knff
34 Dee: =eh- an' you goin' off to live in two roo¯:ms
35 Mark: hhNo:.

(29) Holt May 88: Side 2 Call 4
14 Dee: .p.t.hhh Uh:: but quite honestly the prices that 'ey've
15 'ad to- 'ave to pay up[here is absolutely]'orrifi:c you=
16 Mark: [((fidget)) h h h h]((fidget))
17 Dee: =kno:[w,
18 Mark: [Yerah,h So I gather I mean they're .hhhh they're
19 → they're fantastic aren't[they n o : w,]
20 Dee: [That's ri:ght,] they're taw-
21 they're payin a[hundred 'n ten Mark]

Notice then that in both cases a tag question is followed by some small bit of further talk – by "really" in (28) and by "now" in (29). In both cases this post-tag-question talk is overlapped by a next speaker who has apparently treated the tag question as constituting TCU completion.

Turn increments constitute another kind of "marked" completion in so far as an increment involves a recompletion of an already possibly complete turn unit.

(30) NB 1.1
09 Guy: 'Av ↑you go(.)t uh: ↑Seacliffs phone number?h
10 (1.1)
11 Guy: by any chance?
12 (0.3)
13 Jon: Yeeah?
14 (2.6)
15 Jon: .k.hhh hIt's uh:< (.) .t.h FI:VE THREE SIX::

Notice that Guy's turn has come to a clear point of possible completion with "phone number?" in line 09. There follows a silence and then Guy speaks again, not with a new TCU but rather with an addition to the one he's just completed. By virtue of its design, the increment "by any chance" shows itself to be parasitic on what came before and thus can be seen to recomplete it. Although in this case the increment follows and is perhaps occasioned by a significant delay in response to the original question, this is certainly not true of all cases. In (31) Wes has come to a possible completion of the turn with "give you." and then, without any delay, recompletes it with the increment "for allowance.".

(31) Virginia
01 Wes: How much didj your momma give you. for allowance.
02 (.)
03 Prudence: °°Golly, I can't >remember it's been so long ago.<

Increments are deployed in response to a wide variety of interactional circumstances. Consider, for instance, the following case in which Emma and Nancy are talking about the news coverage of Robert F. Kennedy's assassination. At line 15 Emma is continuing the talk about reporters following the Kennedys to church (see example (25)) but apparently abandons this in its course to announce, "that was the same spot we took off for Honolulu".[6] This is a news announcement and Emma presents it as a remarkable coincidence and thus as something that might be expected to elicit a response such as the "oh really" which Nancy eventually does produce in line 21.

(32) NB:II:2:R:3–4

15 Emma: =·hh ↑Jackie looked u:p↑ ·h Hey that wz the same spot we
16 took off fer Ho:nuhlulu
17 (0.3)
18 Where they puut him o:n,
19 (0.6)
20 et that chartered pla:[ce,
21 Nancy: [Oh: ri↑ll[y?
22 Emma: [y::Ye::ah,
23 Nancy: ↑Oh: fer ↓heaven ↓sa:[kes.

"That was the same spot" invites Nancy to recognize some specific place that she knows that Emma is talking about. When Nancy does not respond, Emma builds, incrementally, to the turn, adding to it further specifications of "the spot" that might allow Nancy to recognize the place that she is talking about. These specifications take the form of increments which build onto the already completed turn and are grammatically parasitic upon it.

Marked completion of the turn can also involve a combination of tag questions and increments as in the following case:

(33) NB:IV:10:R:15

35 Emma: .hhuhhhh (.) Oh wul weh-uh no:w duh: didju HAVE a hard trip
36 → goin up there Sundee?=That Sunee Anna Canyon's kahna ↓ba:d=
37 Lottie: =[.hh
38 Emma: → =[isn't it [with ahll those ↓li:ghts.=
39 Lottie: [hh
40 Lottie: =I: dint yihknow I wz thinkin I thik (.) God I'm crazy tih
41 go et night yihknow by my[s:elf en the]n I I
42 Emma: [M m h m :]

Here Emma comes to a first possible completion with "kahna ↓ba:d" in line 36 and Lottie's inbreath at line 37 displays her orientation to this as transition-relevant. However, Emma goes on to recomplete the turn first with "isn't it" (and notice the slight breath here from Lottie) and then again with the increment "with ahll those ↓li:ghts.".

Turn increments and tag questions are deployed to deal with a range of interactional circumstances. For instance, increments may be added to a question where an answer is delayed, in this way transforming inter-turn gap into intra-turn pause (see Sacks, Schegloff and Jefferson 1974). Another common environment for increments is illustrated by example (32), in which an announcement of news garners no immediate response from the recipient. The turn is continued and the reference further specified until the recipient eventually responds (for further discussion of the interactional uses to which increments are put see Schegloff 2001, Ford, Fox and Thompson 1996, 2002). Speakers use the other form of marked completion we considered here – tag questions – to deal with quite different interactional contingencies. For one thing, a speaker may use a tag question to select a next speaker and potentially transform what began as a declarative into an interrogative. Heritage and Raymond (2005) also show that tag questions serve as resources in the negotiation of epistemic rights.

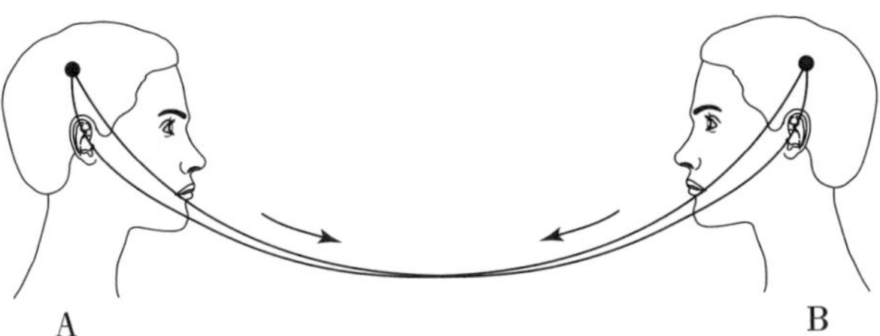

Figure 8.1

Interaction Within the Turn

One common view of how communication works goes like this: The speaker forms an idea and selects the words and grammatical patterns appropriate to its expression. These words and grammatical patterns are then encoded in the sound units of language. The hearer receives the message and decodes the sound units, thus recovering the meaning and, ultimately, if all works as it should, the original idea that the speaker meant to convey. Something like this seems to underlie figure 8.1, reproduced from Saussure's *Cours de linguistique générale*. Interaction in this view is just the "structureless medium" that Schegloff writes about in the following passage (1989: 140):

> What occurs in interaction is not merely the serial externalization into some joint arena of batches of talk, hatched in private (or even socialized) intentions, and filled out with the docile artifacts of "language" (as in many versions of speech act theory, discourse analysis and the like). This treats the mind/brain as the scene of all the action, and the space of interaction as a structureless medium, or at least a medium whose structure is beside the point with respect to what is transmitted through it, as the composition of telephone cable is beside the point for the conversation transmitted through it. But interaction is that for which the talk is conceived; its character is shaped by the structure of opportunities to deliver a message in the first place. . . .

As Schegloff indicates, conversation analysis challenges these rather pervasive ideas about the way communication works. The studies we have considered in this book so far suggest that when we talk we don't form an idea and spit it out like a machine. Rather, talk is shaped in profound ways by the structure of interaction. This *social* organization is something that joins the speaker and recipient. It is an organization in which they both participate. We have seen this already in terms of sequence organization, repair and turn-taking. We will now consider two ways in which the turn is itself a product of an interaction between a speaker and a hearer.

Here is the beginning of a telephone call we considered earlier. Madeline has called her friend Gina's mother to ask if she would be willing to rent out the bottom part of her garage.

(34) Madeline 2
07 Madeline: =okay.I was just wundering y'know ·hhh (0.3) could- (·)
08 d'you think you might (·) wanna rent (·) you know like the
09 bottom part a yer: (·) g'ra::ge like to me: fer a whi:le, °a
10 sump'm like that.°

11 (0.3)
12 Marsha: wul[l-
13 Madeline: [(I think [ )]
14 Marsha: [oh- you mean for] living in: madeline?
15 Madeline: ye:ah
16 (0.3)
17 Marsha: ·hh It's just (0.8)
18 Madeline: no:t possible.=h[uh?
19 Marsha: [ye:ah we- gi:na tri:ed that at one
20 ti:[me.=b't-]
21 Madeline: [I: re]member.=she was doin that o[nce.
22 Marsha: [·hhh we could not
23 get it (ta::)/(uh::) (0.4) clo::sed.
24 (0.3)

What we want to see here is the way in which the recipient's actions (or lack of action) help to shape the eventual course of the turn. In that respect, note that there are several points of possible completion within this turn.

(35) Madeline 2 (detail)
07 Madeline: =okay.I was just wundering y'know ·hhh (0.3) could- (·)
08 d'you think you might (·) wanna rent (·) you know like the
09 bottom part a yer: (·) g'ra::ge like to me: fer a whi:le, °a
10 sump'm like that.°

This turn might have been complete then at the end of "g'ra::ge", or "like to me:", or "fer a whi:le,". Had Marsha treated any of these places as the turn's completion, Madeline might have stopped talking. Thus, the extent of this turn is in part a product of an interaction between current speaker and recipient: by *not responding* at these points of possible completion, the recipient treats the turn as incomplete and the speaker is invited to continue. The more general point is that what a recipient is or is not doing *during the course* of a turn's production can have profound consequences in terms of how that turn unfolds.

Some of the clearest examples of this come from the work of Charles and Marjorie Goodwin (see especially M. Goodwin 1980, C. Goodwin 1979b, 1980, 1981, 1986b). In the mid- to late 1970s the Goodwins pioneered the use of video-recordings in conversation analysis and opened up a wide range of phenomena for further investigation. In one of his earliest published studies, Charles Goodwin developed an analysis of a single turn-at-talk between participants sitting around a table having dinner together. Goodwin used these materials to argue that the gaze of the participants plays a crucial role in the organization of the talk and, for this reason, includes it in the transcript which is reproduced below:

(36) Chinese Dinner – from Goodwin 1979
01 John: . . , , ... [Don,, [Don..
I gave, I gave u[p smo]king ci[garettes::.=
02 Don: =Yea:h
03 John: . . . [Beth__________. . . [Ann__________
I-uh: [one-one week ago t'da:[y. acshilly

Transcription conventions
The top line of each numbered segment represents the gaze of the speaker.
. . . indicates movement towards the person named in the "gaze" line
[the bracket indicates that gaze is now focused on the person named
__ underlining in the "gaze" line indicates that gaze is maintained

Goodwin's analysis is based on one of Sacks's most basic and crucial observations: that speakers orient to their recipients. This has at least two important consequences for the analysis. First, a basic consideration for a speaker is, obviously, to secure a recipient for their talk. Recipients orient to this in so far as they don't just listen to a speaker's talk but in various ways *display* that they are listening to it. In face-to-face interaction one basic resource for displaying that one is attending to the talk of a speaker is by gazing at them. A second very basic rule or principle of recipient design is that one should not tell a recipient what they already know (or should know, or can be assumed to know, etc.). Taking these considerations into account, Goodwin shows how this turn is modified in its course to solve various problems of recipiency.

Thus, in this fragment, John begins by telling Don that he gave up smoking cigarettes. This accords with the recipient design rule since Don does not already know that John has given up smoking.

However, there is also a knowing recipient at the table, John's wife Beth. In order to involve her as a recipient, John modifies this sentence in its course. Specifically, John changes this from a report about quitting smoking to the announcement of an anniversary: a one-week anniversary of the event of quitting smoking. Notice then that by emphasizing the word "today" John conveys that he has discovered the anniversary in the course of telling the news. However, although he has apparently designed this talk specifically for *her*, Beth does not return John's gaze. Ann, however, gazes at Beth thus indicating she has found in John's talk a change in recipient. Apparently taking this into account, John adds "actually" so as to transform the announcement of the discovery of the anniversary to a report of its discovery. Thus rather than being asked to recognize the anniversary (which presumes a *knowing* participant – Beth) the recipient is being told that the event marked by the anniversary did happen a week ago. By shifting his gaze once again, now to Ann, John shows that this talk is specifically intended for *her*. Goodwin's detailed analysis of this fragment (which includes many more important observations than we have dealt with here) thus shows that a single turn is a complex product of an interaction between speaker and recipients.

It is a concern for such interaction *within the turn* that led Moerman (1988: 181) to write: "At various points in the course of an utterance, various others may be required, proposed, invited, or allowed to speak next, or discouraged or enjoined from doing so. And 'next' can be 'right now'." C. Goodwin and M. Goodwin (1987) raise similar issues, contrasting the usual emphasis in CA on next-turn position with the possibility of looking at what happens in the course of a turn's production:

> One very productive strategy for uncovering the interactive organization of talk has focused on ways in which subsequent utterances display an analysis of prior ones (Sacks, Schegloff and Jefferson 1974: 728). However, despite the great power of this methodology, and in particular its ability to reveal how participants themselves analyze prior talk in a way relevant to the activities they are engaged in, there are limitations to it. For example, with it it is difficult to determine precisely how participants attend to utterances as they are being spoken. The treatment that a bit of talk gets in a next utterance may be quite different from the way in which it was

> heard and dealt with as it was spoken; indeed, rather than presenting a naked analysis of the prior talk next utterances characteristically transform that talk in some fashion – deal with it not in its own terms but rather in the way in which it is relevant to the projects of subsequent speaker. Thus while subsequent utterances can reveal crucial features of the analysis participants are making of prior talk they do not show how participants hear the talk as it is emerging in the first place, what they make of it then, and what consequences this has for their actions, not in a next turn, but within the current turn. . . . In brief it would be valuable to begin to uncover the types of organization that a strip of talk provides, not simply for subsequent talk, but for the organization of action as it is being spoken.

So in these passages we see the authors contrasting the kind of relevance established for *next* position at the possible completion of a turn with relevances that may be established *within* the course of a current turn. Of course, participants in conversation engage in a range of activities that are not, or at least are not solely, organized in relation to utterance completion.[7] An obvious example is recipient gaze (M. Goodwin 1980, C. Goodwin 1979, 1986), which as we've just seen can be made relevant, and found to be missing, at various points *within* the course of turn's production. Another example is laughter, about which Lerner remarks (1996: 259):

> Jefferson (1979) has shown that in-speech (and therefore TCU-internal) laughter makes recipient laughter specially relevant as a demonstration of understanding or affiliation. There are, of course, ways of asserting or showing understanding through talk, but ordinarily these must wait until transition to a next turn becomes relevant at TCU completion. (But see M.H. Goodwin 1980, and C. Goodwin and M.H. Goodwin 1987.) In the case of laughter – since it is not turn organized – a recipient need not delay affiliation until next turn.

Here I want to discuss two other activities in which we find that recipient response may be made relevant *within* the course of the ongoing turn and before its first possible completion.

The first of these activities is the pursuit and display of recognition. If a speaker is uncertain as to whether a recipient will be able to recognize a person, place or thing being talked about, they may mark it with rising intonation as a "try" at recognitional reference and by this invite the recipient to display that recognition has indeed been achieved (see Sacks and Schegloff 1979). The point is that all this can, and routinely is, done within the bounds of a single TCU quite independently of utterance completion. The following case from interaction between a teacher and three 5-year-old children provides a particularly clear example.

```
(37) KIDS SKT7 12:00
01  Alison:       I think I'm gonna use this [(        )]
02  Ben:      →                              [Cindy?]
03  Teacher:  →   Yes
04  Ben:      →   Has these.
05  Teacher:      Has?
06  Ben:          [The melter beads]
07  Cari:         [(               )]
08  Teacher:      Oh ok, did you guys- were you guys
09                with Cindy last year?=
10  Cari:         =yeah
```

Notice then that at line 02 Ben starts a TCU which will eventually become "Cindy has these.". This is an announcement directed at the teacher and as a first action clearly initiates an adjacency pair. However, embedded *within* this TCU is another sequence-initiating action that invites response: specifically, the try-marked reference to "Cindy" invites a display of recognition from the teacher which it gets at line 03. The TCU is then completed at line 04 with "has these.".

So during the course of the ongoing turn a display indicating that recognition has been achieved may be made relevant. Such pursuit and display of recognition is not limited to person reference. Consider also the following case in which Mom, Dad and Cindy are having dinner together. The day this recording was made, Mom had accompanied Cindy on a class trip to a restaurant, and earlier in the dinner Dad had asked to hear about what happened there. This fragment begins with Mom asking Cindy what she had for lunch. After Cindy answers that she had hamburger Mom turns her gaze away from Cindy and towards Dad saying "it looked good.". Dad then invites elaboration of this report saying, "Oh didju, you had a hamburger, and it was good?". In this way, Dad displays a hearing of Cindy's talk as indicating that she had a single hamburger. In line 27 Mom corrects this understanding, saying "two little ones". She goes on to produce a recognitional reference form at line 28, "thuh sliders" – apparently an item on the menu at this restaurant which she believes Dad should be able to recognize.

(29) Stew Dinner:
20 Mom: What d'ju have.
21 (0.2)
22 Cindy: Hamburger,
23 (1.0)
24 Mom: It 'ooked goo:d. ((with mouth full))
25 Dad: Oh didju, you had a hamburger, and it was good?
26 Cindy: [°(Yeah.)°
27 Mom: → [Two little ones like when they- (wu- wu- wh'n) they put
28 → [thuh (sliders) [on thuh- (.) On thuh (0.2) appetizer menu?,
29 Dad: → [#huh# [UH HU:H?,
30 Mom: ((sniff)) Bu:t they didn't gi- bring any condiments.
31 (0.2)
32 Mom: except ketchup; so_ (.) it would've been boring for an adult
33 tuh have uh burger like that cuz there's nothing on it=>except<-
34 (0.2)
35 Dad: M[m hm,
36 Mom: [bun an' burger an:' ketchup.

As Mom produces the recognitional form "thuh sliders" here she uses both hands to create a gestural accompaniment to the talk. This gesture begins before Mom says "Two little ones" and is fully formed at "like when they- (wu- wu- wh'n) they put". At this point Mom brings her own gaze to the gesture she has created. The gesture is held long enough for Dad to turn his head towards Mom and to display, with "UH HU:H?", that he has recognized the object being referred to. At this point the gesture is retracted and Mom continues with her turn-at-talk. This TCU comes to completion in line 28 with "menu" but Mom continues the turn with a series of increments beginning at line 30.

So we've seen that a display of recognition can be made relevant within the course of an ongoing turn-at-talk. The question remains as to whether that display can be found to be absent if it is not produced. Do participants orient to the non-production of such an intra-turn display of recognition? One sort of evidence that they do is provided by example (39):

(39) SBL 2/2/4 (Sacks & Schegloff, 1979:19)
01 Ann: . . . well I was the only one other than
02 .hhh than thee uhm (0.7) mtch! Fo:rds.
03 Uh Missiz Holmes Ford? (0.8) You know the-
04 [the the cellist?
05 Bev: [Oh yes. She's- she's (a)/(the) cellist.
06 Ann: Ye: s.
07 Bev: ye[s
08 Ann: [Well she and her husband were there, . .

Here Ann initially has trouble finding the name of the person(s) to whom she means to make reference and engages in a word search, the outcome of which is "Fo:rds." at line 02. This is immediately followed, however, by the try-marked item "Missiz Holmes Ford?". As we've seen, such a try-marked recognitional form makes an immediate display of recognition by the recipient relevant. In this example we can see the participants' orientation to this relevance. Thus, after the first recognitional form is produced, Ann stops speaking, thereby conveying that recognition is required for the development of the sequence and, moreover, providing a place for Bev to produce a token of recognition (e.g. uh huh) in the clear. When no such token of recognition is produced, Ann treats it as missing by pursuing it with further material that might allow for recognition of the person being talked about. Finally, we may note that when, after these two tries at recognition, Bev does respond, she does it with something more than a simple token of recognition. Bev's repeat of "the cellist" prompts Ann's acceptance with "ye:s", and the turn continues at line 08. This elaborate display is occasioned, it would appear, by the fact that Bev initially failed to recognize the person being talked about and thus provides further evidence that she also orients to the fact that a display of recognition was initially missing (see Heritage 2007).

Another case of an activity not solely organized in relation to utterance completion is similar in that it also involves a recipient's display of recognition. In the examples discussed so far a recipient is invited to in some way convey that they have recognized something or someone to which the speaker is making reference. In the next set of examples, what the recipient is invited to recognize is something worthy of assessment. In other words, in each of these examples a speaker produces an item which is thereby made available to the recipient for assessment. Consider first the following case, in which Vivian and Shane are telling Michael and Nancy that Shane had lobster for lunch. Their description of the meal makes immediate response from the recipients relevant and does in fact elicit such response at lines 30, 54, 58, 61, 63 and 67:

(40) "Lobster Lunch" Chicken Dinner p. 16
28 Vivian: u-Shane ate lobster (0.5) 's afternoon
29 (0.2)
30 Nancy: [R i l l [y?
31 Michael: [(He) di[d?
32 Shane: [Yeah:,=
33 Nancy: =Where[a:t.
34 Vivian: [A half Maine lobster in u-that ma::ll? They have

35 this (.) pl_ace ih wz Cafe: M_andarin?
36 Michael: Ya-a_[h¿
37 Vivian: [So ih had this spe_cial. (0.4) So h_e thinks is thet
38 l_o:bster's gunnuh be all cut u:p en evrythin:g 'ee
39 [c 'n j's:]t sti_ck it i_n'n e_at it'n'e_re they bri_ng=
40 Nancy: [ee(h)eeYa:h.
41 Vivian: =this a[n i m a l ,]
42 Michael: [Wiz it a who]le lobster?=
43 Vivian: =Th w[z a h_a : l f.]
44 Shane: [A half a lobs]ter.
45 Vivian: But it wz a:ll (.) yihknow,
46 Shane: One claw en then: half'v[: yihkno]w,=
47 Vivian: [Mm hm,]
48 Michael: =How m-How mu:c[h.
49 Shane: [th'body
50 (0.4)
51 Vivian: Si[x ni] nedy]five.]=
52 Shane: [Six] ninedy]five.]=
53 Vivian: =·hh I[h wz with]appeti[zer s[o u : p ,]
54 Michael: [Ri l l y?] [[ ]
55 Shane: [I got[evrything.]
56 (0.5)
57 Vivian: Chicken chow mein r[ice en the lo]bst[er
58 Nancy: → [W_o : : : w .] [
59 Shane: [Ah- ih wz ih wz
60 a full mea:l.
61 Michael: We:w.
62 Shane: Six[ninedy five]I c'nt b'lieve it.]
63 Nancy: [S_u c h a] d e a : l .]
64 Shane: =Ye:a[h.
65 Nancy: [uhh-huh-huh-huh
66 Shane: Really.
67 Michael: °mNe:h. We shoulda been ther[e.°
68 Shane: [Yeh heh heh heh hih

Here Vivian is telling Michael and Nancy about Shane having lobster for lunch. The story has been occasioned by Nancy remarking that she "had a light lunch", to which Vivian notes in apparent contrast, "Shane ate lobster (0.5) s' afternoon". This contrast is made explicit in the subsequent talk where Vivian explains that Shane was expecting lobster "all cut up" but to his surprise received "this animal,". Notice then that Vivian's "Chicken chow mein rice en the lobster" elicits from Nancy a prosodically enhanced marker of appreciation with which Nancy displays her recognition of this as an assessable item (at line 58). Notice further that Nancy's assessment is completely "contained within" Vivian's turn-at-talk. Consider also the following case from Goodwin and Goodwin's 1987 study of assessments:

(41) G.126:22:40
01 Paul: Tell y- Tell Debbie about the dog
02 on the golf course t'day
03 Eileen: °eh hnh [h_nh ha has! [ha!
04 Paul: [hih hih [Heh Heh! ·hh hh

05 Eileen: ·h Paul en I got ta the first *gr*een,
06 (0.6)
07 Eileen: ·hh an this beautiful, ((swallow))
08 Paul: I[rish Setter. ((reverently))
09 Eileen: [Irish Setter
10 Debbie: → Ah:::,
11 Eileen: Came tear[in up on ta the first *gr*ee(h)n,=
12 Paul: [°Oh it was beautiful
13 Eileen: =an tried ta steal Pau(h)l's go(h)lf ball. ·hh
14 Paul: Eh *h*nh hnh.
15 Eileen: ·hheh! ·hh

Here Eileen explicitly marks Irish Setter as an assessable item with the adjective "beautiful" and secures from the recipient Debbie a return assessment in line 10. The key point for present purposes (though see the original article for many other important observations) is that Debbie's assessment comes at a place at which the current speaker has clearly *not* reached possible completion of the current unit. Goodwin and Goodwin (1987: 11–12) write:

> It can be noted, first, that recipient's action does not occur at the end of speaker's current turn-constructional unit, the characteristic place for recipient response, but rather at a point where her current sentence has recognizably not reached completion. Structurally, the assessments of both speaker and recipient are placed in the midst of a turn-constructional unit.

C. Goodwin (1986b) has argued that the placement of such recipient assessments *within the course of a single turn at talk* is quite systematic and contrasts with, for instance, continuers, which tend to come at boundaries between units. He writes (1986b: 209):

> rather than bridging two turn-constructional units, assessments in the midst of another's extended talk come to completion before a new unit is entered. . . . An active orientation by participants toward placement of the assessment within the current unit is demonstrated by cases in which the assessment has the potential to extend into a subsequent unit. In such a situation participants actively work to prevent this from happening. . . .

Goodwin illustrates this with the following example:

(42) HGII:35
01 Hyla: One time I member, ·hh 's girl wrote
02 end her, ·hh she wz like (·) fifteen er
03 six[teen end] her mother doesn let'er wear
04 Nancy: [Uh hu:h,]
05 Hyla: ·hh nail polish er sh(h)ort ski:::rts
06 → 'er:[:: ·hhhhhh]=
07 Nancy: → [Oh: wo:(h)w]=
08 Hyla: =Oo::h no I remember what yesterday was

Here the "recipient's assessment extends past the end of the speaker's current turn constructional unit. However by producing an inbreath, the speaker delays production of a subsequent unit until recipient's assessment has been brought to completion" (Goodwin 1986b: 210). Compare in this respect the placement of the continuer "uh hu:h" in line 4. This item comes at a point where Nancy can anticipate a point of possible completion, and it bridges two units: [she wz like fifteen er sixteen] [and her mother doesn't let 'er wear nail polish er short skirts]. So there is evidence that recipient assessments are properly placed *within* a current turn unit, and where they threaten to extend past such a unit speakers may take action to prevent this from happening.

The Goodwins go on to show that recipients may not only respond to assessable items as they are being produced but, furthermore, may project their occurrence and produce simultaneous and congruent responses even before the item itself is actually articulated. Consider:

(43) G.50:03:45
01 Dianne: Jeff made en asparagus pie
02 it wz s::*so*[: *goo*:d.
03 Clacia: [I love it.

(44) HGII:12
01 Hyla: an it's j's r:*r*il[l y s::: [s a : : d,]
02 Nancy: [Guy that [sounds so goo] : : d?

In these instances we see a recurrent structure of the following sort:

PRONOUN	COPULA	INTENSIFIER	ADJECTIVE
it	was	so	good
it	's	just really	sad

The authors note that the placement of a recipient's assessment, in each case before the assessing adjective has been produced, suggests that these recipients are anticipating the talk that is to come (see also Jefferson 1993). In doing so they are able not just to respond to the assessment but also in some sense to participate in it as it is produced.

Now this of course means that a speaker may monitor the recipient to see if an appropriate assessment will be produced *within the course of the current unit of talk*. If the speaker suspects that, for whatever reason, the recipient is not prepared to do this, the speaker can engage in reparative work in an attempt to have their talk properly understood and responded to. Specifically, if the speaker of an assessable item hears that an assessment is not immediately forthcoming and not projectable within the same unit of talk, they may attempt to revise and extend the current turn (or "unit of talk") so as to provide further opportunities for the recipient to produce the assessment in the appropriate place. To this end, speakers have available to them specific practices of speaking which both mark the absence of the assessment and provide further opportunities for the assessment to be done. For instance, in the following example, Dee is telling Mark how much money her daughter and son-in-law have to pay each month in mortgage payments.

(45) Holt p. 224, lines 39–42, QT 13.00
39 Dee: [↑Oo it's about[five hundred pounds a month the um:
40 (.)
41 Mark: ↑Uhh::::,h[hhh
42 Dee: [repayments. But uh-he get[s'
43 Mark: [↑↑'OW TH' ELL D'
44 YOU ↑DO ↓it ehh[heh huh (.) .hk .hh[hhhh
45 Dee: [( ) [Well there you ↑a:re.

At lines 39–42 in extract (45), Dee tells Mark that her daughter and son-in-law are paying 500 pounds a month in mortgage installments. There are several places in the course of this turn at which Mark might have produced an assessment that conveyed his understanding that five hundred pounds is "a lot of money". By the time Dee has produced the first syllable of "hundred" the content of the turn is projectable (it is unlikely to turn out that they have to pay 500 pence, shillings, pesos etc.!). At the completion of "pounds", Dee has come to a point of possible turn completion and again at the completion of "month". However, in both cases, when Dee reaches these places within the unfolding course of her turn she has no evidence to suggest that Mark has recognized something assessable in her talk. When Mark fails to produce the assessment, Dee delays the progress of the turn by the production of first "um:" and then a micropause. Such features of the talk may alert the recipient to the fact that the assessment is missing while at the same time extending the turn-at-talk so as to allow the recipient further opportunities to produce it before the current speaker's turn reaches completion. Notice then that Mark finally does produce an elaborate display of recognition beginning with "↑Uhh:::::,hhhh" and continuing with "↑↑'OW TH' ELL D'YOU ↑DO ↓it". Extract (13) presents a similar case. Here Dee is telling Mark what the same couple have had to pay in rent.

(46) Holt [224–225 QT13:00]

01	Dee:		[An:d um:n (0.3) but he gets quite a- a very very: (.) u-
02			reasonable rent allowance being in the po[lice(it's a)=
03	Mark:		[Oh:: ye:s:,
04	Dee:		=pe:rk
05			(0.6)
06	Dee:		But even so it's stih- I think it wz (.) i:t wz (O.2)
07			'bout six
08			(0.3)
09	Mark:		.hhhhhhh[hhhhh- [huhh-h u h h h h h h h h h h ((YAWN))
10	Dee:		[six (0.3) [hundred (.) six hundred'n fifty
11			pou:nd if 'e 'adn' got iz rent[allowance
12	Mark:	→	[↑.hhho:hhhh
13			(0.6)
14	Mark:		hho:h ( ) people couldn(.)'t even (.) dlook at
15			tha[↑:t,hhh
16	Dee:		[Well ex↑actly. ↑Course you ↓couldn't.

At line 01 Dee explains that the burden of the rent is lessened slightly by the husband's rent allowance. In doing so, Dee self-repairs, replacing "quite" with "very". At line 05, she is on the way to saying "it's still" and thus projectably about to report the cost. This is however abandoned and replaced by the epistemically downgraded "I think it wz – it wz about six" This once again presents Mark with a place where he could assess the amount of money being spent. Although she has not prosodically come to a clear point of possible completion at this point, Dee suspends her talk, thereby allowing a slight gap to develop. However, instead of producing an assessment, Mark begins a very audible and obvious yawn. By the initiation of the yawn, Dee can see that Mark is now unavailable to do the assessment. Persevering throughout the yawn, Dee produces "six", "hundred", and subsequently corrects this with "six hundred and fifty pound" and then adds the conditional phrase "if he hadn't got his rent allowance". Finally, and in overlap with the last component of Dee's turn, Mark produces the appreciative gasp at line 12 and once again elaborates the assessment in his subsequent talk (lines 14–15).

In extracts (45) and (46) the production of an assessment is delayed. Rather than let the assessable item pass without comment from the recipient, the speaker builds on additional components to their turn. These both mark the absence of the recipient's assessment and provide further opportunities for its production. A final example of this phenomenon comes from the Goodwins' 1987 paper on assessments.

(47) G.126:31:40
01 Debbie: oh we had homemade ice cream today.
02 Eileen: Ah::[:
03 Debbie: [They had big- (0.4) We-
04 I don't know what they're like.
05 =I never *s*aw 'em before.
06 But you put ice and salt around them?
07 =And there'sa a little can in the middle
08 and you just pert- We had
09 pea:ch? *H*omemade *p*each, en [strawberry.
10 Eileen: ↑ [A*h*oh:,

Eileen begins assessment head shake

The authors (1987: 17–18) provide the following analysis:

> The second version of "peach" is treated by recipient in a way that the first wasn't, and this change in alignment appears to be responsive to the details of the way in which speaker organizes her emerging description. First, by interrupting that talk before it has reached a point of recognizable completion speaker shows recipient that for some reason it is no longer appropriate for that talk to continue moving towards completion. What speaker does next, in part by virtue of its status as a repair of the talk just marked as flawed, provides some information about what she found to be problematic with the earlier talk. In so far as the second version differs from the first primarily through the addition of the word "homemade" that term is marked as in some sense essential for proper understanding of the description in progress. However, recipient has already been told in line 1 that the ice cream was homemade. Thus speaker is not telling recipient something new, but instead informing her that something that she already knows has not yet been taken proper account of. . . . In brief it would appear that the problem being remedied with the repair lies not so much in the talk itself as in the way in which recipient is visibly dealing with it. Moreover speaker is able not only to see this problem but to initiate action leading to a remedy of it while the description itself is still in progress.

To conclude this discussion, we've seen that a number of activities appear not to be organized primarily in relation to utterance completion. Rather, gaze, laughter, displays of recognition and recipient assessments may become relevant *within the current TCU*. I've provided evidence that where such displays or assessments are not undertaken within the TCU, participants may orient to them as missing.

Collaboratively Built Turns

Collaboratively built turns provide another clear case of interaction between speaker and hearer *within* the bounds of a single turn-at-talk. In collaboratives, or what are sometimes called "anticipatory completions", one speaker starts the turn and another finishes it (or refinishes it). Let's begin with the example from the conversation between Madeline and Marsha:

(48) Madeline 2 detail
14 Marsha: [oh- you mean for] living in: Madeline?
15 Madeline: ye:ah
16 (0.3)
17 Marsha: ·hh It's just (0.8)
18 Madeline: no:t possible.=h[uh?
19 Marsha: [ye:ah we- gi:na tri:ed that at one
20 ti:[me.=b't-]

Here Madeline has asked Marsha if she'd be willing to rent out the bottom part of her garage. Very early on there is reason for Madeline to suppose that the request will not be granted, and here Marsha seems to be on the way to producing an account for that rejection, having already queried the request with "oh- you mean for living in Madeline?". Marsha's turn beginning with "It's just" is however suspended and a substantial pause develops. Notice that this turn is quite clearly *not* complete at this point and in that respect it may be found to invite completion by the recipient. It is, in the end, Madeline who breaks the silence and completes the turn with "not possible.". Rejection of a request is a delicate matter and here the practice of collaborative completion is nicely fitted to dealing with it: by completing the turn, Madeline shows that this is not a totally unexpected, and thus not an unreasonable, response to the request she has made. However, the collaborative construction creates another problem. This is *Marsha*'s garage being talked about, and, clearly, whether it is rented out or not is not up to Madeline. More specifically, whether the arrangement is possible or not is for Marsha rather than Madeline to decide. So while Madeline's completion nicely dealt with the delicacy involved in the rejection of a request, it has also involved Madeline saying something that was, in a sense, not for her to say. She deals with this by appending a tag, "huh?", which marks this as something requiring confirmation from Marsha – and confirmation it gets. And another nuance to notice about this is that Marsha's confirming "yeah" does not in fact come in response to the "huh?" tag but rather overlaps it. So Marsha treats this as something requiring her confirmation, quite apart from whether this has been invited by Madeline's tag question.

Gene Lerner (1991, 1996, 2004) has studied collaboratively built turns extensively, looking at both the grammatical resources which provide for them and the interactional functions they serve.[8] Lerner notes that many of the turn-constructional units out of which collaboratives are built are composed of more than one component: they are made up of what he calls "compound TCUs". Mom's talk in the example below is an instance:

(49) [Virginia] Simplified
01 Mom: if you save(d) yer allowance, an:' um: you could get=
02 =these little extra things.

Although Mom's turn contains only a single TCU, it is nevertheless composed of two units. The first unit is "If you save(d) your allowance," and the second is "you could get these little extra things.". Now you can see that many collaborative completions are constructed out of just such compound TCUs.

(50) GTS Schegloff collaboratives handout
01 D: They haftuh run programs for them to rehabilitate
02 them tuh- to deal with the new materials. And if
03 they ca:n't,
04 R: they're out.
05 (.)
06 D: Mm hm,

(51) Unknown, Schegloff collaboratives handout
01 Boy: 'cause if we get to go (0.7) to Toys R Us,
02 (0.5)
03 Girl: Den get tuh buy something hhhuhhh.
04 Boy: Uh huh,

(52) GTS Schegloff collaboratives handout
01 Dan: when the group reconvenes in two weeks=
02 Roger: They're gunna issue strait jackets

In each case the second speaker completes the utterance by producing the second component of a compound TCU. Lerner (1996: 241) notes that in some environments production of a collaborative completion initiates a small sequence "in which the acceptance or rejection of the proffered completion becomes a specially relevant responsive action". Notice then that in (50) and (51) the first speaker accepts the completion that the other has produced with a minimal acknowledgement token. And again in the following cases the initial speaker accepts the completion with "yeah" or "yes".

(53) MDE – Madeline and Marsha – Madeline has called to ask her friend's mom (Marsha) if she can rent the bottom part of her garage.
14 Mar: [oh- you mean for] living in: Madeline?
15 Mad: ye:ah
16 (0.3)
17 Mar: .hh It's just (0.8)
18 Mad: no:t possible.=h[uh?
19 Mar: [ye:ah we- Gi:na tri:ed that at one
20 ti:[me.=b't-]

(54) Schegloff collaboratives handout
01 Carol: Wuhd she do:.
02 (0.4)
03 Chris: Oh nothin she's just a:
04 (0.4)
05 Carol: bitch.
06 Chris: tch! Yeah:.

(55) Schegloff collaboratives handout
01 B: Well do you think she would fit in?
02 A: Uhm, uh I don't know, what I'm hesitating about is
03 uh- uhm maybe she would, (1.0) uhm but I would
04 hesitate to uhm
05 B: recommend her.
06 A: Yes,

The initial speaker, however, need not accept a completion so unequivocally. In (56), for instance, the completion is accepted but not as the thing the original speaker would have said:

(56) Dad and daughter (Lerner 2004)
01 Daughter: Oh here dad (0.2) a good way to get tho:se corners out
02 (0.2)
03 Dad: is to stick yer finger insi:de.
04 Daughter: well, that's one way.

In (57) the completion is disattended and an alternate completion offered by the original speaker.

(57) Labov: TA (Lerner 2004)
01 C: Kids can eat twice as much as you (.)
02 D: En' it doesn't mean [anything
03 C: [en' not gain any wei[::ght.
04 D: [Right

And in (58) the completion is rejected:

(58) (H and M) (Lerner 2004)
01 Hal: and the answer is perhaps, though I don't really know,
02 that it isn't a substitution,
03 Max: it's a transformation
04 Hal: no it's not even a transformation.

There are a number of observations we can make about this phenomenon of collaboratively built turns. First, it provides further, particularly strong evidence for the projectability of the turn-in-progress in terms of its grammar, content/action and intonation. Second, projectability seems to be maximized by certain kinds of grammatical structures. Thus, collaboratively built turns often (though certainly not always) involve some kind of compound structure (if–then, said+quotation, when . . . , etc.). Third, in some cases the first part of the turn is designedly incomplete (see Koshik 2002), suggesting that initial speakers may in fact set out to prompt or invite completion by another. Fourth, in some cases the completion is followed by a turn from the original speaker which accepts, rejects or modifies the completion. There is here an issue of who "owns" the utterance as a whole. Fifth, such collaboratively built utterances provide a very strong way for the recipient to demonstrate understanding of what is being said. Sixth, they also allow a recipient to show agreement and alignment. And, finally, such collaboratively built turns appear to be a resource for speakers who find themselves in the position of having to say something potentially delicate. Collaboratively built turns allow the burden of responsibility for the saying of something delicate to be shared between participants (see examples (53), (54), (55)).

Before leaving this topic, I want to very briefly consider the issue of what to do with "related" cases. Consider the following case (59) from later in the conversation between Madeline and Marsha. Marsha has remembered that "the woman next door" has little rooms that she rents out. However, after Madeline receipts this news with "oh that's good.", Marsha seems to have remembered something else that may be a problem. Marsha begins by saying "but she's uh" and then stops speaking, allowing a significant pause to develop. Up to this point the case is remarkably similar to the example we looked at from earlier in this call. Notice that, rather than attempt a completion of this clearly incomplete turn, Madeline prompts Marsha to complete it by asking "she's what?". And note that Marsha does not actually complete the turn at all. Rather, she restarts it, saying "wull she was moved out:.".

(59) Madeline 2

10	Marsha:		cuz the woman nextdoor has little(-) (1.0) little rooms and
11			so=f : : or[th.]
12	Madeline:		[(does she?)]
13	Marsha:		=·hh[h
14	Madeline:		[oh that's good.=
15	Marsha:	→	=which she rents. but she's: uh
16			(1.2)
16	Madeline:	→	she's what?
17	Marsha:	→	°hhh wull she was moved ou:t. she's ninety and terribly
18			senile.=I think she finally went(-) (0.6) they sent her
19			to live with a chi:ld. ·hhh and I don't know who's in
20			charge of . . .

There are then alternative practices available for speaking in particular interactional circumstances. Many cases of collaborative completion are alternative to the kind of thing Madeline does here – prompting completion by the original speaker. Others are alternative to repair by means of an understanding check. Participants thus select among alternative ways of speaking – alternative practices – and this in turn has consequences for the ways in which sequences of talk develop.

In this section we have reviewed two ways in which the sentence, utterance or turn which a speaker ultimately produces is the product of an interaction between a speaker and a hearer. This is true even where the speaker is silent, since the absence of response has consequences just as significant as the presence of one. Examining transcripts, it is easy to be taken in by what Merleau-Ponty described as the "retrospective illusion" (Merleau-Ponty 1968, 2003), whereby we project onto the participants our own disembodied, abstract sense of the conversation as a whole. Instead, conversation analysis demands that, as far as is possible, we adopt the perspective of the participants for whom whatever happened later hadn't happened yet. Participants in a conversation do not have a transcript to tell them what will happen next. All they have are the projections that the talk-of-the-moment affords them.

Conclusion

We began this chapter by considering different positions within turns-at-talk. Turn beginnings are important for what they project about the type of turn that is being produced, and it is at turn beginning that we find the various tokens such as "oh", "well", "anyway", "by the way", and so on that convey a relation between the current turn and what has gone before. We saw that a turn need not end with a completion. Rather, speakers may construct their turn so as to end it with a completion or with something else. Moreover, once completed a turn may be recompleted. Whereas turn-prefaces like "oh" and "look" and "well" apparently mark a relation between a current turn and a prior, turn increments and tag questions mark a sequential relation between the current turn and a projected next.

We then considered various ways in which the turn-at-talk is the product of an interaction between speaker and recipient. Here we noted that in the course of its production a turn may pose certain tasks for a recipient, such as displaying recognition of some referent or displaying that some item in the talk is worthy of assessment. Failure by the recipient to display recognition may be treated by the current speaker as evidence that her talk has not been properly understood, and this may occasion various kinds of reparative work. Collaborative completions provide another clear case of interaction within the bounds of a single turn-at-talk. Taken together, the studies reviewed in this chapter indicate that turns, and even TCUs, do not constitute the minimal unit of interaction. Rather, the evidence suggests that recipients monitor a turn word by word (perhaps sound by sound) so as to find not only that it is now beginning, now continuing, now reaching completion but *also* where, in the course of its production, they may be called upon to respond either with talk (as in the case of a designedly incomplete utterance) or something else (e.g. laughter, gaze, display of recognition, etc.). And of course a speaker may monitor the recipient at precisely this level of detail, and thus may find that she has not done the thing that the talk made relevant. This can then lead the current speaker to make adjustments to what she was saying, or how she was saying it. It is in this sense that the recipient can be seen as the co-author of the talk (Goodwin 1986a, Duranti and Brenneis 1986).

Notes

1 There are exceptions, of course. A turn beginning with "What" may end up as "What a week!" or "What a beautiful baby!".

2 Students sometimes insist that Jon is in fact proposing these as possible places to play golf. The evidence against this otherwise intuitively appealing interpretation is not restricted to the design of both Jon and Guy's turns at talk (as I have sketched) – it is also found in the fact that after Guy recovers "Shorecliffs" from Jon's talk, converting it into a proposal, Jon indicates that although it might be possible to "get on there", "they charge too much". Thus, in saying "can you get in there" Guy has anticipated one possible reason for passing over Shorecliffs but, as it turns out, this is not why Jon has done so. The point then is that the subsequent talk provides further evidence that Jon was not proposing that they play at Shorecliffs.

3 This issue of what difference the "oh" makes in a case like this is one of considerable complexity and subtlety that cannot be adequately dealt with here. My suggestion of the kind of difference it makes in this case is based partly on an ongoing study of receipts such as "you're kidding" and "oh you're kidding". In that case, the presence of an "oh" registers the news in what has been said and, as such, *accepts* it. Receipts without "oh" do not register the news and thus are routinely heard as challenging.

4 And indeed its absence in this and other similar contexts (such as in response to advice), and alternation with a form such as "right" or "okay", can itself be heard as claiming that the questioner already knew the answer given.

5 I have not been able to detect any differences in the use of "look" and "lookit".

6 In another call, Emma raises this topic even more abruptly:

(60) NB:II:1:3–4
Emma: =This's rilly been a wee:k hasn'it.
Lottie: Oh: ↓Go:d a lo:ng wee[k. Yeah.]
Emma: [O h : my] ↓God I'm (.) glad it's
over I won't even turn the teevee o[:n.
Lottie: [I won'eether.

Emma: °aOh no. They drag it out so° THAT'S WHERE THEY WE TOOK
OFF on ar chartered flight that sa:me spot didju see it?
(0.7)
·hh when they took him in[the airpla:ne,]
Lottie: [n : N o : : : .] Hell I wouldn'
ev'n wa:tch it. I think it's so ridiculous.

7 On this matter see also the work of Hayashi, e.g. 2004, 2005.
8 See also Lerner and Takagi 1999, and Hayashi 1999, 2001, 2003a.

9

Stories

One of the things that people recurrently do in conversation is tell stories and, as Sacks (1995b: 222) puts it, a "bland fact" about stories is that they require more that one utterance to tell. Since, as we saw in chapter 3, the turn-taking system allocates a single TCU at a time, telling a story can be seen as something of an interactional problem. Specifically, how can a teller secure an extended turn-at-talk within which a story can be told? In this chapter we will begin by considering one solution to this problem – a solution built out of the sequential resources of adjacency pairs: the story preface. But, as Sacks notes, it is possible also to turn things around and see stories not as the source of an interactional problem but rather as themselves a solution. A story can be seen as a package or format which affords its speaker unique opportunities for delivering what it is she has to say. Sacks (1995b: 222–8) points out that, if stories are to function in this way as a solution to the interactional problem of how to produce an extended, multi-unit turn-at-talk, they must be recognizable as stories to their recipients. Furthermore, it's no good if they are recognizable as stories only retrospectively (at their completion for instance). Rather, in order to serve as solutions, the story format must be recognizable *before* the speaker reaches a first point of possible completion. So this raises the question of what it is about a story that makes it recognizable as such.

The interactional environment in which stories emerge can be examined not only in relation to the taking of turns but also to the organization of sequences. A basic distinction here is between stories that embody first actions and make relevant particular seconds and those that are occasioned as responses to first actions.

The embedding of stories in a particular interactional environment has a number of other important dimensions. For instance, a story-telling is significantly shaped by the way in which knowledge of the events being talked about is distributed among the co-participants. Sacks drew attention to one particularly relevant aspect of this in his discussion of how tellers position themselves in relation to the events they talk about – showing, that is, how they know a story. Whether the teller witnessed the events, participated in them, heard about them from a friend has a range of consequences for how the story is told.

Equally significant in shaping the story-telling is the knowledge of the other co-participants. As C. Goodwin (1986a) has shown, an audience need not be composed of a single, undifferentiated group of recipients. Rather, it is quite typical for an audience to contain some who know significantly more about the events being recounted than others. The particular and diverse ways in which different recipients are informed with respect to the events, people, activities and settings being talked about again has important consequences for the telling. Sacks (1995b: 437–43) discussed one particularly clear case of this in his lecture titled "Spouse Talk". There he noted that a speaker may recurrently find himself or herself telling a story that his or her spouse has already heard or otherwise talking about events in which his or her spouse also participated. Telling a story in the company of another participant who already knows the details of what is being told appears to conflict with a basic principle of recipient design: "do not tell others what they already know." Looked at from the other side – that of the recipient – this recurrent situation means that a spouse may find himself or herself listening to a story which he or she already knows. Such situations, notes Sacks, provide for particular kinds of joint-telling.

Bland Fact: Stories Take More than One Utterance

Anthropologists, linguists and folklorists often isolate stories from the processes of interaction within which they emerge before submitting them to analysis. Indeed, by eliciting narratives through the use of interview questions, the researcher effectively treats as inconsequential the interactional context within which such narratives are situated. In contrast, for participants stories are accountably occasioned, which is to say that a story is told for a reason. Indeed, a story-teller who does not make clear why *this* story is being told in *this* way at *this* moment is likely to be met with a question such as "so?", "so what?" or "what's that got to do with what we were talking about?". In order to see how stories are occasioned we need to consider the manner in which they are initiated. One way in which this can be done is through the use of a "story-preface" (Sacks 1974).

The following example is taken from a recording of a dinner-time conversation. The participants are three siblings, Virginia, Wes and Beth, their mother, and Wes's girlfriend Prudence.

(1) Virginia qt 15:20
23 Virginia: [Um(>binwin<) (.) Mom, (·hh) w'd you talk t'Beth
24 becuz (0.8) EVERY MORNIN', ·hh she will not turn off
25 her alarm clock. An' she comes in there an' tells me
26 her alarm clock is singin', Mom.
27 Mom: ( )
28 Prudence: (Mm n(h)ot)
29 Mom: huh huh
30 Prudence?: mm hm [hm ·hh hh ·hh
31 Virginia: [Mom I(s)- I swear she's flippin' out.
32 ???: (Ooh yeah)
33 (0.2)
34 Prudence: Whaddya mean she said it was singin'?
35 (0.5)
36 Virginia: ([ )]
37 Prudence: → [You know what she said] one ti:me?

38		(.)
39		((dog bark))
40		(0.4)
41	Prudence:	One [night we were talki- we had porkchops fer dinner an'=
42	Virginia:	[( )
43	Prudence:	=thuh next mornin' I went tuh wake her u(huh)p ·hm! an' she
44		was in thuh bed goin' (1.1) they're porkchops. They're all:
45		porkchops. People are porkc(h)ho(h)ps sih hih high heh
46	Wes:	heh heh heh
47		(.)
48	Prudence:	·hhhh uhh! A(h)ll thuh p(h)eop(h)le a(h)re p(h)orkcha(h)
49		·hh ·uh ·h[hh

As we saw in chapter 3, the organization of turns-at-talk is locally managed on a turn-by-turn basis. As Sacks, Schegloff and Jefferson (1974) demonstrated, participants anticipate points where the current turn will be complete. Such projected points of possible completion constitute "discrete places in the developing course of a speaker's talk . . . at which ending the turn or continuing it, transfer of the turn or its retention become relevant" (Schegloff 1992b: 116). Story prefaces, such as Prudence's "You know what she said one time?", solve a problem generated by this system. In telling a story, a speaker often reaches completion of a turn-unit (e.g. in line 41 "we had porkchops fer dinner") without at the same time completing the story. As such, in order to allow for the telling of a story in its entirety, the usual association of turn completion and transition relevance must be suspended. A story preface allows recipients to see that points of possible turn completion which fall within the scope of the story-telling are not transition-relevant and do not constitute opportunities for another speaker to take a turn.

But this raises another issue. How do recipients determine that "dinner" in line 41 is not the last element of the story, or "up" in line 43, or "porkchops" in line 44? In short, how do participants locate the story's completion, at which point transition to a next speaker might relevantly take place? Story-prefaces help to solve this problem as well. A preface provides the recipients with clues regarding what the story will consist of and, therefore, what it will take for the story to reach completion. So, in the example given, the recipients can monitor Prudence's telling to locate "something that Beth said" and, upon hearing such a thing, will have reason to expect the completion of the telling is imminent. Tellers also typically provide recipients with resources with which to determine what kind of a response is due at story's completion, if not in the preface then elsewhere in the telling. Prudence, for instance, punctuates the final lines of her story with laugh tokens (e.g. line 45's "porkc(h)ho(h)ps"), thereby marking this as something funny and the story as a whole as "humorous". Notice also in this respect that Prudence's story is touched off by something else. That is, we can see that there is some relation between what Virginia has said in lines 20–8 and what Prudence says in lines 41–8. Both are about Beth and in both tellings Beth is reported as saying something unusual, funny, or strange. We will see that stories often come clumped together like this and, when they do, subsequent stories are specifically designed to display a relation to previous ones.

Story prefaces do more than simply carve out a place for a story within an unfolding course of talk. Consider the following example from the same occasion as our last example. Here Wes and Virginia discuss Beth's excessive drinking.

(2) Virginia

Virginia: pt! You know the other weeken' [when she went downta=
Prudence?: [·uhh
Virginia: =Charleston?
Wes: She tried tuh quit smokin', I know that.B't she couldn'
do that.
(0.3)
Virginia: (Well,) (.) she wen' downta Charleston the other
weeken' with Paul?
(0.9)
Virginia: An' Paul s[aid ( )
Beth: [(They were) down there, stu:pid.
(0.4)
Prudence: An' wha'd Paul say?
Virginia: Paul said she was laughin' 'er head off an' she was so:
bombed.
(0.2)
Prudence: eh huh huh [huh

According to Sacks, the principle of "recipient design" entails that a speaker should not tell a "recipient what they already know" (1995: 438). In aligning participants as story-recipients then, tellers are concerned to determine whether the story they propose to tell is "news" for the recipient(s) – that it is not already known to them. We can see this in example (2). Here Virginia initiates a telling by eliciting Wes's recognition of a recent event. Wes responds by telling Virginia something that he knows about this event (that Beth tried to quit smoking) but this turns out not to be the thing that Virginia wants to tell. Wesley's response then treats Virginia's recognition solicit in lines 32–4 as advertising a telling and he makes a guess at what this might be by telling something he knows about Beth's trip to Charleston. However, by not getting it right, Wes suggests that he does *not* in fact know the thing Virginia is proposing to talk about and thus he invites its telling. Virginia begins the story but, at line 42, Beth attempts to arrest and block it by suggesting that telling it violates the rule of recipient design: according to Beth, Virginia is telling Wes and Prudence what they already know ("They were down there, stu:pid."). Beth's effort to block the telling appears successful and the story is only resumed after Prudence asks at line 44 "What did Paul say?", thereby suggesting that she is uninformed with respect to at least this component of the projected story. We can see then that issues of newsworthiness are crucially implicated not only in the initiation of a story but also across the course of its production. Indeed, participants can be seen to monitor a telling for parts of it that they or other intended recipients do or do not know about.

As noted, in conversation, stories are accountably occasioned, which is to say that tellers need to show *why* they are telling *this* story at *this* moment in this conversation. As Jefferson notes, "techniques are used to display a relationship between the story and prior talk and thus account for, and propose the appropriateness of, the story's telling" (Jefferson 1978: 220). According to Jefferson's analysis, techniques for introducing stories into the ongoing talk often consist of two discrete devices: (1) a "disjunct marker" such as "oh" or "incidentally" which signals that the talk to follow is not topically coherent with the adjacent prior talk, and (2) an "embedded repetition" which "locates, but does not explicitly cite, the element of prior talk which triggered the story". Here is one of the examples she gives to illustrate:

(3) GTS:II:2:64
Ken: The cops, *o*ver the hill. There's a place up in
*Mul*holland where they've- where they're building those
Hous[ing projects?
Roger: [*Oh* have you ever taken them Mullhollan' time trials?
.hh You go up there wid a girl. A buncha guys'r up there
an'
((STORY follows))

Jefferson goes on to note that whereas some stories are touched off by prior talk, in other cases they are shown by their tellers to be occasioned by something in the local physical environment such as the tee-shirt someone is wearing.

Recognizability: Story Format

The units of conversation, be they stories, turns, requests, complaints or whatever else, do not typically come with labels attached. Occasionally someone will preface a request by saying, "Can I ask you a favor?" or a story by saying, "Lemme tell you what happened to me today" but more often than not speakers will launch directly into a request or story without providing any such label.[1]

This means of course that requests, complaints, stories and so on must be designed in such a way as to provide for their own recognizability as possible requests, complaints, stories and so on by their recipients. We have dealt with this issue at several places in earlier chapters; here we need to consider how it is relevant to the telling of stories in conversation. Sacks (1995b: 222) writes:

> A question that one eventually comes to raise is: Although something may be callable a "story," is it recognizable as a story? Is it produced as a story? Specifically as a story? And is there some relationship between its production as a story and its recognition as a story? And why should it be produced and recognized as a story?

Of course, there are many parts of a conversation that *might* be called "stories". Here Sacks suggests that if we are looking specifically at stories we want to consider spates of talk that were designed by their tellers to be recognizable to their recipients *as* stories.[2] "We're assigning the candidate name 'story' to something for which that name is provably warranted, provably relevant to the thing coming off as a story. If it isn't provably relevant then it's of no particular interest that it's a story or not" (Sacks 1995b: 223). Before considering the larger significance of "recognizability" in this context, let's treat the issue as an empirical matter and ask what makes stories recognizable as such to their recipients. How is recognition that a story-telling is being initiated (or is continuing) displayed in conversation? Consider the following cases.

(4) Virginia
32 Virginia: → pt! You know the other weeken' [when she went downta=
33 Prudence: [·uhh
34 Virginia: → =Charleston?
35 Wes: She tried tuh quit smokin', I know that.B't she couldn'
36 do that.
37 (0.3)
38 Virginia: → (Well,) (.) she wen' downta Charleston the other
39 weeken' with Paul?

(5) GTS:II:2:64
04 Roger: *Oh* have you ever taken them Mulhollan' time trials?
05 .hh You go up there wid a girl. A buncha guys'r up there
06 an'

(6) Rip yer hand
01 Ron: ere ere Matt
02 don't rip your hand off (.) it's uh uh it's uh pop
03 Matt: °oh man cool [thanks°
04 Dave: [hahaha
05 Matt: I was tryin to be really macho 'n [stuff
06 ?: [hahhahha
07 Ron: → wn I wuz in Mexico?
08 Gina: mmhmhm
09 Ron: → an' an' the du::de that we wen- we wen on a crui::se?

Assuming for the moment that each of these is in fact a story, we can ask whether their beginnings share any features. The arrows have been placed to pick out one, particularly obvious, thing that they have in common. Each story begins with an indication of the setting in which the to-be-narrated action took place. So one thing that may make a story recognizable as a story is the provision of a setting for the action. Of course not all stories start with such a clear specification of the physical or geographic setting, but many do and those that don't often foreground some other *alternative* kind of context of the narrated action that is particularly relevant.

So a recurrent feature of story beginnings is the characterization of the setting in which the action takes place. In fact there is evidence that participants orient to the specification of setting as a required feature of some story beginnings. Consider in this respect the following case:

(7) Chicken Dinner
16 Shane: [Uh wz goi:n
17 crazy tihday uh on th'on the roa:d
18 (0.2)
19 Vivian: We' yih know w't he di[↑:d?
20 Shane: [Wen'outta my fuckin'mi[:nd.
21 Vivian: [He maHHde
22 (.)
23 Vivian: → a right- it wz- in Sanna Monig'yihknow have- theh have:
24 [all those: right]

25 Shane: [O h : shit I ma]de a left (.) le[ft
26 Vivian: [They have (0.2) w:one
27 way stree:ts'n evrihthi:ng? En then two way streets (.)
28 He made e- (0.3) a lef'tu:rn fr'm a one way stree:t,
29 (0.2) into a ↑two way street ·hh bu[t ↑h e thought it]=

Here it appears that Vivian has begun to produce a news announcement ("a right onto a one way street . . .") but, upon finding that the news cannot be told in a single TCU, self-repairs and initiates, instead, a story telling. Relevant in the current context is that, once Vivian decides to tell this as a story rather than a single TCU news announcement she immediately provides a setting for it: "Santa Monica", the place where the action happened.

Now consider the following case which begins with Vivian responding to a complaint from Shane that the potato he is eating is not fully cooked.

(8) Chicken Dinner
15 Vivian: They were bi:g.That's ↓why. I[mean rilly bi]g.
16 Shane: [Y a y yea:h.]
17 (0.4)
18 Nancy: Yeah where'dju git tho:se. Gah ther hu:[ge.
19 Vivian: → [Well w't happ'n
20 was we picked'p a ba:[g
21 Shane: [Oh yeh it wz ba:[:d
22 Vivian: [en they w'r
23 ro:tt'n.
24 (0.7)
25 Vivian: So they said (1.7) go back en pick anothuh ba:g. _____
26 (1.1)
27 ((bang)) (1.2)
28 Shane: All[the bags w'rott'n they w-all ↓s:me:lled. _____
29 Vivian: [Theh-
30 (0.2)
31 Shane: Ri[ght'nna]
32 Nancy: [O h :](g)[Go:d
33 Shane: [Right'nna maw:kits.=
34 Shane: =(The[stu[ff wuh)/(di[sgu:[sting)
35 Vivian: [So [then I picked the]b e s t p'↓tato]es
36 Michael: [Where dju sh-]Where dju sho:p)]
37 (.)
38 Vivian: An' I js put'm in th'ba:g.[·h .t ·h]=
39 [(0.3)]=
40 Michael: =[Where'dju sho:p.]
41 Vivian: =[An: we walked ou][:t.
42 Shane: [We wen'[tuh Alpha]Beta:.=
43 Nancy?: [nghhhn,]
44 Shane: =En ther usually very good.
45 (0.4)
46 Nancy: Yah they a:re.
47 Shane: Usually bettuh th'n Ra:lphs,

Notice that after Vivian explains that the potatoes are not completely cooked because they were big, and then "rilly big.", Nancy agrees with "yeah". Nancy follows up by asking "where'dju git tho:se. Gah ther hu:ge." Although it was a negative consequence, their being undercooked, which initially occasioned Vivan's characterization of the potatoes' size, here Nancy's "gah ther huge" is positively valenced and clearly appreciative.[3] In the context of this positive assessment, Nancy's question "where d'ju git those" can be heard as seeking a recommendation – that is, as asking, where can *I* get some of those?

Now notice that Vivian does not immediately answer the question "where d'ju git those". Rather she begins to respond to Nancy with "well what happened was we picked up a bag.". This is not unambiguously the beginning of a story but it is also not an answer to the question as put and therefore is hearably incomplete in this context. There are aspects of this utterance that, as we shall see, recurrently characterize the beginnings of stories. First of all, we find the framing by "What happened was . . .". Secondly, with "we" Vivian establishes characters for a possible story to be told (she and Shane) (see Lerner 1992). Finally, continuing a bit, we find that this utterance continues with "en they w'r ro:tt'n." With this Vivian establishes something of a problem – something that might be expected to be resolved within the story.

So we can see that Vivian does not provide a characterization of the setting in which the action took place. Given that this is a recurrent feature of story beginnings, we can ask if perhaps there is a systematic basis for its absence here? Recall that the telling of this story was prompted by a question from Nancy about where Vivian bought the potatoes. If Vivian had provided a setting for the story, the question would have thereby been answered without the story as yet being told. Moreover, as we noted, that question is at least hearable as seeking a recommendation and as the story makes clear, Vivian's opinion of the place where she got the potatoes is not, in the end, positive. So the story here is in a sense a solution to a problem created by Nancy's question. To answer this simply would be to imply an endorsement of the place where the potatoes were purchased but, as Vivian makes clear, this is something she wishes to avoid. A story in this position allows for a much more nuanced response to the question.

A recurrent position for stories, then, is in answer to questions, and this sequential positioning constrains the shape that stories take in particular ways. In the following example, Nancy and Hyla are talking about a play that they are to see later in the evening. Nancy asks Hyla, who has made the plans, "How didju hear about it from the paper?" By adding a candidate answer ("from the paper") Nancy designs this as a yes–no interrogative that makes a type-conforming "yes" or "no" response relevant (Raymond 2003, chapter 5). Hyla seems initially prepared to answer the question with a type non-conforming confirmation but self-repairs saying "A'right when was it".

```
(9)  Hyla and Nancy
07   Nancy:  [How did]ju hear about it from the pape[r?
08   Hyla:                                           [·hhhhh I sa:w-
09                  (0.4)
10   Hyla:   A'right when was:(it,)/(this,)
11                  (0.3)
12   Hyla:   The week before my birthda:[y, ]
13   Nancy:                             [Ye] a[:h,
14   Hyla:                                    [I wz looking in the Calendar
15           section en there was u:n, (·) un a:d yihknow a liddle:: u-
16           thi:ng, ·hh[hh
17   Nancy:             [Uh hu:h,=
18   Hyla:   =At- th'-th'theater's called the Met Theater it's on
```

Point[setta.]
Nancy: [The Me]:t,
(·)
Nancy: I never heard of i[t.
Hyla: [I hadn't either. ·hhh But anyways, .-en
theh the moo- thing wz th'↓Dark e'th' ↓Top a'th' ↑Stai[:rs.]
Nancy: [Mm-h]m[:,
Hyla: [EnI
nearly wen'chhrazy cz I[: I:lo:ve]that] mo:vie.]
Nancy: [y:Yeah I kn]ow y]ou lo:ve] tha::t.=
Hyla: =s:So::, ·hh an' like the first sho:w,=
Nancy: =M[m hmm,]
Hyla: [wz g'nna] be:,
(·)
Hyla: on my birthday.=
Nancy: =Uh hu[h,]
Hyla: [I'm] go'[n awhh whould hI love-
Nancy: [(So-)
(·)
Hyla: yihknow fer Sim tuh [take me tuh that.]
Nancy: [Y a y u : : h ,]

Notice then that the story here is occasioned once again by a question. The question includes the presupposition that Hyla "heard about" the play but the story that follows reveals that this is not quite right. As Hyla makes clear, it was not that she "heard about" the play by some happy coincidence but rather that, a week before her birthday (line 12), she was "looking" (line 14) in the Calendar section. Here then an initial answer to the question starting with "I saw . . ." is abandoned and replaced by a story which addresses a problem with the way in which the question was formulated.

We can note a parallel with the story about Shane's driving. Here we find Vivian producing the pre-announcement "We' yih know w't he di:d?" and subsequently beginning the projected announcement "He made a right". The attempt to tell what happened as an announcement and perhaps as a single event – i.e. "He made a right onto a one way street" – is abandoned and what we get instead is the beginning of a story indicated by the provision of a setting ("it was in Santa Monica"). In both cases then an initial attempt to do the telling is abandoned and the teller proceeds instead to provide background to the events in terms of a temporal ("a week before my birthday") or spatial ("Santa Monica") setting. As we've seen, a description of the temporal or spatial setting, background, may provide for the recognizability of the talk in progress as a story. Notice in this respect what Nancy does in line 13. Specifically, in responding with "Yeah" in this position Nancy treats the talk as incomplete and as a multi-unit turn (Schegloff 1982). This then is evidence that she has heard "the week before my birthday" as the first component of an extended telling or story.

A story may then be thought of as a "package" or format which provides its speaker with particular opportunities not available with a single TCU. Specifically, stories are (typically) composed of multiple units which may be deployed to provide background information and complex formulations of story-relevant actions. Moreover, stories provide their speakers with an opportunity to describe something, Shane's driving for instance, in terms of a series of ordered and interrelated actions rather than as a single event.

Stories may also be initiated by some participant other than the one who eventually comes to tell the story. Lerner (1992) describes a practice he terms a story prompt, in which "one participant solicits a story from another participant, while casting others present as recipients."

(10) Schenkein
01 Leni: Oh you haftuh tell'm about yer typewriter honey,

(11) G.126:22:40
01 Paul: Tell y- Tell Debbie about the dog
02 on the golf course t'day
03 Eileen: °eh hnh [*h*nh ha has! [ha!
04 Paul: [hih hih [Heh Heh! ·hh hh
05 Eileen: ·h Paul en I got ta the first *gr*een,

In cases where the proposed teller does not take up the story the prompter may expand the preface as in the following instance:

(12) Auto 75:15 – 78:7 QT 2:11 – 3:58
15 Phyllis: → =Mike siz there wz a big fight down there las'night,
16 Curt: Oh rilly?
17 (0.5)
18 Phyllis: → Wih Keegan en, what. Paul [de Wa::ld?]
19 Mike: [Paul de Wa:l]d. Guy out of,=
20 Curt: =De Wa:ld yeah I [°(know] ['m.)
21 Mike: [Tiffen.] [D'you know him¿
22 Curt: °Uhhuh=I know who'e i:s,

Lerner (1992) writes:

> Phyllis's utterance at line 15 foreshows a possible story. However, she is setting up the story for someone else to deliver. This is accomplished by formulating the news of the "big fight" as a report by the copresent source of that news. By formulating the news as a second hand account (as "hearsay") she shows Mike to be the authoritative source for unpacking the events summarized by "big fight."

When Mike does not take up the story, Phyllis does not go on to tell it herself. Rather, she builds a syntactically fitted increment onto the preface turn she began in line 15, now naming the fight participants. As Lerner notes, not only does this increment continue the relevance of the projected telling, "naming makes relevant an appraisal of the recognizability of the principal characters by Curt." If recognition is achieved, the telling of the story becomes even more relevant than before since it is now established that it involves people Curt knows about. However, as Lerner shows, the naming is used to produce a concurrent action, one that implicates a next action by Mike and thus selects him as next speaker. Phyllis accomplishes this by producing the names in the form of a "reference check" by which she invites confirmation or correction. Lerner writes:

> Soliciting a confirmation of the names of the principal characters from Mike (while, and as, a solicit of recognition of those same persons from Curt) continues her alignment as a less authoritative prior recipient of the story, continues Curt's alignment as a story recipient and

again makes relevant Mike's entry at a place the story could begin. If Mike, on whose behalf the announcement is being made, does not provide or confirm the reference he would clearly be withholding it. This is a powerful way to prompt a reluctant storyteller.

Entry into a story may thus be a collaborative accomplishment in which one participant shows that a story is available (or, as in this case, actively encourages its telling) while another tells it. We will consider other aspects of what Lerner (1992) describes as "assisted story-telling" below.

Entitlement

In telling and listening to stories participants hold one another accountable in terms of what each is warranted or obligated to know. This helps to explain why tellers often situate themselves within the events of the story as witnesses or as participants and in this way design their stories so as to make visible both the epistemic and the moral basis of their account. In the set of lectures which was published as "Doing Being Ordinary," Sacks (1984b) discusses two stories. In one of them Ellen tells Jean about an incident at a shop called Cromwell's. After remarking "I just thought I'd re-better report to you what's happened at Cromwell's tod:y=", Ellen goes on to say "Well I: got out of my car at fi:ve thirty I: drove arou:nd and of course I had to go by the front of the sto:re,=". In this way, Ellen incorporates within the story, as a constituent feature of that telling, a display of the epistemic grounds upon which the report is based. In this case, Ellen's story is epistemically grounded in first-hand access as a witness. Moreover, by saying "I just thought I'd re-better report", Ellen provides a warrant for her telling in the form of an obligation to tell the recipient her news – an obligation to report on events that have special relevance for this recipient. So Ellen builds into this story both the warrant for its telling and the epistemic grounds which provide an entitlement to tell it. Sacks notes that Ellen is completely comfortable in acting as a witness and never once shows any concern that she might herself have been implicated in the scene.[4]

In the second fragment Sacks examines, Madge is telling Bea about an accident that she witnessed as she was driving "down to Ventura". Madge says: "And on the way home we saw the – most gosh awful wreck." and continues "we have ev- I've ever seen. I've never seen a car smashed into sm- such a small space." Sacks focuses attention on the "entitlement to have experiences" (1984b: 424) asking under what conditions someone is considered to have rights to tell a story, to convey their feelings with respect to it, in short, to transform some set of events into *their* experience. In Madge's story we see once again the way in which the teller claims credentials to tell the story, and that this again involves a display of the epistemic grounds on which the telling is based (here, what she saw). An interesting wrinkle here is to be found in the way Madge self-corrects her assessment from "the most gosh awful wreck we have ever seen" to "the most gosh awful wreck I have ever seen". With the first assessment Madge claims access to her companion's set of experiences against which the current crash might be compared. The corrected assessment is not only downgraded in relation to the first but at the same time does not claim the companion's experiences as a basis for comparison (see Lerner and Kitzinger 2007).

Sacks also picks up on the fact that Madge tells how this accident inconvenienced her, saying: "We were s-parked there for quite a while." He writes (1984b: 424):

I want to suggest that, in having witnessed this event, and having suffered it as well, in some way (for instance, having had to stop on the freeway in a traffic jam by virtue of it), she has become entitled to an experience. That she is entitled to an experience is something different from what her recipient is entitled to, or what someone who otherwise comes across this story is entitled to.

In part, I am saying that it is a fact that entitlement to experiences are differentially available. If I say it as "entitlement," you may think of it as not having rights to it, but that is only part of it. It is also not coming to feel it at all, as compared to feeling it and feeling that you do not have rights to it. The idea is that in encountering an event, and encountering it as a witness or someone who in part suffered by it, one is entitled to an experience, whereas the sheer fact of having access to things in the world, for example, getting the story from another, is quite a different thing.

Issues of entitlement are also implicated in cases where more than one participant may claim knowledge to the events being talked about – a recurrent situation, Sacks suggests, for spouses (see below).

Second Stories and Listening Techniques

We have seen in our discussion of stories produced in response to questions that the sequential position in which a story is produced may be reflected in various aspects of its design. As Sacks and later conversation analysts have noted (e.g. Jefferson 1978, Ryave 1978), stories commonly occur in a series, with a first story followed by a second, a second by a third and so on. The relationship between a first and a second story was something that interested Sacks very much and provided him with materials for a broad range of profound observations. We should begin as Sacks does, with some of the most basic observations. Consider the following example in which Matt, Ron, Dave, Jake and Gina are sitting around on a couch intermittently watching sports on television and chatting. Where the fragment given as (13) begins, Matt is trying to open a bottle of beer with his hand and Ron, noticing this, draws his attention with a summons (line 01) before tossing over a bottle opener. He accounts for his own action by saying "don't rip your hand off (.) it's uh uh it's uh pop" meaning by "pop" that it is not a "twist off" cap.

(13) Rip yer hand
Ron: ere ere Matt
don't rip your hand off (.) it's uh uh it's uh pop
Matt: °oh man cool [thanks°
Dave: [hahaha
Matt: I was tryin to be really macho 'n [stuff
?: [hahhahha
Ron: → wn I wuz in Mexico?
Gina: mmhmhm
Ron: an' an' the du::de that we wen- we wen on a crui::se?
(0.5)
an this guy opnzit with his mouth like this
(0.8)
Dave: yes

14			(1.5)
15	Gina:		ouch
16	Dave:	→	uh guy at my house a- um (.) fourth of <u>july</u> did that
17			(0.7)
18			'n I wuz all wha::t?=I looked at iz teeth and jstall
19			f:::ucked [uh:p
20	Jake:		[hahaha
21	Ron:		[hahahha, Oh Shi:t=
22	Jake:		=haha
23	Ron:		[I dunnit like <u>this</u>] y'know on the table (.)
24	Jake:		[don't drink much huh?]

Here at line 07 Ron launches directly into a story with a turn that introduces the setting ("in Mexico") and a character ("I"). Ron then goes on to tell about someone opening a beer bottle with his teeth. Much of the story is conveyed through gesture, indexed by "like this" (see Sidnell 2006). After Gina responds to the story with "ouch", Dave tells a second story which bears a clear resemblance to the first. One basic yet important observation we can make is that there is a clear relation between these two stories: in a fundamental way they are *about* the same thing. This is manifested in part through Dave's use of "did that" to refer to talk about opening a beer bottle with one's teeth. "Did that" links back to Ron's "like this" and his accompanying gesture, which is actually better described as a "re-enactment" (see Sidnell 2006). So there is a very basic similarity between the two stories but there are also some rather more subtle connections. Consider for instance that each story has exactly two characters – the person who opened the bottle with his mouth and the person who witnessed this. Notice further that in each story there is a consistent mapping of character to teller. Specifically, in both stories the teller is the witness in the story (not the one who opened the bottle). And finally for now let us note that although Ron starts to introduce the main character of his story with "the dude that we wen-" he eventually settles on "this guy" at line 11, and Dave uses this same term in line 16 to refer to the character in his story. Both "this guy" and "uh guy" are non-recognitional reference forms (see chapter 5) but, more than that, they seem decidedly neutral in terms of the stance they take towards the person being talked about. This can be seen if we compare "this guy" with the initial reference form "the dude", which adopts a clearly and unambiguously positive stance towards the person being talked about. In a sense then both tellers introduce their main characters in such a manner as to give away as little as possible as to how they feel about them (and their actions).

It can also be noted that each story has two components. In the first story by Ron, those components are:

1 "We" went on a cruise.
2 This guy opened the bottle with his mouth.

Dave's story has the following two components:

1 A guy did that on the fourth of July at "my" house.
2 "I" saw how it damaged his teeth.

So in terms of their content, their characters, and even their structure these two stories exhibit a relationship to one another. That is, it is not just that after Ron finishes his story, Dave tells his. Rather, Dave's story can be found to have been occasioned by Ron's story; indeed, Dave's story is told in *response* to Ron's. Just as Ron's story is touched off by an event in the world – Matt's attempt to open the bottle he is holding – so Dave's is touched off by the story it follows.

Now there are aspects of Dave's story that clearly reflect its positioning as a second story. Apart from the similarities noted above, we may also note that Dave's story is in certain basic respects "parasitic" on the first. As we have already observed, Dave uses Ron's story as a resource when he glosses the action in his own telling with "did that". Whereas much of Ron's story is taken up with a description of that action, Dave can simply index what Ron has already established and use this in the presentation of his own story.

As Sacks showed, a second story such as Dave's displays an analysis of a first, a hearing of its import. At least, participants treat a second story in this way, which is to say they listen to it for the understanding it displays of a first story. The analysis of a first story embodied by a second is not "neutral" or "objective". Rather, a second story necessarily takes up a certain stance on the first whether that be supportive, appreciative, skeptical or whatever else. The hearing or understanding that it conveys of a first story is one among many possible. It is, as they say, a particular take on it. Consider then that Ron initially introduces the protagonist in his story using the referring expression "the dude", thereby conveying an unambiguously positive stance towards him. Even though he eventually replaces this with the more neutral "this guy", his story seems to express a generally positive stance towards the protagonist in so far as it tells about something Ron takes to be remarkable. Notice also that this story is being told in the shadow of Matt's "I was tryin to be really macho 'n stuff" and is hearable, therefore, as providing an example of behavior characterizable as "really macho 'n stuff".

If we compare Dave's story in this respect we find that although the action is the same – opening a beer bottle with one's mouth – Dave puts the emphasis on the consequences of this action and his own surprise, perhaps even concern, upon seeing someone do this. The stance towards the protagonist is not obviously positive and by characterizing his teeth as "jstall fucked up" Dave clearly foregrounds the negative consequences of this action. We can see then that in Ron's story the action of opening a beer bottle with one's mouth is characterized positively as a demonstration of machismo. In Dave's story, in contrast, the same action is cast as comic, foolish and resulting in personal injury.

Audience Diversity

In the last example we saw how a second teller can provide an alternate understanding of a previous speaker's story. C. Goodwin (1986a) shows that audience members can provide alternate templates for understanding a story even as it is being produced. Goodwin analyzes a story the beginning of which we saw as example (8). Here it is in its entirety.

(14) Auto 75:15–78:7 QT 2:11–3:58
15 Phyllis: =Mike siz there wz a big fight down there las'night,
16 Curt: Oh rilly?
17 (0.5)

Phyllis: Wih Keegan en, what. Paul [de Wa::ld?]
Mike: [Paul de Wa:l]d. Guy out of,=
Curt: =De Wa:ld yeah I [°(know] ['m.)
Mike: [Tiffen.] [D'you know him¿
Curt: °Uhhuh=I know who'e i:s,
(1.8)
Mike: Evidently Keegan musta bumped im in thee,
(0.6)
Gary: W'wz it la:st week sumpn like th't ha[pp'n too?
Mike: [Ohno:,thi[s:
Gary: [Somebody
bumped somebody else'n [t h e y- spun] aroun th'tra:[ck
Mike: [I don't kno:w.] [(02:30)
Mike: [Oh that
wz:uh a'week be[fore last in the late (model .)]
Phyllis: [(Yeah really feulin)en den ney go down'n] ney
thrrow their hhelmets off'n nen n(h)ey [l : lo]ok-et each
[But,] [othe][r
Mike: [But,][this]
Curt: [=Ye::h=
hh[heh heh
Phyllis: [°ehhehhhhh
Mike: [This:: uh:::.
Gary: (They kno:w [ )
Phyllis: [ehh heh!
Curt: [Liddle high school ki[ds,=
Gary: [(No [matter what
[ju:re) [
Mike: [=[This,
[De Wa::ld spun ou:t. 'n he waited.
(0.5)
Mike: Al come around'n passed im Al wz leadin the feature,
(0.5)
Mike: en then the sekint- place guy,
(0.8)
Mike: en nen Keegan. En boy when Keeg'n come around he come
right up into im tried tuh put im imtuh th'wa:ll.
Curt: Yeh¿
Mike: 'n'e tried it about four differn times finally Keegan
rapped im a good one in the a:ss'n then th-b- DeWald
wen o:ff.
(0.5)
Curt: [Mm
Mike: [But in ne meantime it'd cost Keegan three spo:ts'nnuh
feature.
Curt: Yeah¿ (03:00)
Mike: So, boy when Keeg'n come in he- yihknow how he's gotta
temper anyway, he js::: °wa:::::h sc[reamed iz damn
e:ngine yihknow, [
Curt: [Mm
(0.5)

69 Mike: settin there en'e takes iz helmet off'n clunk it goes
70 on top a' the car he gets out'n goes up t'the trailer
71 'n gets a °god damn iron ba:r¿ ·hhh rraps that trailer
72 en away he starts t'go en evrybuddy seh hey you don't
73 need dat y'know, seh ye:h yer righ'n 'e throws [that
74 son'vabitch down- ·hhhhhhh [
75 Curt: [°Mn hm hm
76 Mike: So they all [go dow[n
77 Gary: [A:ll [All show.
78 (0.2)
79 Curt: Yeah, th[ey all,=
80 Mike: [They all-
81 Gary: =hn-[-hn!
82 Mike: [They all go down th[ere,=
83 Gary: [°Gimme a
84 [be[er Curt,
85 Mike: =[N [o some- somebuddy so:mebuddy,]
86 Carney: [It reminds me of those wrestl(h)]ers.
87 Carney: ·hhh
88 Mike: So:me[body ra:pped=
89 Carney: [hhh(h)on t(h)elevi[sion. °( ).
90 Gary: =[Bartender how about a beer.
91 While yer settin[there.
92 Carney: [°( ).
93 Mike: So:mebuddy rapped uh:. (03:30)
94 Curt: °((clears throat))
95 Mike: DeWald'nna mouth.

Goodwin notes that members of a telling's audience have resources available to them for

1 analyzing the talk that is being heard;
2 aligning themselves to it in a particular way;
3 participating in the field of action it creates.

Goodwin (1986a: 297) suggests that by making use of these resources Phyllis "is able to offer a way of understanding the events that Mike is describing that undercuts the seriousness and drama he attributes to them. . . . The effect of this is that Mike faces serious problems when he attempts to produce the climax of his story, as many of his recipients treat it in a way that he finds quite inappropriate." As noted above, the telling is initiated by Phyllis in line 15. Here, however, Phyllis does not propose to tell the story herself but rather to have it told by Mike. Moreover, although the event to be told about is characterized as a "big fight" this assessment is attributed to Mike, and Phyllis's own interpretation of the event is "left unspecified" (Goodwin 1986a: 299). Phyllis goes on to offer an understanding of the events quite different from the one that Mike is proposing.

(15) Auto 75:15 – 78:7 QT 2:11 – 3:58 (Detail)
26 Gary: W'wz it la:st week sumpn like th't ha[pp'n too?
27 Mike: [Ohno:,thi[s:
28 Gary: [Somebody

```
29            bumped somebody else'n [t h e y- spun ] aroun th'tra:[ck
30   Mike:                           [I don't kno:w.]             [      (02:30)
31   Mike:                                                        [Oh that
32            wz:uh a'week be[fore  last  in  the  late  ( model . ) ]
33   Phyllis:                [(Yeah really feulin)en den ney go down'n] ney
34            thrrow their hhelmets off'n nen n(h)ey [l : lo]ok-et each
35                                                   [But, ]  [othe][r
36   Mike:                                                    [But,][this]
37   Curt:    [=Ye::h=
38            hh[heh heh
39   Phyllis:   [°ehhehhhhh
40   Mike:      [This:: uh:::.
41   Gary:    (They kno:w          [              )
42   Phyllis:                      [ehh heh!
43   Curt:                         [Liddle high school ki[ds,=
44   Gary:                                               [(No [matter what
45            [ju:re)                                          [
46   Mike:    [                                               =[This,
47            [De Wa::ld spun ou:t. 'n he waited.
```

Goodwin notes that Phyllis's "en en den ney go down'n ney thrrow their hhelmets off'n nen n(h)ey j's l:lookit each other" belittles the "drama, power and even seriousness" of the events Mike is describing. Curt picks up on this alternative understanding by describing the characters as "Liddle high school kids,". As Goodwin also notes, Phyllis's alternative template draws on what Gary has just said. Specifically, by asking whether "something like that happened last week too" (line 26) Gary impugns the newsworthiness and authenticity of the events. "Instead of being dramatic and unusual the kind of events that Mike is talking about happen all the time." Goodwin continues:

> Phyllis picks up on these possibilities in Gary's talk by portraying such violent confrontations as not newsworthy and dramatic, but rather empty show: e.g., despite the violent bravado of the protagonists (for example throwing their helmets off) they end up "just looking at each other": Phyllis explicitly ties what she says to what Gary has just said (in addition to the "Yeah" that begins her talk in line 33 the videotape reveals that she nods toward Gary just before she starts to talk). By doing so, she is able to cast her description of how the prospective fighters just bluster at each other as representative of a series of repetitive events (note her use of present tense) and thus to formulate this as typical of the way in which the fights that Mike finds so dramatic in fact come off, i.e. they regularly end up as just empty bravado. Phyllis thus undercuts the telling that Mike is about to produce by proposing an alternative framework for interpreting the events he will describe.

In addition, Phyllis inserts laugh tokens into her talk and thus marks these events as humorous – as laughables. Laugh tokens regularly serve as invitations to others to laugh and thus Phyllis can be seen to be recruiting others to her view of these events as comedic rather than dramatic (see Jefferson 1979).

Goodwin argues that Mike orients to this challenge to his own presentation of the story. One way he does this is by emphasizing, perhaps upgrading, the seriousness of the story. This is seen in the way Mike describes the events to highlight their violent character: the iron bar "raps" the trailer, the helmet hits the car with a "clunk". Goodwin goes on to note that Mike does some additional work to include profanity in his telling. "Placing 'god damn' before 'iron bar' . . . adds nothing to the description of the bar itself." The profanity then does not contribute to the facts being told but rather helps Mike convey his stance towards them. Finally, it may be noted that, like Phyllis, Mike also tries to recruit audience members to his view of these events. Notice the way he treats Curt, to whom the talk at lines 24–6 is directed, as a co-expert, "So, boy when Keeg'n come in he- yihknow how he's gotta temper anyway, he js::: °wa:::::h screamed iz damn e:ngine yihknow,". With this, Mike treats Curt as someone who could confirm or disconfirm what he is saying and in this draws on his authority in talking about Keegan.

Despite his efforts, Mike's attempt to impose his interpretation of the events in the face of Phyllis's challenge appears unsuccessful. As it turns out, although someone is eventually reported as rapping "De Wald in the mouth", for much of Mike's story the characters behave in just the way Phyllis described them – "throwing off their helmets and staring at each other" but never actually coming to blows. For instance, Keegan's actions are described as: "he gets out'n goes up t'the trailer 'n gets a °god damn iron ba:r¿ ·hhh rraps that trailer en away he starts t'go en evrybuddy seh hey you don't need dat y'know, seh ye:h yer righ'n 'e throws that son'vabitch down-". Goodwin notes that by using the verb "start" in "and away he starts to go" Mike alerts the audience that the action being described was never brought to completion since, if it was, the character would have been described as performing it rather than as beginning it. Gary's response "All show" is then consistent with the interpretation of the events that Phyllis has proposed earlier. Carney's "it reminds me of those wrestlers" further impugns the drama and seriousness of the events. In his detailed and subtle analysis of this story Goodwin shows that an audience may be composed of story recipients who are variously situated relative to the events being talked about and that this diversity in the audience has significant consequences for how the story is told.

Spouse Talk, Co-tellership

Recall the definition of recipient design from the turn-taking paper: "the multitude of respects in which the talk by a party in a conversation is constructed or designed in ways which display an orientation and sensitivity to the particular other(s) who are the co-participants" (Sacks, Schegloff and Jefferson 1974: 727). Sacks elaborated this notion of recipient design in his discussion of stories. In a lecture (1995 vol. 2: 437–43) entitled "Spouse Talk" he begins by noting several occurrences of "completing another's sentence" in a transcript.[5] In his analysis of this phenomenon, Sacks invokes the principle of recipient design, which he now formulates as "a speaker should, on producing the talk he does, orient to his recipient", and goes on to note that one specification of that is, "If you've already told something to someone then you shouldn't tell it to them again; or if you know in other ways that they know it then you shouldn't tell it to them at all." Put most baldly the rule can be simply stated as, "Don't tell your recipient what they already know" (1995 vol. 2: 438). Sacks then goes on to notice that the principle of recipient design – and this specification of it in particular – presents a difficulty in certain "standardized situations", one of these being a situation in which "couples are present and talking in the presence of others, possibly other couples . . . where for various reasons it is usual for spouses to have already heard news that is tellable."[6] According to Sacks this fact prevents spouses from following a basic rule for listening to stories, which he states as, "listen to a story to find out if a similar thing or the same thing happened to you. At the end of the story, if you've found such a thing, tell it." Sacks asks if there are techniques for listening to stories which are specifically adapted to a situation in which one has already heard the story being told, a situation that he suggests spouses recurrently encounter.

> One such listening technique is present in our materials and is altogether kind of common; and that is a spouse listens precisely to the story they already know, for its more or less correct presentation and engages in monitoring it – as listeners should – utterance-by-utterance. But now however, for whether it's correctly presented as they know it. If not, what they do is put in corrections at the proper places.

Indeed as Lerner (1992) shows, speakers orient to a knowing participant as a monitor of story correctness by producing "verification requests" which anticipate the possibility of correction if an error is made. So in the following case Michael seeks confirmation from his spouse/partner as to whether they were "loaded" at the time the narrated events took place.

(16) Chicken Dinner
16 Michael: ↑First'v ↑ah:ll (1.1) °W'w'r° (0.2) Wir- W'r we loaded?
17 (0.8)
18 I don'kno[w if we w'loaded er n]ot.
19 Nancy: [I d o n' r:emember.]
20 (0.8)
21 Michael: But (0.7) first'f all we see this car goin down the street
22 ↑side↓ways.

A story recipient can also orient to the possibility of intervention by a knowing participant, for instance by checking on a detail of the story with *him* rather than with the teller herself. Lerner illustrates with the following case:

(17) Chicken Dinner
26 Vivian: [They have (0.2) w:one
27 way stree:ts'n evrihthi:ng? En then two way streets (.)
28 He made e- (0.3) a lef'tu:rn fr'm a one way stree:t,
29 (0.2) into a ↑two way street ·hh bu[t ↑h e thought it]=
30 Shane: [B't in the wro(h)ng]=
31 Vivian: =[wu:z:
32 Shane: =[la:ne·hih hih hi[h
33 Vivian: [He thought it wz a ↑one way street so
34 he's tra:veling do:wn- Right? er w'tche wih tellin me?
35 ·hh He's travelling[d o : w n ,]
36 Michael: [the wrong wa]y?
37 (0.2)
38 Vivian: The wrong [↑wa:[y
39 Shane: [.hh [All'fa sud' dis g[uy go EH::::::::::]:[:)

At line 36 the recipient Michael checks a detail "the wrong way?" with Shane, a knowing participant and Vivian's spouse, although up to this point it is Vivian who has told the story with only occasional interventions from Shane. As he says "the wrong way?" Michael turns his gaze to Shane and Shane confirms this candidate understanding with a head nod. Shane then continues the story.

Elaborating Sacks's observations, Lerner (1992) shows a variety of ways in which what he calls "story consociates" can participate together in the telling. Lerner describes two practices for the entry of a consociate. First, a consociate may enter so as to repair aspects of the story or its delivery; second, a consociate may enter so as to tell their own version of the events told by another.

Lerner describes four types of trouble that may occasion entry: trouble in event sequencing; trouble in delivery; trouble in the facts of the story; trouble in story elaboration. The last of these is similar to what Sacks described in his lecture on spouse talk – where a knowing participant enters a telling to add extra information via a "clarifying appendor". As Lerner notes, such entry may be occasioned by insufficient uptake by the recipient:

(18) From Lerner 1992

Cathy:	She 'ad this big hairy mole y'know
	those kinds r(h)eally gross ones,
Cindy:	o(h)n her neck.=
Terri:	=Oh how d'sgusting,

Lerner writes that in this instance "the storyteller seems to be pursuing a strong recipient assessment. The story consociate produces a clarification to aid in proper recipient understanding." It is apparently Terri's initial failure to produce a sufficiently strong negative assessment (indeed any assessment at all) that prompts Cindy's clarification.

As Lerner notes, a consociate may also enter specifically to tell their own side of things. Consider in this respect the following.

(19) Jeopardy Question (JS.V:9:34.06)

Beth:	oh: honey. What wuz the jeopardy question
(Ann):	hhhmph
Beth:	maybe somebody could answer it.
	(0.2)
	we watch jeopardy.=we play together.
	an: he was late coming home so he called me
	to say: tape it.
	(.)
	anso I taped it.
Ann:	[hehihih
Beth:	[I got home,
	(0.2)
	an I ( ) think its over,
	an I turn the teevee on:,
	(0.2)
	an it wasn't over
	it was like the final jeopardy question?
Roger:	so she pressed stop.
Beth:	so I [pressed stop on] the video recorder
Roger:	[on the recorder]
Beth:	instead a [turning the teevee back off]

Ann: [( ) oh::: no:::::]
Beth: [AN SO WE']re watch [ing the whole jeopardy]
Ann: [( )] [he he he h heh heh heh]
Beth: (an feelin' [soo dumb)]?
Roger: [it goes like this
they got the question
an then th-they turned up
the f[irst person,
Ann: [that is soo funny
Roger: who got it wrong.
Beth: right.
Roger: they turned up the second person.
Beth: who got it [wro:ng.
Roger: [who got it wrong.
an it goes off.
Beth: an then it went off an.

Here Beth tells a story about a time when she mistakenly pressed stop on the video recorder instead of turning the television off. The result was that the recording cut off just before the climax of the show (final *Jeopardy*). Notice then that in her story Beth tells how she made this mistake. Then at line 30 Roger, Beth's spouse, tells how the couple *discovered* the mistake she had made – in watching the recorded television program they found that it cut off at the final crucial moment.

Conclusion

In this chapter we've reviewed a range of studies concerned with story-telling in conversation. Following on Sacks's pioneering work in this area, conversation analysts have shown that stories emerge within a larger context of ongoing talk which dramatically shapes the details of their design and construction. Moreover, stories are told to accomplish various sorts of action in conversation: as Schegloff writes, "to complain, to boast, to inform, to alert, to tease, to explain or excuse or justify, or to provide for an interactional environment in whose course or context or interstices such actions and interactional inflections can be accomplished". Recipients of stories are then oriented not only to the story as a recognizable unit of talk distinguished by a variety of formal features, but also to *what is being accomplished* through its telling. In order to explicate this aspect of conversational story-telling it is necessary to situate stories within the particular sequences in which they are encountered by the participants, since it is this location that provides the participants with the resources needed to discern what action is being performed through the story.

Notes

1 Clearly even in those rather rare cases in which speakers name the action they are about to do, the naming is not always a very accurate guide to the action that is ultimately done. Consider for instance that one way of introducing a warning or a bit of advice is to begin with "Let me tell you a story . . .".

2 Of course the point is much more general. Sacks (1995b:222) writes, "For pretty much any object it turns out there are various things we could call it. We want to know, not so much is some name correct, as how is it that that name is relevant."

3 This is consistent with the stance Nancy has taken earlier – specifically, when Shane suggests that he can't mash the potato and characterizes it as "hard as rock", Vivian asks "It's not done? Th' potato?" and Shane replies "Ah don't think so,". Nancy, however, contests this, saying that hers "seems done". And somewhat later she remarks, "theh: fuck them it's goodd.okay?"

(20) Chicken Dinner p. 4
29 SHA: Ah can't- Ah can;t[get this thing ↓mashed.
30 VIV: [Aa-ow.
31 (1.2)
32 NAN: You[do that too : ? tih yer pota]toes,
33 SHA: [This one's hard ezza rock.]
34 SHA: ↑Ye[ah.
35 VIV: [It i:[s?
36 SHA: [B't this thing- is ↑ha:rd.
37 (0.3)
38 VIV: It's not do:ne? th'potato?
39 SHA: Ah don't think so,
40 (2.2)
01 NAN: Seems done t'me how 'bout you Mi[chael,]
02 SHA: [Alri']who cooked
03 this mea:l.
04 MIC: ·hh Little ↓bit'v e-it e-ih-ih of it isn'done.
05 SHA: Th'ts ri:ght.
06 (1.2)
07 MIC: [°('T's alright)°
08 SHA: [No it's a(h)lr(h)i(h)ght['t's (h)air(h)i(h)ght]
09 NAN: → [Theh: F u c k t h e]m it's
10 goo:d.o[kay?
11 SHA: [he-he

4 Sacks is suggesting that this is a manifestation of her privilege (see Kitzinger 2000).

5 The lecture is the fourth from Fall 1971 (*Lectures on Conversation*, vol. 2: 437–43). The transcript, updated slightly, runs as follows:

(21) Sacks 1995b
01 Ben: When're yer folks comin' down.
02 Lori: They should be he:re.
03 (1.5)
04 Ben: There wz the one spot there, — they must have hadda,
05 [some kind'v a
06 Lori: [Will they get into it too? 'r wz it- more up by yer house.
07 Ben: Yeah.
08 Ben: No, no they'll get into it. They must'v had some type
09 of a showing. A camper sho:w or uhm- [flea market
10 Ethel: [At the great big drive
11 in theater. =
12 Ben: =or they mighta hadda swap meet, and there were, so many cars
13 parked there en' so many people walkin' on the bridge across
14 the freeway thet people were slowin' down tuh look.

Bill: Huhh
Ethel: Brother I mean it slowed up [a:ll, the traffic y' know
Ben: [An' there-there wz at least ten
mi:les of traffic bumper tuh bumper.
Ethel: -because a' that,
(1.0)
Ben: [Damn idiots,
Lori: [An' how long did it- So-so it took a while tuh get through-
What time [didju leave.
Ethel: [Mm hm, Well, let's [see, we
Ben: ['Leven thirty,
Lori: But that wz- Then you wentuh Fre:d's.
Ethel: We, [we left- we left-
Ben: [No. That's the time we left Fre:d's.

6 Sacks notes that "another aspect of it is spouses will jointly have participated in some of the events that they will have occasion to tell in the company of others." On the topic of "couples" telling stories, see also Mandelbaum 1987, 1989.

10

Openings and Closings

In this chapter we examine two basic problems of interaction: how, on the one hand, participants begin occasions of talk-in-interaction and how, on the other, they bring them to a close. Although our examination of these issues will focus on telephone calls, it is important to see that for the most part the organizational problems involved are not specific to such occasions. Rather, many of the problems are generic and are worked through in any spate of interaction, be it conducted on the telephone or otherwise. That said, some of the tasks involved in opening and closing occasions of talk-in-interaction take on a specific cast when the parties to talk are not visually accessible to one another. We will begin, however, with a consideration of "pick-ups" – a topic from Sacks's lectures – before moving to look in some more detail at the sequences of talk which constitute the beginnings and endings of telephone calls.

Pick-ups

How *do* conversations get started? For the most part the procedures that lie behind this accomplishment are hidden from view by their complete ordinariness; they are so much a part of us that we hardly notice them. It will take some detailed analysis of several recorded instances to reveal the interactional organizations at work here. However, one kind of opening is very much consciously available. In fact you can find whole books about them – books which promise love, companionship and friendship. I'm talking, of course, about "pick-up lines". These are devices for beginning a conversation with a stranger – a conversation that might lead to some kind of intimate connection. Now, it's rather obvious that although many conversations start with greetings, some cannot start that way. To greet someone essentially presupposes an already existing relationship of some kind and thus the possibility of mutual recognition. Presumably this is why, if you go up to a stranger on the street and say "hello", they are as likely to give you a cold look and walk away as they are to return the greeting.[1]

But if "hello" (or "hi") as a way of starting a conversation presupposes some kind of relationship – some warrant for starting a conversation – how do conversations start when the persons involved do not already know each other? This, of course, is the problem that "pick-ups" or "pick-up lines" are meant to solve – specifically, how to start a conversation when there is no already established warrant for doing so. Sacks suggests that one way in which pick-ups can work is by embodying their own warrant. An extreme case of this would be something like "your pants are on fire", but the same idea informs the design of the less dramatic, "excuse me but I think you dropped this", or, "your bag is open." And there is a thing that people can do which actually involves setting up some specific other to do a pick-up of this sort, like prominently dropping some item and pretending not to notice. "Dropping the handkerchief" is a well-known ruse in this genre.[2]

Sacks (1995a: 49) reports on an interesting experiment in which he had students write down a pick-up line. Of the 60 he collected in this way, "just under 60 were questions" (Sacks 1995a: 102). The thing about questions, Sacks explains, is that they have a kind of special capacity to get the conversational ball rolling by virtue of the conditional relevance they establish. Sacks notes that the questions used in pick-ups typically exhibit other interesting design features. For instance, the pick-up "Don't I know you from somewhere?" "formulates a first conversation as a version of an nth" (Sacks 1995a: 103). It gets around the problem of not being in the proper relationship to have a conversation by questioning whether that is the case.

Other pick-ups may use something in the local environment to co-categorize speaker and hearer. For instance, "Do you know when the bus is scheduled to arrive?" co-categorizes speaker and hearer as potential passengers and thus invokes something that they have in common. Such questions can also be seen to derive some of their effectiveness from being recipient-designed, which is to say they display a special attention to the details of the recipient's situation.

A final pick-up Sacks discusses is "do you have a light?" (Sacks 1995a: 50–1). His discussion is now somewhat dated as smoking has become less common, but it is still possible to appreciate Sacks's Goffman-like insight on this practice. Asking for a light of course works to effect a co-categorization of the persons as "smokers" but, more than that, with it a suitor can gain entry to the highly "sacred" and regulated territory of self that each person maintains. When lighting a cigarette, hands can touch and eyes can meet in a way that might not otherwise be possible.

Pick-ups then illustrate something about the more common situation in which an exchange of greetings is used to begin an occasion of talk. First, such an exchange, along with other aspects of the participants conduct (such as stopping and gazing at one another), can show a preparedness to begin a conversation. Second, such uses of "hello" presuppose that the participants stand in a particular kind of relationship to one another – that they are possible co-conversationalists.

In face-to-face conversations opened with an exchange of greetings, the participants work through a number of issues which remain all but invisible to the casual observer (but see Kendon 1990). The telephone makes some of these organizational issues visible and brings the practices by which they are accomplished to the interactional surface.

Telephone Openings

Opening an encounter involves a series of jobs or tasks. Schegloff (1986) suggests that, in openings, participants are oriented to the accomplishment of at least three jobs: gate-keeping, (re)constituting the relationship, establishing what will be talked about.

1 Gate-keeping: The issue here is whether or not some co-present persons are going to engage in a sustained episode of interaction. We can easily think of two, quite different, kinds of occasions in which an initial greeting does not lead to a conversation. There are, for instance, "passing" situations. Think, for instance, of professors and students who pass each other in the hallways or fellow employees who acknowledge one another on the way to the water cooler. So greetings may be done without necessarily opening an encounter and it is an interesting question as to how participants distinguish a greeting which is intended to open an episode of sustained interaction from one which is not. Another occasion in which initial talk does not constitute the beginnings of a conversation is what we will call a "switchboard request". Here's an example.

(1) House Burning

		((Ring))
01	Ans:	Hello:,
02	Penny:	.pt .hhh hhHi, this is Penny Rankin from:Lincoln I'm a
03		friend'v Pa:t's. ken I speak t'her et all?
04	Ans:	She:ur.
05	Penny:	[Okay.]
06	Ans:	[Just one] sec'nd.
07		(4.0)
08	Pat:	Penny?
09	Penny:	.khh-HHI:[:
10	Pat:	[Hi::. How are you. hh [(hh)

Here, Penny's turn at 02–03 is not the beginning of a conversation but instead a request to speak to someone other than the person who has answered the phone.

2 (Re)constituting the relationship: Another job involved in openings is described by Schegloff (1986: 141) as "constituting or reconstituting" the relationship. One aspect of this involves mutual recognition by the participants of whom it is they are speaking to. As we shall see, this job takes a characteristic form in telephone conversation. Another aspect of it involves figuring out who the participants are for one another. That is, it is not just that participants must recognize in some absolute sense who it is they are speaking to, but also how they stand vis-à-vis that person. There are obvious consequences for the conversation depending on whether the other party is one's mother-in-law, a telemarketer or an old college buddy.

3 Establishing what will be talked about: Thirdly, as we will see, openings are involved in the organization of what gets talked about (or what gets done) in the conversation and, where there are multiple topics to be broached, the order in which they get talked about. If you think, for a minute, about a meeting rather than conversation you can see that this aspect of openings is particularly important. Meetings typically begin with an agenda and, although this certainly does not, indeed cannot, determine what ends up getting talked about in what order, it nevertheless provides a set of priorities to which the participants may orient ("we're getting off-track . . ."). In conversation the practices by which participants launch the first topic are quite subtle and intricately organized. As we will see, although it need not happen there, there is, in fact, a position reserved for the introduction of first topic – what we will call, following Schegloff (1986), "anchor position". How participants arrive at, exploit and even avoid this position is the focus of the first part of this chapter.

Conversation Openings: The Core Sequences

Consider again the beginning of the conversation we examined in some detail in chapter 4. Here it is again:

```
(2)  XTR. 1 (detail)
               <<ring>>=
01   Anne:     =Hello::
02   Janet:    Oh=hi:_=it's Janet_ [Cathy's mom]
03   Anne:                         [hi:      Janet]
04             How eryou(h) .h hh
05   Janet:    I'm goo:d,how are y[ou
06   Anne:                        [I'm fi:ne.h[we're actually: uhm
07   Janet:                                   [°good°
08             (0.2)
```

We shall see that this short fragment of talk contains no less than four overlapping and interdigitated sequences. First, a summons–answer sequence (see chapter 6):

```
(3)  XTR. 1 (detail)
               <<ring>>=                               SUMMONS
01   Anne:     =Hello::                                ANSWER
```

Next, a greeting sequence and identification/recognition sequence:

```
(4)  XTR. 1 (detail)
02   Janet:    Oh=hi:_=it's Janet_ [Cathy's mom]  GREETING+SELF-IDENTIFICATION
03   Anne:                         [hi:      Janet]  GREETING+RECOGNITION
```

And, finally, reciprocal "how-are-you" inquiries.

```
(5)  XTR. 1 (detail)
04   Anne:     How eryou(h) .h hh
05   Janet:    I'm goo:d,how are y[ou
06   Anne:                        [I'm fi:ne.h
```

Of course, this call exemplifies just one possible way in which these individual sequences and the larger trajectory which they together constitute can be brought off. We will consider briefly each of these "core sequences" before turning to discuss alternative trajectories to anchor position.

Summons–answer

In the first published conversation-analytic study, Schegloff (1968) noted that two-party conversations have a basic, alternating structure:

A – B – A – B – A – B – A – B – A – B – A – B – A – B . . .

Schegloff (1968: 1076) goes on to note that this "formula describes the sequencing of a two-party conversation already underway. It does not provide for the allocation of the roles 'a' and 'b' (where 'a' is a first speaker and 'b' is a second speaker) between the persons engaged in the conversation." In other words the basic alternating pattern does not itself provide a means for determining the first speaker of the conversation. This may seem an absolutely obvious and trivial matter: the person who answers the phone (in the case of telephone conversations) is the first person to speak (with "hello"). However, as it turns out, the matter is neither obvious nor trivial. With respect to the latter, as Schegloff notes, what we are dealing with here is the coordinated entry of parties into a conversation which is surely a fundamental and utterly generic problem of social interaction.

So how do telephone conversations get started? How do the participants decide who will speak first? A simple rule might be "answerer speaks first." Schegloff (1968) called this a "distribution rule" and found that it could handle all but one of the approximately 500 telephone openings he examined in his study. The problematic case for the distribution rule goes as follows:

(6) Exception to the distribution rule – Schegloff (1968)
Police make call
RING-receiver lifted.
(1.0)
01 Police: Hello
02 Other: American Red Cross
03 Hello: Hello, this is Police headquarters . . .
04 er, officer Stratton

This case clearly doesn't fit the distribution rule since here it is the police desk who makes the call and the police desk who speaks first whereas the distribution rule says that it should be the Red Cross, the answerer, speaking first. Schegloff (1968: 1079–80) asks, "is this best treated as a deviant case, or would a deeper and more general formulation of the opening sequencing reveal properties of the initiation of talk that the distribution rule glosses over?" In fact, rather than treat this as a deviant case, Schegloff proposes a more general analysis which can cover this and all the other 499 cases. Schegloff begins the more general analysis one step back, asking not "who speaks first?" but rather "how do these sequences begin?"

We speak of "answering" the phone but what in that case is being answered? The ringing of a telephone is not "posing a question" in any obvious sense, even one so banal as "is anybody at home?" If it is not a question that is being answered then what is it? Consider the following case.

(7) Mom and kid
01 Child: Mom?
02 Mom: Yes dear.
03 Child: Why don't mommies have beards?

What does this turn at line 02 answer? C's "Mom" is not a question but rather a request for Mom to attend to the child. It is what Schegloff (1968) called a "summons". Schegloff proposes that we should see the first part of telephone calls as constituting a summons–answer sequence which begins with the ring itself. Summons–answer sequences have a number of interesting features. Most importantly for the present discussion, a summons–answer sequence has a "prefatory" character. It is what we called in chapter 6 a "pre-sequence". Schegloff described this in terms of the "non-terminality" of summons–answer sequences: "A completed summons–answer sequence cannot properly stand as the final exchange of a conversation" (1968: 1081). This non-terminal character of the summons–answer sequence is seen in the particular ways in which summonses are answered. Thus one typical way in which a summons gets answered is with a question such as "what is it?" or, if you summon a clerk in a shop with "excuse me?", you may get "yes, may I help?", etc. Exasperated parents may even answer the repeated summonses of a child with "what is it *now*?" or "not now dear". If the one summoned is unable or unwilling to extract themselves from a current and ongoing engagement they may respond with "hold on a minute", thus attempting to defer the business projected by the summons–answer sequence. Indeed, the non-terminality feature of summons–answer sequences can be put in an even stronger form: the production of a summons–answer sequence not only creates an expectation of further talk by the summoner but, moreover, an obligation to produce it. If that talk is not forthcoming on completion of the summons–answer sequence, the answerer may follow up with "well, what is it?" Non-terminality is, then, an outcome of the obligation of the summoner to speak again and a corollary obligation of the answerer, having answered the summons, to listen further (see Schegloff 2002: 342).

So summons–answer sequences establish a framework of participation, a very basic kind of alignment, between the parties. By answering, the answerer shows herself to be ready to hear whatever it is the other intends to say, while by producing the summons, the summoner obligates herself to produce that talk. This then is a mechanism for the coordinated entry of parties into conversation. "Summons–answer sequences establish and align the roles of speaker and hearer, providing a summoner with evidence of the availability or unavailability of a hearer, and a prospective hearer with notice of a prospective speaker" (Schegloff 1968: 1093).

Notice also that a summons–answer sequence solves the problem of how to allocate to the parties the roles of first and second speaker and, moreover, accounts for the case which looked "deviant" when examined under the "distribution rule". There it was the caller who spoke first with "hello" rather than the called. But this is easily explained if we see this as comprising a sequence of summons and answer. The ring of the telephone is a first summons. Although the receiver is picked up, the summons is never answered. The police desk's "hello" can then be seen to redo the unanswered summons – that is, to pursue the answer which the telephone ring has not received (see chapter 4 and 5 on pursuit). Schegloff concludes that, because an answer is made conditionally relevant by the occurrence of a summons, "should it not occur it is officially absent and warrants a repetition of the summons. Hearing, now, the 'Hello' as such a repetition provides for its status as the second summons in such an occurrence. The structure of the datum thus is seen to be summons, no answer, summons, answer" (1968: 1088).

Identification–recognition

The summons–answer sequence is remarkable for the fact that it can be accomplished without the parties in talk-in-interaction having recognized one another; in this respect it is very nearly unique among sequences in talk-in-interaction. As Schegloff (1986: 118) notes, "nearly everything in conversational interaction is sensitive to the individual or categorical identity of the interlocutor." Mutual identification and recognition of the parties to the conversation is thus an issue that must be worked through more or less directly after the summons–answer sequence. In fact, the answer to the summons can convey to the caller that they have or have not reached the person they intended. This is most obvious in cases where the call is answered by a self-identification. Consider:

(8) YYZ 5a
((ring))
01 A: → Hospital for sick children=
02 B: =·hh Oh hi, is there a-um an information line?

(9) YYZ 8
((ring))
01 A: → Hello Beck Taxi,
02 B: Hi: ken I've a cab at seven . . .

But even "hello" may reveal to the caller that they have or have not reached the intended answerer. Recall the following telephone opening which we considered in chapter 3:

(10) Dick and Deb
(ring)
(r[
01 Deb: → [Hello:?hh
02 Dick: → Good morning.=
03 Deb: =Hi:, howareya.
04 Dick: Not too ba:d. Howareyou?

Here it is particularly clear that Dick's "Good morning." embodies a claim to have recognized the answerer and moreover claims that the answerer should be able to recognize the caller. And with her turn in 03 Deb claims to have done just this. How do these turns embody claims of this sort? One crucial aspect of this seems to involve their recipient-designed character. That is to say, a stand-alone "Good morning." in this position is clearly not appropriate to just any recipient. As such, its use here conveys that it has been selected or designed for some specific person and thus that its speaker knows to whom it is that he is speaking. Similar observations could be made about the selection of "hi" and the pronunciation of "howareya." in line 03. It is generally assumed that "hi" is simply the informal variant of "hello", but in the context of telephone openings at least there is a more basic significance to the distinction. Specifically, in this context, "hello" may be heard as the default form whereas "hi" is selected as appropriate for some but not all recipients. The consequence, of course, is that "hi" can be found to have been recipient-designed and thus to embody a claim by its speaker to have recognized the recipient. Consider then:

(11) Schegloff 1979 (p. 32, ex. 37) LL, 9
01 L: H'llo::,
02 M: H'llo:: ((intended intonation echo)
03 (1.0)
04 L: H'llo?=
05 M: =H'llo?
06 L: Oh hi.

Here, the initial utterances of "hello" apparently withhold any claim to have recognized the other and it is not until line 06 that L's "oh" and recipient-designed "hi" show that this has been achieved.[3]

In these examples, recognition is achieved and displayed *en passant* – embedded in turns that are engaged in other tasks such as answering a summons or issuing a greeting. Here is another example of this:

(12) Hyla & Nancy
01 ((ring))
02 Nancy: H'llo:?
03 Hyla: Hi:,
04 Nancy: ↑HI::.
05 Hyla: Hwaryuhh=
06 Nancy: =↓Fi:ne how'r you,
07 Hyla: Oka:[y,
08 Nancy: [Goo:d,

Here there is no exchange of names and mutual recognition of the parties is accomplished through the exchange of greetings with each participant recognizing the other on the basis of a short voice sample.[4] There is an elegance to this highly efficient means of identification. At the same time, because the participants are able to do it without any sign of trouble or difficulty, recognition via voice sample can be found to reaffirm the relationship between the parties in a way that self-identification does not.

Not surprisingly, then, recognition by other is preferred over self-identification.[5] In order to see how this works we need to consider in a bit more detail the caller's first turn-at-talk (T2). We've seen, for instance in example (12), that one option in this position is for the caller to produce a greeting and, by this, claim to have recognized the answerer and at the same time to convey that the answerer should be able to reciprocate by recognizing the caller on the basis of the voice sample. Another option is for the caller to append a downwardly intoned address term to the greeting, in this way demonstrating (rather than claiming) that they have recognized the answerer.

(13) Schegloff 1979: 37 (CF, #145)[48]
((Rings))
01 Charles: Hello?
02 Yolk: Hello Charles.

(14) Allison & Clara
01 Allison: Hello:
02 (.)
03 Clara: Hi=Allison,

In chapter 5 we saw that a first pair part not only makes a specific set of responses relevant in the next turn but typically also conveys a preference for one of them. So, for instance, requests make grantings and refusals relevant next actions but clearly prefer the former over the latter. Occurrence of delay after the first part has come to completion is regularly treated as foreshadowing a dispreferred response. In the context of telephone openings, identification of the called by the caller makes reciprocal identification the preferred next action and if this is not produced, caller may treat this as evidence that reciprocal recognition was not possible and go on to self-identify in the next turn.

(15) Schegloff 1979: 37 (CF, #145)[48]

			((Rings))
01	Charles:		Hello?
02	Yolk:		Hello Charles.
03		→	(0.2)
04	Yolk:	→	This is Yolk
05	Charles:		Oh hello Yolk.
06	Yolk:		How are you heh heh
07	Charles:		Alr(hh)ight hah hah It's hh very
08			Funny to hear(hh) from you.

Notice that in 15, Yolk treats the 0.2-second delay which follows his turn at 02 as evidence that the recipient has been unable to reciprocate recognition, and goes on to self-identify in line 04. Notice also that Charles eventually provides an account for failing to recognize Yolk, remarking that his phone call is unexpected ("Funny to hear(hh) from you.").

At this point we should pause to consider what kind of a resource for recognition is being provided by the use of an address term. Of course, appending an address term significantly expands the length of the "voice sample" and in this way may aid the called in determining who it is calling. At the same time, the answerer can assume that this address term has been selected by the caller to be appropriate to the relationship that these two people have. So the answerer can use the term to "search", as it were, all the people "who might address me by this term". Now in some cases, for instance where the address term is something like "my love" or "big boy", the search may end with a single result such as "my spouse" or "Daryl, my old college buddy". But even where the address term is a perfectly ordinary first name (as opposed to a nickname used only by a few people) its use will significantly narrow the field of possibility. Sacks examined the telephone opening given as (16)

(16) From Sacks 1995 vol. 1: 160

01	Jeanette:	Hello,
02	Estelle:	Jeanette,
03	Jeanette:	Yeah,
04	Estelle:	Well I just thought I'd- re- better report to you
05		what's happen' at Bullocks toda::y?

and went on to observe:

> "Jeanette" as a first utterance by the caller does a series of jobs. It claims recognition of the answerer and, as well, informs that person that its user feels entitled to address them in the way they have just done. So that, leaving aside whether the caller can, from its enunciation, recognize the caller, "Jeanette" is markedly different in the information it gives the called than would be, say, "Mrs Jones." (Sacks 1995b: 161)

He goes on to remark specifically about names that they put "you in the position of choosing among such things as you can use with respect to the recipient. And by that choice you then inform the recipient about what you take it your rights are with respect to them" (Sacks 1995b: 161). So use of a name in fact provides the recipient with an important resource for recognition.

Let's now look to see how answerers may respond in T3 to these downwardly intoned address terms. We noted earlier that selection of "hi" in T2, rather than "hello", as in the call between Hyla and Nancy (12), is often treated as embodying a claim to have recognized the caller. Answerers may respond in the same way in T3 to an address term produced in T2, as in the following case:

(17) Allison & Clara
01 Allison: Hello:
02 (.)
03 Clara: Hi=Allison,
04 Allison: → Hi:

However, as Schegloff notes, "the import of these unevidenced recognition claims can be equivocal. Regularly they are taken by callers to display recognition. Sometimes, however . . . the caller proceeds to a self-identification in his second turn anyway" (1979: 53). And so notice what Clara does in the expanded version of (17):

(18) Allison & Clara
01 Allison: Hello:
02 (.)
03 Clara: Hi=Allison,
04 Allison: → Hi:
05 Clara: → It's Clara, howyadoin',
06 Allison: Good.How are you Clara.

Schegloff (1979) provides a number of similar examples of which the following is one:

(19) Schegloff 1979: 53
01 Bonnie: .hhh Hello,
02 Barbie: Hi Bonnie,
03 Bonnie: Hi.=
04 Barbie: =It's Barbie.=
05 Bonnie: =Hi.

Notice then that here Barbie treats Bonnie's "hi" at line 03 as insufficient evidence of recognition and goes on to self-identify in next turn. So the preferred action in T3 appears to be reciprocal other-identification, and *any other* action, including a greeting with "Hi", is vulnerable to being heard as evidence of a failure to recognize the caller.

We've begun to consider some of the alternatives for the caller's talk at T2. One option is to issue a greeting such as "Hi" as in (12) by which Hyla (the caller) claims to have recognized Nancy (the called) and simultaneously invites reciprocal recognition. Another option, which we've just briefly considered, is for the caller to produce a downwardly intoned address term thereby demonstrating recognition of the answerer and also, as we've just seen, making reciprocal recognition relevant in T3. A third alternative in T2 is for the caller to produce an upwardly intoned address term with or without a greeting as in (20) below.

(20) Schegloff 1979 p. 51#67, JG#65a
Connie: Hello.
Joanie: Connie?
Connie: Yeah Joanie

Here Joanie's "Connie?" invites and receives a reciprocating display of recognition. But whereas a downwardly intoned address term presumes that the caller has recognized the answerer, the upwardly intoned address term questions this. As such, it makes confirmation of the proposed identification (Connie) the first-order relevant next action. So notice that at line 03 Connie first confirms the identification with "yeah" before identifying the caller (Joanie). The key thing to notice then is that where the answerer is not able to recognize the caller, that failure need not rise to the interactional surface, since use of an upwardly intoned address term in T2 provides for simple confirmation as a sequentially relevant next turn.

(21) Shawn & Allison pt.1
Shawn: Hello:
Allison: °tch° Oh hi (.) Shawn?
Shawn: → Yep.
Allison: Hi:: it's Allison upstairs:=

(22) Shawn & Allison pt.2
Allison: Hello::
Shawn: Hi Ali?=
Allison: → =Yeah
Shawn: It's Shawn downstairs
Allison: Hi Shawn

Schegloff (1979) calls "interrogative address terms" in T2 "pre-self-identification" and argues that their use exhibits a preference for other-recognition over self-identification. This is just one manifestation of a more general preference to "oversuppose and undertell". So how does such a turn serve as a "pre-self-identification" and how does it exhibit a preference for other-recognition over self-identification?

1 It constitutes a voice sample which answerer may use as a resource for recognizing the caller.
2 By virtue of its upward, interrogative intonation it displays some uncertainty that the answerer will be able to recognize the caller.
3 It provides for a next turn in which the recipient *may* display recognition if it is achieved.
4 But, at the same time, it provides for another option in next turn which will not explicitly exhibit failure if recognition is not achieved (confirmation with "yeah").

To summarize, the issue of identification and recognition of the parties is pervasively relevant in talk-in-interaction. This is related to the fundamental principle of recipient design: the expectation that talk is specifically designed for the particular others who are the recipients. Obviously, to so design the talk one needs to determine who – in some categorically or relationally relevant sense of "who" – those others are. In telephone calls, where the participants do not have visual access to one another, a specially adapted set of practices are in operation. As we've seen, these are largely organized around a basic preference for other-recognition over self-identification. This preference goes to the basic, socially reaffirming core of talk-in-interaction, since recognizing others rather than them having to self-identify allows the terms of the relationship to be presumed without being articulated. There's an obvious intimacy in the way Hyla and Nancy begin their conversation that is indexed, in part, by their ability to recognize one another so assuredly and on the basis of the most minimal resources.

How-are-you Inquiries

After sequences dedicated to summons–answer and identification–recognition, the next sequence is often one that involves an exchange of "how-are-you" inquiries. Although these can be extraordinarily complicated, it's best to begin with something relatively simple – an example we considered at various earlier points in this book (see chapter 1):

(23) Deb and Dick
01 Deb: Hello:(hh)?
02 Dick: Good morning=
03 Deb: =Hi:, howareya.
04 Dick: Not too bad.How are you?
05 Deb: I'm fi::ne.
06 Dick: Howdit go?

Here Dick responds to Deb's "howareya." with "Not too bad." and she in turn responds to his "How are you?" with "I'm fi::ne.". "How are you?", "How have you been?", "How are you doing?" and so on may be usefully thought of as belonging to a class of "personal state inquiries". Sacks (1975) noted that answers to such questions fall into three subsets:

[0] neutral, e.g. "fine", "okay",
[+] positive, e.g. "great", "terrific", and
[-] negative, e.g. "awful", "terrible".

Responses from either the [+] or [-] subsets have quite different sequential relevance from those in [0]. With respect to [-] responses, Sacks (1975: 68) writes:

> Given the occurrence of an answer from subset [0], e.g., ok, fine, etc., no further inquiries are appropriate. Given the occurrence of an answer from the [-] subset, a sequence is appropriately launched, directly, to determining "what's the matter." . . . the sequence launched on the occurrence of an answer from the [-] subset, . . . I call a "diagnostic sequence," and it has at one point in it the offering of such an account as explains how it is that the answerer is in the [-] subset.

Now Sacks makes these remarks in the context of a discussion of the expression "everyone has to lie." He is concerned to show how it is that such a statement as "everyone has to lie" could come to be seen as true. The point about answers to "personal state inquiries" is, of course, that not uncommonly one finds oneself saying "fine" even though one feels "terrible", "lousy", "bored to tears", or whatever else. In responding "fine" to the question "how are you?", a speaker may, in fact, be lying. In some sense, however, Sacks suggests, we are forced to lie by the very sequential organization of conversation. We've already seen that an answer from the [-] subset (that is, a possibly "truthful" answer from one who feels "lousy", etc.) will establish the relevance of a diagnostic sequence devoted to finding out "what's the matter". Consider next that the information contained in such "diagnostic sequences" is information which is highly regulated.

> Let us consider the information that may stand as the "diagnostic information." In particular, let us consider the regulation of its exchange as between any two parties. It seems, in the first instance (grossly), that it may be said that for any two parties not any item of such information may be offered to any given other. Stated otherwise, exchange of information serving as an answer to a diagnostic inquiry is independently regulated – independently, that is, of the regulations that provide for the relevance of the occurrence of diagnostic answers. (Sacks 1975: 71)

So here Sacks points to a potential interactional problem. If the recipient of a personal-state inquiry answers honestly with "lousy" she makes relevant the production of a "diagnostic sequence", in which an account for why she answered in the way she did will be given. The problem, however, is that such "diagnostic information" (e.g. my wife left me, I feel terribly alone, my kid is failing grade two) is the kind of thing you can't share with just anybody: it is, as Sacks says, highly regulated, and regulated independently of "personal-state inquiries" which might establish the relevance of its telling. Sacks writes, "for such information as constitutes an answer to the question *Why?*, given the answer *Lousy!* to the question *How are you?*, regulations that exist concern such matters as what it is that should be held within the family, what should be told only to your doctor or a priest, and the like" (Sacks 1975: 71). He goes on:

> What we have arrived at is that any person feeling lousy and having some trouble as the explanation of feeling lousy, if asked how he is feeling by someone who ought not to hear that trouble or hear it now, may control that one's access to that information by avoiding the diagnostic sequence, and the diagnostic sequence is avoided by choosing a term from a subset other than the subset the monitoring operation comes up with; that is, he may lie.

Sacks goes on to note that such interactional constraints are consistent with advice given by authorities on etiquette such as Emily Post and Ann Vanderbilt. The latter says, "In greeting people we say 'How do you do.' We do not really expect an answer, but it is all right to reply 'Very well thank you,' even if it is a blue Monday and you feel far from well" (Vanderbilt 1963, cited in Sacks 1975: 77).

But of course recipients of questions such as "how are you?" do sometimes answer with a negatively valenced response and by this occasion diagnostic inquiries, as in the following case:

(24) Holt SO88(II):2:2:1–2
01 Les: Hello↑:?
02 ((dog barking))
03 Ron: Hello Leslie it's Ron Lo:per ↓he↑:[re
04 Les: [.tlk ↑Oh ↑hell↓o↑:
05 Ron: How'r ↓yo[u.
06 Les: [.hh Oh::, alri:ght missing Gordo-:n,
07 (.)
08 Les: .hhhh[hh
09 Ron: [What's happ'ning to ↓Go:r[don.

Les: [Well he's in naw- (.)
i-in um↑ hmhhhh .tch Oh where is 'ee now..hhh uh:m: .tl
↑up the No:rth Newcastle. huh huh .hh[hh
Ron: [He's at college't
Newca[stle.
Les: [ihYes:.
(.)
Les:[6] Ye[s..≠hh-.≠hh
Ron: [So:- (0.2) that means you're all on your lone[some.=
Les: [.hhh
Les: =↑Ye:s yes,h↑ Un[fortche'ly]
Ron: [↓Aw:::::::]:[ ]
Les: [ ]hAh:::::,
(.)
Les: .hhh[hh
Ron: [Never ↓min[d
Les: [eh: ↓hhuh huh↓

Although Leslie begins her response to Ron's "how are you" with what Jefferson (1980) described as a "mildly downgraded" neutral response (considered below), she adds "missing Gordon", which pushes this over onto the negative end of the scale and makes a "diagnostic sequence" relevant. The diagnostic sequence is launched by a directed inquiry – "What's happening to Gordon" – and, after Leslie answers, Ron formulates the upshot of the answer in line 18 with "that means you're all on your lonesome."

Mildly Downgraded Versions: "Trouble-Premonitory" Response to Inquiry

A study by Gail Jefferson (1980) revealed how subtle differences in answers to "personal-state inquiries" could have significant consequences for how an interaction unfolds. Jefferson considers what she refers to as "mildly downgraded versions" of neutral answers. These are responses to "how are you" such as "oh pretty good, I guess", "I'm pretty good", "Oh surviving I guess", "Oh no complaints" and the like. Jefferson notes that while such responses sometimes introduce a "report on a trouble" and may be treated by recipients as having "negative import", in other cases they are treated as "conventional responses, even if downgraded ones; that is, they are not followed by troubles-talk but by whatever might follow something like 'Fine' " (1980: 158). Jefferson goes on to argue that such a downgraded conventional response does not necessarily premonitor a report on a trouble: "It can, but it need not." So while "pretty good" and other downgraded responses can project that the speaker has a trouble to report, responses which are not downgraded (such as "Fine"), "appear to project that a speaker will not proceed to deliver a report". Moreover, Jefferson argues, mildly downgraded neutral responses propose "that if the trouble is to be reported on, it will be by virtue of some further pursuit by the inquirer, and not on the basis of an inquiry that might or might not be a request for an update by someone who might or might not be acquainted with the trouble." Jefferson (1980: 158) summarizes:

> On the one hand, then, there appear to be response-types that specifically do not project that a speaker will proceed to deliver a report on a trouble. On the other hand, a downgraded conventional response, such as "Pretty good," can but need not make such a projection. Thus, while some responses seem to be clear as to their sequential import, the downgraded conventional response may specifically be equivocal, possibly projecting a report, possibly not. It turns out, however, that while a downgraded conventional response to an inquiry need not project an immediately forthcoming report on a trouble, it may nevertheless mark the presence of a trouble.

That is, a minimally downgraded response can be picked up by the recipient and pursued for its negative import *or not*. If it is not pursued, the trouble will likely not be told – at least, it will not be told *here*. As it turns out, in many of the cases in which a recipient attends to the conventional rather than negative import of a mildly downgraded response, a trouble *does* eventually surface. So even if a trouble is not picked up immediately, it may eventually be aired and, when it is, the recipient may be able to see that it was foreshadowed or adumbrated by the downgraded response.

Jefferson then highlights the tension between attending to "trouble" and attending to "business as usual" (for further discussion of this tension see Jefferson's original report). Another way to put this is to say that a question such as "how are you" can be heard for what it literally is – an inquiry into the recipient's well-being – *or* as a merely *pro forma* civility. In some contexts, one hearing is more likely than the other. For instance, in conversations between non-familiars or non-intimates, "how are you" may be heard as a nicety and nothing more, whereas between friends or family it may be heard as a real expression of interest and concern. Thus the way in which "how are you" is treated is something of a test for a relationship. In responding, a recipient can choose to be "polite" if distant, answering with "fine" and returning the inquiry, or to be intimate and indicate – by using, for instance, a minimally downgraded response – a willingness to talk at a "personal" level. This tension is much in evidence in the following opening:

(25) Holt May 88: Side 2: Call 4
Dee: . . . lie?
Les: Oh is that Deena,=
Dee: =↑Hello[dea:r↑[
Les: [.hhh [↑Hello::,[hhh
Dee: [How ↑are yo[u↓:
Les: [.hhhh ↑Oh alright
→ 'n you↑hh
Dee: → ↑Ye::s. You ( ) alri:ght I mean are you
→ we↓:l[l.
( ): [([ )
Les: → [↑Yes're you:↑
(0.2)
Dee: → [Yes alright dea[r thank y[ou.
[((door slam)) [[
Les: [gn- [Goo:d heh heh[.hhhh
Dee: [Lovely to speak
to you an[y↓wa[y::s.]
Les: [.t [.hhhh]And you ↑here's uh::↑ (.) Skip.
Dee: Oh:.

Here Dee has called for Skip but the phone has been answered by Skip's wife Leslie. Now this situation is somewhat ambiguous. Skip is Dee's cousin and she has in fact called to speak *to him*. However, speaking to Skip clearly cannot be handled as a mechanical "switchboard" request (see example (1)); Leslie and Deena should properly greet one another and thereby reconstitute *their* relationship. At line 05, after Leslie has recognized her, Deena produces a prosodically enhanced "How ↑are you" to which Leslie responds with ".hhhh ↑oh alright". This is a mildly downgraded neutral response which, as we have seen, can invite pursuit from a recipient. However, in an apparent attempt to foreclose the possibility of further pursuit by Deena, Leslie appends " 'n you" to her answer. This elicits only the most minimal of answers and Deena continues by transforming her question from one that is equivocal in its import ("How are you?") to one which is unambiguously attentive to the well-being of the recipient. By adding "I mean are you well", Deena pursues a trouble which the downgraded response indexed. Notice, however, that Leslie responds with a minimal answer and, once again, a reciprocal question, saying "Yes're you." In this way she not only gets out from under the conditional relevance of the question, she treats it is a mere formality – as something to be reciprocated rather than answered candidly. Deena responds to the reciprocal question, and, treating the matter as closed, remarks, one suspects with some irony, "lovely to speak with you anyways."

Trajectories to Anchor Position

The foregoing discussion should be enough to show that getting through the opening of a phone call to the first topic is not a straightforward matter. There are numerous ways in which the opening can be expanded or contracted, a few of which we have briefly touched upon. The last thing to discuss here, then, is how the different core sequences come together in any particular case to produce a trajectory to anchor position. Anchor position is the term we use (from Schegloff 1986) to refer to the position, after the core opening sequences reviewed above, in which callers may be expected to raise a first topic – the "reason for the call". Recall, for instance, the following:

(26) Dick and Deb

			(ring)
			(r[
01	Deb:		[Hello:?hh
02	Dick:		Good morning.=
03	Deb:		=Hi:, howareya.
04	Dick:		Not too ba:d. Howareyou?
05	Deb:		I'm fi::ne.
06	Dick:	→	Howdit go?

Here Dick has called Deb. After the core sequences of summons–answer, identification–recognition and personal-state inquiries are complete, Dick asks, in anchor position, "Howdit go?". By asking this question in this position, Dick conveys that asking this question is his reason for calling. We can see this by comparing a call in which the participants reach anchor position but the caller does not use it to raise a first topic and show what she is calling about.

(27) Hyla & Nancy

01			((ring))
02	Nancy:		H'llo:?
03	Hyla:		Hi:,
04	Nancy:		↑HI::.
05	Hyla:		Hwaryuhh=
06	Nancy:		=↓Fi:ne how'r you,
07	Hyla:		Oka:[y,
08	Nancy:		[Goo:d,
09			(0.4)
10	Hyla:		·mkhhh[hhh
11	Nancy:	→	[What's doin,
12			(·)
13	Hyla:	→	aAh:, noth[i : n :,]
14	Nancy:	→	[Y'didn't g]o meet Grahame?=

So here Hyla has called Nancy. A reciprocal exchange of "how are you"s (both answered with neutral responses) ends with Nancy's assessment "good" at line 08. Here the participants have reached anchor position, but instead of the caller raising a first topic there is silence and some audible breathing from Hyla at lines 09–10. This occasions Nancy's "What's doin," at line 11. Nancy's "What's doin," pursues and thereby displays an orientation to the relevance of first topic in this position. Finally, by responding to the question with "ah nothing" Hyla suggests that she does not need a reason to call Nancy. Nancy's question "Y'didn't go meet Grahame" is a more focused news solicitation (see chapter 11).[7]

Openings may be highly contracted. Consider in this respect the following:

(28) NB:II:5:R

01	Lottie:	Hello:,=
02	Emma:	=Are you answering the pho::ne? ((smile voice))
03	Lottie:	ehh ↑hhah .hh I WZ J'S GUNNUH CA:LL YUH ehh[huh]huh]
04	Emma:	[I]JIS]GO:T
05		HE:RE.hh
06		(0.3)
07	Lottie:	Rea:ll[y?
08	Emma:	[Oh: it's u-been so: foggy we didn' come do:wn. Oh
09		it's so fo:ggy Lottie ahll ar way-ahl'p ar way 't's
10		-terrible ·hf
11	Lottie:	No: ↑ki:ddin:g.
12	Emma:	Ya:h we came down Ro:semead ri:l slo::w,
13		(0.7)
14	Emma:	·hhhh ↑Oh:[yah they w]a↑:rned you tuh stay away from thum
15	Lottie:	[°Oh ::::::°]
16		(0.4)
17	Emma:	five ten mi:les on the freeways la:s'ni:ght. yihkno:w so
18		(.)
19	Lottie:	Yeh I know it but you know ih wa:sn't b- i:t wasn't ba:d
20		here it a::ll.

Emma: That's: w't ↑Gladys js tells me but it's ba:d ↑inlind it's
↑te:rrible yih on'y have abou:t a blo:ck visibility. It's
jis:t (.) ↑AW:↓fu:l.
(0.7)
Lottie: Yeah becuh-uh see yesterday it was'm oh: beautiful. En then
abou:t noo::n: the fo:g came in.=

Here the caller (Emma) begins with "Are you answering the phone?". This turn embodies a claim to have recognized the called and suggests that she should be able also to recognize the caller. The question "Are you answering the phone?" makes little sense if taken literally, so what is the speaker doing in asking this? One thing that seems to be involved is that with a question such as this the caller displays an orientation to the particular circumstances of the called, specifically, the possibility that Lottie may not have wanted to answer the phone and has only done so out of a sense of obligation. We can ask then how Emma might have arrived at this conclusion. Before we consider this though, notice also that with "are you answering the phone?" the caller intercedes into the normative structure of telephone openings that we have described in previous sections. We have already seen (for further evidence see Schegloff 1986) that this question occurs in a position in which the caller typically initiates a recognition–identification sequence. That is, although the turn here may consist only of a greeting, whatever is done here will be understood by reference to the task of a called party to recognize who is calling and a caller to recognize who has answered the phone. As noted, with "are you answering the phone" the caller here treats these tasks as a *fait accompli*. Moreover, rather than setting up a return greeting, a confirmation of the called's identity, a display of recognition of the caller and possibly an exchange of "how-are-you"s as relevant next actions, "are you answering the phone" establishes the relevance of an answer to the question. The funny thing is, it's not entirely clear how that question *could be* relevantly answered. Here, what it gets as a response is not an answer but rather some initial laughter followed by "I was just going to call you." If "are you answering the phone" shows some attentiveness to the state of the recipient – that she might have not wished to answer the phone, that she might be avoiding people – "I was just going to call you" suggests that the called party had already planned to make contact.

One thing that seems to be at issue in this exchange is who should call whom. That is, in "are you answering the phone" one can hear the caller's attentiveness to the possibility that the called may not wish to talk, that they may be avoiding contact. How, we may ask, might Emma have arrived at such a conclusion? One possibility is that Emma has been expecting to hear from – that is, to receive a call from – Lottie and, when she received no such call, she figured Lottie did not want to talk to her or anyone else. One way of avoiding contact is by not answering the phone; another is by not making any calls. So by a rather complex and convoluted route one can perhaps see that with "are you answering the phone" Emma is suggesting that Lottie should have been the one to call *her* and of course with "I was just about to call you" Lottie can be seen to respond to just such a possible complaint.

Closings

In their well-known study "Opening up closings", Schegloff and Sacks (1973: 290) observe that a conversation "does not simply end, but is brought to a close". Clearly, one cannot simply hang up the phone at just any point in a call. Likewise, it would be considered extremely rude to suddenly walk away in the middle of a conversation. While you do eventually have to hang up or walk away, a rather specific place, or context, must be prepared for such actions if they are to be properly understood as simply ending the conversation rather than as expressing annoyance or anger, for instance.

So we can readily see that conversations are "brought to a close" and can surmise that there are some methods for doing this. It is those methods that Schegloff and Sacks set out to describe in their paper. As we shall see, as a piece of the "overall organization" of an interaction, closings intersect and draw together a number of different concurrently operative organizations.

What is the Closing Problem?

As described in chapter 3, at one level of organization conversation is composed of turns-at-talk, produced by different participants who alternately inhabit the roles of speaker and hearer so as to produce serial exchanges. Furthermore as we saw in chapter 3, the system that organizes the distribution of turns-at-talk operates locally, organizing just current and next turn. Opportunities to speak, in conversation, are distributed on a turn-by-turn basis and the system is locally managed by and for the participants.

Now just as the turn-taking system provides for the organization of a conversation already in progress but not for its beginning (see above), so it does not provide a way for it to end. Remember that each point of possible completion is transition-relevant: each such place presents an opportunity for one or another of the participants to take a turn-at-talk. In a sense, then, the turn-taking machinery *creates* the closing problem which can be thought of in the following terms: "how can a possible completion be so constructed that it will not be understood as an opportunity for another speaker to take a turn?"

The solution involves a special kind of adjacency pair which Schegloff and Sacks describe (1973: 295) as a "terminal exchange". With the first part of such an exchange ("bye" or "good-bye") a speaker can propose to end the conversation, and with the second part the other can accept that proposal. The effect, of course, is to suspend the usual connection between possible completion and transition relevance at the end of the second speaker's "bye". Thus, such an exchange is capable of terminating a conversation by suspending the transition relevance recurrently activated by the turn-taking machinery at the possible completion of every turn-at-talk.

But it's not quite that simple, and in fact Schegloff and Sacks characterize the terminal exchange as merely a "proximate solution" to the closing problem. The terminal exchange is a proximate solution because it works only at the level of turn-taking organization. But, of course, as we have already seen, conversation is organized not only as a series of turns but also as a sequence of actions. So there are two particularly obvious ways in which the terminal exchange is ultimately an incomplete solution to the closing problem. First, there is the "placement problem". By this Schegloff and Sacks mean to draw attention to the fact that the first part of a terminal exchange is not "freely occurrent", which is to say that it cannot go just anywhere in a conversation. If I say "how's your mom?" and you respond with "bye" I'll figure I've said something terrible. Even if you were to reply to my query with "oh fi:ne, back from Florida", thus completing the adjacency pair, it would still sound either very rude or extremely odd if my next utterance were an attempt to initiate a terminal exchange with "bye". Think then about the two parts of a terminal exchange ("bye" and "bye", etc.). There are restrictions on where each part can be placed. For the second part, it's pretty obvious that it can only come after a first. The placement problem for this item is solved at the level of adjacency pair organization. But how is the placement problem solved for the first part of a terminal exchange? Where does this item properly fit in a conversation? Clearly not after the second part of just any adjacency pair (e.g. A: "how's your mom?" B: "oh fi:ne, back from Florida." A: "Bye."). Schegloff and Sacks argue that the first part of a terminal exchange is properly placed at the possible end of a closing section. That is, a terminal exchange is the last piece of a larger organization – a section devoted to closing down the conversation.

> Addressing considerations of placement raises the issue: what order of organization of conversation is the relevant one, by reference to which placement is to be considered. We dealt earlier with one kind of placement issue, i.e., the placement of second parts of terminal exchanges, and there the order of organization by reference to which placement was done and analyzed was the adjacency pair, which is one kind of "local" – i.e., utterance, organization. It does *not* appear that *first* parts of terminal exchanges, which is what we are now concerned with, are placed by reference to that order of organization. While they, of course, occur after some utterance, they are not placed by reference to a location that might be formulated as "next" after some "last" utterance or class of utterances. Rather, their placement seems to be organized by reference to a properly initiated closing *section*, and it is by virtue of the lack of a properly initiated closing section that the unilateral dropping in of the first part of a terminal exchange is only part of the solution to the closing problem. (Schegloff and Sacks 1973: 300)

Problems of placement are typically accompanied by problems of "recognition". Notice that, although we have been talking about "bye" or "goodbye" as if they were the only items that could be used in a terminal exchange, this is clearly not the case. "Okay" can also be used in a terminal exchange, for instance. But then, this raises the question of how any particular instance of "okay" can be analyzed as the first part of a terminal exchange. How does the recipient of such an item figure out that, in using it, the speaker is proposing to end the conversation, since "okay" can be used in any number of ways. That is, how can a recipient recognize some instance of "okay" as the first turn in a terminal exchange? The solution to this is, once again, formulated in terms of placement (Schegloff and Sacks 1973: 299):

> Past and current work has indicated that placement considerations are general for utterances. That is: a pervasively relevant issue (for participants) about utterances in conversation is "why that now", a question whose analysis may also be relevant to finding what "that" is, That is to say, some utterances may derive their character as actions entirely from placement considerations.

So a consideration of closings leads to the recognition of an interactional problem which we can paraphrase from Schegloff and Sacks as "how to so construct things that a point of possible completion will not be heard as transition relevant, and thus as a place for another to take a turn." The terminal exchange stands as an obvious solution to this problem but also raises further questions. Most relevant at this point is the problem of where in a conversation a first part of a terminal exchange can be properly produced? We have already noted that this problem cannot be solved by reference to adjacently paired actions. Instead, the first part of a terminal exchange is placed in relation to a "closing section". This of course begs the question, what is a closing section? In earlier chapters we have made occasional reference to a distinction between actions and activities (or sequences and activities). The "closing section" is perhaps best thought of not as a single action or as a single sequence but rather as an activity which is initiated, managed in its course and completed.

There are a number of ways in which entry into a closing section may be proposed. One that Schegloff and Sacks (1973) discussed in some detail involves the use of what they describe as "possible pre-closings". Consider the following cases:

(29) Joyce and Stan p. 9
31 Joyce: [·uhhh! Well:, you know, you never know.<Maybe: I'll see
32 somewhere tomorr[ow,
33 Stan: [°Yeah,
34 (1.2)
35 Stan: → Okay (Joyce),
36 Joyce: → Arright Stan,
37 Stan: Gihbye.
38 Joyce: Buhbye.
39 ((receiver down))

(30) John and George – Source (Unknown)
01 John: Why don't we all have lunch
02 George: Ok so that would be in St. Jude would it?
03 John: Yes
04 (0.7)
05 John: → Okay so:::
06 George: One o'clock in the bar
07 John: Okay
08 George: Okay
09 John: Okay then thanks very much indeed George=
10 George: =All right [See you there
11 John: [See you there
12 George: → Okay
13 John: → Okay [bye
14 George: [Bye

(31) Bev and Ann
38 Ann: wul what should I bring?
39 Bev: But uhm: (0.5) If you wanna bri:ng: (0.5) uh- some wi::n:e (0.7)
40 Ann: that's it
41 Okay. No food?
42 (0.2)
43 Bev: No we have all the food covered.
44 Ann: Okay
45 Bev: We're having such a good dinner too
46 Ann: Wonderful
47 Bev: → Okay Bahbe(h)=
48 Ann: → =Okay Honey=
49 Bev: bye.
50 Ann: bye.

It is not difficult to see a recurrent pattern here. In each case the participants are talking about a possible next meeting. Thus in (29) at lines 31–2, Joyce says "Maybe I'll see you tomorrow", in (30) at line 10 George says "see you there" in reference to a plan to meet "in the bar", and in (31) Ann and Bev are discussing a dinner they have planned for the weekend. If we consider the turns that immediately follow these parts we find the following:

(32) Joyce and Stan p. 9
34 (1.2)
35 Stan: Okay (Joyce),
36 Joyce: Arright Stan,
37 Stan: Gihbye.
38 Joyce: Buhbye.

(33) John and George – Source (Unknown)
12 George: Okay
13 John: Okay [bye
14 George: [Bye

(34) Bev and Ann
47 Bev: Okay Bahbe(h)=
48 Ann: =Okay Honey=
49 Bev: bye.
50 Ann: bye.

What we find then, with great regularity, before the production of terminal items such as "bye" is an exchange of "okay" or "alright". What we want to notice about such an item as "okay", *in this context*, is that with it the speaker passes an opportunity to take a more substantial turn-at-talk. In each case, the speaker of the first "okay" might have produced some further talk on an already established topic, or alternatively might have raised some further topic of conversation. So with a first "okay" a speaker may be seen to be passing an opportunity to raise additional topics of conversation and thus as proposing that the conversation should come to a close. With a second such item a recipient likewise passes the opportunity to raise further talk on a topic and may thus both display an understanding of that proposal and accept the move to closing.

Such an exchange of possible pre-closings establishes a warrant for closing the conversation – the warrant being that neither participant has anything more to talk about. As Schegloff and Sacks noted, in such a case the warrant for closing the conversation is *embodied* in the very practices used to close the conversation. Now there are other ways in which a conversation may come to a close, and it is useful to consider those in which the warrant for closing is announced rather than embodied as it is in an exchange of possible pre-closings. In the following example, Shirley is telling Geri about an apartment that a mutual friend (Michael) has found. In the course of her description Geri's dog, Shiloh, begins to bark. At first the dog's barking is disattended by the participants, but at line 13 Geri interrupts Shirley, saying "wait hold on the dog." After the dog is addressed and directed to "cool it", Shirley notes that she "c'n hear it fr'm this side.". The problem then is one to which both participants orient. It is in precisely this environment that Geri says, "Okay w'l lemme get o:ff", thereby proposing that the relevance of closing has been occasioned by the disturbance of the dog's barking. Notice, however, that in her response Shirley treats the closing as warranted by the need for Geri to get back to work.

(35) Geri and Shirley

04 Shirley: a:nd, (.) a bathroom j's li[ke a hundred other apartments.=
05 Dog: [ar-krugh-((f)) roo!
06 Dog: =ar-[ar!
07 Geri: [Yeah.=
08 Shirley: =Right?h
09 Geri: Ye[ah.
10 Dog: [Ragh!
11 Shirley: .hhhhh[So, you kno[:w,
12 Dog: [Ragh!
13 Geri: [Wait hold[on the do:g.=
14 Dog: [Ragh!
15 Shirley: Ye:ah,
16 Dog: [Aghwoo
17 Geri: [SHI:LO:::H!
18 (0.4)
19 Geri: Coo[l it.
20 Dog: [ragh ragh!
21 Shirley: I c'n[hear it fr'm[this [side.
22 Dog: [ragh! [ragh[ragh!
23 Geri: → [Okay w'l lemme get o:ff,
24 Shirley: → Yeh go do yer work,
25 Geri: Yeh,
26 Shirley: .t.hh Okay?=
27 Geri: =En tell Joey ah'll be over in awhi:[le.
28 Shirley: [Okay,
29 Geri: Okay.[.hh-
30 Shirley: [Okay beh-bye,=
31 Geri: =Bah-bye.

In announcing a warrant for closing, participants may make use of materials in the local environment (such as a dog barking) or items mentioned earlier in the conversation ("I should let you get back to your show/dinner/to sleep", etc.). There are warrants available strictly to calleds (e.g. "this is costing you a lot of money") and to callers (e.g. "I'll let you go, I don't want to tie up your phone"). Moreover, a warrant may be alternately embodied and announced in the same call with some subtle shading between the two. To see this, let's consider the following call in its entirety.

(36) Dick and Deb

(ring)
(r[
01 Deb: [Hello:?hh
02 Dick: Good morning.=
03 Deb: =Hi:, howareya.
04 Dick: Not too ba:d. Howareyou?
05 Deb: I'm fi::ne.
06 Dick: Howdit go?
07 Deb: hhOh, just great,=everybody:-st=still here.
08 Dick: (.) Oh reall(h)y,
09 Deb: Yea(h[hh)
10 Dick: [Oh they stayed. Okay,=

Deb: =Yeah
Dick: [( )]
Deb: [pool]'s kind of (.) yucky: bu:t what can I say
Dick: What, (0.2) The pool?
Deb: Yeah.
Dick: O[h.]
Deb: [b]ut so's the Wymer's too so I think it was just thee
-uhm -the rain an everything [you know,
Dick: [(oo dit) rain. yeahmhm,
Deb: yeah
Dick: Oh. that's too ba[d]
Deb: [s]o don't you have all your
family coming today?
Dick: Well: they're coming around two and I °hhh left
messages with Brian an:d mydad to(uh) see if
they wanted to come but=ah
(0.2)
°hh that's all I could do was leave messages.
Deb: owh
(0.4)
Dick: °Gotsome° °hhhh five pound lasagna thing to(hh)
throw in the oven=an
Deb: o(h)h(h)=huh (.) well: I'm sure you'll have a
good time.
Dick: [oh
Deb: [<at least it's inside. And it didn't rain
yesterday so we were lucky [l- looking at it
Dick: [mmhm yeah
Deb: today god. woulda been awful.
Dick: Well were gonna probably hit the squash court en the ah
pool so ah[::
Deb: [well thanks for all the work ya d[id here
Dick: [Oh honey. ( )
listen -( ) -duh- anyway (hhh)
Deb: Anywa::y.
I shall talk to ya [later okay.
Dick: [Did the-
Did the kids get in the- the water.
[( )
Deb: [Oh yeah. It was - was quite a few kids. Heidi popped by,
and Terry and Kirk are here en [: : :] yup.
Dick: [mhm]
Deb: (0.2) Got a full house.
Dick: heh heh Oh jeez
Deb: s-so: (0.2) oka::y?
Dick: alright then=
Deb: =okay talk to yu later=
Dick: Are they leaving today?
Deb: I don't know

Dick: O-(hhh)-kay(hh)
Deb: Okay.
Dick: Talk to you later.
Deb: Bye bye.
Dick: Bye.

If we were to point to where in the call Deb makes her first move to initiate closing, what would we say? An obvious candidate would be lines 46–7, "Anywa::y. I shall talk to ya later okay." But there are less obvious signs that Deb is moving towards closing earlier in the call. Perhaps "moving towards closing" is too strong. It would be more accurate to say that Deb appears to be building in materials which might be used later in the conversation to warrant the initiation of closing. In chapter 3 we considered Deb's answer to the question "Howditgo", noting that she seems intent on correcting the mistaken assumption embedded in the question that "it" (a party held the night before) is over. When an event has reached its completion it is often appropriate for others to ask how it went. While it is in progress, however, one can ask only "how is it going?" But it is not simply that Dick has selected the wrong grammatical form for the question. Rather, Deb's answer suggests that a report of the kind the question invites is not appropriate at this time. Given that this inquiry is presented, by virtue of its position, as the reason for the call, Deb's answer can perhaps be heard as suggesting that the call itself is somehow coming at the wrong time.

More obviously, by saying that her guests "are still here" Deb indicates that she is still playing the role of hostess and thus that she is otherwise engaged. This, of course, provides material that she will later use to warrant closing down the conversation. Thus, in line 54, after listing some people who "are here" as part of a list of people who used the pool, Deb remarks "got a full house.". Deb then goes on to produce a stand-alone "s-so:", which elliptically indexes the upshot of "got a full house" (see Raymond 2004). After she proposes closing with "okay" and Dick appears to go along with "alright then" Deb moves straight away to closing with "okay talk to yu later". Notice the way in which, at line 59, Dick displays his orientation to the relevance of the guests, asking "are they leaving today?"

So it seems that Deb is at least anticipating a warrant for closing (and building in materials to be used in this regard) much earlier in the conversation. Although our observations are now significantly more speculative, it is at least worth registering Deb's very first turn-at-talk. It is difficult to see this in the transcript, but at line 01 Deb's answer to the summons is produced with a heavy and clearly audible breathiness which extends beyond the word so that it trails off, and becomes almost a sigh. There is something to her voice, in this very first utterance, which suggests exhaustion and perhaps even that she is "out of breath". Now, why would someone be out of breath in saying "hello?". Certainly the act of producing the "hello" could not, under normal circumstances, be responsible for someone being out of breath. Rather, the person must have been engaged in some other activity just prior to answering. Thus, in producing this single-word utterance in the way she does, Deb gives at least a hint of being inconvenienced by the call, of having to stop doing something else in order to attend to the phone. That something else, of course, turns out to provide her with a reason for initiating closing and ultimately for terminating the conversation.

We can see then that conversation is finely organized at this *overall* level, and that openings and closings are designed to deal with the specific sorts of organizational problems involved in both beginning and ending an encounter.

Conclusion

In chapter 1 we considered the utterance "that was fun" in terms of intersecting organizations of turn-taking, action sequencing, repair and so on. We began that discussion by considering an organization relation to occasions: "an overall structural organization". There it was noted that this utterance came at the conclusion of the visit which it assessed. In this chapter we've considered various aspects of this overall structural organization in somewhat more detail. Specifically, we've seen that talk can be analyzed in terms of its positioning at the outset or at the close of an occasion. We've seen that in these positions particular kinds of interactional work are relevant and that particular practices are routinely used to accomplish that work.

Notes

1 And when greeting strangers on the street we may do it in such a way as to discourage the production of a return greeting, e.g. "Hi there, uhm: sorry to bother you but could you tell me the way to Bloor?"

2 A gambit frequently pictured in silent movies. See, for instance, *It*, a silent film from 1927 starring Clara Bow and Antonio Moreno, in which "Betty Lou drops her handkerchief, and Cyrus picks it up to return it to her. However, she's disappointed because he doesn't even look at her." From: www.silentsaregolden.com/featurefolder2/itscenes.html, accessed August 3, 2009.

3 Where the answerer is unable to reciprocate recognition claimed by a caller's "hi" they may select default "hello" in T3:

((ring))
A: Hello
B: Hi:
A: Hello?

Another relevant practice involves repeating, indeed replicating, in T3 the caller's turn in T2, presumably on the grounds that, although I don't recognize who it is I'm talking to, it is reasonable to assume that I should use the same form that they use with me.

4 Of course there's more for the recipient to work with than simply a voice sample. There is, for instance, the recipient's sense of who might be calling me *now*.

5 Not surprising because it conforms with a much more general preference to "over-suppose and under-tell".

6 The crosshatch [≠] indicates a wheezing sound.

7 As we will see in chapter 11, there is evidence here that Hyla has called to talk about Grahame but would rather have Nancy elicit the story than volunteer it herself.

11
Topic

In chapter 4, I contrasted an analysis of conversation based on action with one based on topic: that is, a focus on what a given stretch of talk is *doing* rather than a focus on what it is *about*. For the purposes of that chapter it made sense to treat these as though they were more or less mutually exclusive ways of approaching conversation. In terms of how these notions are applied within the wider field of sociolinguistics and discourse analysis that is not totally inaccurate. But of course people *do* talk on topics and sometimes they can be seen as trying to get *off a topic*, change the topic, etc. These are robust intuitions that we have for ordinary conversation and the fact that we talk in these ways about conversation suggests that there is something out there that requires an account. There are, however, some rather well-known problems involved in the use of a notion of "topic" in analysis. Schegloff (1990), for instance, notes the following complications:

1 There are problems in determining "what the topic is" for a given unit of talk (sentence, stretch of sentences and so on).
2 The practices of topic-shading (Schegloff and Sacks 1973) and stepwise transition (Jefferson 1984), which allow for the gradual transition from one topic to another, complicate the problem identified in 1.
3 The practice of "formulating the topic" is something that may be done *by the participants*. However, when this is done it is not done in an unconstrained way, and is typically the vehicle for some *other* activity or action.
4 A focus on topic may obscure important questions about what the participants were doing in and by talking about whatever it was they were talking about. Talk gets treated as "talk-about" rather than "talk-that-does" (Schegloff 1990: 52).

Sacks, noting that he was "in the first instance a bit leery of beginning to do work on the phenomenon of 'topic'" (1995 vol. 1: 752), raises another issue: it seems to be the kind of thing in which "direct content considerations would seem to be involved." Sacks writes that with respect to topic it seemed "I couldn't proceed in my usual fashion, which would be to try to extract relatively formal procedures which persons seem to use in doing whatever they are doing." Sacks did eventually find a way of analyzing topic in terms of formal procedures rather than "content". This began with the basic question, "How do persons go about doing topical talk?" or "How do persons show respect for a topic?"

One of the phenomena where one sees this most clearly according to Sacks is in the selection of "referring expressions". So for instance in one of the fragments he shows, there is reference to someone via the expression "the woman who lives there now" – an expression that seems perfectly suited to a discussion of a house for rent (but not the speaker's marital situation!).

> We note of course that this person could be referred to in a variety of other ways, and indeed in other places in the conversation she's referred to in other ways. So that, e.g., when it's being explained how come she's moving, she's called a "widow." At other places she's called a "tenant," and she could be called numerous other things, were other sorts of "topics" up in the conversation. (1995 vol. 1: 753)

By the selection of a reference form, a speaker exhibits a respect for the topic and attention to it. This is one of a set of technical features, part of a machinery, for doing topical talk (see also Maynard 1980).

Having established "that persons orient to the fact of topical organization, and that they have a variety of ways of doing respect for topical organization" (Sacks 1995 vol. 1: 540), Sacks goes on to ask what kind of an organization it is.

> Assuming you've got your hands on some order of fact, you want to try to find what sort of order of facts it is, i.e., where does it fit, what is it derivative of, what's consequential on it. Can you say, e.g. topical organization of conversation is a consequence of X phenomenon, and X phenomenon is more primary then topical organization. (1995 vol. 1: 540)

According to Sacks topical organization is, ultimately, "a direct consequence, almost an artifact, of the tying structures" (ibid.) since "if you're going to have tying structures as a fundamental organizing principle of conversation, then you're going to have topics as a consequence."

The idea here is that "tying structures" provide the basic means by which participants display to one another that and how they understood the talk to which they are responding. For instance, in the following case Betty has called her mother Amy. Amy is apparently informed via a call display who is calling and forgoes an opening sequence. Rather, guessing what it is Betty is calling about, Amy asks "what do you want me to pick up?". Amy has it wrong and Betty responds by asking "I want to know how you boil an egg". Amy goes on to give some advice on how to do this. We can see many different tying structures at work in this short conversation. Let's track those that tie together references to "egg" or "eggs".

(1) XTR.3.boilanegg.mov		**Reference Forms**
((Telephone rings))		
Amy:	What do you want me to pick ↑up?	
Betty:	Nothi:ng.but I want to know how you boil an egg	"an egg"
	(1.0)	
	(h)hard boil.	
	(0.4)	
Amy:	↓Oh oka::y an' I just read this you know 'cause	
	I always let the water boil but you're not supposed	
	to (.hh) put it in and you (.hh) bring it to a boi:l	"it"

09		(.) but then turn it down 'cause you're really not	
10		suppose' to boil the e::gg	"the egg"
11	Betty:	hhh=	
12	Amy:	=ya'let it- (.) uh simmer:, or you know on me:dium,	
13	Betty:	Ri:ght	
14	Amy:	fo:r [tw]elve minutes.	
15	Betty:	[((sniff))]	
16		(.)	
17		Twelve minutes?	
18	Amy:	Wull I always do it faster than th(h)at[(hh)	
19	Betty:	[okay=	
20	Amy:	=I jus' boil the shit out of it. [but(h)	"it"
21	Betty:	[How dihy'know when	
22		it's done	"it's"
23		(1.0)	
24	Amy:	You don't.	
25	Betty:	Okay. (.) [This is for Easter egg colouring. (.) so	
26	Amy:	[I-	
27		O::h hell then boil the hell out of [them	"them"
28	Betty:	[Uh	
29		they won't kra- they won't crack?	"they"
30	Amy:	We::ll that's why you simmer them.	"them"
31	Betty:	[Ri(hh)ght(hh)	
32	Amy:	[I jus' put a bunch in an' the:n:, bring the water	"a bunch"
33		up, an' then lower it and let it simmer fer (hh)	
34		twelve minutes	
35	Betty:	O:ka:y	
36	Amy:	Okay	
37	Betty:	B[ye: :]	
38	Amy:	[Bye.]	

Sacks (1995 vol. 1: 541) remarks, "tying is a two-utterance phenomenon, in which the basic components are the pro-terms." In the example, we see that, after an initial mention of "an egg" in the phrase "boil an egg", Amy refers to the egg in line 08 using a pro-term, "it". "It" is also used to refer to the water in line 08 and again in line 09. It is perhaps this multiple use of "it" that leads Amy to use "the egg" in line 10 (as a matter of disambiguation where "it" in this position might refer to the water). At lines 20 and 22 Amy and then Betty refer to the egg again using "it". However, after Betty explains in line 25 that this is for "egg coloring", the reference form is transformed from "it" to "them". Easter egg coloring typically involves boiling multiple eggs so that by using "them" instead of "it" at line 27, Amy displays a subtle understanding of Betty's talk while at the same time maintaining the tying structure relation between utterances.

Another tying-structure is illustrated in the following fragment:

(2) XTR.3.boilanegg.mov (detail)

27			O::h hell then boil the hell out of [them
28	Betty:		[Uh
29			they won't kra- they won't crack?
30	Amy:	→	We::ll that's why you simmer them.

Here at line 27 Amy suggests that Betty can just "boil the hell out of them" prompting Betty to ask "they won't crack?" In her response, Amy uses the demonstrative "that" to tie back to the possibility that the eggs might crack. Like the "pro-terms", so-called "deictics" such as "this" and "that" exhibit a kind of "indexical" or "linking" relation between the current utterance and previous talk. They invite the recipient to locate such links and thus perform a basic tying function. Here's another example in which the deictic "this" ties back to "how you boil an egg":

(3) XTR.3.boilanegg.mov (detail)
02 Betty: Nothi:ng.but I want to know **how you boil an egg**
03 (1.0)
04 (h)hard boil.
05 (0.4)
06 Amy: → ↓Oh oka::y an' I just read **this** you know 'cause

Sacks notes that such considerations "permit us to treat the machinery for orienting to 'preserving a topic' as something fitting onto the tying structures, as an accessory to those" (1995 vol. 1: 541). So, according to Sacks, the whole phenomenon of topic in conversation is an outgrowth of more basic forms of organization. This being the case, it should be possible to locate a set of practices in conversation by which topics are generated, maintained, pursued and so on and through which "respect for topic" is displayed. It is to this set of issues that we now turn.

The Practices of Topic Talk

In accordance then with the basic CA principle of focusing on what a given bit of talk is doing rather than what it is about, in examining topic in this chapter we will consider the various practices of speaking which conversationalists use to generate, to locate, to pursue and to resist talk on a topic. These can be thought of as practices of topic talk. By way of introduction, consider the following short telephone call:

(4) Bev and Ann (Transcribed 4/25/04)
01 Ann: Hi::,
02 Bev: Hellu:[:::
03 Ann: [How are you:.
04 Bev: >Fine<
05 Ann: Everything good,
06 Bev: S-stalker hasn't been arou:nd since that day=
07 Ann: =Oh good hh=.
08 Bev: =>I mean I haven't logged onto the ga:me or to
09 the-im-my old messenger account though so=
10 Ann: =Right wul (.) jus as well(.) °hhh good hh
11 Bev: How's life with you.
12 Ann: Oh fi:ne, hh
13 (0.2)
14 Bev: Are you writing away,

Ann: Uhm: Not right now=my mom's here. hh
(0.5)
it's a PD day.
Bev: Oh Good.
Ann: So I got the kids hom:e an my mom's here.
[(0.4) [an the kids are screaming at each other
Bev: [°hhhhh[h
hh[hhh
Ann: [huh ha ha
Bev: Okay wul listen ((smile voice))
.hh (.) >Are=you gonna be at my house at what time on
ah Fri:- on Sund[ay?
Ann: [What time am I (.) to be there at.
Bev: I think a little before se:ven.=
((Call continues with arrangement
making sequence to close))

Here then we find a standard opening for intimates in which no self- or other-identifications are necessary (see chapter 10). Ann then asks at line 03 "How are you.". As we saw in chapter 10, a "neutral" answer to such a personal-state inquiry regular invites the inference "no news to tell". Now in this case, although Bev gives the standard, neutral and therefore "no news" response, it is delivered very rapidly in a manner one could describe as clipped. This contrasts quite strikingly with her greeting (Hellu::::) which is not only massively elongated but also marked by a highly noticeable vowel substitution (the final vowel "u" as in the name Lou rather than "o" as in the word "low"). Moreover, Bev does not follow up her "fine" with a reciprocal personal-state inquiry and thus provides Ann the opportunity to speak next. So there are several aspects of this utterance that seem to convey that it is not a plain and simple "neutral" response and Ann, apparently picking up on this, pursues the matter further with "everything good,". This time round, Ann's question elicits from Bev some news which apparently bears on her personal state. After this talk is brought to a close (through Ann's positive assessments) Bev asks Ann "How's life with you.". Ann treats this as a personal-state inquiry (equivalent to "how are you?"), answering with "Oh fine,", and Bev follows up with "are you writing away," (Ann is a novelist). Ann answers negatively and follows with an explanation – that her kids are home from school – that turns out to be strongly closing-implicative and the participants move into an arrangement-making sequence. So we have here a recurrent structure of personal-state inquiries followed by neutral responses which are followed by turns that, we will come to see, pursue a recipient's topic.

How are you.	How's life with you.	PERSONAL-STATE INQUIRY
>Fine<	Oh fi:ne,	NEUTRAL RESPONSE
Everything good,	Are you writing away,	PURSUIT
. . .	. . .	

One the tasks being worked through in the beginning of a telephone call like this, then, is "what we will talk about", and as we saw in chapter 10 the beginnings of telephone calls are specifically organized to accomplished the generation of a topic.

Three Topic-Generating Sequences

Button and Casey (1984, 1985) described a set of sequences through which topic is interactionally and mutually generated in environments where it does not flow out of a prior topic. As noted above and as I discuss in more detail below, a systematic feature of topic organization is that topics recurrently flow from one to another in "stepwise" or gradual fashion, thereby obscuring beyond recognition any boundary between them. However, Button and Casey (1985) isolate three environments in which this is not the case: the opening of a conversation, the point where closure of a previous topic has been accomplished, and the closing of a conversation. In these environments there is no topic out of which another can emerge and thus, if the participants are to talk on a topic (rather than making a request or an offer, etc.) it must be generated. Button and Casey make a basic distinction between practices for eliciting and practices for nominating topic. What they describe as a topic-initial elicitor is designed to "elicit a candidate topic from the next speaker whilst being mute with respect to what that topic might be" (Button and Casey 1985: 4). Example (5) illustrates:

(5) Hyla & Nancy
10 Hyla: ·mkhhh[hhh
11 Nancy: → [What's doin,
12 (·)
13 Hyla: aAh:, noth[i : n :,]

Topic nominations on the other hand are "oriented to particular newsworthy items". An itemized news inquiry is oriented to a recipient's newsworthy item:

(6) Holt 2:2:6
01 Ron: =three is the code isn' i[t
02 Les: [Yes.
03 (1.0)
04 Ron: → An' whils' we're chatting how is ↓Ski:p,?

A news announcement is oriented to a speaker's newsworthy item.

(7) Geri–Shirley
01 Geri: Howyih doin.h
02 Shirley: Okay how'r you.
03 Geri: ↑Oh alri:[:ght,
04 (Shirley): [(.hhhhhh)
05 Shirley: → Uh:m yer mother met Michael las'night.

Button and Casey argue that participants are oriented to the mutual and interactional generation of topic in conversation; that is, one participant typically does not mandate what is to be talked about. The mutual and interactional generation of topic through the use of topic-initial elicitors, itemized news inquiries, and news announcements, stands in rather stark contrast to other practices. For instance, in the following Dad selects a topic for Cindy to talk to.

(8) Stew Dinner, p. 3
Mom: Yeah it's bee:n: crockin' (in thuh [crock pot.)
Dad: → [So Ci:n (0.2) tell me
about your day.
(0.5)
Cindy: Uh::_ .h
Dad: → Wha'd=ju (d) learn.
(1.0)
Dad: [O:^::H yeah (we) went to thuh- we went to uh: (.)
Cindy: [Uh:m-
Cindy: Claim Jumper.
Dad: Claim Jum[per today.

Rather than immediately presenting a topicalizable item, the recipient of a topic-initial elictor may respond with a no-news response and this may in turn occasion the production of an itemized news inquiry which pursues talk on a particular topic. Consider the following:

(9) Hyla & Nancy
Hyla: ·mkhhh[hhh
Nancy: [What's doin,
(·)
Hyla: aAh:, noth[i : n :,]
Nancy: [Y'didn't g]o meet Grahame?=
Hyla: ·pt·hhhhhahh Well, I got ho::me,=
Nancy: =u-hu:h?
(·)
Hyla: Ayu:::n:: ·hh he hadn' called yet'n there weren't any
messages'r anythi[n: g] e-]
Nancy: [Uh h] u] :h?=

By asking about some specific recipient-related activity in the face of a "no news" response, itemized news inquiries can be heard as "accusatory" – in essence suggesting the existence of a possible news item which has been withheld. Button and Casey suggest that the form of the no news response may be important here. Specifically by neither accounting for the "no news" (saying for instance, "I didn't leave the house today") nor proposing an alternate activity with a reciprocal topic-initial elicitor ("nothing, what's doin' with you?), Hyla's response is vulnerable to being heard as "withholding".

A question arises as to why a recipient of a topic-generating move might "withhold" a possible news item when presented with an opportunity to tell it. Button and Casey's analysis suggests this may be a consequence of a preference for delivering news as a "response to a request to tell" over "volunteering it on its own behalf". So notice, in the case above, that by withholding her news, Hyla ends up answering Nancy's question rather than simply offering her news about Graham on its own account.

It is important to note that both topic-initial elicitors and itemized news inquiries recurrently take the form of questions. Consider for instance the "a" arrows in the following examples:

(10) Deb and Dick p.1

21 Dick: Oh that's too ba[d]

22 Dee: a→ [s]o don't you have all your family coming

23 today.

24 Dick: b→ Well they're coming around two and I hhh left messages with

25 b→ Brian and my dad to see if they wanted to come but ah (0.4)

26 b→ that's all I could do was leave messages.

27 Dee: c→ oh

(11) Holt 2:2:6

01 Ron: =three is the code isn' i[t

02 Les: [Yes.

03 (1.0)

04 Ron: a→ An' whils' we're chatting how is ↓Ski:p,?

05 Les: b→ .k Oh fi:ne?

06 (.)

07 Les: b→ Ye:s? [We've we've]jus' come back fr' Newcastle an'=

08 Ron: [And- a n d]

09 Les: b→ =Yo:r[k,.hhhh.hhh ↑Kath'rine's ↓doing very we↑:ll?[ ]

10 Ron: c→ [Oh:? ↓yes [ ]Goo:d?

11 (0.2)

12 Les: .hh[hh hhhhhhhhhhhh

13 Ron: c→ [Is she: 'as she completed her ↑stu[dies?

14 Les: [.hhhhh We:ll she

(12) Holt 2:4:14/15

01 Dee: a→ [So ↑anyway how a::re uh

02 Katherine an:d um[:

03 Mar: b→ [Oh Katherine's very well thank you?=

04 Dee: =[( )

05 Mar: b→ =[uh she wz: down at- uh Easter,[m-w: s h e] t- .hhhhhhh

06 Dee: c→ [Yeh b't wuh]↑where is she

07 Dee: c→ now[Mark?↑

It can be observed that in each of these cases an initial topicalizing move is made through the use of a question which might have occasioned a minimal response either in the form of a "yes" or "no" (10) or a "no news response" such as "oh fine" or "fine" (11) and (12). The elaborated answers which the recipients of these questions *do* provide display an orientation to the question as doing something more than requesting that a gap in knowledge be filled. Moreover, recipients build these answers to be recognizably incomplete. So for instance, Dick's answer leaves open the question of what will happen with respect to his family gathering and how he will deal with it, Leslie indicates that Katherine is doing "very well" but does not specify in what sense (at work, her personal life, her health . . .) and, finally, although Mark notes that Katherine was down at Easter he does not indicate from where she had come. Recipients of news inquiries thus recurrently produce elaborated answers which are recognizably incomplete and thereby invite further topicalization. Next speakers may collaborate in this further development in a number of ways. In (11) and (12) we see next speakers addressing the incompleteness of the news through further topically fitted questions. In other cases, next speakers mark the possible further development of the news through the use of a continuer. In (10), by way of contrast, Deb's "oh" appears to curtail the development of the topical trajectory.

Some itemized news inquiries are what Button and Casey describe as "news generational"; they display in their design an orientation to the relevance of doing more than filling in a gap in knowledge.

(13) Holt 2:4:?
07 I s[poze Leslie working has obviously helped her a little=
08 Mark: [.h h h h h h
09 Dee: =bi:[t [or- or you,
10 Mark: [.t.hhh[hYe:s.
11 (.)
12 Mark: Yes that's ri:ght.
13 Dee: Ye::[h
14 Mark: [Ye:h.
15 Dee: a→ An' what about your own job Mar[k
16 Mark: [.hhhhh[↑W E : : l l :-:]=
17 Dee: [You're still (in]=
18 Dee: =↓pap[er)?
19 Mark: [↑Pard'n?
20 Dee: You're still[there
21 Mark: b→ [↑Oh yeh still the:re b'course we're
22 b- ↓struggling becuz the ay::gricultural ↓problem:s=

Here, after a previous topic has been mutually closed by reciprocal confirmations at lines 13 and 14 (see below and Jefferson 1993), Dee's initial topic-generating move is produced in two parts. She first asks "what about your own job Mark" and follows with "you're still in paper?". This two-part question clearly invites more than simple confirmation – what is being requested here is an update on how things are going at work and this is exactly what Mark goes on to provide.

Participants' orientation to the use of itemized news inquiries to generate topic rather than simply fill a gap in knowledge may be seen quite clearly in the following example.

(14) Hyla & Nancy 14
26 Nancy: Didja a'ready get the mai:l,=
27 Hyla: =·hhhh Yes, hh-hh-h[h,
28 Nancy: [Oh, hhhmhh[hh
29 Hyla: [hh-hh
30 (·)
31 Nancy: Sorry I brought it uhhhp
32 (·)
33 Hyla: Yeah,

Here, at line 26, Nancy asks Hyla, who is waiting on a letter, whether she got the mail. Hyla treats the itemized news inquiry as a knowledge gap inquiry, answering with a simple "yes" in line 27 (but notice also the breathy quality of the response, which ends in a sigh). This is receipted with "oh", and when Hyla does not elaborate any further Nancy apologizes, saying "sorry I brought it up". Here then Hyla has been presented with an opportunity to talk on the topic of her mail. When she answers the topic-generating move with a simple and unelaborated "yes", Nancy treats this as indicating that Hyla does not want to talk about it.

Recipients of itemized news inquiries can thus be seen to collaborate in the production of a topic by producing elaborated yet recognizably incomplete responses to them. However, a recipient may construct her response in such a way that it does not address the relevancies projected by the itemized news inquiry, a non-elaborated and possibly complete response serving to curtail the topic. Consider for instance the following:

(15) Goodwin 91: 1–2
01 A: How's Tina doin'
02 (.)
03 J: → Oh she's doing goo:d.
04 A: Is she I heard she got divo:rc:ed.=
05 J: =Mmhm?
06 (.)
07 A: Is she?
08 J: (sh)sposeuh get rema:rried again thou:gh, next couple
09 a'wee:ks,=
10 A: =↑Oh yer ↑kiddee:n. Who's she marryin'.

A response such as "Oh she's doing goo:d" in line 3 is topic-curtailing in so far as it treats the initial inquiry as one that can be simply answered. Button and Casey suggest that one possible response to such topic-curtailing moves is to produce a "recipient's version of a news announcement", as here, "I heard she got divorced.". While this reveals more of what the inquirer knows about the proposed topic and further reveals the particular topical trajectory she is attempting to establish, by virtue of its epistemically downgraded character it maintains an orientation to the asymmetry of knowledge embodied in the initial question.

News announcements are unlike both topic-initial elicitors and itemized news inquiries in so far as they propose a topic which is speaker- rather than recipient-related. That said, news announcements engaged in topic nomination recurrently contain components which display an orientation to the recipient as having some knowledge of the topic being proposed.

(16) Geri–Shirley
01 Geri: Howyih doin.h
02 Shirley: Okay how'r you.
03 Geri: ↑Oh alri:[:ght,
04 (Shirley): [(.hhhhhh)
05 Shirley: → Uh:m yer mother met Michael las'night.
06 Geri: Oh rilly?=
07 Shirley: =Ye:ah.
08 ( ): .hh-.hh
09 Geri: ↑Oh:::.=
10 Shirley: =Yeah.She wz taking Shiloh out.just ez we w'r coming back
11 fr'm dinner.

Here Shirley's news announcement includes reference to Geri's mother; moreover, it makes reference to "Michael", and in using the recognitional reference form conveys that Geri should know who it is Shirley is talking about and thus indexes the recipient's knowledge about the topic. A further feature of news announcements related to topicalization is their recognizably incomplete or partial character. Button and Casey (1985: 23) write that news announcements "selectively present aspects of the activity whilst projecting that there is more that could be told. Therefore, these announcements do not in themselves constitute 'news deliveries', but rather 'headline' news which, following an appropriate response . . . may then be delivered." Button and Casey go on to note that following an appropriate response, such as Geri's "oh really", the news announcer may, rather than deliver the news, simply confirm it, as, in fact, Shirley does above. This may then again set up a situation in which the news is delivered in response to a "request to tell". Consider also (17) which develops along the same lines.

(17) FD:Finger
01 B: Oh I got hurt a li'l bit las' night.
02 C: You did.
03 B: Yeah,
04 C: → Wut'app'n tih you.
05 B: Well ah(,) like tuh cos' much little finger they had me
06 in surgr'y f'about three'n a haf hours gettin ( )

Here then the news is headlined with "Oh I got hurt a li'l bit las' night." When the recipient marks this as newsworthy with "You did.", B merely confirms with "Yeah,". C pursues the news with "Wut'app'n tih you." and B then delivers it in response to this "request to tell". Where, in response to a simple confirmation of the news, no request is made to have it told, the speaker can go on and deliver it without any request from the recipient.

(18) Geri–Shirley
05 Shirley: Uh:m yer mother met Michael las'night.
06 Geri: Oh rilly?=
07 Shirley: =Ye:ah.
08 ( ): .hh-.hh
09 Geri: ↑Oh:::.=
10 Shirley: =Yeah.She wz taking Shiloh out.just ez we w'r coming back
11 fr'm dinner.

Here after Shirley confirms the news in response to Geri's news mark, Geri does not produce a follow-up "request to tell". Shirley however continues with the news delivery. So although the organization of news announcements suggests a preference to tell news in response to a "request to tell" rather than to volunteer it, in the absence of such a request, the speaker may still continue to tell it.

To summarize, the studies by Button and Casey show that topics in conversation are interactionally and mutually generated. Moreover, the various topic-initiating sequences they describe appear to be organized so as to maximize the chance that news will be delivered in response to a request to tell rather than volunteered on its own behalf.

Topic Shift

So far we've seen some ways in which topics are generated where no topic is already in play. It is obvious, though, that topics change and transform over the course of a conversation. You may start out talking about one thing and find yourself later talking about something quite different. Such transitions and shifts may be accomplished in more or less subtle ways. We begin here with the less subtle practices of topic shift.

What I want to consider then are instances in which the participants are talking away on one topic and one of them, in ways to be discussed, proposes that they turn to some other topic of conversation. A topic shift of this kind is a delicate matter especially where the moved-away-from topic concerns a speaker's trouble. Given that delicacy it is hardly surprising to find that participants regularly display some attention to a previous topic, even if fleeting, before launching their own. The most minimal version of this involves the use of an acknowledgement token such as "yeah" or "yes". Consider (19):

(19) [NB:IV:1:R:2]
01 Emma: I ↓think I ought to go↓ home,
02 (0.2)
03 Emma: I don't know maybe Bud would like me to stay hh
04 I do(h)n't ↓kno[:w.
05 Lottie: [hhhh[h °↓h[n°
06 Emma: [h [I think he'd like t- me to
07 sta-:-:y khhh[°hhh
08 Lottie: [°hm h[m°
09 Emma: [BUT FOR ORNERINESS I'm
10 going ho:me, mhh!=
11 Lottie: → =Ye:ah.=
12 Emma: =hnh huh, °hhh[h
13 Lottie: → [↑God I see in the paper there's sure
14 a lot of halibut being cau:ght down that coa:st,
15 (0.3)
16 Emma: Ye:ah. Bo:y well: it sure is ↑goo::d, we had some it was
17 really goo:d.

As Jefferson (1993) notes about this and the other fragments like it that she shows, the pre-shift token used is different from the speaker's prior exhibits of recipientship. Thus the pre-shift token here is "Ye:ah.", whereas earlier Lottie responds to Emma's talk with "light laughter", "hhhhh °↓hn°" and "°hm hm°" (lines 5–8). With such a pre-shift token, then, a participant can be exhibiting attention to a previous topic while introducing her own. Jefferson writes that here "the display of recipientship is fleeting – a merest nod to the other's materials before launching one's own" (1993: 9). Slightly more "interactionally engaged" than an acknowledgement token is a pre-shift assessment. Jefferson argues that assessments are more "interactionally engaged" because "they at least exhibit a position." So in (20) below, Lottie responds to Emma's itemized news inquiry with a report about complications encountered in renting out a property. In line 15 Lottie begins a turn which is projectably on the way to summarizing the situation and Emma completes this with a terminal item ("business") which Lottie then accepts with "Yea::uh" (see Lerner 2004). Emma's topic shift in lines 19–20 follows a summarizing assessment "that's goo:d".

(20) [NB:II:3:10:R]
01 Emma: You haven't got the Hawaiian House rented ↓then °huh?°
02 Lottie: ·kh·hh We:ll u-no: I (.) u-We k- we ke:pt it open for a
03 couple weeks 'cause I want the-uh: Doctor Livingston
04 wanted to come down gee I want to: (.) pay him
05 for you know giving me that stuff for my
06 arthri:ti[s and I mean]: he won't =take any money=

07 Emma: [°m-Hm: hm,°]
08 Lottie =and everything ·hh ·hhh and then (.) Earl's gonna ha:ve
09 uh:: (0.2) a guy from:: Central. (0.3) do:wn,
10 (.)
11 Emma: [M m] hm:]
12 Lottie: [for a] wee:]k so: h You kno:w
13 (.)
14 Emma: Mm hm,
15 Lottie: •k I mean it's jus::t
16 (.)
17 Emma: ih bu[siness,]
18 Lottie: [(ta:kes)] Yea::uh, (.) Ye[a : h .]
19 Emma: → [yeh tha]t's
20 → goo:d.u-How is your arthritis, you still taking sho:ts?

Jefferson goes on to suggest however that "assessments need be no more topically engaged than the acknowledgement tokens". She shows this with respect to the following example.

(21) [Her:I:6:3]
01 B: I got your ca:rd. Thank you [very much.]
02 I: [ih-] Goo:d.h·hhh
03 (.)
04 I: e-So: what are you doi-]w
05 B: [A : n d the dogs are s]::u:pe:r,
06 I: [u-Wot- ↑Mm::?
07 B: The dogs are a:bsolutely lovel[y.
08 I: → [Oh good. I'm hoping for
09 another litter shortly
10 (0.2)
11 B: Ah:: h[AH([ )]
12 I: [Uh:: [Mitzie] wuh (.) Mitzie was mated
13 about uh:m ·tch·h two weeks ago:.
14 (0.3)
15 B: → Oh: ↓love[ly.
16 I: [So: if it's taken they should be here in about
17 six weeks but I ↓don't know yet of course you can't
18 tell, (.) until,][[about a month,]
19 B: →][O[h h o w r e a]lly lovely.
20 °hh As a matter of fact I was going to ↓a:sk you,
21 °p °hhh eh:m (.) Is there anyone very reliable that does
22 clipping you know their ↓cla:ws.

Jefferson notes (1993: 11) that the pre-topic shift assessment in line 19 ("Oh how really lovely") is "thoroughly misfitted to the utterance it is positioned upon" (". . . but I don't know yet of course you can't tell, until . . .", lines 17–18). Jefferson goes on:

> That is, although the assessment is highly interactionally engaged, it is thoroughly disattentive to the current state of talk. This particular case of an assessment, with its topical misfittedness, may be seen as a rather blatant exposure of a feature of all the assessments cited here; that is, although they are more interactionally engaged than the acknowledgement tokens, they are every bit as topically disengaged.

Looking across a collection of such assessment turns, Jefferson noticed a recurrent phenomenon in which a speaker "starts up somewhere in the course of what turns out to be the recipient's assessment". So for instance in the following case A begins an "uh"-prefaced continuation of her turn, in the course of M's "Oh: well tha:t was: thoughtful hh".

(22) [Detail]
27 A: . . . I did the same thing for he:r,h
28 M: → Oh: well tha:t [was: thou]ght[ful hh
29 A: [U h : :] [the day before yesterday

Jefferson (1993: 14) asks whether the "somewhere" where A starts speaking in line 29 might, in fact, be "specifiable as the point at which a speaker can recognize that a recipient is producing an assessment". If so, by interrupting the course of such an assessment the speaker might be "counteracting a recognizable move toward closure of the topic or topical line underway". That is, in these interruptions, a speaker may be orienting to such assessments as topic pre-shift items. So there are really two questions here. First, do these interruptions really come in a recurrent position specifiable as the point at which it becomes recognizable that the recipient is producing an assessment? And, secondly, do these interruptions counteract a move to topic closure? Consider the following cases:

(23) [NB:V:4–5]
01 P: She's up at uh: Ronny's mo:m's no:w, she went up
02 (.) Sunday ·hhh-·hh-·hh They came down for dinner=
03 E: =[Mm: -hm:]
04 P: =[And then] uh: she'll I'll go get her tomorrow.
05 E: → Oh. Well that's [°wonderful°]
06 P: → [And then uh,] (.) too- e-she has
07 an old frie:nd Oh well she's u:an old friend of
08 uy a:ll of us. You know. [·h- ·h- ·h]
09 [M m h m,]
10 But she's eh she:'s uh up in Lodi.hh
11 E: O[h : : :.]
12 P: [So she's] gonna come down . •

(24) [Rah:II:3]
01 J: And is he any ↑be(.)tter. Is it u[h
02 I: [wOo- ih- Ye:s
03 his back has been much better the last two: da:ys?=
04 J: → aOh: that's [good] ↓the:n.]
05 I: → [It ha]:d The] pai:n's go↑:ne:=
06 J: =eeYe:s::

(25) [TCI(b):l6:77–8:R]
01 A: That's what really made me ma:d.=
02 D: =Hu:[:h.
03 A: [·hhhhh And I thought maybe they've got uh
04 some: supply: °hhh A::nd a::nd (.) that uh:m ·tk·hh
05 since she was a dea:ler then they sold them to her.
06 D: Hm::.
07 (0.2)

A: ·t[°I don't kno:w.°]
D: [°I don't ↑kno:w.°]
(0.3)
A: ·t·hh [hhhh]
D: → [Well] tha[t's u too ba:d]
A: → [But a:nyway it] really makes me:
(.) kind of disgusted, ·hhhh Fay says ↑I'd write them
a letter and tell them just what you think about
that kind of bu(h)si(h)nes[s °hhhehh
D: [Ye:ah,
A: And I said ye[:ah,
D: [I hope I don't have too much trouble,

(26) [NB:IV:12:R:2]
E: So all the kids are STANDING OU:T here the
maRI[nes get o]ut=
L: [°heh heh°]
E: =of [↑the CA [: R] the st(h)a](h)tion wa:gon
L: [°°he°° [°eh°] henh henh]
E: [And u-]: huhh]
L: [Oh: th]a t ']s wo[nder f u l.]
E: → [The:re's th]e (.) two young
→ girls you know that's across the street
and every[thing they're-a:l]l ik- They're gonna take
L: [°Ye oh:: y e h.°]
E: them down to the beach now and wa:lk them down
the beach

In each of these cases the assessment turn takes an utterly standard form such as "Well that's u too ba:d" (in (25)) or "Oh: that's wonderful." (in (26)). The format can be represented schematically as:

turn-initial component		assessment term
Oh/ Well	*that's*	*too bad, good, wonderful*

Work by Charles and Marjorie Goodwin (1987) has shown that recipients are quite able to parse and project the course of an assessment turn (see pp. 165ff.). Moreover, in this sequential position, a turn beginning such as "Oh that's . . ." or "Well that's . . ." strongly projects an assessment turn next (see Schegloff 1987 for discussion of turn beginnings). It therefore seems quite reasonable to suppose that here the speakers are in fact interrupting the assessment at just the point at which its status as such becomes recognizable. As to the second question (whether these interruptions counteract a move to topic closure), we can see that in each of these cases the speaker interrupts a recipient's assessment to specifically *continue* with what they were saying. Indeed, in (23) and (25) the continuation is explicitly marked as such with a conjunction-type item, "and", in (23) and "but anyway . . ." in (25). So there is good evidence not only that assessments are topic-shift implicative but further that current speakers-on-a-topic orient to this implicativeness. By interrupting an assessment in the course of its production, current speakers-on-a-topic may attempt to prevent its closure.

Assessments are well fitted to the work of topic closure because they allow a recipient to show attention to the preceding talk while at the same time delivering a "summary" or "upshot" of it (see Jefferson 1984: 212). Paul Drew and Elizabeth Holt (Drew and Holt 1998, Holt and Drew 2005) have provided a detailed account of the use of "figures of speech" in making such assessments so as to facilitate topic transition. They illustrate some of the basic issues involved with the following example (Drew and Holt 1998: 499–500):

(27) [Field:X(C)85:1:1:1:6]
(Lesley is telling her mother about an acquaintance that has recently died.)
Lesley: . . . He wz a (0.2) .p a buyer for the hoh- i- the
only horse hair fact'ry left in England.
Mum: Good gracious,
(0.3)
Lesley: And he wz their buyer,
(.)
Mum: Hm:::
Lesley: .t
Mum: Hm:.
Lesley: So he had a good inni:ngs did[n't he.
Mum: [I should say so:
Ye:s.
(0.2)
Mum: Marvellous,
Lesley: .tk .hhhh Anyway we had a very good evening o:n
Saturda:y.

Here Lesley and Mum are discussing a mutual acquaintance who has recently died. At lines 01–05 Lesley is explaining that the person in question was a buyer for the only horsehair factory left in England. With this Lesley is perhaps implying that the man in question had a long life and near the end of it was living in conditions very different than those he knew as a younger man – the "only horse hair fact'ry left in England" is a synecdoche for a broad range of social and economic changes (see Drew and Holt 1998 for a detailed analysis of "a good innings"). In line 10 Lesley summarizes the situation using the figurative expression "he had a good innings." Holt and Drew (2005) note that the phrase is metaphorical: "'Innings' (used in a literal sense to refer to a person's turn at batting in cricket) is applied to someone's life." After Mum agrees emphatically with "I should say so: Ye:s.", Lesley begins an entirely new topic, reporting on what she has done earlier in the week. Holt and Drew (2005: 36) write:

> This new topic is introduced in a disjunctive manner: It is not linked to the previous talk. The figurative phrase acts as a summary and positive assessment of the preceding detailing regarding the man's life. This, together with Mum's agreements in lines 11, 12, and 14, brings the topic to a point at which it can be terminated, and Lesley consolidates this move by initiating a topic transition to an unrelated matter.

Drew and Holt go on to argue that, used in this way, figurative expressions such as "had a good innings" and "you can't win" serve as "summary assessments". They are assessments because they convey a positive or negative value "to be attached to the circumstances that the speaker has been describing" (1998: 502). Moreover, with a figurative expression, a speaker moves away from or steps out of "their report of empirical details" (1998: 503).

That such a figurative expression is summarizing can be seen in the fact that the assessment it embodies is not connected particularly or exclusively to the immediately preceding talk. Rather it relates back to a larger stretch of talk on a topic, organizing it under the "heading" of a single evaluation.

> In producing a figurative expression, the speakers are becoming empirically disengaged. They are not contributing further details but rather are assessing and summarizing the previously reported empirical information. Employing a figurative expression can be a device to summarize a topic, and thereby to draw it to a conclusion. (Drew and Holt 1998: 503)

On the basis of their analysis of many examples, Drew and Holt propose "a standard sequence", represented as follows:

1	→	Speaker A:	Figurative summary
2	→	Speaker B:	Agreement (or other expression of contiguity)
3	→	Speaker A:	Agreement/confirmation
4	→	Speaker A/B:	Introduces next topic (Drew and Holt 1998: 506)

However, in a later paper the same authors note that a number of cases did not fit this pattern. They provide the following case as an illustration:

(28) [F1 MAY.8:9–10]
(D is talking about bumping into someone she went to school with and how she thought he would never amount to anything.)

D: .hhh hhh And I- You know it- for some
reason he struck me as never even being
able to get out of high school well I's
talking to him well he's go-he's got a year
left at SMU in law school.
M: hh [h huh huh] huh [huh .hhh].hhh=
D: [hh h] [h h h h]
D: =and he's rea:l cute now
M: .hhh We:ll see that just goes to show you
he's a late bloomer
D: Yeah he was re:al handsome
(1.0)
M: You know (0.4) sometimes the late bloomers
'll fool you
(0.6)
D: Yeah that's true
M: I told you about my friend who's son
graduated from .hhh A and [M:]
D: [ye:]ah and he wen
straight to law schoo:l and
(0.5)
M: all that kind of [stuff and now he's]
D: [and now he's workin] as a
painter
(0.6)
M: driving a trailer or something

Here then D is initially talking about meeting someone with whom she attended school. She reports her surprise in learning that he is now in law school and, moreover, in finding him "real handsome", which is evidently not what she expected from him in school ("he struck me as never even being able to get out of high school."). M then provides a figurative expression which assesses and summarizes the previous talk, saying "he's a late bloomer". Although D concurs in line 11, the figurative expression is not followed by a marked or disjunctive change in topic. Rather, M repeats the expression in the turn at lines 13–14, saying "You know (0.4) sometimes the late bloomers 'll fool you", and follows this up with a related story about someone who followed a trajectory opposite to a "later bloomer": M's friend's son went straight to law school and is now working as a truck driver. On its second use the expression "later bloomer" is not "used to refer to the man D has been talking about, but to 'late bloomers' in general, thus providing an explicit link to a related story". Holt and Drew (2005: 38) note:

> In this extract, the participants discuss two distinct matters: D's encounter with an acquaintance from school and M's friend's son. The figurative expression used to respond to D's story and then repeated by M at the start of her telling manages the transition between them. It explicitly portrays M's story as related to D's (being another instance of "late bloomers [who]'ll fool you"), thus creating a stepwise transition from one story to the next. Thus, in this instance as in the others in our collection, a figurative phrase forms a pivot between two matters. In the extracts that make up the corpus on which this article focuses, there is a figurative phrase (or several phrases) that forms a connection between two related matters (or matters made to relate through the phrase), bringing one matter to an end while simultaneously opening up the opportunity of introducing the next. The figurative expressions contribute toward managing transitions that would otherwise seem disjunctive or would require handling as disjunctive (or would need explicitly connecting to the previous matter through some other mechanism).

Here then we see a transition between topics that is not disjunctive but rather "shaded" (Schegloff and Sacks 1973): the transition is managed in a stepwise manner. Such stepwise transitions are absolutely pervasive in conversation. Indeed, in a certain sense this is the normal or unmarked way for topic change to occur. It is thus to stepwise topic transition that we now turn.

Stepwise Transition

In a lecture from 1972, Sacks noted:

> It's a general feature for topical organization in conversation that the best way to move from topic to topic is not by a topic close followed by a topic beginning, but by what we call a stepwise move. Such a move involves connecting what we've just been talking about to what we're now talking about, though they are different. I link up whatever I'm now introducing as a new topic to what we've just been talking about [in such a way that] so far as anybody knows we've never had to start a new topic, though we're far from wherever we began and haven't talked on just a single topic, it flowed. (Sacks 1995 vol. 2: 566)

And in another lecture Sacks notes: "If you have some topic which you can see is not connected to what is now being talked about, then you can find something that is connected to

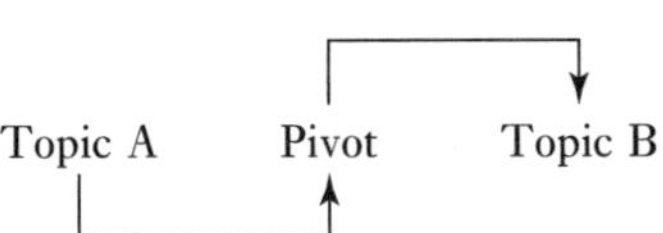

Figure 11.1

both, and use that first" (1995 vol. 2: 300). These observations then lead us back again to consider the idea of "topical pivots" in conversation – items which by virtue of a connection to different topics can be exploited to effect transition without any disjuncture (see figure 11.1).

An example of such stepwise transition between topics is shown below (from Jefferson 1984).

(29) [NB:IV:14:12–14]

Lottie: But eh-it's-it's terrible to keep people ali:ve and
[you know and just let them suffer [day in and day=
Emma: [Right. [r:Right.
Lottie: =out, [it's-
Emma: [They don't do that with an animal.((sniff))
(0.5)
Emma: (You kno[:w,)
Lottie: [Yeah.
Emma: Oh well [bless his heart Well, we don't know what=
Lottie: [((sniff))
Emma: it's all about I g-I-((sniff)) Don't get yourself=
Lottie: =[O h I' m n o t . I j u s t- you know I wish]=
Emma: =[Honey you've got to get aho:ld of your- I know]=
Lottie: =I'd- I'd kind of liked to gone out there but I was
afraid of the fog I was gonna drive him in::- l-·hh
last [ni:ght. but,
Emma: [·hh Oh it was terrible coming down ev[en this=
Lottie: [But-
Emma: =morning.((sniff))
Lottie: But San Diego? I c- I couldn't believe it last
night. We left there about, ·hh eleven thirty (.)
and it w- (.) it[was clear all the way up until we=
Emma: [((sniff))
Lottie: =hit, (1.0) u-uh:: the, thee uh Fashion Square here
in Balboa. [I couldn't believe it [and we went into,=
Emma: [((sniff)) [( )
Lottie: =you couldn't even see:.
Emma: Oh God it's terrible. ((sniff)) That's why well we
didn't get home til two o'clo:ck. God it's-
(0.2)
Emma: [beautiful-]
Lottie: [It was ter]rible in to:wn?
Emma: ·hhh[hh

34 Lottie: [((snort))
35 Emma: ·h Oh we just got into bed at two:.I wasn't gonna
36 (.) go down, wait let me turn this fa- uh:
37 (0.5)
38 Emma: You know we w-this par:ty and then we went to
39 another little party a:fterward.s and oh I met so
40 many f:fa::bulous pees- (.) people and danced with
41 my poor old toes with no t(h)oenails and I was
42 [in-. ·hhhh hh(h)igh (h)h(h)eels and ·hahhh and oh:=
43 Lottie: [hmh hmh
44 Emma: =we (.) just had a (.) beautiful time.

A first observation is that although the fragment begins with Lottie describing the extremely poor health of her husband's mother, it ends with Emma reporting what a good time she had at a party. Nowhere in between do we see the kind of marked, disjunctive topic shift that characterized some of the examples we considered earlier (e.g. (23)–(26)). Thus the story about the party is woven into the current conversation in such a way that, to paraphrase Sacks (1995 vol. 2: 566), a new topic has not been started, though we're very far from where we began. Jefferson's analysis shows that the "arrival at a report of a good time may be seen to be systematically achieved" (1984: 201).

As Jefferson notes, then, the fragment begins with "summing up the heart of the trouble", beginning with Lottie's "But eh- it's-it's terrible to keep people ali:ve . . ." at line 01 through to the trouble recipient Emma saying "Honey you've got to get aho:ld of your (I know)." at line 13. At this point, the troubles teller (here Lottie) "turns to matters that, although on-topic with and part of the trouble, are not at the heart of the matter, but are ancillary" (1984: 202). Here, explains Jefferson, in saying "I'd- I'd kind of liked to gone out there but I was afraid of the fog I was gonna drive him in::- l-.hh last ni:ght.", Lottie is accounting for not having driven her husband in to the airport by reference to the fog. In the third step of stepwise transition, the troubles recipient produces talk that "stabilizes the ancillary matters". So here, Emma agrees with Lottie's assessment of the weather conditions by producing a second assessment, "hh Oh it was terrible coming down even this= =morning" (see Pomerantz 1984). Jefferson notes that although the talk here "can be seen to be working on behalf of a telling in progress" it also "potentiates further talk by the troubles recipient". Emma's second assessment establishes the relevance of her own experience "via which she was enabled to make such an observation". And she eventually does produce this further talk, remarking "Oh God it's terrible. ((sniff)) That's why well we didn't get home til two o'clo:ck." This is the pivotal utterance, allowing Emma to move to other, though analyzably related, matters via the mention of "fog". Notice that it is not just the concept of "fog" that provides for this. It is "fog as inconvenience" or "fog as impediment". Of course in Emma's story the fog has warranted her staying at several parties longer than she might otherwise have.

Stepwise transition thus works via the medium of a pivotal utterance or item. Sacks discussed these pivot utterances in terms of their construction (Sacks 1995b: 300): "utterances can be built in such formats, starting with something connected to the prior topic, with, then, the second part using something else which is connected to the first part of the utterance, not to the prior topic." Schegloff (1996c: 66–7) examines a number of these utterances. Here is one of the examples he cites:

(30) SN-4p.2
10 Mark: w'll (jat'll) jus' be fanta:stic. ·hh So what've y'called any
11 other hotels (r) anything?
12 (.)
13 Sherri: → Y:eah I called thee Embassader 'n stuff. I've go so much
14 → work that I don't believe it.so I'm j'st not even thinking
15 → about that [·now.
16 Mark: [In schoo:l yih mea[:n?
17 Sherri: [Ye:ah,
18 (0.2)
19 Mark: (Y')havent been 'n school in five weeks doesn' matter.
20 Sherri: hhmh hih hmh=

Here Mark is initially asking Sherri about her plans for her upcoming wedding. The first component of her response to this connects back to that topic by answering the question ("Yeah I called thee Embassader 'n stuff). The second unit connects to that answer by raising something that is competing for Sheri's attention, and the third unit completes the turn by relating the two. Mark initiates repair with "In schoo:l yih mea:n?" in such a way as to topicalize "work" and, after the candidate understanding is confirmed, Mark develops that as the new topic. Sacks writes, "A given part of an utterance can be analyzed to find that it has some (actually many) class statuses. Having found some class status for that given item, one may in the next utterance present such a term as stands in co-class membership with a term used in the last. So A talks about cigars, B can talk about pipes" (Sacks 1995 vol. 1: 757), the implication being that B might just as well have talked about Groucho Marx or Cuba.

What seem to be crucial for stepwise movement are the recognizable co-class relations between different topics. In example (30) above, for instance, the participants are initially talking about "wedding preparations", which belongs to the class of topics "things that Sherri has to do". They then move stepwise into another member of that same class – "schoolwork".

Now although this relationship of co-class membership appears to be absolutely central to the organization of topic in conversation, it raises a number of puzzles. As Sacks notes, "it really isn't very discriminative to say that, e.g., pipes and cigars are co-class members – cigars and horses may be co-class members also" (1995 vol. 1: 757). Sacks goes on to explain that, while there are lots of "natural classes" (cats, dogs, horses; orchids, roses, tulips, etc.), "some items are co-class members by virtue of being members of a class for a topic" (1995 vol. 1: 757). Consideration of the example Sacks provides here gives a sense of what he is getting at:

(31) From Sacks 1995 vol. 1: 757
01 A: I have a fourteen year old son.
02 B: Well that's alright.
03 A: I also have a dog.
04 B: Oh I'm sorry.

Sacks explains "the status of kids and dogs as co-class members may turn on that you're renting an apartment; otherwise they may seem a strange pair" (1995 vol. 1: 757).

Speakers can help to shape the topical trajectory of talk, then, by selecting particular items. Sacks argues that if one person says "I went surfing yesterday" it's perfectly available to a recipient to develop the topic by finding the co-class member for "things you did yesterday" and so you get "Oh yeah? I went for a ride." If however, the first speaker, rather than saying that they went surfing, says "I was at County Line yesterday", which is a well-known place to go surfing, "one gets specifically a discussion about what surfing conditions were like over the weekend along the Southern California coast" (1995 vol. 1: 758). Sacks proposes that "the place focus doesn't provide for the generation of other activities as topically coherent next utterances whereas an activity name might be treated as 'one activity' which could suggest that one would be talking topically if one presents another activity" (1995 vol. 1: 758). This leads Sacks to suggest a set of connections between topic, place and memory – a kind of machinery for memory.

Conclusion

We began this chapter by reiterating from chapter 4 some of the complications involved in the use of "topic" in conversation-analytic work. Moving from there, we considered some of Sacks's earliest discussions of topic, in which he linked it to very basic tying structures in conversation. We then reviewed some CA studies of the various practices by which topic is generated and topic transitions are managed. Finally, we very briefly considered some of Sacks's analyses of topic and co-class membership. In fact, Sacks's discussion of these issues is quite extensive; the interested reader should pursue these themes in the lectures.

12
Context

Approaches to Context

"Context" is clearly crucial to understanding even the seemingly most straightforward utterances. For instance, the utterance "can I walk?" will be understood in very different ways if it is asked of a doctor by a patient after he has undergone surgery or, alternatively, of a local by a tourist who is looking for the Eiffel Tower. This much is clear. But it is much more complicated to determine what counts as the context for a given utterance in any particular case. Where does the context of an utterance begin and where does it stop?

Broadly speaking, there are two main ways in which ideas about "context" have been brought to bear in the study of language and social interaction. On the one hand, there is the context that is established by the structures of preceding talk and conduct. For instance, as we saw in chapter 4, by virtue of the conditional relevance it establishes, a question creates a particular context for whatever happens next. And as we touched upon in the last chapter, talk about an argument with my boss, about the weather, about the need to deal with climate change, likewise creates a context for whatever happens next. In the broadest formulation, context in this sense includes the particular type or kind of interaction the participants understand themselves to be engaged in: a scholarly discussion, a petty dispute, an intimate chit-chat or whatever else.

The other sense of "context" makes reference to what are typically thought of as "larger" or "macro" aspects of the social world – social stratification, class, race as well as social institutions such as the law, medicine and so on. As Schegloff (1992c) puts it, here we are talking about

> aspects of social life long central to the social sciences – the class, ethnic, and gender composition of an interaction, each of these understood either as a distinctive source of ordering of and constraint on social life, or as an embodiment of more general properties such as "power" (in various of the senses in which that term is used). Here as well are found the various institutional matrices within which interaction occurs (the legal order, economic or market order, etc.) as well as its ecological, regional, national, and cultural settings, all of which may be taken as "shaping" what goes on under their auspices or in arenas of social life on which they have a bearing.

As it turns out these two conceptions of context are not entirely disjunct. Consider then that in the second notion of context there are indefinitely many ways in which a context *might* be formulated: the same occasion might be characterized as talk between men, as a cross-examination, as a middle-class interaction, etc. The sheer correctness of a description "is equivocal in its import; for we know that not everything that goes on in a courtroom has anything to do with the law, and we know as well that endless numbers of other descriptions would also be 'correct' (e.g. that it was in a north-facing room)" (Schegloff 1992c: 195).

As Schegloff notes, following Sacks, "macro" invocations of context necessarily face a hurdle; they must be shown to be relevant to the participants themselves, for if such invocations are not grounded in the actual orientations of the participants one may legitimately question why *this* aspect of the context as opposed to some other is being invoked. This, then, is where the two conceptions of context link up. Prior talk has the capacity, as we have seen, to invoke the relevance of particular *aspects* of the context. For instance, when, in the midst of a game, one child says to another, "this is my house so I get to go again", he invokes the relevance of the identities of host and guest. When the other child responds by saying, "that's not fair, you just had a turn," he denies the relevance of the host–guest identity in favor of those tied specifically to the rules of play (see C. Goodwin and M. Goodwin 1990). Take another example: when the lecturer of the course interrupts the pre-class chatter to say, "Alright, where were we last time?", she invokes the relevance of the pedagogical setting and the identities of teacher and student.

In an influential argument based on considerations such as those outlined above, Schegloff suggested that invocations of context should satisfy two methodological or analytic constraints. First, any aspect of context invoked by the analyst should be demonstrably relevant to the participants themselves. If one wants to claim that someone said something as a woman, or a doctor, or a lawyer one should show that the speaker (and perhaps the recipient) was themselves oriented to this aspect of their identity and not some other (see also Kitzinger 2000). The task then is to show "from the details of the talk or other conduct in the materials that we are analyzing that those aspects of the scene are what the parties are oriented to. For that is to show how the parties are embodying for one another the relevancies of the interaction and are thereby producing the social structure" (Schegloff 1991: 51). Second, argues Schegloff, we should be able to show that some aspect of context is not only relevant for the participants but, moreover, has some "procedural consequentiality" which Schegloff explains in the following way: "how does the fact that the talk is being conducted in some setting (say, 'the hospital') issue in any consequences for the shape, form, trajectory, content, or character of the interaction that the parties conduct?" (1991: 53). He concludes:

> When a formulation of the context is proposed, it is ipso facto taken to be somehow relevant and consequential for what occurs in the context. It is the analyst's responsibility either to deliver analytic specifics of that consequentiality or to abjure that characterization of the context. Otherwise, the analysis exploits a tacit feature of its own discursive format, but evades the corresponding analytic onus. A sense of understanding and grasp is conveyed to, and elicited from, the reader, but is not earned by the elucidation of new observations about the talk. (ibid.)

In what follows we will consider several ways in which these constraints may be satisfied. In the next section, however, we turn to consider Heritage's (1984) formulation of the context problem.

Talking Context into Being

Heritage's (1984b) account of the context problem is developed in response to an earlier article by Levinson (1979). In that paper, titled "Activity Types and Language", Levinson argued that speakers and hearers draw upon knowledge about the institutional context or ongoing activity in interpreting talk. For instance, the interpretation of a simple utterance like "out!" will be quite different depending on whether the speaker is a line judge in a tennis match or a mother talking to children who have just walked across a clean floor in muddy boots. Heritage (1984) suggests that though the logic here seems inescapable the fact that Levinson treats the "context of interpretation" as something exogenous to the talk presents a problem. Specifically, this raises the question of how participants know to bring *these* assumptions and not others to bear on the talk. As noted above, the physical setting (e.g. a classroom) alone cannot serve as a reliable guide here since, on the one hand, non-pedagogical interaction may take place in the classroom, and, on the other, pedagogic interaction may take place outside the classroom. Heritage suggests then that we begin to think of context as something generated endogenously, *within* the talk itself.

We usually think of context as surrounding or enveloping the talk, so it may at first be quite difficult to understand just what Heritage is suggesting here. Thankfully he provides a very clear illustration, drawing on his analysis of the response particle "oh". In his "A Change of State Token and Aspects of Its Sequential Placement", Heritage shows that "oh" is used "to propose that its producer has undergone some kind of change in his locally current state of knowledge, information, orientation or awareness" (1984a: 299). Heritage (1984a: 314) writes:

> Through the use of the particle, informed, counterinformed, questioning parties can assert that, whereas they were previously ignorant, misinformed or uninformed, they are now informed. Correspondingly, the informing, counterinforming, or answering party is reconfirmed as having been the informative, knowledgeable, or authoritative party in the exchange. By means of the particle, the alignment of the speakers in their sequence-specific roles is confirmed and validated.

As we saw in chapter 6, one recurrent place in which "oh" occurs is in a sequence which consists of question (first position), answer (second position) and "oh" in third position. Here are some examples of this usage:

(1) YYZ – 11/18/06 Call 1
110 S: are you talkin' to m:e?
111 (1.0)
112 B: yeah
113 S: → oh::haha.HHH I'm like who the hell is she talking to? .hh
114 anyway ummm::=

(2) Virginia p.19
24 Wes: Whadduz that boy do.'Uz he work- work fur 'is father?
25 Prudence: Mm mm. He works fer First National Bank.
26 Wes: → Oh 'e does?
27 Prudence: Mm hm.

As the remainder of the turn in each case indicates, these "oh" tokens convey that the questioner has been informed by the answer.

Drawing on a distinction first made by Searle (1969), Heritage suggests that such "real" questions in which "the questioner proposes to be ignorant about the substance of the question" contrast with "exam"-type questions in which the answer is known to the questioner. Exam-questions are a characteristic feature of classroom interaction and produce sequences quite unlike those we see in examples (1) and (2). Here are some examples from the work of Hugh Mehan (1979; see also Mehan 1985):

(3) Mehan 1979
Teacher: What does this word say? Beth
Beth: One
Teacher: Very good

(4) Mehan 1979
Teacher: Edward, what's it about?
Edward: The Map
Teacher: The map. That's right, this says 'the map.'

In each instance the sequence begins with a question from the teacher directed to a specific student. The student selected then responds with an answer. In the third turn, rather than mark the answer as informative, the teacher evaluates it as "very good" in (3) and "that's right" in (4).

These examples and those from conversation may be further contrasted with question–answer sequences in court. Consider the following taken from the cross-examination of the plaintiff in a sexual assault case:

(5) Chmura Trial, LD = Lawyer for the Defense, W=Witness/Plaintiff
LD: my question is
(0.6)
LD: when you went into the bathroom with
Mr. Chmura nobody saw that.
W: to the best of my knowledge.[no.
LD: [w'll there
wud'nt anybody out there.
W: no. ((sniff))
LD: Mr. Cleber wasn't there.
W: no
LD: he wasn't standing so he could see you.
W: not that I am aware of=
LD: =well he says that you stopped. after
he told you not to go in there. and the
language thet I've just used or
(.)
you didn't
turn at him, look at him, smi:le,
an go in anyway. he's lying about that.=
W: =he's lying.
LD: that's a lie.
W: that's a lie.
LD: so he did not see you go into the bathroom.

Here the lawyer says "my question is (0.6) when you went into the bathroom with Mr. Chmura nobody saw that.". The question is answered with "to the best of my knowledge. no.". At this point the lawyer neither marks the answer as informative (with "oh" or some other token) nor does he evaluate the answer. Rather, the lawyer immediately moves to the next question, asking "w'll there wud'nt anybody out there.". Looking through this fragment one can see that this is a recurrent pattern. In court there is typically neither receipt nor evaluation of the answer but rather an immediate move to the next question. Drew (1985) argues that such a pattern reflects the fact that, in court, testimony is elicited *not* for the benefit of the questioner but rather for participants (the jury) whose rights to speak are severely curtailed.

Where there is receipt, it typically takes the form of acknowledgement via repetition or reformulation as in:

(6) Chmura Trial
19 LD: an go in anyway. he's lying about that.=
20 W: =he's lying.
21 LD: that's a lie.
22 W: that's a lie.

Note also that in this sequence the lawyer is asking what is essentially the *same* question several times. For instance:

(7) Chmura Trial
09 LD: Mr. Cleber wasn't there.
10 W: no.
11 LD: he wasn't standing so he could see you.
12 W: not that I am aware of=

As was noted in chapter 4, questioners who feel they have not been adequately answered may pursue a response to a question and, in this way, display their own sense that something which was due is missing. In the context of courtroom cross-examination then, a lawyer can convey that a question has not been adequately (or truthfully) answered by asking what is recognizably another version of the same question.

The more general point to be made about these examples is that in them we see a pervasive orientation on the part of the participants to the institutional context in which they are operating. This orientation shapes the ways in which the participants speak and thus they can be seen to talk the context into being. As Heritage (1984) remarks, "participants routinely assure and reassure one another that it is 'this' and not some 'other' sense of context that is operative for the local organization of 'this segment' of interaction." This of course is what Heritage means when he speaks of context as endogenously generated and as something that participants "talk into being".

A further point is that these orientations are pervasively relevant, shaping the whole trajectory of the talk. Indeed, it is not just that one participant is *invoking* or *imposing* the institutional context but, rather, that all the participants are co-constructing it. It is the participants' common and for the most part unquestioning engagement in this or that kind of sequence that provides for the felt presence of the institutional context.

In their introduction to *Talk at Work* (1992), the volume that stands as the touchstone for conversation-analytic research on institutional interaction, Drew and Heritage make a threefold proposal. They write:

1 Institutional interaction involves an orientation by at least one of the participants to some core goal, task or identity (or set of them) conventionally associated with the institution in question. In short, institutional talk is normally informed by *goal orientations* of a relatively restricted conventional form.
2 Institutional interaction may often involve special and particular constraints on what one or both of the participants will treat as allowable contributions to the business at hand.
3 Institutional talk may be associated with inferential frameworks and procedures that are particular to specific institutional contexts.

These authors go on to describe some particular aspects of institutional talk, focusing on lexical choices, turn design, sequence organization, overall structural organization and finally what they describe as "social epistemology and social relations". Under the last heading Drew and Heritage discuss such features of institutional talk as "professional cautiousness" and neutrality, as well as participants' orientation to various asymmetries of knowledge, expertise and so on (Drew and Heritage 1992: 45–53). Since it is impossible to discuss all of these matters within a single chapter, in what follows I present a case study of talk in legal inquiries that illustrates many of the points that these and other researchers in this area have made.

A Case Study: Talk in Inquiries

Public inquiries represent a special kind of courtroom talk in which lawyers elicit testimony from witnesses. Inquiries are officially characterized as "fact-finding" missions, in contrast to other kinds of legal activities which are explicitly concerned with allocating blame and responsibility (though see Sidnell 2004). The basic procedural rules of public inquiries are, however, similar to those that characterize other legal activities: lawyers are mandated to ask questions and witnesses to answer them. The commissioner (who plays a role similar to that of a judge in other legal contexts) makes occasional, typically corrective or reparative, interjections.

As we saw in chapter 3, in ordinary conversation, turn-taking is locally managed by the participants. In inquiry, turn-taking is tied to the organization of questions and answers and the roles of lawyer and witness. Witnesses orient to the recognizable completion of the lawyer's question as a place for speaker transition, specifically as the place where the witness should begin a response to the lawyer's question. Similarly, the recognizable completion of the witness's answer constitutes a place for the lawyer to begin a next question. Thus turn-taking and the organization of actions into sequences are tightly interwoven in the normative organization of inquiry. A great deal of evidence could be presented to show that this is the case. For instance, it is possible to show, as Clayman and Heritage (2002) have done for news interviews, that although lawyers often produce quite complex, multi-unit turns, witnesses typically withhold their responses until the point at which a recognizable question is produced. That is, witnesses do not treat points of possible completion *within* such turns as transition-relevant until they have heard that a question has been put. Deviations from this are treated as breaches and thus also reveal participants' orientation to the organization of inquiry testimony. Consider the following instance:

(8) Walkerton pp. 140–1
01 Lawyer: °hh Now- (.) as you know, after Wa:lkerto:n,
02 (.) in August of two thousand,your government
03 did (.) pass a law. did pass a regulation
04 °hh that cleared up the notification protocol
05 so that it's clear now that la:bs and the
06 owner (.) must (.)°h notify the appropriate
07 officials,
08 (0.2)
09 The protocol obviously is now aba- a binding
10 law and a regulation, °hh=
11 Witness: =°yeah°
12 Lawyer: an' that mandatory accreditation is now
13 (0.2)
14 a law
15 (0.2)
16 for the private labs doing the testing.
17 (0.4)
18 Now this was done in August of two thousand.=
19 → =Would you agree with me: thet (.)
20 the fact that it was done then is
21 an-a-acknowledgment that that regulation
22 should have been there in May of two thousand?
23 Witness: → (0.4) uhm:: (.) No, I wouldn't sa:y that.
24 I:-I:-I would say thet Walkerton was a
25 wake up call,
26 (0.2)
27 for all of us. including our government=
28 =including other governments. who if you know,
29 subsequently ah-°hhh made a number of changes-
30 aa number of regulatory ah-uhm changes.
31 thee
32 (0.2)
33 tchh thee ah change ah that was made on ah:
34 on the ah: thee protocol? Ah:: is not the one
35 that was recommended to the Minister=but
36 I believe it is the appropriate ah::- change.
37 (0.2)
38 an' I think thee-thee former Medical Officer
39 of Health has acknowledged that-that in
40 hindsight ah- the regulation we ultimately
41 passed ah-thet-thet that would have been ah:
42 better than his recommendation.

Here we see the lawyer producing a long, multi-unit turn in the course of which there are several points that might have been treated as completions. For instance, in terms of both syntax and prosody the turn is possibly complete at lines 16 and 18. Notice also that at line 16 the lawyer pauses after reaching possible completion. Even so, the witness does not treat this place as transition-relevant. Instead he waits until a point at which the lawyer has produced a clear question; this comes in the form of a turn component marked both by interrogative syntax and rising intonation as a question (at lines 19–22).

Similar remarks might be made about answers. Answers, as Button (1992) and Halkowski (1992) point out, are also interactional products. In inquiry testimony, the beginning of a lawyer's next question treats the previous answer as having come to completion. Therefore, what counts as an answer is the product of an interaction between these two participants. Lawyers may thus interrupt the ongoing production of witness's turn so as to launch a next question and thereby treat the preceding answer as complete. On the other hand, a lawyer can withhold the production of a next question and thereby treat the answer as incomplete.

The participants sometimes locate deviations from the normative framework of question and answer and thus make their orientation to it visible. Consider, for instance, the following example, in which the lawyer insists on "finishing the question" before the witness speaks and, indeed, asserts his right to do so, saying "that's why I went to law school (.) so I could ask the questions" (lines 18–20):

(9) Walkerton [p. 73]
Lawyer: right. °hh And (.) y-you should be aware
as well of course what the Common Sense
Revolution talked about °hh ah-was a 15
percent reduction. an-and what that meant
for the Ministry of the Environment was
something like three hundred and sixty-five
(.)
positions
Witness: Well the [commo- [no [no
Lawyer: [look [can=I [could=I
Witness: no
Lawyer: → excuse me [could I [finish the question?
Witness: [Well [just with
respect, tha-that's ah yes go ahead.=
Lawyer: =okay let me finish the question thank you.
°hh
(.)
That's why I went to law school.
(.)
so I could ask the questions.
Witness: well
Lawyer: alright.
Witness: that's why I didn't.
Lawyer: [okay
All: [heh-heh hhhh
Witness: Eventually what happened Premier is that
there were seven hundred and fifty

Here the lawyer is spelling out the implications of budget reductions to the Ministry of Environment as matters about which the witness "should be aware" (line 01). The witness treats the completion of "positions" as the turn's completion and, at this point, begins his own turn prefaced by "well". As we've seen (in chapter 5), turn-initial components such as "well" routinely project disagreement, and the rest of the talk here further suggests that this is the direction in which the witness is headed. However, before such disagreement might be articulated, the lawyer marks the witness's talk as interruptive by asking permission to finish the question with "can I, could I" (line 06). Although the witness seems initially intent on expressing his disagreement and produces further talk along these lines (e.g. "with respect"), he eventually relinquishes the turn, saying "yes go ahead".

This example illustrates the manner in which participants may invoke the normative framework of inquiry testimony and, in so doing, use it to hold one another accountable to the constraints it specifies. At the same time we see that, although inquiry testimony is normatively organized as a series of lawyer's questions and the answers given in response to them, the participants' actions are not in any sense determined by such a framework. Rather that framework is a pervasively relevant resource which participants themselves use to produce and interpret the unfolding course of talk (see Atkinson and Drew 1979).

Participants also orient to the right and responsibility of a witness to *answer* the question. We can see this, for instance, in cases where lawyers complain that the witness is not answering the question (see Sidnell, forthcoming, for examples). There is another side to this norm, in so far as witnesses are expected not only to answer the question, but to answer the question and no more. Thus, we find that witnesses routinely "request permission" to do something in addition to providing an answer to the question. Consider the following cases:

(10) Walkerton
34 Lawyer: ah:: reduction that was cited in thee:
35 Common Sense Revolution.
36 (1.0)
37 So that Environment was hit substantially
38 you would agree with me, >seven hundred
39 an' fifty-two positions r- °hh which thee
40 figures show an' I-I'm not quoting now
41 but it's approximately thirty to thirty-
42 five percent of the workforce
43 (0.4)
44 was let go:.
45 (0.2)
46 Witness: → °h yes. and uh if- if I can put all of
47 that intuh context as well ah: ther- there
48 at no time did we identify (.) that uh
49 that fifteen percent (.) uh:: uh was across
50 the board,

(11) Walkerton 65–6 qt 1.08:45
13 Lawyer: uh reduced level of front-line service,
14 slower response times to complaints,
15 reduced technical ah- (.) assistance".
16 (2.0)
17 Witness: → Yes. These- these ah: ugh uh uh-uh let me put
18 → this into context too.=uh Cabine- or-uh the
19 Caucus wer-were sworn in. uh: an Oath of Secrecy
20 similar to the senior staff or to- to Cabinet.
21 for this process. because not only was this (.)
22 ah: the first time business plans had ever been
23 shared outside the Ministry .hh uh normally

(12) Walkerton 225 qt 11:18

Lawyer: So uhm
(0.3)
I take it then you're quite prepared at least
to commit to having a very crow- close and
critical look at the need for additional funding
an' sta:ff (.) .h in the MOE if that's the
opinion of your Minister.
(0.2)
Witness: → Ah: yes an- an' let me sa:y. as we:ll:. thet uh
ah that unlike nineteen ninety five, (0.4) we
are now in a position (0.2) to take a look (0.2)
ah: at requests.for increased funding.

In fragment (10) at line 46, the witness first answers the question with "yes" thereby confirming the facts that the lawyer has been citing. He then goes on to do something more – "to put all of that into context" – prefacing this with a permission request, "If I can . . .". By prefacing talk which is recognizable as something more or other than an answer to the question (which after all called only for a "yes" or "no" confirmation), the witness displays an orientation to the context of inquiry testimony – specifically the norm that witnesses' talk should consist exclusively of answers to questions. It is again instances in which the practice deviates from the norm that make that norm visible and available for analytic inspection. To repeat an earlier point: norms create expectations for what *should* happen and participants hold one another (and themselves in this last example) accountable to those norms even though they do not always act in accordance with them.

In a few cases from a very large collection, an opposing counsel will object that a lawyer's turn does not constitute a question (see Sidnell 2010a). Example (13) below comes from an inquiry into spending in a government office responsible for promotion and marketing of matters of national interest (in Canada). The inquiry investigated charges of patronage; specifically, members of the office were accused of siphoning off hundreds of thousands of dollars of government money into the hands of cooperating marketing firms. In this fragment the lawyer is asking "Didit ever occur to you that you might want to qualify a firm fer permer-promotional items." This is obviously not a neutral question. Rather, the lawyer conveys (by the use of "ever" among other things) that it *should* have occurred to the witness to do this, that any reasonable person would have done this. After the question is answered at line 06, the lawyer continues with the apparently ironic, "was much better to pay seventeen point sixty five percent . . .". When the witness subsequently questions this (line 18), the lawyer withholds an answer and instead complains "If you had looked at the invoices, you might have found out." The question is then reasked at 22–5 and answered at 26. The lawyer then appears to be repeating what he has said earlier at line 08, but instead suggests, "It was a perk for these guys, no?", with this imputing a motivation for the witness's behavior (suggesting, in effect, that the reason for not qualifying firms had to do with a system of "perks"). The witness rejects this and offers his own alternative reason, saying, "We did it because it was: (.) fav- fa:st an' quick an'". It is the lawyer's turn at lines 32–4 to which the witness's lawyer objects in 37–8. Notice that in terms of its design, this turn is clearly ironic. Thus, on the surface, "Oh yeah:, Christmas balls in March an' golf balls in December?" agrees and affiliates with the witness's prior answer. However, it clearly also *implies* quite the opposite (see the discussion of irony in chapter 4). There is then about this turn an evident lack of neutrality in so far as the lawyer can be heard as conveying his stance towards the witness and his testimony. Moreover, this turn is marked as a comment upon the previous answer by the "oh yeah" preface. In these ways, it can be seen to occupy third position in the sequence – a post-expansion (see chapter 6). This is despite the fact that "Christmas balls in March an' golf balls in December?" could, in another context, be heard as a garden-variety B-event question asking about something to which the recipient has obviously greater access than the speaker.[1]

(13) trans20563 (L = Lawyer, W = Witness, C = Commissioner, L2 = Lawyer for the Witness)

01 L: Didit ever occur to you that you might want to
02 qualify a firm fer permer-promotional items
03 (0.8)
04 W: [No.
05 L: [through- (.) competition?
06 W: No.
07 (0.2)
08 L: was much better to pay seventeen point sixty five
09 percent. (.) .h and in some instances .h (.)
10 seventeen point sixty five: (.) percent for one
11 agency and sixty fi- seventeen point sixty five
12 percent for a second agency (.) because there had
13 been a subsubcontract_
14 (0.8)
15 W: I don't understand you- we've never paid seventeen
16 point six five twice.
17 L: You did.
18 C: Well, you did.
19 W: Where? (.) [( )
20 L: [If you had looked at the invoices,
21 you might have found out.
22 (3.0)
23 and it never occurred to you that it would be a
24 good idea,
25 (0.4)
26 to make a call for tenders,=these are for a
27 particular contract or at least to qualify a
28 firm for permish-promotional items?=
29 W: =No. We did it through the sponsorship agencies.
30 L: It was much better.
31 (0.4)
32 It was a perk for these guys, no?
33 (2.0)
34 W: No. We did it because it was: (.) fav- fa:st
35 an' quick an'
36 L: → Oh yeah:, Christmas balls in March
37 (0.4)
38 an' golf balls in December?
39 (7.0)

40 Is that a ye:s a no o[r
41 L2: [Commissioner, I am not
42 sure that that's actually in fa[irness a
43 W: [no
44 L2 question.
45 C: tch [well
46 L2: [It's a statement. You've heard that
47 evidence.
48 C: It's a little argumentative and well I'm sure
49 Mr. (.) Lussier is wanting to make a point
50 rather than get an answer.
51 L: So the answer is
52 (0.2)
53 you did not think of qualifying promotional
54 items firms?

By withholding an answer and thus allowing a long silence to develop (7.0) at line 39, the witness refuses to treat the lawyer's turn as a question. The lawyer however presses ahead, asking "is that a yes or no?" This then prompts the witness's lawyer to object, saying, "Commissioner, I am not sure that that's actually in fairness a question." Notice also that, when the lawyer again presses ahead at line 51 with "So the answer is", the question that is re-asked is the one initially produced at lines 01–02 and again at 24–5. In proceeding this way, the cross-examining lawyer himself treats the intervening talk as "not a question".

We can see, then, across these examples a pervasive orientation to the basic structuring norms of inquiry testimony, which specify a right and obligation of lawyers to ask questions and a right and obligation of witnesses to answer them. Of course, as we've noted and seen in various places, this does not imply that participants strictly adhere to these norms, only that they are accountable to them. We've seen this accountability in participants reporting or explaining a deviation (as in example (9)), requesting permission to do something other than what is normatively expected (examples (10)–(12)) and, finally, in raising formal objections to the commissioner (example (13)).

Conclusion

Although this book is focused on conversation I felt that it was important to include some discussion of the way conversation analysts have approached talk in institutions, for several reasons. First, this is a major area of contemporary research. Conversation analysts have examined talk in the practice of medicine, in the court, in educational contexts, in various forms of news and media broadcasts. This research has not only illuminated *those* domains; it has, by way of contrast, thrown light on the organization of ordinary conversation (see e.g. Greatbatch 1988). Second, a consideration of talk in institutions allows us to probe the notion of "context" in general, and specifically the way in which conversation analysts have dealt with this complex, multifaceted problem in the social sciences. Obviously we've only scratched the surface by gesturing at a sizeable literature on this topic, but it is hoped that this chapter provides at least an indication of the various ways in which the issue of context has arisen within conversation-analytic studies.

Notes

1 Questions may be designed as assertions of what Labov (1970) described as "B-events". Putting things somewhat crudely, these are events (or whatever else) about which the recipient knows more or better than the questioner. The assertion of a B-event is routinely understood as constituting a request for confirmation and thus as doing questioning. B-events typically involve characterizations of what the recipient knows, feels, believes or, alternatively, what they did or said.

13
Conclusion

Focusing on a single extract but looking also at multiple instances of a practice across different occasions, the aim of this chapter is to bring together the analytical resources developed in the course of the book so as to develop a more sustained analysis of a single fragment of conversation. I want to begin with a quotation from one of Sacks's last recorded lectures. He remarks (1995 vol. 2: 562):

> a given object might turn out to be put together in terms of several types of organization; in part by means of adjacency pairs and in part in some other type of organizational terms, like overall structural terms or topical organizational terms. And one wants to establish the way in which a series of different types of organizations operate in a given fragment . . . So one sort of thing I engage in doing is to take a particular fragment apart in terms of a collection of different types of organization that may operate, in detail, in it. Where the question is, in part, how to bring that kind of a consideration off in a possibly integrated way, i.e. to also show the relationships between the types of organization *in* the particular object. I want, then, to inhibit a consideration of actual objects in terms of single types of organization, i.e. saying of something that it is a "question," and then saying that it's adjacency-pair orderly in a variety of ways, and that's that, as though one is finished with it. The question of what sorts of things, even for the sequential organization of conversation, can be pulled out of a piece of talk needs to be open, and having found it orderly in one way doesn't mean that you've done all there is to make it operate in the ways that we can, perhaps, make it operate.

In the introduction to this book I cited some suggestive remarks from Sacks in which he talked about "machineries", and I suggested that along those lines we might see any particular fragment of conversation as the unique product of multiple, intersecting organizations of practices. In this quotation Sacks seems to me to be echoing those ideas but now with an emphasis on method, the point being that, if it's the case that any bit of talk is the product of multiple organizations, in developing an analysis of it we have to be prepared to look at it from any number of different directions. This is the animating idea of the present chapter. In it, I have a go at taking apart a single fragment of conversation with an eye to the various organizations that operate within it.

In talking together, people are typically engaged in getting something done. We can examine talk then in terms of trajectories of action, asking what these people were attempting to accomplish in speaking the way they did. So, drawing on the resources provided in the preceding chapters, let's consider the fragment of interaction from a family dinner given as example (1) below. Schegloff (2005), introducing another extract from the same recording, writes:

> The occasion is dinner at the home of a family at or near an air force base in South Carolina in the early to mid-1970s. Mom is at the head of the table – whether because the paterfamilias is on duty, or dead, or separated we do not know. On her left is her 14-year-old daughter Virginia, on her right (and across from Virginia) is older brother Wesley. Next to Wesley, and only occasionally visible on camera, is Wesley's intended, Prudence – whether fiancée or longtime girlfriend we do not know. And invisible to the camera but to Virginia's left is middle child Beth, who is taping this for a course at a local college, and has apparently been told not to speak, but just to record.

In the talk leading up to the extract we will consider, Virginia has asked her mother to give her a dress which Mother has in her store (Mother is apparently the owner of this store). When Mom responds to this by saying that Virginia could buy it for herself if she saved her allowance, Virginia treats this as a ludicrous suggestion, complaining that she only gets five dollars a week. According to Virginia this is not only insufficient to allow for saving, it is not enough to cover her ordinary, regular expenses. Accordingly, she has requested a raise in her allowance. In the fragment presented below, Mom is questioning the claim that Virginia's allowance is insufficient, asking at line 08, "W'll what do you spen:d your allowance on." This leads Virginia, and intermittently Wesley, to list various expenses. Virginia cites "McDonalds" (line 13), "Gas" (line 18); Wesley offers "beer" (line 19). After Virginia suggests ten dollars would be fair (lines 27–8), Mom renews the question (Virginia remarks "Not to throw away, to spe:nd." Mom responds at line 36 with "On WHAT? That's what I been tryin'a find out."). Just as Mom questioned Virginia's citing of McDonalds with "You don't really need t'eat that much junk.", here, when Virginia claims makeup as an expense, Mom comes back with "I buy all'uh your makeup¿" and "=I buy your shampoo:. I buy your clo:thes¿". The question as to how Virginia spends her allowance has not, then, been answered to Mom's satisfaction. Not only has she re-asked the question in the face of the answers given, she has challenged each item that Virginia has listed. Mom's attempt to discover where the money goes has been frustrated – notice that she characterizes herself as *trying* to find out how Virginia spends her money, which implies that this has been unsuccessful. Given Mom's expressed frustration, the context is perhaps ripe for explanations from someone other than Virginia, and Wesley tries twice. In a preview of what is to come, at line 19 Wesley has suggested "She- she buys the beer wit' it." This elicits laughter from both Virginia and Prudence, but Mom responds, straight-faced, with disagreement, saying "I don't think she drinks any beer." And at lines 52–4 Wesley offers another possible explanation, saying "They- they chargin' more on thuh- thuh uh nickel ba:g now." One way of seeing this is as an "upgrade" of "She- she buys the beer wit' it.", smoking marijuana being further along the normative scale of "bad things that teenagers do". But there is also a transformation from the earlier tease about beer, in so far as here Wesley is teasing Mom as much as he is Virginia. Notice in this respect that he uses the vernacular expression "nickel bag" – a phrase he can perhaps expect Mom not to know. Use of a term like this can effect a categorization of the participants, dividing them into those "in the know" on the one hand and those not on the other. That categorization can have real, observable consequences for the subsequent conduct of the participants. Notice then that Mom initiates repair in line 56 with "a bag?", while Prudence explicates the reference in lines 57–8. Indeed, as I discuss in greater detail below, Mom,

Virginia and Prudence all respond to this one utterance in a different manner, showing, in doing so, the alternate ways in which they find it consequential specifically for each of them.

(1) Virginia 7–9, 4:00–5:35

Virginia: (w)you do[n't understand.=an' Mom, it's not=
Prudence: [(uh)
Virginia: =fai[:r, (five dollars a week?)]
Mom: [I ' m n o t t h a t o l d .]
Prudence: [(What a daughter)
Prudence: uh huh! ((laughter))
(1.0)
Mom: W'll what do you spen:d your allowance on.
That's [what I have |NEVER b]een able tuh find out.=
Virginia: [E V R Y |THA:n:'!]
Mom: =·hh·hh ((holds breath)) You get it on Satihday¿ (0.7)
Wensdee? You nevuh have a penny.
Virginia: I know.That's 'cause we go ta McDonald's, an:' goes places,
'n (0.7)
Mom: You don't really need t'eat that much junk.
Virginia: Wul- ·hh (hh) (0.4) You don't spend it on junk, yuh spend it
on impaw:tant things like-suh-say: I can't drive yet,so I have
tuh pay everybody for ga:[s.
Wes: [She- she buys the beer wit' it.
Virginia: Mmnu(h)h-u(h)hho(h)[hh
Wes: [ih hih hih hih hih
Prudence: [ehh heh [heh huh
Mom: [I don't think she drinks any beer.
Prudence: uhhhh! heh hah!=
Virginia: =Nuh-uhh.
(1.4)
Virginia: But- you know, you have to have enough mo:ney¿ I think
ten dollars'ud be good.
(0.4)
Mom: ·hhh Ten dollahs a week?
Virginia: Mm hm.
Mom: Just to throw away?
(0.5)
Virginia: Not to throw away, to spe:nd.
(.)
Mom: ((shrilly)) On [WHAT? That's what I been tryin'a find=
Prudence?: [eh hih hih
Mom: =out. [besides McDo:nalds¿ (·hh) And yu[h eat here. I=
Prudence?: [uh! ·hh |
Virginia: [Well,
Mom: =have(d)-u-haven't seen yuh skip a single mea:l!
(0.2)
Virginia: eWell:¿ uhh! (.) yuh just need it >fer things like< if you
go downtown an' you wanna buy a coke er some'in er:an::' you
buy makeup er you °see a different thing you'wanna'buy.
(0.8)
Mom: I buy all'uh your makeup¿

```
48  Virginia?:   °mh ih hh= ((whimpering-like sounds))
49  Mom:         =I buy your shampoo:. I buy your clo:thes¿
50               (0.2)
51  ???:         [((sniff))
52  Wes:         [They- they char[gin' more on thow- (for thuh)- uh nickel=
53  ???:                         [((hiccup?))
54  Wes:         =ba:g now.
55               (0.7)
56  Mom:         A [ba:g?
57  Prudence:      [W(h)e(h)sl(h)e(h)y s(h)he d(h)oe(h)s(h)n't u(h)se
58               [a(h)ny marajuana! ·ih[h! eh huh huh [^huh huh!=
59  Wes:         [ehhhh ·ih!           [(     ?)      |
60  Wes?:                                              [khhh!
61  Wes:         =·ihhh! hih [(hmh)
62  Mom:                     [Wesley I'M tellin' you, I: don'[t think I=
63  Prudence:                [^·IH uh huh huh huh huh ·ih |
64  Wes:                                                   [ihh ((hoarse))
65  Mom:         =c(h)a[n  st(h)  a  (h)  n  d] ·hhh [coming from=
66  Prudence:          [·uhhh! eh huh huh!] ·ih   [m·hh (        ) huh!
67  Mom:         =[both  s  i  :  :  d  es,]
68  Virginia?:    [(       ) Wesley I don]'t [do tha:t!
69  Prudence:                                [huh!
70               (.)
71  Wes:         eh huh huh=
72  Prudence:    =ehhh!
73               (0.2)
74  ???:         ·hh hhh
75               (0.2)
76  Prudence:    eh heh huh
77               (1.0)
78  Mom:         Great (.) goodness!
79  Prudence:    £She's past all that. eh huh(uh)!
80               (.)
81  Virginia:    I don't do tha:t¿
82               (2.3)
83  Virginia:    °It's ridiculous.
```

We've described this trajectory of action in gross organizational terms, following the main line of action through a series of exchanges. We have noticed that, although the talk begins with a complaint from Virginia to Mom, Mom quickly turns this around so that Virginia is on the defensive and having to explain how she spends her money.

Let's turn to consider now the final part of this fragment in more detail. We will focus first on Wesley's turn at lines 52–4, and following that we will consider the responses it elicits from Mom, Prudence and Virginia.

We've seen then that Mom's "On what?" has established the relevance of a listing of Virginia's expenses. However, when Virginia offers "makeup" Mom counters that she buys Virginia's makeup and continues with "shampoo" and "clothes". The result, for the participants, is an unsolved mystery – how exactly does Virginia spend the five dollars a week she receives? It is in this context that Wesley's "They- they chargin' more on thuh- thuh uh nickel ba:g now." is produced, and it is by virtue of the particular sequential context in which it occurs that this utterance is recognizably an answer to Mom's question to Virginia ("What do you spend your money on?") and a solution to the mystery of what happens to Virginia's money.

We can make a series of initial observations about Wesley's turn here by comparing it to his earlier suggestion that "She buys beer with it." That turn was ostensibly concerned with exactly the same matter – explaining what it is that Virginia spends her money on – but, interestingly, these two turns are strikingly different in design. Notice then that "She buys beer with it", as an assertion, establishes the relevance of agreement or disagreement. Indeed, as we noted, this is exactly how Mom treated it – as an assertion – and she disagreed, saying "I don't think she drinks any beer." In contrast, while "They- they chargin' more on thow- (for thuh)- uh nickel ba:g now." is also an assertion, it does not assert anything about Virginia. It only *implies* that Virginia is spending her money on marijuana and thus does not invite agreement or disagreement with this. It thus has the character of an observation produced for its possible relevance to the question of where the money goes.

In terms of its design, we may note that the turn is self-repaired twice, first on "they- they" and then again on "thuh- thuh uh".

(2) Virginia 7–9, 4:00–5:35 (Detail)
52 Wes: [They- they char[gin' m̲ore on thow- (for thuh)- uh nickel=
53 ???: [((hiccup?))
54 Wes: =b̲a:g now.

The first self-repair appears to be produced in an effort to draw Mom's gaze. Thus as he starts speaking Mom is looking down at her food, having just retracted her gaze from Virginia, at whom she was looking when she said "I buy your clo:thes¿". By the time he reaches "charging", however, Mom has begun to open her mouth to receive food and has started to adjust her head in his direction. By the time Wesley reaches "more", Mom is gazing at him. Now, although it's not unusual for speakers to, in various ways, request the gaze of their recipients, this has some special significance here (C. Goodwin 1979b, 1980). First, as we already noted, Wesley's talk here is not, by virtue of its design alone, obviously addressed to Mom as an answer to her question. It would perhaps be possible to hear this as an unrelated observation about the rising prices of marijuana. So, that this is directed to Mom is something that Wesley may be at pains to convey in part by establishing mutual gaze during its production. More importantly, although produced without laughter – that is "straight-faced" or "deadpan" – it is both a joke and a tease which is meant to be amusing to the participants. The problem in this respect is that Wesley has used, again as already noted, a word that he may suspect his Mom not to know: "nickel bag". So, there is an issue here of how Wesley can deliver this in a "straight-faced" manner while at the same time conveying to the participants that it is a joke. And in this respect securing Mom's gaze is crucial, for as he produces "bag" Wesley subtly but clearly raises his eyebrows. He allows the moment in which, for Mom, what he is up to is not completely clear to develop, but by the end of the silence and by the time Mom starts speaking he is clearly grinning. The talk and the facial expression then work hand in hand, at first to convey "serious" and subsequently to convey "joke".

The second self-repair here is associated with the formulation "nickel bag". Jefferson (1974) noted that an "error correction" format can convey that a word or phrase eventually selected is not the first to come to mind. That is, an error-correction format can make visible to the recipient(s) that the speaker has encountered a word-selection issue of some kind. Now here that seems important in so far as Wesley uses a phrase that, though fitted to the *action* he is performing (teasing Mom), constitutes a recipient design error. Wesley, after all, has used a word that Mom does not recognize/know. The self-repair here may convey to Mom not only that there is something special about this phrase but also that this is not a term Wesley habitually uses.[1]

Having considered the design and sequential context of Wesley's utterance, let's now turn our attention to the responses it elicits. As we have already noted, all of these responses are significantly delayed, but Mom is the first to speak, initiating repair with "a bag?". With this Mom conveys not only a problem of understanding but more specifically a problem with the referring expression "nickel bag". We've already noted the relevance of this word selection; here let's just register that by initiating repair in this way Mom shows that this is, indeed, a word or phrase or use of a word with which she is not familiar. Notice also that Wesley has, at this point, conveyed by the expression on his face that he is joking. Mom's response does not, however, show that she has picked up on this (though she may have). Rather, she responds to this in a way consistent with its delivery as a serious observation. We will see that once the meaning of "nickel bag" is explicated she responds to this quite differently, as the tease it was intended to be rather than as the serious observation it was disguised as.

Prudence then responds in a way which does several things at once. First, as I discuss below, Prudence reprimands Wesley for teasing his Mom and sister Virginia. Secondly, she appreciates the joke with laughter. Finally she explicates and unpacks the meaning of the term "nickel bag" by substituting "Marijuana".

Once Prudence has unpacked the meaning of "nickel bag", the nature of the tease becomes clear to Mom and she responds to it as such with a warning to Wesley. The first component of this turn ("Wesley, I'm telling you") helps to bring it off as a warning – a warning of what might happen if Wesley continues. In saying "both sides" here, Mom equates what Wesley is doing here with Virginia's prior conduct – characterizing herself as the target of "attacks" from both her son and her daughter. In saying this, then, Mom registers that this tease is directed at her as much as at Virginia. Notice also that the talk here is now inflected by laughter ("c(h)an st(h)a(h)nd").

And finally, Virginia responds to what Wesley has said with a denial, thereby showing that she has heard in this an accusation to the effect that she uses marijuana, saying "I don't do that" and "That's ridiculous".

Though we've still really only scratched the surface, we've nevertheless developed a slightly more nuanced account than was afforded by our initial gross description by zeroing in on this smaller fragment of talk. The other way to develop an analysis, as we've seen, is to look across collections at stable and recurrent practices. Let's see if we can't now make some headway on that front, working horizontally, as it were, and focusing on a particular practice. Notice then that Prudence, Mom and Virginia all preface their response to Wesley by saying his name. Notice also that Prudence says this in a way markedly different than the other two. Not only does Prudence insert laugh particles into the saying of "Wesley", she also produces it with clear emphasis and lengthening of the first syllable. I want to propose then that by producing the name in the way she does, and in the place she does, Prudence is doing something more than just addressing him. Specifically, I want to suggest that this is a practice for reprimanding another.[2] The basic evidence for this analysis of the practice is in its recurrent context-of-use. Thus, in the case we've have been considering, the name comes as the first component of a response to something "objectionable" that Wesley has done. Wesley has implied that his sister is using marijuana, thereby teasing his mother. This, of course, is conduct that a spouse (like Prudence) may find untoward and thus worthy of reprimand. In this case the name is followed by further talk, both by Prudence and by Mom, that supports this analysis. In the rest of her turn, Prudence not only explicates the meaning of "nickel bag" and appreciates the joke-character of Wesley's turn, she also *disagrees* with what Wesley has implied, thereby "defending" Virginia. In other instances, the name, with emphasis on the first syllable, is produced as a stand-alone item. Again the context-of-use suggests that it serves as a reprimand for an untoward action by the recipient. Consider the following case in which couples Curt and Pam, Gary and Carney, Mike and Phyllis have come together for a backyard barbecue. At the point where we pick up the action, Curt and Gary are sitting on one side of the table, Carney, Phyllis and Mike on the other. At line 01 Carney rises from the table, stands up and walks around to the other side. As she approaches Gary (her spouse) and Curt, Mike produces the utterance at line 06. At line 10 Carney sits on Gary's knee/lap and at lines 18–23 she falls off. As Carney falls off of Gary's knee she produces a small "shriek" and there is some laughter, and then Carney says, through laughter, "Gary", once again with emphasis on the first of the two syllables.

(3) Auto discussion Fragment

???: [·e-·hhh!
???: [·hhhh
(0.3)
Carney: °I gotta move.
Carney: (1.0)
Mike: Oh look-eh-she gonna g'm down here'n break those two u:[p.
Carney: [ehhhh!
Mike: se[e:?
Curt: [Aw[: ma:n,]
Mike: [hah hah] hah hah[hah.
Gary: [(You)talk about[j e alous.]
Curt: [°( ).[ ]
Carney: [I'm gonna-]
Curt: ehh he:h he:h, (00:30)
Carney: S::
Curt: [hn
Carney: [cramp yer sty:le [( )
Curt: [ehh!
(0.4)
Gary: Mh, mh-[-mh-[-mh-mh-[-mh-
???: [°Mh [[
Curt: [eh-huh,[huh-huh!
Carney: [((little shriek)) Ohh!=
Gary: =[ah!ah!ah! [ah! ah!=
Phyllis: =[ehhuh-h- [-huh huh
Curt: [hhah: hha:=
Gary: =[ah! ah! ah! ah! ah! ah! ah! ah! ah! ah!=
Carney: → =[Ga(h)ry(h)y haha
Curt: =[hha:huh, °hn-n-hn!
Gary: =[ah! ah! ah!

31 Curt: =[Never spilled a[dro:[p=
32 Carney: [·hh [·hhh[h! ·huh-
33 Curt: =[Look it that.
34 Mike: =[ah ah ah- hah!
35 Gary: =[ah! ah! ah! ah! ah! [ah! ah! ah!=
36 Curt: [Outstanding.
37 Carney: [Wahddiyuh mea::n!

Let's just notice then that in both cases the "name" is produced through laughter, by the female member of a couple to the male member, immediately after the male member has done something that can be seen as untoward. Gary has at best allowed Carney to fall off his lap and at worst caused her to fall. Wesley has suggested, to his mother, that his sister is using marijuana. We may also note that in both cases the untoward action is treated in a light-hearted way by the participants – as joking or as "horsing around" – this being conveyed by laughing while producing the name. In a final instance of the practice to be considered here, the name is produced again with the same pattern of emphasis (see below) but now without inflection by laughter. In this case Shane and Vivian and Michael and Nancy are having dinner of chicken, potatoes and peas together. In line 08 of the fragment below Michael asks Shane, who is at that moment struggling somewhat to scoop some butter onto his potato, to pass the butter when he's "through". The request is done with what can be described as jocular familiarity – "L'mme have that" – and the addition of "when yer through there" provides for a certain delay in performing the action that has been requested. However, by the time Michael has completed the turn Shane has visibly moved on from the job of scooping butter and is looking over on the other side of the table. As he returns his upper body to the position it was in before he began the unsuccessful search, he rotates his head and leans in slightly to Vivian who is seated on the floor to his right. At line 13 he says something to her *sotto voce*. By this time Michael, who has already let out a possible laugh at line 11, is gazing at Shane and grinning slightly. When Vivian knocks a utensil off her plate onto the floor she gasps and Shane produces his first "good" (line 17). Michael now reinvokes the request, saying "Butter please", and Shane produces his second "good", but now in a way that disattends Michael's request by being clearly misfitted to it. It is in this context that Vivian says Shane's name.

(4) Chicken Dinner p. 3
01 Shane: °Oh:.°
02 (1.8)
03 Shane: .t 'S too ↑ba:dhh hhheh heh heh[heh
05 [((cork being pulled-(1.5))
06 Vivian: Yea:h.we need some more wine over he:re.
07 (5.6) ((wine being poured))
08 Michael: → L'mme have that butter when yer through there
09 (3.3)
10 ((clank))
11 Michael?: °hnh°
12 (1.8)
13 Shane: ( )
14 (0.8)
15 Vivian: ↑·hu:hh
16 (0.3)

Shane: °Goo[d.°
Michael: [Butter please,
(0.2)
Shane: Good.
Vivian: → Sha:ne,
Michael: ↑(Oh ey adda way)
Shane: eh hu[h huh hih hih hih-]hee-yee hee-ee] [aah=
Nancy: [eh-heh-hih-hih-hnh-hnh]h n h-h n h hnh]-hn[h
Shane: =aah aah

After the name, Michael says something that apparently constitutes an "inside joke" among these participants, there is laughter and Shane passes the butter. But Shane extends the tease a little bit further. Just as he is handing off the butter to Michael, and as Michael is reaching his hand out to receive it, Shane pulls back momentarily, retracting the butter dish and forcing Michael to wait, hand extended, a moment more. So once again, we see the name produced in response to an untoward action which it thereby marks as a norm infraction. Here, it should be noted that Shane and Vivian are the hosts, and thus by actively ignoring Michael's request for the butter Shane is failing to behave in a way appropriate to his role within this occasion.

Another interesting aspect of the example has to do with the name itself. It would seem that the action of reprimanding another by saying his name is conveyed in part by a particular prosodic pattern. Specifically, the first syllable of "Wesley" or "Gary" is both emphasized and extended. Now, in this last instance the name is "Shane", which of course consists of only one syllable. Vivian is able to adapt the name so as to carry the prosodic pattern constitutive of this practice by breaking it into two parts: a heavily stressed and elongated "shay" is followed by a short but clearly distinct "en" (notice the transcript, "Sha:ne,").

We can ask, I think, why saying a recipient's name with this prosodic pattern should come to convey the action of reprimanding as it apparently does. In order to at least begin to explain that, we need to consider who, specifically, is saying the name. We can assume that recipients hear the name as having been selected out of a range of alternatives. That is to say, there are multiple forms of address just as there are multiple ways in which one can describe the weather (stormy, rainy, clear, ominous and so on). But it is clear that a given set of possible "forms of address" is specific to some particular relationship: to my wife, I am "Jack", "Honey" or "Darling" whereas to my students I am, occasionally, "Jack" and, more often, "Sir" or "Professor". Sacks remarks:

> Alternatives are an obvious way to go about locating what something is doing or what something means. But the question of alternatives does not have an easy answer. It is, for any given thing, an empirical issue and not simply a transparent semantic issue to be gotten by lexical considerations. In saying what I figure to be the kinds of things that are alternatives here, . . . I'm saying something that has to discovered from a consideration of the way the world works that produces these kinds of sequences. This obviously produces a massively complex set of problems in analyzing things like a small question–answer sequence. For each one of them, if we're going to use alternatives to find out what it means, then we're going to have to go into a discovery of what the alternatives are. (1995 vol. 2: 538)

So in this case we have to figure what the alternatives are for addressing within *this* relationship. And here the fact that in each case the name-reprimand is done by the recipient's spouse or "life partner" seems to be highly relevant, since it means that in each case the name has been selected as an alternative to some "endearment term". So, for instance, taking the example of Gary and Carney we can see that each uses "honey" or "hon" in addressing the other on separate occasions:

(5) Auto discussion ((After Carney has fallen from Gary's knee))
26 Carney: → Thanks hon,
27 (0.1)
28 Carney: W'make a good=
29 Gary: ME::=
30 Phyllis: =°Go sit by [Curt.
31 Carney: =[couple.
32 Gary: Yer the one thet did it!

(6) Auto discussion ((A joke has been told, Carney has not laughed at it))
92 Mike: ·hh You heard d'one about=
93 Gary: → =D'you understand that [honey
94 Mike: [eh heh [hhh
91 Curt: [eh

So in the examples we have considered it would seem that using the name has the significance it does precisely because it is selected from some particular set of alternatives that includes, as one option, an "endearment term". Given the availability of that option, use of a name can be found to be specifically alternative to it, and thus can come to have meanings it might otherwise not have. This suggests that the practice of reprimanding with a name is tied to a specific category of people – people who have available to them "endearment terms" as an alternate possible form of address.

Conclusion

In this brief concluding chapter we've seen then that an analysis of some fragment of talk may require attention to turn-construction and design, the orientation and organization of the participants' bodies and movements, the sequential location in which the talk occurs, the deployment of practices of repair and directed gaze, and so on. The point, which I initially made in the introduction to this book, is that any bit of talk is the product of multiple, intersecting organizations. This book is divided into chapters, each of which deals with some particular set of practices such as turn-taking, turn construction, repair and so on. But these should not be thought of as independent of one another. Not only is any bit of talk the product of multiple, intersecting organizations of practice, those organizations are themselves organized by their relation to one another. The repair mechanism is shaped by the organization of turns-at-talk which provides that a speaker will have first crack at repairing anything that she says in the course of her turn. The repair mechanism is further shaped by the organization of sequences in so far as anyone other than the speaker of the trouble source typically finds herself initiating repair in next-turn position and by this initiating a digressive sequence of talk directed not to the business at hand but rather to the problem of fixing some problem of speaking, hearing or understanding, and so on.

This has implications both for the kind of research we can do and the way we should do it. Specifically, a conversation analyst must be a generalist in a basic way. To take a real example, in order to develop an account of gaze behavior in conversation, one has to simultaneously consider turn-taking, repair, action-sequencing and so on. It's no good looking just at the gaze behavior, since it is not organized in isolation from everything else that it is going on (see Goodwin 1979, Rossano nd). As Sacks puts it, one has to be open to the possibility that the thing one is looking at is connected to an indefinite number of other features of the talk (including features we do not yet know anything about). An alternative way to put the matter is to say, as Schegloff (2005) does, that

> conversation analysts cannot disassociate themselves from language or culture or gesture or posture or facial displays without violating the integrity of their undertaking. Their undertaking is defined by a domain of naturally occurring events – talk and other conduct in interaction; that undertaking is committed to the study of any observable doings that are treated as relevant by the parties to those interactions.

It is to the study of those naturally occurring events of talk-in-interaction that conversation analysis is committed. I hope that this book provides the reader some tools for pursuing that study.

Notes

1 Notice how neatly Wesley's tease is fitted to the circumstances: Virginia only gets "five dollars a week". The standard price of a "nickel bag" is five dollars (hence the name "nickel"). If prices went up, Virginia would of course be short.

2 The practice is tied to the category of persons whose members take it as their responsibility to police and to sanction the behavior of the recipient. "Wife" is perhaps the prototypical member of the category but I do not discount the possibility that "Mother" may occupy this role too and that Mom's "Wesley" in line 62 is an instance of the practice.

In this respect there may be a distinction here between, on the one hand, cases in which the name is said by the person offended by the action (e.g. Carney) and, on the other hand, cases in which someone other than the offended party says the name. The restriction to "spouses" and so on may be a feature of the latter only. Thus, we find in interaction between children that an offended party may use the name or the name alone as a reprimand. The following cases from interaction among 4- and 6-year-old children respectively illustrate.

(6) KIDS_02_02_06(1of2)JKT1.mov 10:55 – Erika is building a structure with blocks. Jude bumps the table and the structure wobbles.

Erika: → Ju::de: yer makin' (me) knock it dow:n.
(0.4)
be more careful next time.
Jude: I: wi:ll:. I we:ll, I will, I will.
Tina: He sounds like a (actin) hhh
kinda like (ss) (0.2) ba:(h):by,
(0.8)
Jude: Ba::by?
(0.4)
Tina: he he ha ha oh .hhhh

11 Jude: sshhh.
12 (0.2)
13 You sound like a baby (to Adult)

(7) KIDS_SKT7a.mov. Sophie is building a structure with blocks. When Gwyer bumps the table one of the pieces falls off this structure.
01 Sophie: → Gwy:er
02 Gwyer: I didn't mean to knock that Kay(h)t(h)ie (.) I mean-
03 Katie: Sophie
04 Gwyer: K(hh!)ih
05 Katie: I'm KayDEE
06 Sophie: .HH I'm Sophie
07 Gwyer: Ok'a:y I: sometimes get mixed up because last time
08 I was with two girls also

(8) KIDS_G2_T1 – 29:45
01 Alex: Mi::::::a
02 Mia: I didn't do that.
03 Alex: yes you did
04 Mia: No all I did was that

(9) G2_t1 35:25
(Alex has earlier recruited Mia to help hold her structure; at line 01 she complains "pay attention". Mia has now gone back to work on her own structure and Alex is visibly struggling to balance her own.)
01 Alex: Mi::::A
02 Mia: yes what
03 Alex: Help!
04 Mia: Oh okay.
05 I don't have three arms
06 Alex: You broke it.
07 Mia: I didn't break it
08 Alex: you broke it in the first place

Here Mia disattends the reprimand in the saying of her name and treats it as a summons. The reprimand character of the name-use is subsequently unpacked: as the person who broke the structure, Mia is obligated to help rebuild it and she has abandoned Alex to this job.

In interaction between children the alternative form in relation to which this use of the name derives its force appears to be not endearment terms but rather "pet" terms such as "silly billy" or "funny bunny". The following cases illustrate the use of such terms in interaction between children of this age:

(10) KIDS_12_09_05(1of1)SK_T15.mov
01 Bigkid: Who's Sasha?
02 Jer: Sahsoo
03 Ant: Not Sashoo
04 (.)
05 Sa:sha: [hih heh he
06 Jer: [he heh he
07 Ant: You funny bunny.

(11) KIDS_11_22_05(1 of 2)T4_00:02:09

01	Sasha:	Wanna 'tach this?
02	Will:	This is an airplane you silly goose

(12) KIDS_11_29_05(2of2)SK_T11_00:16:06

01	Ant:	that's the worst dog I've e[ver Seen.]
02	Margot:	[HHhheh]
03		(0.6)
04	Ant:	.HH! .HHH! .hhh hhh [.hhh)]
05	Margot:	[(yeah)] hh hh hh
06		hnh .hh! heh heh
07	Margot:	heh?
08		(0.8)
09		.HHhh! it's a poodle silly.
10		(0.4)
11	Ant:	it's a (puh- dh- yuh:::)? but poodles
12		a:re dogs.

References

Antaki, Charles. 1994. *Explaining and Arguing: The Social Organization of Accounts*. London, and Thousand Oaks, CA: Sage.

Atkinson, J. M., and Paul Drew. 1979. *Order in Court: The Organisation of Verbal Interaction in Judicial Settings*. London: Macmillan.

Barker, Roger. 1963. The stream of behavior as an empirical problem. *The Stream of Behavior*, ed. R. Barker. New York: Appleton-Century-Crofts, pp. 1–22.

Barker, Roger, and Herbert Wright. 1951. *One Boy's Day: A Specimen Record of Behavior*. New York: Harper & Row.

Bateson, Gregory. 1956. The message "this is play". *Group Processes: Transactions of the Second Conference*, ed. B. Schaffner. New York: Josiah Macy, Jr. Foundation, pp. 145–242.

Bateson, Gregory. 1972. *Steps to an Ecology of Mind*. New York: Ballantine Books.

Bateson, Gregory, and Margaret Mead. 1942. *Balinese Character: A Photographic Analysis*. [New York]: New York Academy of Sciences.

Bauman, Richard, and Joel Sherzer. 1974. *Explorations in the Ethnography of Speaking*. Cambridge: Cambridge University Press.

Bavelas, Janet B., Linda Coates, and Trudy Johnson. 2000. Listeners as co-narrators. *Journal of Personality and Social Psychology* 79: 941–52.

Button, Graham. 1992. Answers as interactional products: two sequential practices used in interviews. *Talk at Work*, ed. P. Drew and J. Heritage. Cambridge: Cambridge University Press, pp. 212–31.

Button, Graham, and Neil Casey. 1984. Generating topic: the use of topic initial elicitors. *Structures of Social Action: Studies in Conversation Analysis*, ed. J. M. Atkinson and J. Heritage. Cambridge: Cambridge University Press, pp. 167–90.

Button, Graham, and Neil Casey. 1985. Topic nomination and topic pursuit. *Human Studies* 8: 3–55.

Chomsky, Noam. 1957. *Syntactic Structures*. The Hague: Mouton.

Chomsky, Noam. 1965. *Aspects of the Theory of Syntax*. Cambridge, MA: MIT Press.

Clayman, Steven, and John Heritage. 2002. *The News Interview: Journalists and Public Figures on the Air*. Cambridge: Cambridge University Press.

Clift, Rebecca. 1999. Irony in conversation. *Language in Society* 28: 523–53.

Curl, Traci. 2006. Offers of assistance: constraints on syntactic design. *Journal of Pragmatics* 38: 1257–80.

Curl, Traci, and Paul Drew. 2008. Contingency and Action: A Comparison of Two Forms of Requesting. *Research on Language and Social Interaction* 41: 129–53.

D'Andrade, Roy. 1995. *The Development of Cognitive Anthropology*. Cambridge: Cambridge University Press.

Davidson, Judy. 1984. Subsequent versions of invitations, offers, requests, and proposals dealing with potential or actual rejection. *Structures of Social Action*, ed. J. M. Atkinson and J. Heritage. Cambridge: Cambridge University Press, pp. 102–28.

Drew, Paul. 1981. Adults' corrections of children's mistakes. *Adult–Child Conversations*, ed. P. French and M. MacLure. London: Croom Helm, pp. 244–67.

Drew, Paul. 1984. Speakers' reportings in invitation sequences. *Structures of Social Action*, ed. J. M. Atkinson and J. Heritage. Cambridge: Cambridge University Press, pp. 152–64.

Drew, Paul. 1985. Analyzing the use of language in courtroom interaction. *Handbook of Discourse Analysis*, vol. 3, ed. T. A. Dijk. New York: Academic Press, pp. 133–48.

Drew, Paul. 1997. "Open" class repair initiators in response to sequential sources of troubles in conversation. *Journal of Pragmatics* 28: 69–101.

Drew, Paul, and John Heritage. 1992. Analyzing talk at work: an introduction. *Talk at Work*, ed. P. Drew and J. Heritage. Cambridge: Cambridge University Press, pp. 3–65.

Drew, Paul, and Elizabeth Holt. 1998. Figures of speech: figurative expressions and the management of topic transition in conversation. *Language in Society* 27: 495–522.

Duranti, Alessandro. 1997. *Linguistic Anthropology*. Cambridge: Cambridge University Press.

Duranti, Alessandro, and Donald Brenneis. 1986. The Audience as Co-Author. Special issue of *Text* 6 (3): 239–347.

Durkheim, Emile. 1964. *The Rules of Sociological Method*. New York: Free Press of Glencoe.

Edwards, Derek. 2000. Extreme case formulations: softeners, investment, and doing nonliteral. *Research on Language and Social Interaction* 33: 347–73.

Egbert, Maria M. 1997. Some interactional achievements of other-initiated repair in multiperson conversation. *Journal of Pragmatics* 27: 611–34.

Ehrlich, Susan, and Jack Sidnell. 2006. "I think that's not an assumption you ought to make": challenging presuppositions in inquiry testimony. *Language in Society* 35: 655–76.

Enfield, N. J., and T. Stivers (eds.). 2007. *Person Reference in Interaction: Linguistic, Cultural, and Social Perspectives*. Cambridge: Cambridge University Press.

Evans-Pritchard, E. E. 1937. *Witchcraft, Oracles and Magic among the Azande*. Oxford: Oxford University Press.

Ford, C. E., B. Fox, and S. A. Thompson. 1996. Practices in the construction of turns: the TCU revisited. *Pragmatics* 6: 427–54.

Ford, C. E., B. Fox, and S. A. Thompson. 2002. Constituency and the grammar of turn increments. *The Language of Turn and Sequence*, ed. C. E. Ford, B. Fox, and S. A. Thompson. Oxford: Oxford University Press, pp. 14–38.

Fox, Barbara A., Makoto Hayashi, and Robert Jasperson. 1996. Resources and Repair: A Cross-Linguistic Study of Syntax and Repair. *Interaction and Grammar*, ed. Elinor Ochs, Emanuel A. Schegloff, and Sandra A. Thompson. Cambridge: Cambridge University Press, pp. 185–237.

Francis, David, and Stephen Hester. 2004. *An Invitation to Ethnomethodology: Language, Society and Interaction*. London: Sage.

Freud, Sigmund, Angela Richards, and James Strachey. 1975. *Introductory Lectures on Psychoanalysis*. Harmondsworth: Penguin.

Gardner, R. 2001. *When Listeners Talk: Response Tokens and Listener Stance*. Amsterdam: John Benjamins.

Garfinkel, Harold. 1967. *Studies in Ethnomethodology*. Englewood Cliffs, NJ: Prentice-Hall.

Garfinkel, Harold. 1974. On the origins of the term "ethnomethodology". *Ethnomethodology*, ed. R. Turner. Harmondsworth: Penguin, pp. 15–18.

Garfinkel, Harold. 2002. *Ethnomethodology's Program: Working Out Durkheim's Aphorism*. Lanham, MD: Rowman & Littlefield.

Garfinkel, H., and H. Sacks. 1970. On formal structures of practical actions. *Theoretical Sociology: Perspectives and Developments*, ed. J. C. McKinney and E. A. Tiryakian. New York: Appleton-Century-Crofts, pp. 337–66.

Garfinkel, H., and D. L. Wieder. 1992. Two incommensurable, asymmetrically alternate technologies of social analysis. *Text in Context: Contributions to Ethnomethodology*, ed. G. Watson and R. M. Seiler. Newbury Park, CA: Sage, pp. 175–206.

Glenn, P. 2003. *Laughter in Interaction*. Cambridge: Cambridge University Press.

Goffman, Erving. 1955. On face work. *Psychiatry* 18: 213–31.

Goffman, Erving. 1956. The nature of deference and demeanor. *American Anthropologist* 58: 473–502.

Goffman, Erving. 1957. Alienation from interaction. *Human Relations* 10: 47–60.

Goffman, Erving. 1961. *Encounters: Two Studies in the Sociology of Interaction*. Indianapolis: Bobbs-Merrill.

Goffman, Erving. 1971. *Relations in Public: Microstudies of the Public Order*. New York: Harper & Row.

Goffman, Erving. 1972. The neglected situation. *Language and Social Context*, ed. P. P. Giglioli. Baltimore: Penguin, pp. 61–6 (reprinted from the *American Anthropologist* 66: 133–6, 1964).

Goffman, Erving. 1976. Replies and responses. *Language in Society* 5: 257–313.

Goffman, Erving. 1978. Response cries. *Language* 54: 787–815.

Goffman, Erving. 1983. The interaction order. *American Sociological Review* 48: 1–17.

Goodwin, Charles. 1979a. Review of Starkey Duncan, Jr. and Donald W. Fiske, *Face-to-Face Interaction: Research Methods and Theories*. *Language in Society* 8(3): 439–44.

Goodwin, Charles. 1979b. The interactive construction of a sentence in natural conversation. *Everyday Language: Studies in Ethnomethodology*, ed. G. Psathas. New York: Irvington, pp. 97–121.

Goodwin, Charles. 1980. Restarts, pauses, and the achievement of mutual gaze at turn-beginning. *Sociological Inquiry* 50: 272–302.

Goodwin, Charles. 1981. *Conversational Organization: Interaction between Speakers and Hearers*. New York: Academic Press.

Goodwin, Charles. 1986a. Audience diversity, participation and interpretation. *Text* 6(3): 283–316.

Goodwin, Charles. 1986b. Between and within: alternative treatments of continuers and assessments. *Human Studies* 9: 205–17.

Goodwin, Charles. 1986c. Gesture as a resource for the organization of mutual orientation. *Semiotica* 62(1/2): 29–49.

Goodwin, Charles. 1987. Forgetfulness as an interactive resource. *Social Psychology Quarterly* 50(2): 115–30.

Goodwin, Charles. 1993. Recording interaction in natural settings. *Pragmatics* 3: 181–209.

Goodwin, Charles, and Marjorie Harness Goodwin. 1987. Concurrent operations on talk: notes on the interactive organization of assessments. *IPrA Papers in Pragmatics* 1(1): 1–52.

Goodwin, Charles, and Marjorie Harness Goodwin. 1990. Interstitial argument. *Conflict Talk*, ed. Allen Grimshaw. Cambridge: Cambridge University Press, pp. 85–117.

Goodwin, Charles, and John Heritage. 1990. Conversation analysis. *Annual Review of Anthropology* 19: 283–307.

Goodwin, Marjorie Harness. 1980. Processes of mutual monitoring implicated in the production of description sequences. *Sociological Inquiry* 50: 303–17.

Goodwin, Marjorie Harness. 1983. Aggravated correction and disagreement in children's conversations. *Journal of Pragmatics* 7: 657–77.

Goodwin, Marjorie Harness. 1990. *He-Said-She-Said: Talk as Social Organization among Black Children*. Bloomington: Indiana University Press.

Goodwin, Marjorie Harness, and Charles Goodwin. 1986. Gesture and coparticipation in the activity of searching for a word. *Semiotica* 62(1/2): 51–75.

Greatbatch, David. 1988. A turn-taking system for British news interviews. *Language in Society* 17(3): 401–30.

Gumperz, John J., and Dell Hymes (eds.). 1964. The Ethnography of Communication. Special issue of *American Anthropologist* 66(6), part 2.

Gumperz, John J., and Dell Hymes (eds.). 1972. *Directions in Sociolinguistics: The Ethnography of Communication*. New York: Holt, Rinehart and Winston.

Hacking, Ian. 1999. *The Social Construction of What?* Cambridge, MA: Harvard University Press.

Halkowski, Timothy. 1992. Hearing talk: generating answers and accomplishing facts. *Perspectives on Social Problems* 4: 25–45.

Hayashi, Makoto. 1999. Where grammar and interaction meet: a study of co-participant completion in Japanese conversation. *Human Studies* 22: 475–99.

Hayashi, Makoto. 2001. Practices in joint utterance construction in Japanese conversation. PhD dissertation, University of Colorado.

Hayashi, Makoto. 2003a. *Joint Utterance Construction in Japanese Conversation*. Amsterdam: John Benjamins.

Hayashi, Makoto. 2003b. Language and the body as resources for collaborative action: a study of word searches in Japanese conversation. *Research on Language and Social Interaction* 36: 109–41.

Hayashi, Makoto. 2004. Discourse within a sentence: an exploration of postpositions in Japanese as an interactional resource. *Language in Society* 33: 343–76.

Hayashi, Makoto. 2005. Referential problems and turn construction: an exploration of an intersection between grammar and interaction. *Text* 25: 437–68.

Heritage, John. 1984a. A change-of-state token and aspects of its sequential placement. *Structures of Social Action*, ed. J. M. Atkinson and J. Heritage. Cambridge: Cambridge University Press, pp. 299–345.

Heritage, John. 1984b. *Garfinkel and Ethnomethodology*. Cambridge: Polity Press.

Heritage, John. 1998. Oh-prefaced responses to inquiry. *Language in Society* 27: 291–334.

Heritage, John. 2002. *Oh*-prefaced responses to assessments: a method of modifying agreement/disagreement. *The Language of Turn and Sequence*, ed. C. E. Ford, B. Fox, and S. A. Thompson. Oxford: Oxford University Press, pp. 196–224.

Heritage, John. 2007. Intersubjectivity and progressivity in person (and place) reference. *Person Reference in Interaction: Linguistic, Cultural, and Social Perspectives*, ed. N. J. Enfield and T. Stivers. Cambridge: Cambridge University Press, pp. 255–80.

Heritage, J., and J. M. Atkinson. 1984. Preference organization. *Structures of Social Action: Studies in Conversation Analysis*, ed. J. M. Atkinson and J. Heritage. Cambridge: Cambridge University Press, pp. 53–6.

Heritage, John, and Geoff Raymond. 2005. The terms of agreement: indexing epistemic authority and subordination in talk-in-interaction. *Social Psychology Quarterly* 68: 15–38.

Heritage, John, and Sue Sefi. 1992. Dilemmas of advice: aspects of the delivery and reception of advice in interactions between health visitors and first time mothers. *Talk at Work*, ed. P. Drew and J. Heritage. Cambridge: Cambridge University Press, pp. 359–417.

Heritage, John, and Marja-Leena Sorjonen. 1994. Constituting and maintaining activities across sequences: *and*-prefacing as a feature of question design. *Language in Society* 23: 1–29.

Holt, Elizabeth, and Paul Drew. 2005. Figurative pivots: the use of figurative expressions in pivotal topic transitions. *Research on Language and Social Interaction* 38: 35–61.

Hutchby, Ian, and Paul Drew. 1995. Conversation analysis. *Handbook of Pragmatics*, ed. J. Verschueren, J.-O. Ostman, and J. Blommaert. Antwerp: IPrA.

Hutchby, Ian, and Robin Wooffitt. 2008. *Conversation Analysis*. Cambridge: Polity.

Jefferson, Gail. 1972. Side sequences. *Studies in Social Interaction*, ed. D. Sudnow. New York: Free Press, pp. 294–338.

Jefferson, Gail. 1974. Error correction as an interactional resource. *Language in Society* 2: 181–99.

Jefferson, Gail. 1978. Sequential aspects of storytelling in conversation. *Studies in the Organization of Conversational Interaction*, ed. J. Schenkein. New York: Academic Press, pp. 219–48.

Jefferson, Gail. 1979. A technique for inviting laughter and its subsequent acceptance/declination. *Everyday Language: Studies in Ethnomethodology*, ed. G. Psathas. New York: Irvington, pp. 79–96.

Jefferson, Gail. 1980. On "trouble-premonitory" response to inquiry. *Sociological Inquiry* 50: 153–85.

Jefferson, Gail. 1983. *Two Explorations of the Organization of Overlapping Talk in Conversation*: "Notes on some orderlinesses of overlap onset" and "On a failed hypothesis: 'conjunctionals' as overlap-vulnerable". Tilburg Papers in Language and Literature 28. Tilburg, Netherlands: University of Tilburg.

Jefferson, Gail. 1984. On stepwise transition from talk about a trouble to inappropriately next-positioned matters. *Structures of Social Action*, ed. J. M. Atkinson and J. Heritage. Cambridge: Cambridge University Press, pp. 191–221.

Jefferson, Gail. 1985. An exercise in the transcription and analysis of laughter. *Handbook of Discourse Analysis*, vol. 3, ed. T. A. Dijk. New York: Academic Press, pp. 25–34.

Jefferson, Gail. 1987. Exposed and embedded corrections. *Talk and Social Organisation*, ed. G. Button and J. R. E. Lee. Clevedon: Multilingual Matters, pp. 86–100.

Jefferson, Gail. 1988. On the sequential organization of troubles-talk in ordinary conversation. *Social Problems* 35(4): 418–41.

Jefferson, Gail. 1990. List construction as a task and interactional resource. *Interaction Competence*, ed. G. Psathas. Washington, DC: International Institute for Ethnomethodology and Conversation Analysis and University Press of America, pp. 63–92.

Jefferson, Gail. 1993. Caveat speaker: preliminary notes on recipient topic-shift implicature. *Research on Language and Social Interaction* 26: 1–30.

Jefferson, Gail. 2004. "At first I thought": a normalizing device for extraordinary events. *Conversation Analysis: Studies from the First Generation*, ed. G. Lerner. Amsterdam: Benjamins, pp. 131–67.

Jefferson, Gail, Harvey Sacks, and Emanuel A. Schegloff. 1987. Notes on laughter in the pursuit of intimacy. *Talk and Social Organisation*, ed. G. Button and J. R. E. Lee. Clevedon: Multilingual Matters, pp. 152–205.

Kendon, Adam. 1990. Conducting interaction: patterns of behavior in focused encounters. Cambridge: Cambridge University Press.

Kitzinger, C. 2000. Doing feminist conversation analysis. *Feminism and Psychology* 10: 163–93.

Koshik, Irene. 2002. Designedly incomplete utterances: a pedagogical practice for eliciting knowledge displays in error correction sequences. *Research on Language and Social Interaction* 35: 277–309.

Labov, William. 1970. The study of English in its social context. *Stadium Generale* 23: 30–87.

Lerner, Gene H. 1991. On the syntax of sentences in progress. *Language in Society* 20: 441–58.

Lerner, Gene. 1992. Assisted storytelling: deploying shared knowledge as a practical matter. *Qualitative Sociology* 15: 247–71.

Lerner, Gene. 1996. On the "semi-permeable" character of grammatical units in conversation: conditional entry into the turn-space of another speaker. *Interaction and Grammar*, ed. E. Ochs, E. A. Schegloff, and S. Thompson. Cambridge: Cambridge University Press, pp. 238–76.

Lerner, Gene. 2003. Selecting next speaker: the context-sensitive operation of a context-free organization. *Language in Society* 32: 177–201.

Lerner, Gene. 2004. Collaborative turn sequences. *Conversation Analysis: Studies from the First Generation*, ed. G. Lerner. Amsterdam and Philadelphia: John Benjamins, pp. 225–56.

Lerner, Gene, and Celia Kitzinger. 2007. Extraction and aggregation in the repair of individual and collective self-reference. *Discourse Studies* 9: 526–57.

Lerner, Gene, and T. Takagi. 1999. On the place of linguistic resources in the organization of talk-in-interaction: a co-investigation of English and Japanese grammatical practices. *Journal of Pragmatics* 31: 49–75.

Levelt, W. 1989. *Speaking: From Intention to Articulation*. Boston, MA: MIT Press.

Levinson, Stephen C. 1979. Activity types and language. *Linguistics* 17: 365–99.

Levinson, Stephen C. 1983. *Pragmatics*. Cambridge: Cambridge University Press.

Levinson, Stephen C. 2005. Living with Manny's dangerous idea. *Discourse Studies* 7: 431–53.

Levinson, Stephen C. 2006. On the human "interactional engine". *Roots of Human Sociality: Culture, Cognition and Interaction*, ed. N. J. Enfield and S. C. Levinson. Oxford: Berg, pp. 39–69.

Livingston, Eric. 1987. *Making Sense of Ethnomethodology*. London: Routledge.

Local, John, and John Kelly. 1986. Projection and silences: notes on phonetic and conversational structure. *Human Studies* 9: 185–204.

Local, John, and Gareth Walker. 2004. Abrupt-joins as a resource for the production of multi-unit, multi-action turns. *Journal of Pragmatics* 36: 1375–1403.

Mandelbaum, Jenny. 1987. Couples sharing stories. *Communication Quarterly* 35: 144–71.

Mandelbaum, Jenny. 1989. Interpersonal activities in conversational storytelling. *Western Journal of Speech Communication* 53(2): 114–26.

Maynard, Douglas. 1980. Placement of topic changes in conversation. *Semiotica* 30: 263–90.

McQuown, Norman A. (ed.) 1971. *The Natural History of an Interview*. Chicago: University of Chicago Library. (Microfilm collection of manuscripts on cultural anthropology, 95(xv).)

Mehan, Hugh. 1979. *Learning Lessons*. Cambridge, MA: Harvard University Press.

Mehan, Hugh. 1985. The structure of classroom discourse. *Handbook of Discourse Analysis*, vol. 3, ed. T. A. Dijk. New York: Academic Press, pp. 120–31.

Merleau-Ponty, Maurice. 1968. *The Visible and the Invisible: Followed by Working Notes*. Evanston, IL: Northwestern University Press.

Merleau-Ponty, Maurice. 2003. *Nature: Course Notes from the Collège de France*. Evanston, IL: Northwestern University Press.

Moerman, Michael. 1988. *Talking Culture: Ethnography and Conversation Analysis*. Philadelphia: University of Pennsylvania Press.

Parsons, Talcott. 1937. *The Structure of Social Action*. New York: McGraw-Hill.

Peräkylä, A., C. Antaki, S. Vehviläinen, and I. Leudar (eds.). 2008. *Conversation Analysis of Psychotherapy*. Cambridge: Cambridge University Press.

Pittenger, Robert E. 1960. The first five minutes: a sample of microscopic interview analysis. Ithaca, NY: P. Martineau.

Pomerantz, Anita. 1975. Second assessments: a study of some features of agreements/disagreements. PhD dissertation, University of California at Irvine.

Pomerantz, Anita. 1978. Compliment responses: notes on the co-operation of multiple constraints. *Studies in the Organization of Conversational Interaction*, ed. J. Schenkein. New York: Academic Press, pp. 79–112.

Pomerantz, Anita. 1984. Agreeing and disagreeing with assessments: some features of preferred/dispreferred turn shapes. *Structures of Social Action: Studies in Conversation Analysis*, ed. J. M. Atkinson and J. Heritage. Cambridge: Cambridge University Press, pp. 57–101.

Pomerantz, Anita. 1986. Extreme case formulations: a way of legitimizing claims. *Human Studies* 9: 219–29.

Quirk, Randolph, Sidney Greenbaum, Geoffrey Leech, and Jan Svartvik. 1985. *A Comprehensive Grammar of the English Language*. London and New York: Longman.

Radcliffe-Brown, A. R. 1954. Social sanctions. *Structure and Function in Primitive Society*. New York: Free Press, pp. 205–11.

Raymond, Geoffrey. 2003. Grammar and social organization: yes/no interrogatives and the structure of responding. *American Sociological Review* 68: 939–67.

Raymond, Geoffrey. 2004. Prompting action: the stand-alone "so" in ordinary conversation. *Research on Language and Social Interaction* 37: 185–218.

Reddy, Michael J. 1979. The conduit metaphor: a case of frame conflict in our language about language. *Metaphor and Thought*, ed. A. Ortony. Cambridge: Cambridge University Press, pp. 164–201.

Robinson, Jeffrey D. 2006. Managing trouble responsibility and relationships during conversational repair. *Communication Monographs* 73: 137–61.

Robinson, Jeffrey D. 2009, Managing counter informings: an interactional practice for soliciting information that facilitates reconciliation of speakers' incompatible positions. *Human Communication Research* 35: 561–87.

Robinson, Jeffrey D. and Heidi Kevoe-Feldman. Forthcoming. Using full repeats to initiate repair on others' questions. *Research on Language and Social Interaction*.

Rossano, Federico. nd. Gaze and the sequentialization of conversation. MS, Max Planck Institute, Nijmegen.

Roth, Andrew. 2002. Social epistemology in broadcast news interviews. *Language in Society* 31: 355–81.

Ryave, A. L. 1978. On the achievement of a series of stories. *Studies in the Organization of Conversational Interaction*, ed. J. N. Schenkein. New York: Academic Press, pp. 113–32.

Sacks, Harvey. 1963. Sociological description. *Berkeley Journal of Sociology* 8: 1–16.

Sacks, Harvey. 1967. The search for help: no one to turn to. *Essays in Self-Destruction*, ed. E. Schneidman. New York: Science House, pp. 203–23.

Sacks, Harvey. 1972. Notes on police assessment of moral character. *Studies in Social Interaction*, ed. D. N. Sudnow. New York: Free Press, pp. 280–93.

Sacks, Harvey. 1973. On some puns with some intimations. *Report of the Twenty-Third Annual Round Table Meeting on Linguistics and Language Studies*, ed. R. W. Shuy. Washington, DC: Georgetown University Press, pp. 135–44.

Sacks, Harvey. 1974. An analysis of the course of a joke's telling in conversation. *Explorations in the Ethnography of Speaking*, ed. R. Bauman and J. Sherzer. Cambridge: Cambridge University Press, pp. 337–53.

Sacks, Harvey. 1975. Everyone has to lie. *Sociocultural Dimensions of Language Use*, ed. M. Sanches and B. G. Blount. New York: Academic Press, pp. 57–80.

Sacks, Harvey. 1984a. Notes on methodology (edited by Gail Jefferson from various lectures). *Structures of Social Action: Studies in Conversation Analysis*, ed. J. M. Atkinson and J. Heritage. Cambridge: Cambridge University Press, pp. 21–7.

Sacks, Harvey. 1984b. On doing "being ordinary". *Structures of Social Action*, ed. J. M. Atkinson and J. Heritage. Cambridge: Cambridge University Press, pp. 413–29.

Sacks, Harvey. 1987 [1973]. On the preferences for agreement and contiguity in sequences in conversation. *Talk and Social Organisation*, ed. G. Button and J. R. E. Lee. Clevedon: Multilingual Matters, pp. 54–69.

Sacks, Harvey. 1995. *Lectures on Conversation*, 2 vols. Oxford: Basil Blackwell.

Sacks, Harvey. 2004. An initial characterization of the organization of speaker turn-taking in conversation. *Conversation Analysis: Studies from the First Generation*, ed. G. Lerner. Amsterdam and Philadelphia: John Benjamins, pp. 35–42.

Sacks, Harvey, and Emanuel A. Schegloff. 1979. Two preferences in the organization of reference to persons and their interaction. *Everyday Language: Studies in Ethnomethodology*, ed. G. Psathas. New York: Irvington, pp. 15–21.

Sacks, Harvey, Emanuel A. Schegloff, and Gail Jefferson. 1974. A simplest systematics for the organization of turn-taking for conversation. *Language* 50: 696–735.

Saussure, Ferdinand de. 1959. *Course in General Linguistics*, ed. Charles Bally and Albert Sechehaye in collaboration with Albert Riedlinger, translated from the French by Wade Baskin. New York: Philosophical Library.

Schegloff, Emanuel A. 1963. Toward a Reading of Psychiatric Theory. *Berkeley Journal of Sociology* 8: 61–91.

Schegloff, Emanuel A. 1968. Sequencing in conversational openings. *American Anthropologist* 70: 1075–95.

Schegloff, Emanuel A. 1972. Notes on a conversational practice: formulating place. *Studies in Social Interaction*, ed. D. N. Sudnow. New York/London: Free Press/Macmillan, pp. 75–119.

Schegloff, Emanuel A. 1979a. Identification and recognition in telephone openings. *Everyday Language*, ed. G. Psathas. New York: Erlbaum, pp. 23–78.

Schegloff, Emanuel A. 1979b. The relevance of repair for syntax-for-conversation. *Discourse and Syntax*, ed. T. Givón. Syntax and Semantics 12. New York: Academic Press, pp. 261–88.

Schegloff, Emanuel A. 1980. Preliminaries to preliminaries: "Can I ask you a question?" *Sociological Inquiry* 50: 104–52.

Schegloff, Emanuel A. 1982. Discourse as an interactional achievement: some uses of "uh huh" and other things that come between sentences. *Georgetown University Round Table on Languages and Linguistics 1981: Analyzing Discourse: Text and Talk*, ed. D. Tannen, pp. 71–93.

Schegloff, Emanuel A. 1984. On some questions and ambiguities in conversation. *Structures of Social Action*, ed. J. M. Atkinson and J. Heritage. Cambridge: Cambridge University Press, pp. 28–52.

Schegloff, Emanuel A. 1986. The routine as achievement. *Human Studies* 9: 111–51.

Schegloff, Emanuel A. 1987a. Between micro and micro: contexts and other connections. *The Micro-Macro Link*, ed. J. Alexander, B. Giesen, R. Munch, and N. Smelser. Berkeley and Los Angeles: University of California Press, pp. 207–34.

Schegloff, Emanuel A. 1987b. Recycled turn beginnings: a precise repair mechanism in conversation's turn-taking organisation. *Talk and Social Organisation*, ed. G. Button and J. R. E. Lee. Clevedon: Multilingual Matters, pp. 70–85.

Schegloff, Emanuel A. 1988a. Goffman and the analysis of conversation. *Erving Goffman: Exploring the Interaction Order*, ed. P. Drew and A. Wootton. Cambridge: Polity Press, pp. 89–135.

Schegloff, Emanuel A. 1988b. On an actual virtual servo-mechanism for guessing bad news: a single case conjecture. *Social Problems* 35(4): 442–57.

Schegloff, Emanuel A. 1988c. Presequences and indirection: applying speech act theory to ordinary conversation. *Journal of Pragmatics* 12: 55–62.

Schegloff, Emanuel A. 1988d. From interview to confrontation: observations on the Bush/Rather encounter. *Research on Language and Social Interaction* 22: 215–40.

Schegloff, Emanuel A. 1989. Reflections on language, development and the interactional character of talk-in-interaction. *Interaction in Human Development*, ed. M. Bornstein and J. S. Bruner. New York: Erlbaum, pp. 139–53.

Schegloff, Emanuel A. 1990. On the organization of sequences as a source of "coherence" in talk-in-interaction. *Conversational Organization and Its Development*, ed. B. Dorval. Norwood, NJ: Ablex, pp. 51–77.

Schegloff, Emanuel A. 1991a. Conversation analysis and socially shared cognition. *Perspectives on Socially Shared Cognition*, ed. L. Resnick, J. Levine, and S. Teasley. Washington, DC: American Psychological Association, pp. 150–71.

Schegloff, Emanuel A. 1991b. Reflections on talk and social structure. *Talk and Social Structure*, ed. D. Boden and D. H. Zimmerman. Berkeley: University of California Press, pp. 44–70.

Schegloff, Emanuel A. 1992a. Repair after next turn: the last structurally provided for place for the defense of intersubjectivity in conversation. *American Journal of Sociology* 95: 1295–1345.

Schegloff, Emanuel A. 1992b. To Searle on conversation: a note in return. *(On) Searle on Conversation*, ed. H. Parret and J. Verschueren. Amsterdam: Benjamins, pp. 113–28.

Schegloff, Emanuel A. 1992c. In another context. *Rethinking Context: Language as an Interactive Phenomenon*, ed. A. Duranti and C. Goodwin. Cambridge: Cambridge University Press, pp. 191–227.

Schegloff, Emanuel A. 1993. Reflections on quantification in the study of conversation. *Research on Language and Social Interaction* 26: 99–128.

Schegloff, Emanuel A. 1995. Introduction. *Lectures on Conversation*, ed. G. Jefferson. Oxford: Basil Blackwell, pp. ix–lxii.

Schegloff, Emanuel A. 1996a. Some practices for referring to persons in talk-in-interaction: a partial sketch of a systematics. *Studies in Anaphora*, ed. B. Fox. Amsterdam: John Benjamins, pp. 437–85.

Schegloff, Emanuel A. 1996b. Confirming allusions: toward an empirical account of action. *American Journal of Sociology* 104: 161–216.

Schegloff, Emanuel A. 1996c. Turn organization: one intersection of grammar and interaction. *Interaction and Grammar*, ed. E. Ochs, S. Thompson, and E. Schegloff. Cambridge: Cambridge University Press, pp. 52–133.

Schegloff, Emanuel A. 1997a. Third turn repair. *Towards a Social Science of Language: Papers in Honor of William Labov. Vol. 2: Social Interaction and Discourse Structures*, ed. G. R. Guy, C. Feagin, D. Schiffrin, and J. Baugh. Amsterdam: John Benjamins, pp. 31–40.

Schegloff, Emanuel A. 1997b. Practices and actions: boundary cases of other-initiated repair. *Discourse Processes* 23: 499–545.

Schegloff, Emanuel A. 1998. Reflections on studying prosody in talk-in-interaction. *Language and Speech* 41: 235–63.

Schegloff, Emanuel A. 2000a. Overlapping talk and the organization of turn-taking for conversation. *Language in Society* 29: 1–63.

Schegloff, Emanuel A. 2000b. When "others" initiate repair. *Applied Linguistics* 21: 205–43.

Schegloff, Emanuel A. 2001. Increments: where they are and what they do. Paper presented to the Linguistic Institute, Santa Barbara, CA.

Schegloff, Emanuel A. 2002. Beginnings in the telephone. *Perpetual Contact: Mobile Communication, Private Talk, Public Performance*, ed. M. A. Aakhus and J. E. Katz. Cambridge: Cambridge University Press, pp. 284–300.

Schegloff, Emanuel A. 2003. The surfacing of the suppressed. *Studies in Language and Social Interaction: A Festschrift in Honor of Robert Hopper*, ed. P. Glenn, C. LeBaron, and J. Mandelbaum. Mahwah, NJ: Lawrence Erlbaum Associates, pp. 241–62.

Schegloff, Emanuel A. 2004. Lectures on Repair and Categorization (244b/266 Conversational Structures II), UCLA.

Schegloff, Emanuel A. 2005. On integrity in inquiry . . . of the investigated, not the investigator. *Discourse Studies* 7: 455–80.

Schegloff, Emanuel A. 2007. *Sequence Organization in Interaction: A Primer in Conversation Analysis.* Cambridge: Cambridge University Press.

Schegloff, Emanuel A. 2009. One perspective on *Conversation Analysis: Comparative Perspectives. Conversation Analysis: Comparative Perspectives,* ed. Jack Sidnell. Cambridge: Cambridge University Press, pp. 355–406.

Schegloff, Emanuel A., Gail Jefferson, and Harvey Sacks. 1977. The preference for self-correction in the organization of repair in conversation. *Language* 53: 361–82.

Schegloff, Emanuel A., and Harvey Sacks. 1973. Opening up closings. *Semiotica* 8: 289–327.

Schenkein, Jim. 1978. *Studies in the Organization of Conversational Interaction.* New York: Academic Press.

Searle, John R. 1969. *Speech Acts: An Essay in the Philosophy of Language.* Cambridge: Cambridge University Press.

Sharrock, Wes. 1989. Ethnomethodology. *British Journal of Sociology* 40: 657–77.

Sharrock, Wes, and Robert Anderson. 1986. *The Ethnomethodologists.* London: Tavistock.

Sidnell, Jack. 2001. Conversational turn-taking in a Caribbean English creole. *Journal of Pragmatics* 33: 1263–90.

Sidnell, Jack. 2004. There's risks in everything: extreme case formulations and accountability in inquiry testimony. *Discourse and Society* 15: 745–66.

Sidnell, Jack. 2005. Deixis. *Handbook of Pragmatics*, ed. Jef Verscheuren. Amsterdam: John Benjamins.

Sidnell, Jack. 2006. Coordinating gesture, talk, and gaze in reenactments. *Research on Language and Social Interaction* 39: 377–409.

Sidnell, Jack. 2007. "Look"-prefaced turns in first and second position: launching, interceding and redirecting action. *Discourse Studies* 9: 387–408.

Sidnell, Jack. 2008. Alternate and complementary perspectives on language and social life: the organization of repair in two Caribbean communities. *Journal of Sociolinguistics* 12: 477–503.

Sidnell, Jack. 2010a. The design and positioning of questions in inquiry testimony. *"Why Do You Ask?" The Function of Questions in Institutional Discourse*, ed. S. Ehrlich and A. Freed. New York: Oxford University Press, pp. 20–41.

Sidnell, Jack. 2010b. Questioning repeats in the talk of four-year-old children. *Analysing Interactions in Childhood: Insights from Conversation Analysis*, ed. Hilary Gardner and Mike Forrester. Oxford: Wiley-Blackwell.

Stivers, Tanya. 2001. Negotiating who presents the problem: next speaker selection in pediatric encounters. *Journal of Communication* 51: 1–31.

Stivers, Tanya. 2005. Modified repeats: one method for asserting primary rights from second position. *Research on Language and Social Interaction* 38: 131–58.

Stivers, Tanya, and Jeffrey Robinson. 2006. A preference for progressivity in interaction. *Language in Society* 35: 367–92.

Tanaka, Hiroko. 2000. Turn-projection in Japanese talk-in-interaction. *Research on Language and Social Interaction* 33: 1–38.

ten Have, Paul. 2007. *Doing Conversation Analysis*. Los Angeles: Sage.

Terasaki, Alene Kiku. 2004 [1976]. Pre-announcement sequences in conversation. *Conversation Analysis: Studies from the First Generation*, ed. G. Lerner. Amsterdam: John Benjamins, pp. 171–223.

Van Gennep, Arnold. 1960. *The Rites of Passage*. Chicago: University of Chicago Press.

Vanderbilt, Amy. 1963. *New Complete Book of Etiquette: The Guide to Gracious Living. With drawings by Fred McCarroll, Mary Suzuki, and Andrew Warhol*. Garden City, NY: Doubleday.

Volosinov, Valentin Nikolaevic. 1973. *Marxism and the Philosophy of Language*, trans. Ladislav Matejka and I. R. Titunik. New York: Seminar Press. (Original published 1929/30.)

Walker, Gareth. 2003. "Doing a rushthrough" – a phonetic resource for holding the turn in everyday conversation. *Proceedings of the 15th International Congress of Phonetic Sciences*, ed. M. J. Solé, D. Recasens, and J. Romero. Barcelona, pp. 1847–50.

Walker, Gareth. 2006. On the design and use of pivots in everyday English conversation. *Journal of Pragmatics* 39: 2217–43.

Wilkinson, Sue and Celia Kitzinger. 2006. Surprise as an interactional achievement: reaction tokens in conversation. *Social Psychology Quarterly* 69: 150–82.

Wong, Jean. 2000. Delayed next turn repair initiation in native/non-native speaker English conversation. *Applied Linguistics* 21: 244–67.

Wootton, Anthony. 1997. *Interaction and the Development of Mind*. Cambridge: Cambridge University Press.

Index